The Multiple Values of Wilderness

Principal Authors and Editors

H. Ken Cordell

John C. Bergstrom

J. M. Bowker

The Multiple Values of Wilderness

Principal Authors and Editors

H. Ken Cordell

John C. Bergstrom

J. M. Bowker

Venture Publishing, Inc.
State College, Pennsylvania

Production Manager: Richard Yocum
Manuscript Editing: Michele L. Barbin, Valerie Fowler, Richard Yocum

Library of Congress Catalogue Card Number: 2005905697
ISBN-10: 1-892132-58-3
ISBN-13: 978-1-892132-58-1

This book is dedicated to all—past, present, and future—who show compassion for life. The book is especially dedicated to those examining naturalness as a condition necessary for native life forms.

Table of Contents

List of Figures and Tables

List of Color Maps

Acknowledgments

As with any project, large or small, there have to be many people involved in many ways to make the project happen and be a success. This book is no exception. Those involved and contributing to this work are all deeply appreciated, but they are too numerous to list fully. Some stand out, however. The origin of this book lies with the first author's interactions with Jerry Stokes and Liz Close who were in 2000 the national leads for Wilderness Management in the Washington Office of the Forest Service. They expressed concern that agency leadership and others in positions of power over the National Wilderness Preservation System seemed to know little about the NWPS and how this System was of benefit to the country and to them. Ken Cordell, Mike Bowker, Jerry Stokes and Hilda Diaz-Soltero of the Forest Service, along with Tom Bancroft of The Wilderness Society, John Bergstrom of the University of Georgia, Denny Bschor, Chair of the Interagency Wilderness Policy Council, and staff from other wilderness management agencies and university academicians gathered in Washington in July of 2000 to review what was known about the benefits and values of Wilderness and to recommend courses of action to address needs. A primary outcome of that Workshop was identification of the need to assemble and disseminate research results about the values of Wilderness. This book is the primary product of that assembly.

All the authors of chapters are top notch in their fields of expertise. Their names are listed with their respective titles and affiliations in the chapters that follow. What they contributed to this book is beyond valuation, even as we attempt the very illusory task of describing the values of Wilderness. Dr. John Bergstrom, Russell Professor of Public Policy at the University of Georgia and Dr. Mike Bower, Scientist and Southern Center Co-Director for Urban Studies, are especially to be acknowledged for their diligence in authoring some chapters and editing all, many times over. The framework upon which this book is based is theirs. Jay Harvard worked for two years as book research manager and is to be applauded for helping keep the work organized and moving steadily. Behind Jay as he left to work for EPA came Danielle Murphy, who kept the work moving without seeming to miss a beat in transition. Both of these individuals helped write some of the chapters. Carter Betz with the Athens, Georgia research unit of the Forest Service provided numerous analyses and data sets for the book that would not otherwise have been available. Peter Landres with the Aldo Leopold Wilderness Research Institute contributed greatly to shaping the idea of broad-scale spatial analyses and mapping of the Wilderness System for Chapters 5 and 11. Kurt Riitters with the Forest Health Monitoring Institute of the Forest Service made the broad-scale spatial analyses happen by contributing world-class GIS skills (especially interpreting spatial relationships).

Especially, appreciation is felt for Shela Mou for her dedicated management of what seemed to be thousands of drafts of the various chapters, chapter tables and figures, references and miscellaneous bits. Without Shela's ability to make sense out of chaos, there would be no book. She handed off the chapter drafts as they were completed to Venture Publishing and to Michele L. Barbin, Valerie Fowler, and Richard Yocum. Venture has been a joy to work with. They know how to get the job done.

This book has sponsorship in many ways by many different entities. First and foremost, it has been sponsored and encouraged by the USDA Forest Service as one part of the Agency's periodic national resource assessments required under the Forest and Rangeland Renewable Resources Planning Act of 1974 and as amended in 1976 (RPA). The RPA requires an analysis of present and anticipated uses, demand for, and supply of the various renewable resources on all forest and range lands in the United States. The most recent RPA Assessment Update was published in 2005 and can be found at http://www.fs.fed.us/pl/rpa/. The Strategic Planning and Resource Assessment Staff in the national headquarters office of the USDA Forest Service administers funds for the RPA Assessment, and they have provided sustained support and encouragement over many years for the Wilderness Assessment. We would also like to thank the USDA Forest Service's Resource Valuation and Use Research Staff, and especially Linda Langner, David Darr, and David Cleaves for their continued support.

Ken Cordell
Senior Scientist and Project Leader
USDA Forest Service

Chapter 1
The Multiple Values of Wilderness

H. Ken Cordell
Senior Research Scientist and Project Leader
USDA Forest Service, Athens, Georgia

John C. Bergstrom
Russell Professor of Public Policy and
Professor, Department of Agricultural and Applied Economics
University of Georgia, Athens, Georgia

J. M. Bowker
Research Social Scientist
USDA Forest Service, Athens, Georgia

Gone are those of the 1950s and early 1960s who championed preserving wild lands and who influenced and saw through the birth of the National Wilderness Preservation System (NWPS). Gone too are myriad eager managers and proponents of wild land protection of the late 1960s and 1970s who helped rear the fledgling Wilderness[1] system and bring it into adolescence by adding management practices and policy interpretations. In this, the 40th year since the birth of the NWPS, this middle-age federal land system is surrounded by many new faces, as its childhood friends have moved on to other callings, have retired, or are no longer with us. The people who now make up this country's political leadership and the administrators of the federal land management system are all new. These new faces, for the most part, have little first-hand knowledge of the history of Wilderness protection in this country, nor do they have as much knowledge of the compelling reasons for the creation of our system to protect wildlands as did those who helped bring it into world. The 1960s "hype" of birthing an unprecedented new federal lands system has long since faded. Without some form of personal attachment to the Wilderness Act, however, the new players on the scene have little from which to draw in forming a personal position on the National Wilderness Preservation System.

The American public is increasingly detached from wild lands. Part of the reason is that as the country continues to experience economic growth and development, there are fewer wild lands that have escaped commercial and residential development. This includes second and vacation homes which are spreading further into formerly undeveloped rural areas and regions. Another part of the reason is that the vast majority of Americans live and choose to live in urban and suburban areas with little direct contact with wild lands, especially lands that might be considered wilderness. Hence, we cannot take for granted that the average American citizen understands and appreciates the multiple values of Wilderness that fueled public interest in the establishment of the NWPS 40 years ago. Younger generations in particular may need to be reminded, or perhaps even convinced, that the NWPS is not just their parents' or grandparents' Wilderness but theirs as well. The Wilderness values that seemed to be a priority to the general public in decades past may not have the same priority today. Also, the realm of relevant Wilderness values has likely changed over the past 40 years.

In 1964 the U.S. Congress established by law the National Wilderness Preservation System. The rich history and background of the Wilderness Act and the NWPS are discussed extensively in Chapters 2 and 3 of this book. At its birth, the NWPS included just 54 areas and a little over 9.1 million acres.[2] Congress has since added hundreds more areas and millions more acres,

---

[1] This book adopts the convention of capitalizing the word Wilderness when it refers to area or land designated into the National Wilderness Protection System.

increasing the NWPS to 662 areas and nearly 106 million acres of the wildest of federal lands. Most of these additions came early on. As the U.S. population and their elected government representatives and federal land management agency personnel have changed, additions are not only coming more slowly but also questions increasingly arise about the efficacy of the continued protection of federal lands as Wilderness. Increasingly voices are heard that advocate other, more commercial purposes and uses for these wild lands, such as oil exploration, tourism development, grazing, mining, and timbering. However, as illustrated in the recent national debate over allowing increased oil exploration in the Alaska National Wildlife Refuge, there are also strong advocates and public sentiments to protect wild lands and the multiple values these wild places provide to the nation as a whole. As domestic and global changes continue to put new and different pressures on the remaining natural lands in the United States, debates over how much new land to officially protect and how much existing, officially protected Wilderness should be opened up to some level of commercial use and development are likely to continue.

Needed in these new times is a clear, comprehensive articulation of the multiple values of Wilderness. This articulation needs to be factual, wide-ranging, and science-based. Thus, the overall purpose of this book is to tell fully what we know about the range of values Americans hold toward the NWPS. We attempt to clarify the meaning of different types of Wilderness values and to present replicable, science-based evidence of these values. Our intended audience is all those new faces who can and do have power over the future of the United States' National Wilderness Preservation System as well as all who seek to influence those who have this power. The book is also intended for teachers, students, and other inquisitive people involved in formal or informal learning and research programs. We hope as well to better inform interested and engaged members of the general public about the values of *their* public Wilderness areas. After all, it is the American citizen who is ultimately responsible and can influence public policy in the greatest measure through their individual and collective voices and actions.

Setting the Stage

To set the stage and provide a springboard for the inventory and description of Wilderness values provided in this book, a national workshop focusing on what research has shown about the values of the National Wilderness Preservation System was held in Washington, DC, on July 11 and 12, 2000. At this workshop,

---

[2] Wilderness acreage data in this chapter provided by the Bureau of Land Management, Fish and Wildlife Service, Forest Service, and National Park Service (February 2004).

invited national experts from the science and management communities explored the need for and approaches to assessing the values the NWPS adds to American landscapes and quality of life. From workshop participants came the conceptualization of the Framework of Wilderness Values, described in Chapter 4, and a call to inventory, assess, and communicate what we know about these values. The principal means for communicating our findings, it was decided, would be through a book unprecedented in its thoroughness in examining Wilderness values. Great care, too, would be taken to assure the book's contents are credible and its language simple and straightforward. Toward these ends, building the foundation for this book began immediately after the workshop.

As a national assessment of values provided by Wilderness currently under federal government protection, the fundamental question this book is meant to help answer is: "To what degrees and in what ways does the National Wilderness Preservation System add value in 21st century America?" This book inventories and discusses the social, economic, ecological, and ethical value perspectives of Wilderness. Considering the broad spectrum of the values of Wilderness, it was acknowledged early in the development of this book that the NWPS contributes to the welfare of both humans and nonhumans; that benefits accrue within the boundaries of NWPS areas; and that benefits accrue to people, nonhumans, and landscapes outside designated Wilderness areas. It was also acknowledged that development of the story of the broad spectrum of Wilderness values would require the work of a highly qualified, multidisciplinary team to look fully at the range of values and measures.

Multiple Values and Multiple Perspectives

To do the heavy lifting involved in assessing the multiple values provided by the NWPS, a national multidisciplinary team of experts was assembled to address each of the major value perspectives as outlined in the general Wilderness values framework (i.e., social, economic, ecological, and ethical; see Chapter 4). Authors of this book represent the members of this team. As follow-up to the national workshop held in 2000, the values team and key agency and organizational leaders held two additional national meetings, both in Athens, Georgia—one in April 2002, the other in November 2002. The purposes of these meetings were to discuss each of the major Wilderness value perspectives and to detail and map how to integrate these perspectives into the overall values framework. At these meetings and in subsequent interactions to develop this book, the values team followed a multidisciplinary approach to assess the values of the NWPS.

A multidisciplinary approach (rather than an interdisciplinary approach) seeks to better understand Wilderness values by using the best available science-based knowledge and information from the disciplinary fields most closely aligned with each of the framework's four value perspectives. An interdisciplinary approach to assessing Wilderness values seeks to blend perspectives and theories across disciplines to examine each identifiable Wilderness value. Although the values team assembled to produce this book supports future efforts to assess Wilderness values using interdisciplinary approaches, such interdisciplinary assessments of Wilderness values are not currently available. Since the goal of this book is to report on what is currently known about Wilderness values, we attempt to assess state-of-the-art existing knowledge and literature related to each of the major value perspectives described in Chapter 4 in an integrated, multidisciplinary manner.

Multiple Values and Book Organization

The framers of the Wilderness Act and the subsequent establishment of the National Wilderness Preservation System were influenced by early recognition of the special values "untrammeled" wild lands provide the United States. To better understand and appreciate the multiple values of the NWPS in 21st century America, it is useful to first look back, as done in Chapters 2 and 3. These chapters offer historical and institutional perspectives about why the United States was the first nation in the world to demonstrate by legislative action that wild lands are important enough to receive special designation and protection. Although the Wilderness Act mentions specific types of Wilderness values and hints at others, this Act and other Wilderness literature written over the past 40 years fail to provide an integrated, multidisciplinary framework for inventorying and assessing the multiple values of Wilderness. The values framework presented in Chapter 4 provides an overview of social, economic, ecologic, and ethical perspectives of the values of Wilderness. These perspectives are described in detail in later chapters. The Wilderness values framework shows that social, economic, ecologic, and ethical value perspectives ultimately depend upon the various measurable characteristics or attributes that describe the make-up of the NWPS and what can be found there. Chapter 5 describes the objective physical and biological attributes or characteristics of the NWPS, and Chapter 6 surveys the more subjective attributes or characteristics of "wildness."

As outlined by the values framework, Wilderness attributes support its functions, such as preserving wild natural places. In turn, these preserved wild natural places support Wilderness services, such as animal and plant habitat, which then support specific types of Wilderness values, such as existence values of rare and endangered animals and plants. Specific types of Wilderness values, such as existence values of rare and endangered animals and plants, can be described and assessed from social, economic, ecologic, and philosophical disciplinary perspectives. Chapter 7 discusses Wilderness values from a broad social value perspective. Chapter 8 provides a closer look at how the social and cultural backgrounds of people influence Wilderness perceptions and values. Personal values from the perspective of economics are examined in Chapter 9, while Chapter 10 explores local economic development benefits at a community level. Chapter 11 discusses Wilderness values from an ecological perspective, focusing on ecosystem health and life support. Chapter 12 explores intrinsic values from the perspective of philosophers, including tracking down the ethical or moral basis for intrinsic values. Chapter 13 summarizes key messages and implications from the national assessment of Wilderness values this book represents. It also integrates and summarizes what we understand to be known about how and how much Wilderness adds value to 21st century America and discusses the implications of this knowledge for the future of the National Wilderness Preservation System.

Chapter 2
Origins of the National Wilderness Preservation System

Paul S. Sutter
Associate Professor, Department of History
University of Georgia, Athens, Georgia

The Early Years

Although the wilderness idea has a deep history (Cronon, 1996; Nash, 1982; Oelschlaeger, 1991), the notion that Americans ought to preserve wild areas within a discrete federal land system had its origins in the years immediately after World War I. For much of American history prior to that point, Americans abhorred wilderness conditions. The goal of early American settlers had been to transform what they called wilderness into landscapes of economic productivity—mostly through agriculture and resource extraction. But by the mid-19th century, some Americans began to reconsider their culture's drive to transform the entire continent. Figures such as George Catlin, Henry David Thoreau, and John Muir wondered whether it might not be wise to save some significant remnants of wild America. Those reservations about the environmental consequences of progress found their initial form in the movement to create and preserve national parks in the years after the Civil War, beginning with Yellowstone in 1872. But the aesthetic ideal behind park making was not the preservation of wilderness conditions, per se, but what historian Alfred Runte called *monumentalism*. By monumentalism, Runte meant the desire to protect the most monumental natural spectacles and wonders that the country—mostly the West—had to offer (Runte, 1987). Moreover, one did not have to scratch the surface very deeply before one came across promoters who stood to profit from the tourists that national parks would bring (Runte, 1987; Sellars, 1997). National park creation had its commercial aspects from the very beginning. Nonetheless, preservation of the first national parks set the important precedent of pulling lands from control of the General Land Office and forever setting them off-limits to private settlement and development. That precedent was a crucial one for the wilderness system that followed.

The creation of the first federal forest reserves in 1891 also set an important precedent, if only because so much of what became the National Wilderness Preservation System (NWPS) came out of national forest lands. Most early forest reserves were created for the purpose of watershed protection, though it was not clear until the 1897 Forest Management Act that they would also be used for their resources, albeit under the guidance of professionally trained federal foresters. In 1905, Theodore Roosevelt transferred the forest reserves from the Interior Department to the Department of Agriculture—a move that made clear the centrality of sustained-yield forestry to their mission. Gifford Pinchot took charge of the newly created U.S. Forest Service, whose mission was to sustainably and efficiently manage these forest reserves (which were renamed national forests a few years later) for their timber resources. Set up to facilitate the wise use of public resources over the long term, the national forests initially appeared to have little room for wilderness preservation (Hays, 1959; Miller, 2001; Steen, 1976).

Prelude to Wilderness: The 1910s

The National Wilderness Preservation System emerged as a third distinct land classification (a fourth, actually, if one accounts for the system of national monuments created by the Antiquities Act of 1906 which is designed to protect areas of scientific importance) within the interstices of these other systems, and out of their tensions and shortcomings. The mid-1910s were a crucial watershed in this regard. The battle over the Hetch Hetchy Valley, within the bounds of Yosemite National Park, put the increasingly rigid doctrines of utilitarian conservation and aesthetic preservation in full national view. The city of San Francisco wanted to dam the valley to create a public water supply, and utilitarians, such as Gifford Pinchot, supported the effort as an example of the wise use of public resources. John Muir, the nation's arch-preservationist with a particular interest in the Sierras, opposed the plan as an inexcusable desecration of a national park. The city, and by association the argument for wise use, won the day in 1913. The Hetch Hetchy Valley was subsequently inundated behind O'Shaughnessy Dam. John Muir died within a year of the decision, but the case he had made for the sanctity of national parks paid longer-term dividends. The national parks enjoyed a growing national constituency willing to stand up for and protect them, and the National Park Service, created by act of Congress in 1916, gave them the same sort of institutional clout that the Forest Service enjoyed. In losing Hetch Hetchy, the cause of preservation actually won some larger victories (Nash, 1982).

The rise of a preservationist constituency, eager to protect, visit, and expand the National Park System, was also the product of another phenomenon of the 1910s—the proliferation of the automobile and growing federal support for a system of roads motorists could use to get to, and through, the parks and other public lands. Automobile ownership in the United States grew slowly during the first decade of the century, but when Henry Ford began assembly line production in the early 1910s, the automobile became affordable and widely adopted by middle-class Americans. Moreover, in 1916, Congress passed the first of a series of Federal Aid Highway Acts, which committed to substantially funding road improvement and coordinating a national system of roads. Stephen Mather and Horace Albright, the two most important leaders in the early history of the National Park Service, eagerly hitched the Park Service wagon to the star of motor tourism. They recognized that by attracting motorists to the parks, and by building modern roads and other tourist facilities, they could further democratize the preservationist impulse. Tourism also lent park preservation an economic rationale that had been lacking during the Hetch Hetchy conflict, when proponents of water development had easily tarred preservationists as selfish aesthetes who cared more about nature than economic progress. As visitation skyrocketed, the National Park System grew, and so did support for preserving further portions of the public domain as national parks. A few observers began worrying that the Park Service was too enamored of tourism development, which came at the expense of wild lands and opportunities for wilderness experiences, and that driving into wild nature might in fact destroy its very wildness. The modern wilderness idea was born out of such concern (Sutter, 2002).

One of the most perplexing questions that arises when plumbing the history of the wilderness idea is why, just a few years after the creation of the National Park Service and in the midst of swelling national support for park preservation, why did wilderness emerge as a new preservationist standard? The developmental proclivities of the Park Service provide one answer, but one also has to turn away from the national parks and look at the young National Forest System. In the mid-1910s national forests were also at a crucial time in their development. Despite the mandate to harvest timber resources of the national forests for the public good and the professional forester culture that developed around that goal, the national forests remained marginal to the nation's timber markets during their early history. Most timber was still cut from private lands, and private timber interests complained that public timber would only glut markets and drive down prices. Federal foresters thus found themselves unable to do what they were trained to do, so they bided their time by cruising timber and developing an administrative infrastructure of roads, trails, telephone lines and fire towers, all in anticipation of the day when public timber would be needed. As they opened up the remote and wild national forests to their scrutiny and control, they inadvertently provided prime opportunities for recreational users, mostly motorists, to visit and enjoy national forest resources. Not surprisingly, a number of foresters on the front lines of the opening of these forests to both management and recreational use began to express misgivings (Meine, 1988; Sutter, 2002).

Although a number of historians have portrayed the Forest Service's entrance into the recreation field in the years after World War I as part of a growing rivalry with the Park Service, such a thesis misses the deeply ambivalent feelings federal foresters had about embracing recreation as part of their mission. On the one hand, recreation provided foresters with a sense of usefulness that eluded them thus far. On the other hand, embracing recreation meant wading into the domain of the Park Service and confusing a public already unclear about just what the differences were between a national park and a national forest. By and large, the Forest Service opted to accept and provide for the growing recreational use of their lands without directly embracing providing recreation—and by association strict preservation—as part of their mission. In some cases, this meant providing for basic recreational facilities, such as fire rings and pit toilets, in the most heavily used camping and recreational areas. In others, it involved creating a system of recreational permitting, made possible by the Term Permit Act of 1915. The Term Permit Act allowed for the development of private summer cottages, camps, and hotels in the national forests. These structures would be owned privately, but set on leased public land. Recreational visitors were coming of their own volition, and the Forest Service sought to accommodate them without altering their professional mission, or having to devote scarce resources to recreational development. That was easier said than done.

In the late 1910s, a landscape architect named Arthur Carhart found himself enmeshed in this controversy. Carhart had been hired by the Forest Service's District Two office to provide recreational planning for some of the most heavily used forests of the region, including several forests in Colorado and the Superior National Forest in Minnesota. One of Carhart's first assignments, in 1919, was to plan for the development of term permit cabins along the shore of Trapper's Lake in Colorado's White Mountain National Forest. Although Carhart was not against recreational development—in fact, he was an avid proponent of getting the Forest Service into the public recreation business—he was concerned that their term permit system allowed the private monopolization of some of the finest scenic resources the national forests had to offer. And so Carhart suggested to his superiors that the shore of Trapper's Lake be saved from all cabin development. He pushed to have any such developments placed a good distance from the lake. Some argued that Carhart's policy suggestion for Trapper's Lake, which was instituted, represented the first instance of wilderness preservation (Baldwin, 1972). But Carhart never used the term "wilderness." He was more interested in protecting the lake's scenic resources from private "monopolization." Moreover, the scale of the preservationist effort at Trapper's Lake did not quite match the scale of the official wilderness policy as it developed a few years later. Nonetheless, in preserving a portion of a national forest, both *for* recreation (as opposed to resources extraction) and *from* recreational development, Carhart's efforts at Trapper's Lake foreshadowed, and directly influenced, the interests of later wilderness advocates (Sutter, 2002).

Leopold Enters the Fray

In December 1919, a forester named Aldo Leopold, who had been overseeing similar recreational work in the Southwest, visited Carhart to discuss the Trapper's Lake policy. Leopold shared Carhart's concerns about how quickly quasiprivate recreational development was proceeding, but he had a larger vision than simply protecting the "scenic territories" of the national forests from recreational monopolization. He saw in the national forests opportunities for preserving vast areas in a primitive state, free not only from term permit cabins but also from roads, mechanized transport, and most other forms of human land use. Leopold codified his thoughts on "wilderness" preservation, as he called it, in a 1921 article in the *Journal of Forestry* titled "The Wilderness and Its Place in Forest Recreational Policy." Leopold argued not only that the Forest Service ought to preserve some of its lands for recreation and from resource extraction but also that they ought to preserve large expanses from modern recreational development. Indeed, the chief innovation of his argument for wilderness was in distinguishing it from other forms of *recreational* preservation. "By wilderness," Leopold wrote, "I mean a continuous stretch of country preserved in its natural state, open to lawful hunting and fishing, big enough to absorb a two-week pack trip, and kept devoid of roads, artificial trails, cottages, and other works of man." Leopold ended his article by suggesting the headwaters of the Gila River in New Mexico's Gila National Forest as a candidate area (Leopold, 1921). A year later, Leopold formally proposed the Forest Service protect the Gila, and by 1924 they had taken his advice, making the Gila Wilderness Area the first of several national forest areas given similar administrative protection in the mid-1920s (Meine, 1988; Sutter, 2002).

Aldo Leopold lobbied for and wrote extensively about the wilderness idea during the mid-1920s, and in the process became the nation's chief wilderness ideologue. Leopold was particularly keen on getting the National Conference on Outdoor Recreation, created by the Coolidge Administration, to study the nation's outdoor recreation needs and to take wilderness preservation seriously. As road development proceeded rapidly in the West, many national forest de facto wilderness areas had been carved and pared into ever-smaller pieces. If some sort of concerted national action did not take place soon, Leopold feared, more of these large roadless areas would be lost to the juggernaut of "automobility." Some of Leopold's wilderness writings—and he produced a flurry of them in the mid-1920s—were tinged with frontier romanticism. He compared the days of the covered wagon with the modern, motorized era. He lamented the demise of the uncharted and the spiritual loss that would occur once all corners of the earth had been mapped and brought into the human orbit. He also celebrated the virtues of wilderness hunting and criticized the narrowly commercial ethos of 1920s America. But in all of these pieces, he expressed concern about the impacts and threats of roads, cars, and a new modern culture of outdoor recreation (Flader & Callicott, 1991).

Through his writings, and with support from sympathetic colleagues, Leopold convinced the leaders of the Forest Service to create a coherent national wilderness policy. Indeed, the mid-1920s saw a fairly vigorous debate within Forest Service circles over the wisdom of preserving areas as wilderness. Some objected that such a policy was elitist, because it devoted huge expanses of wild land to serve the recreational interests of the few people who were interested in primitive recreation. William Greeley, then chief of the Forest Service, warmed to Leopold's idea. Although he was reticent to put any area within the national forests completely off limits to resource use, he also saw the virtue in protecting a few large areas from road building, recreational development, and other forms of administrative modernization. In fact, Greeley thought wilderness preservation might even help the Forest Service deal with the headaches that came with rapidly growing visitation by recreational motorists. After all, it was a time when there was little demand for national forest timber anyway, and there was little money to handle recreational planning. But Greeley made clear that whatever wilderness designations were made—and they were made at that point by the various district foresters—would last only as long as the timber resources of those areas were not in demand. He did not see wilderness preservation as necessarily permanent.

Forest Service discussions about wilderness culminated in the creation, in 1929, of Regulation L-20, the first explicit national wilderness policy. Regulation L-20 required district foresters to identify areas within their forests with wilderness potential and file a report on how they would be managed. Roads and recreational permits were strongly discouraged in such areas, but not prohibited by rule—that decision was still in the district forester's hands. Regulation L-20 also encouraged foresters to set aside "research reserves," a response to the lobbying of the Ecological Society of America, which had been advocating the preservation of areas in their "natural conditions" for scientific purposes. Finally, and tellingly, L-20 changed the name of these areas from "wilderness" areas to "primitive" areas, the rationale being that the latter term better described the recreational intent of these areas—that is, that they would be used for primitive rather than modern recreation. "Wilderness," Forest Service officials felt, suggested a nature that had not been and would not be developed in any way. Some of the areas they had in mind for protection had been logged and grazed, or would be administered in ways that belied a notion of wilderness as untouched. Forest Service officials of that time felt there was a distinct possibility that they would be opened to resource extraction in the future. As such, "primitive" seemed to better describe the purpose of the areas to be protected than did "wilderness." Not everyone shared the Forest Service's definitions of these two terms, however. In fact, what to call these areas would continue to be an important question as wilderness policy and advocacy evolved over the next several decades.

Despite the impermanence and murkiness of the Forest Service's first wilderness policy, advocates such as Aldo Leopold generally were happy with the result. Leopold certainly would have preferred a stronger prohibition against road, recreational and administrative developments, and he would have applauded more permanent protection. But the areas under consideration were remote and, at that moment, did not seem threatened by resource development. To Leopold, getting the Forest Service to explicitly recognize and preserve lands that had primitive recreational values was a huge victory against the forces that posed the greatest short-term threat—road building and administrative modernization.

With victory in hand, Leopold pulled away from wilderness politics. He had moved to Madison, Wisconsin, in 1924, where he worked for the Forest Service's Forest Product's Laboratory. He left that position in the late 1920s and turned his attention to game management—a field he helped to pioneer. In doing so he refocused his attention on preserving and promoting wildness on the nation's agricultural lands (Meine, 1988). Indeed, as L-20 was being issued, Leopold passed the mantle of advocacy to several other key individuals, although he would return to the wilderness cause during the New Deal years.

Marshall and Other Interwar Advocates

The most important figure to step into Leopold's shoes was Bob Marshall (Glover, 1986; Sutter, 2002). The son of a wealthy New York family, Marshall received a forestry degree from Syracuse University's new forestry school in 1924. He then went to work for the Forest Service in the northern Rocky Mountains. Working out of Missoula, Montana, Marshall was within walking distance of some of the nation's most remote and rugged national forest backcountry. He was known to routinely hike 40 miles a day. Marshall became concerned that plans for roads threatened to whittle away at this vast, wild landscape, and so he dove into the Forest Service's wilderness discussions during the late 1920s, most of which occurred in their in-house *Bulletin*. In the summer of 1928, Marshall entered the fray with an essay titled "Wilderness as Minority Right." This essay was issued in response to an incendiary critique of wilderness by Manly Thompson, who had suggested that wilderness advocates' true aim was to keep the "hoi polloi" out of the forests so that the elite crowd who desired wilderness recreation could enjoy it unmolested.

Marshall rejected Thompson's characterization of wilderness advocates as elitists, but he did recognize that there were relatively few Americans who desired a wilderness experience—at least compared to those who enjoyed autocamping and motor touring. Marshall hoped that would change, and he devoted much of his career to promoting accessible wilderness recreation. But Marshall also realized that defending wilderness from roads and recreational modernization meant relying on a minority rights argument. Even if they were a minority, Marshall reasoned, those who wanted wilderness ought to be afforded areas to meet their needs. Americans had, by the late 1920s, plenty of scenic landscapes into which they could drive; the desires of the majority were well met. The few opportunities remaining for primitive recreation, however, were dwindling because the majority, or those who sought to serve them, continued to press for greater motorized access. Finishing off the wilderness, Marshall wrote, would result in a denial of rights to a minority without substantially augmenting the rights the majority already enjoyed.

More to the point, Marshall, like Leopold before him, insisted that roads and cars did more than provide access. Together they fundamentally changed an area and the recreational experiences possible within it (Marshall, 1928). Two years later, in perhaps his most important published essay on wilderness and one of the seminal wilderness articles of the era, Marshall published "The Problem of the Wilderness" which appeared in *Scientific Monthly* in 1930. In this essay Marshall called for the "organization of spirited people who will fight for the freedom of the wilderness," not only to protect it as a minority right but also to build a constituency for preservation as part of a balanced public lands system (Marshall, 1930). That call would bear fruit several years later.

Several other conservationists and recreational activists joined the wilderness cause in the late 1920s and early 1930s. Robert Sterling Yard, a long-time member of the national parks lobby, had been a publicist for the National Park Service during the first few years of its existence. He had also run the National Parks Association (today the National Parks and Conservation Association) since 1919 (Miles, 1995). A staunch defender of the parks against any sort of invasion, Yard grew concerned as the 1920s progressed about how wedded to motor tourism and tourist development the Park Service had become. Disillusioned with their boosterism, Yard feuded with Park Service leaders, including Stephen Mather (at whose wedding Yard had served as best man) and Horace Albright. By the early 1930s, Yard was convinced that wilderness protection was crucial as an alternative to the increasingly developed national parks. In his hands, and in the hands of many other interwar advocates, wilderness was an idea offered, not as a critique, not of resource exploitation, but of the Park Service's model of preservation (Sutter, 2002).

The most idiosyncratic voice for wilderness during the interwar era was that of Benton MacKaye. MacKaye (rhymes with sky) was, like Leopold and Marshall, a trained forester who in 1921 proposed the construction of an Appalachian Trail (AT). Work on his vision had proceeded rapidly through the 1920s, thanks to dedicated trail activists. But by the end of the decade there was a growing schism within the Appalachian Trail Conference (ATC), the confederation of hiking clubs overseeing trail construction. MacKaye and several trail club leaders opposed a series of skyline drives, including the Skyline Drive in Shenandoah National Park and the proposed Blue Ridge Parkway, then being planned for the Appalachian ridgeline. The construction of such roads was part of the larger New Deal mobilization of labor and resources on the nation's public lands, much of it in the name of opening up such areas to modern recreational use. Indeed, New Deal conservation magnified the fears of all of these wilderness advocates. These skyline roads infringed upon the AT in numerous places, undermining what MacKaye and his hiking club allies had hoped would be a primitive trail experience. They urged the ATC to publicly oppose such roads, but its leadership refused. By the mid-1930s, they had become convinced of the need to defend the AT as a "wilderness trail." In fact, they were preparing to found a splinter group for just such a purpose when Bob Marshall crossed their path and suggested an organization with broader scope. The Wilderness Society was the product of his suggestion and became the first national group to promote the preservation of wilderness. Founded in 1935, at the height of the New Deal, and including Leopold, Yard, Marshall, and MacKaye among its founders, the Wilderness Society would be a leading voice in the fight for passage of the Wilderness Act in the years after World War II (Anderson, 2002; Fox, 1984; Sutter, 2002).

While the Wilderness Society gave an organizational voice to the wilderness idea, Bob Marshall, who became the Forest Service's first Director of Recreation and Lands in 1937, set as a goal a more permanent wilderness policy. In 1939, he realized that goal when the Forest Service announced its new U Regulations. These regulations redefined the wilderness designation process and gave wilderness areas more permanence. The U Regulations did several things. First, they vested the power to recommend wilderness areas in the hands of the Chief of the Forest Service and the power to create such areas in hands of the Secretary of Agriculture. Thus, the crucial process of recommendation and designation was moved up the chain of command from the local district level to the national level. Second, the U Regulations prohibited commercial timber harvests on designated areas—an important departure from L-20. Finally, the U Regulations changed the operative term from "primitive" back to "wilderness," and provided not only for the creation of "wilderness areas" of over 100,000 acres but also for "wild areas" as small as 5,000 acres. In sum, the U Regulations created a stricter and more permanent wilderness system within the national forest system. Fittingly, one of the first areas to be classified under the U Regulations was the Bob Marshall Wilderness Area in Montana. Two months later, Marshall died of what was likely a heart attack; he was only 38. Wilderness areas still lacked the permanence of statutory protection however (Glover, 1986; Sutter, 2002).

Aldo Leopold was brought back into the wilderness debate by New Deal threats and the subsequent founding of the Wilderness Society. It was then, in the late 1930s and through the 1940s, that his wilderness thought headed in a more scientific direction. Leopold was not the first person to apply an ecological rationale to preservation. Members of the Ecological Society of America had been engaged in such advocacy since the early 1920s, and their work culminated in the founding of the Nature Conservancy in 1950. Moreover, such ecological thinking, in relation to wilderness at least, was a late development in Leopold's distinguished career as a wilderness advocate. Although Leopold never abandoned his sophisticated position on modern outdoor recreation (the position that had led him to the idea of wilderness preservation in the first place), he is best remembered for forging a compelling ecological rationale for preserving large, roadless areas. Such an ecological rationale made its first substantial appearance in his 1941 article "Wilderness as Land Laboratory." It was this article that served as one of the cornerstones in his classic, *A Sand County Almanac*, which appeared posthumously in 1949 (Flader, 1974; Leopold, 1941, 1949; Meine, 1988). The wilderness idea postwar advocates inherited was thus a rich one—invested with multiple rationales and values, and supple enough to respond to new conditions.

The Post World War II Era

In the years before World War II, wilderness advocacy and wilderness policy largely was crafted in reaction to the automobile, roads, and modern recreational trends. After World War II, wilderness thinking and politics shifted away from the recreational arena and toward threats posed by the development of public land resources. One should not exaggerate this shift, as there were plenty of continuities from the interwar era. Road building and automobile use continued to fuel an outdoor recreation boom that, in terms of scale, dwarfed what had happened during the interwar years. In the mid-1950s, for instance, the National Park Service embarked on an ambitious modernization effort called Mission 66, an effort that many wilderness advocates found alarming. The Park Service had tentatively begun protecting roadless areas within some of the parks, and in the late 1930s it created parks such as Olympic and Kings Canyon on a wilderness model, with few roads and other developments (Runte, 1987; Sellars, 1997). Parts of the most popular national parks were becoming increasingly urban, however, and wilderness advocates continued to criticize tourist development. Nonetheless, such concerns necessarily took a back seat to two trends that altered postwar wilderness politics: aggressive dam-building plans that threatened to transform the canyon country of the Southwest, and the move of industrial timber production into national forests. Together, these threats reoriented wilderness politics around older debates between utilitarian conservation and preservation, and they made the preservation of wilderness a springboard of the modern environmental movement (Harvey, 1994; Hays, 1987; Hirt, 1994).

    The Bureau of Reclamation emerged from the Depression and World War II as an emboldened agency whose sights were squarely set on impounding western rivers, such as the Colorado. As part of the multidam Colorado River Storage Project, the Bureau proposed, in the late 1940s, to build a dam just downstream from Echo Park, the scenic centerpiece of Dinosaur National Monument. In a battle reminiscent of the one over Hetch Hetchy, preservationists fought—successfully, this time—to keep the Bureau from invading an area within the National Park System and thus violating its integrity. The victory was a galvanizing one for postwar environmental activism. But there was a dark side to the triumph at Dinosaur. As it turned out, wilderness activists saved Echo Park at the expense of spectacular, but as yet unprotected, canyon country downstream. Particularly heartbreaking was the loss of Glen Canyon. From this loss, wilderness activists learned that they would have to do more than safeguard areas already preserved; they would also have to search out and promote the preservation of lesser-known remnants of de facto wilderness in a region that was booming. This lesson fed the growing desire for federal wilderness legislation (Harvey, 1994).

The national forests, too, became a battleground. During the first half-century of their existence, the national forests had seen only modest cutting, as most timber harvesting remained on private lands. But after World War II, as the housing market boomed and private timber supplies dwindled, national forest timber was finally in demand. The Forest Service responded by eagerly facilitating national forest timber cutting, which grew four-fold between 1945 and 1970, and by expanding the system of Forest Service roads by tens of thousands of miles (Hirt, 1994). Faced with this new enthusiasm for getting the cut out of the national forests, wilderness advocates necessarily refocused their efforts away from critiquing motorized recreation and toward opposing overzealous timber extraction. Recreational users of all stripes became crucial allies in a broader battle against resource development, and the alliance between public land agencies and commercial timber interests. Indeed, where national forest wilderness preservation before World War I had largely been a process internal to the Forest Service, after the war it was driven by citizen activists opposing Forest Service timber-cutting plans. The Forest Service did not become entirely hostile to wilderness preservation, but they were increasingly unwilling to include within their wilderness system areas with valuable timber resources (Allin, 1982; Marsh, 2002). No longer able to trust the Forest Service to protect wilderness, activists increasingly pinned their hopes on the statutory protection of a federal wilderness bill.

Although one of the major stories of postwar wilderness politics was this rise of effective grassroots citizen activism, the postwar years also saw the emergence of a dynamic new national leadership among wilderness advocacy groups. This new leadership included Howard Zahniser of the Wilderness Society and David Brower of the Sierra Club. While Zahniser and Brower devoted their energies to the political trenches, another group of writers and artists, including Sigurd Olson, Wallace Stegner, and Ansel Adams, channeled their creativity into wilderness activism (Backes, 1997; Cohen, 1988; Spaulding, 1995). The Sierra Club also began holding biennial wilderness conferences in 1949. According to Douglas Scott, these conferences "were great crucibles of wilderness thought and action" in the postwar years (Scott, 2001). Wilderness advocates made savvy use of the news media and public relations after the war, building a persuasive case for wilderness preservation that a growing percentage of the American population came to support. What remained to be done, however, was the crafting and passage of a comprehensive wilderness bill that would clearly define wilderness, provide for greater citizen access to the decision-making process, and protect wilderness areas in perpetuity on any part of the public domain.

In the immediate wake of the Dinosaur victory in 1956, Howard Zahniser, the Wilderness Act's primary legislative architect, embarked on a tireless campaign to pass a wilderness bill. For Zahniser, as for many postwar advocates, wilderness was a place where humans willingly left their tools of domination at the door, where the land and its flora and fauna existed unhindered by self-interested human intervention. Earlier wilderness advocates made the case for wilderness as self-willed land, but it seemed more compelling in the postwar years when the pace at which Americans transformed the landscape accelerated and when atomic and chemical technologies made our ability to dominate nature seem not only starker but also a decidedly less triumphant achievement. Wallace Stegner would make a similar case in his famous "Wilderness Letter" of 1960, in which he argued that the value of wilderness went well beyond recreation. Wilderness, Stegner insisted, was a particularly American spiritual resource, a "geography of hope" in a world increasingly bent to the human will (Stegner, 1969). The campaign for a wilderness bill, then, not only tapped into a growing desire to see wild nature preserved for primitive recreation; it also grew out of a deeper American unease with technology and progress that undergirded the modern environmental movement.

Conclusion

The Wilderness Act of 1964 created a National Wilderness Preservation System, giving statutory protection immediately to 9.1 million acres classified as wilderness under the Forest Service's U Regulations. It provided mechanisms for wilderness review and designation (Allin, 1982; Scott, 2001). Just as important, it provided the sort of legal permanence that the older systems, beholden as they were to administrative discretion, did not. The Wilderness Act of 1964, then, was the fitting culmination to efforts, begun in the 1920s by figures such as Aldo Leopold and Bob Marshall, to protect the nation's wild lands from development of all sorts. It captured the diverse values and concerns of those who had advocated for wilderness preservation over the previous half century. It also left plenty of room for adding new values to the mix. But as much as it was the climax of a long effort, the Wilderness Act was also the beginning of a new and contentious era of activism, another chapter in the history of an important and controversial environmental idea.

Literature Cited

Allin, C. (1982). *The politics of wilderness preservation*. Westport, CT: Greenwood Press.

Anderson, L. (2002). *Benton MacKaye: Conservationist, planner, and creator of the Appalachian Trail*. Baltimore, MD: The Johns Hopkins University Press.

Backes, D. (1997). *Wilderness within: The life of Sigurd Olson*. Minneapolis, MN: University of Minnesota Press.

Baldwin, D. (1972). *The quiet revolution: The grass roots of today's wilderness preservation movement*. Boulder, CO: Pruett Publishing Co.

Cohen, M. (1988). *The history of the Sierra Club, 1892–1970*. San Francisco, CA: Sierra Club Books.

Cronon, W. (1996). The trouble with wilderness; or, getting back to the wrong nature. In W. Cronon, *Uncommon ground: Rethinking the human place in nature* (pp. 69–90). New York, NY: Norton.

Flader, S. (1974). *Thinking like a mountain: Aldo Leopold and the evolution of an ecological attitude toward deer, wolves, and forests*. Madison, WI: University of Wisconsin Press.

Flader, S. and Callicott, J. B. (Eds.). (1991). *The River of the Mother of God and other essays by Aldo Leopold*. Madison, WI: University of Wisconsin Press.

Fox, S. (1984). We want no straddlers. *Wilderness, 48*(Winter), 5–19.

Glover, J. (1986). *A wilderness original: The life of Bob Marshall*. Seattle, WA: The Mountaineers.

Harvey, M.W.T. (1994). *A symbol of Wilderness: Echo Park and the American conservation movement*. Albuquerque, NM: University of New Mexico Press.

Hays, S. (1959). *Conservation and the gospel of efficiency: The progressive conservation movement, 1890–1920*. Cambridge, MA: Harvard University Press.

Hays, S. (1987). *Beauty, health, and permanence: Environmental politics in the United States, 1955–1985*. New York, NY: Cambridge University Press.

Hirt, P. (1994). *A conspiracy of optimism: Management of the National Forests since World War II*. Lincoln, NE: University of Nebraska Press.

Leopold, A. (1921). The wilderness and its place in forest recreational policy. *Journal of Forestry, 19*(7), 718–721.

Leopold, A. (1941). Wilderness as land laboratory. *The Living Wilderness, 6*(July), 6.

Leopold, A. (1949). *A Sand County almanac*. New York, NY: Oxford University Press.

Marsh, K. (2002). *Drawing lines in the woods: Debating wilderness boundaries on national forest lands in the Cascade Mountains, 1950–1984.* Ph.D. Dissertation. Pullman, WA: Washington State University.

Marshall, R. (1928, August 27). The wilderness as minority right. *Service Bulletin,* 5–6.

Marshall, R. (1930). The problem of the wilderness. *Scientific Monthly, 30*(2), 141–148.

Meine, C. (1988). *Aldo Leopold: His life and work.* Madison, WI: University of Wisconsin Press.

Miles, J. (1995). *Guardians of the parks: A history of the National Parks and Conservation Association.* Washington, DC: Taylor and Francis.

Miller, C. (2001). *Gifford Pinchot and the making of modern environmentalism.* Washington, DC: Island Books.

Nash, R. (1982). *Wilderness and the American mind* (3rd ed.). New Haven, CT: Yale University Press.

Oelschlaeger, M. (1991). *The idea of wilderness: From prehistory to the age of ecology.* New Haven, CT: Yale University Press.

Runte, A. (1987). *National Parks: The American experience* (2nd ed.). Lincoln, NE: University of Nebraska Press.

Scott, D.W. (2001). *A wilderness forever future: A short history of the National Wilderness Preservation System.* Washington, DC: Pew Wilderness Center.

Sellars, R.W. (1997). *Preserving nature in the National Parks: A history.* New Haven, CT: Yale University Press.

Spaulding, J. (1995). *Ansel Adams and the American landscape: A biography.* Berkeley, CA: University of California Press.

Steen, H.K. (1976). *The U.S. Forest Service: A history.* Seattle, WA: University of Washington Press.

Stegner, W. (1969). *The sound of mountain water.* Garden City, NY: Doubleday.

Sutter, P.S. (2002). *Driven wild: How the fight against automobiles launched the modern wilderness movement.* Seattle, WA: University of Washington Press.

Chapter 3
The Wilderness Act and Its Recent History

Doug Scott
Policy Director
Campaign for America's Wilderness, Seattle, Washington

Author's Note: The original text of the Wilderness Act of 1964 in its entirety can be found at http://www.wilderness.net/index.cfm?fuse=NWPS&sec=legisAct. Other legal references for quoted text in this chapter refer to *U.S. Code, U.S. Statutes at Large,* et al. at the time of publication.

Two changes to the Wilderness Act worth noting: (1) The repeal of Paragraph 4(d)(5) and the renumbering of the next three paragraphs in 1978 when Congress enacted stronger protection for the Boundary Waters Canoe Area in Minnesota, rendering that provision in the Wilderness Act obsolete. (2) A broad law in 1995 cancelled many annual reporting requirements across the government, which terminated Section 7.

A National Wilderness Preservation System Is Created

Since its enactment, the Wilderness Act of 1964 has been judged a landmark achievement in the evolution of natural resources conservation policy in the United States (Light, 2000). The law's formal title describes the Act's goal: "to establish a National Wilderness Preservation System for the *permanent* good of the whole people" (Wilderness Act of 1964, 16 U.S.C. National Wilderness Preservation System title, emphasis added).

When President Lyndon Johnson signed it in the Rose Garden on September 3, 1964, the Wilderness Act conferred immediate statutory protection for 54 Wilderness areas totaling 9.1 million acres (3.7 million hectares). All of these first units of the National Wilderness Preservation System were on National Forests and most had been protected by Forest Service administrative decisions since the 1930s. All but four were west of Denver; none were in Alaska.

What became widely known as the Wilderness Bill was first introduced in Congress in the summer of 1956. The bill was a bipartisan proposal from the beginning. The lead sponsors were Rep. John P. Saylor (R–PA) in the House, joined by a number of House cosponsors from both parties, and Sen. Hubert H. Humphrey (D–MN) in the Senate, joined by nine Senate cosponsors, four of whom were Republican. As the senior Republican on the House committee handling the legislation, Representative Saylor championed the bill throughout its eight-year legislative gestation. Senator Humphrey handed off the lead advocate role to senators who chaired the Senate committee that would handle the bill. The first to succeed Senator Humphrey was Sen. James E. Murray (D–MT), followed by Sen. Clinton P. Anderson (D–NM).

From the outset, the essential partner to these members of Congress and their staffs was Howard Zahniser of The Wilderness Society (Harvey, 2005). Zahniser is acknowledged as the architect of the Wilderness Act. He fine-tuned the concepts for such a law in the late 1940s and early 1950s. At the same time, Zahniser worked to build a consensus among conservation leaders that would set the stage to campaign successfully for enactment of a wilderness law. In early 1956, Zahniser created a first draft of the legislation. He remained intimately involved in shaping both the legislation and the campaign to help get it approved until his death on May 5, 1964.

Having spent his career as a professional editor, Zahniser applied his talents to give the Wilderness Act both precision in the technical details and evocative wording to capture the essence of the wilderness concept (Scott, 2002). He sought to make the bill reflect the range of values driving the move to establish legislatively a system for protecting wilderness. While struggling with some of the more complex technical language, Zahniser wrote to a colleague: "I am no bill drafter. If I had to do this again, I would much prefer to state all this in iambic rhyming couplets or even in the sequence of sonnets, than attempt to do this in bill language." (H. Zahniser to George Marshall, personal communication, April 3, 1956). The key phrases of today's Wilderness Act, as shaped by Zahniser's pen over four decades ago, have proven enduring.

- In its statement of policy, the Act acknowledges the *threats* to wilderness lands:

  In order to assure that an increasing population, accompanied by expanding settlement and growing mechanization, does not occupy and modify all areas within the United States and its possessions, leaving no lands designated for preservation and protection in their natural condition, it is hereby declared to be the policy of the Congress *to secure for the American people of present and future generations the benefits of an enduring resource of wilderness.* (Wilderness Act of 1964, 16 U.S.C. § 1131a, emphasis added)

- The Act establishes *contrast* as the foundation of the multiple values for which wilderness is preserved:

  A wilderness, *in contrast* with those areas where man and his own works dominate the landscape, is hereby recognized as an area… where man himself is a visitor who does not remain. (Wilderness Act of 1964, 16 U.S.C. § 1131c, emphasis added)

  As with many such central concepts in the bill, Zahniser drew this idea of contrast from the early founders of the wilderness movement. One of those founders, Bob Marshall, spoke of Americans enjoying

  a twofold civilization—the mechanized, comfortable, easy civilization of 20th-century modernity, and the peaceful timelessness of the wilderness where vast forests germinate and flourish and die and rot and grow again without any relationship to the ambitions and interferences of man. (Marshall, 1936)

- In defining wilderness, the Act first states the *ideal* of wilderness as an area "where the earth and its community of life are *untrammeled* by man" (Wilderness Act of 1964, 16 U.S.C. § 1131c, emphasis added). Zahniser later explained:

  The idea within the word "untrammeled" of their not being subjected to human controls and manipulations that hamper the free play of natural forces is the distinctive one that seems to make this word the most suitable one for its purpose within the Wilderness Bill."

(H. Zahniser to C. Edwards Graves, personal communication, April 25, 1959)

• Working with Zahniser, the Bill's lead sponsors responded to requests "for additional and more concrete details in defining areas of wilderness" by providing the second, *less pure* definition. (Sen. James Murray, *Cong. Rec.*, 86th Cong, 2d sess., 2 July 1960, p. 14454). Note the modifiers in italics:

an area of undeveloped Federal land retaining its primeval character and influence, without *permanent* improvements or human habitation, which is protected and managed so as to preserve its natural conditions and which (1) *generally appears* to have been *affected primarily* by the forces of nature with the imprint of man's work *substantially unnoticeable.* (Wilderness Act of 1964, 16 U.S.C. § 1131c, emphasis added)

Testifying at the final Senate hearing in 1963, Zahniser explained:

the first sentence is definitive of the meaning of the concept of wilderness, its essence, its essential nature—a definition that makes plain the character of lands with which the bill deals, the ideal. The second sentence is descriptive of the areas to which this definition applies—a listing of the specifications of wilderness areas; it sets forth the distinguishing features of areas that have the character of wilderness. (*National Wilderness Preservation Act Hearing*, 1963, p. 68; supplementary statement)

• The Wilderness Act specifies each addition of new Wilderness areas beyond the initial 54 designated by the 1964 Act itself (Wilderness Act of 1964, 16 U.S.C. § 1132a) requires that Congress pass and the President sign a new act (Wilderness Act of 1964, 16 U.S.C. § 1131a, 1132b–c). The Act required agency studies of certain categories of public lands for possible designation—all roadless lands in units of the National Park System and the National Wildlife Refuge System, and five million acres of then-existing "primitive areas" on western National Forests. Within ten years after the Act became law, the President was to provide recommendations to the Congress for adding areas to the original list of designations (Wilderness Act of 1964, 16 U.S.C. § 1132b–d). In 1976, Congress extended this wilderness review process to lands administered by the Bureau of Land Management (Federal Land Policy and Management Act, sect. 603, 43 U.S.C. § 1782). Beyond the lands required to be studied, Congress can also respond directly to citizen proposals and designate areas on its own initiative.

- The Act spells out *permissible uses* of wilderness. Once Congress designates an area as Wilderness, use of motor vehicles and other mechanical forms of transport (e.g., mountain bikes) are prohibited. With very few exceptions, also prohibited are any new extractions of resources, such as timber or minerals (Wilderness Act of 1964, 16 U.S.C. § 1133c). The exceptions are that preexisting nonconforming uses, such as mining or grazing rights, are allowed to remain in effect. Hunting may continue on those lands that were previously open to hunting and designation would protect opportunities for increasingly rare, wilderness-quality hunting where there is no motorized access. Owners of any state or private lands surrounded by a Wilderness area are assured reasonable access (Wilderness Act of 1964, 16 U.S.C. § 1134).

- Both the idea of preserving wild areas and the details of the bill Zahniser helped craft were intensely debated throughout the legislation's eight-year congressional odyssey. One opponent, Sen. Gordon Allott, later recalled, "perhaps there is no other act that was scanned and perused and discussed as thoroughly as every sentence in the Wilderness Act." (*Preservation of Wilderness Areas Hearing*, 1972). As a result of this scrutiny, there is a wealth of legislative history, augmented by precedents established as Congress has designated additional areas since 1964, to guide Wilderness managers and other interests.

A Presumption of Permanence

As the bill to create a Wilderness System was debated, some agency officials objected to the implication that administrative designations might be less permanent and not assured of being overturned at some future time. But for champions of the bill such as Sen. Richard Neuberger (D–OR), the Act would function as a "legislative shield" against development pressures on agency decision makers (*Cong. Rec.*, 85th Cong., 1st sess., 11 February 1957, p. 1906). A 1956 conservationist flyer explains one reason why preservation leaders pushed for congressional rather than administrative designations:

> Our rare, irreplaceable samples of wilderness can be diminished at the will of the administrator, without the sanction of Congress. Under the bill Congress would protect the wilderness interior as well as the

boundaries of all dedicated wilderness. This would strengthen the
hand of the good administrator, and steady the hand of the weak one.
(Trustees for Conservation, 1956)

The crucial impact of the Wilderness Act, compared with the situation before it
became law, is once Congress designates a Wilderness area, it is presumed to be
preserved *in perpetuity*. As referenced in the Act, a congressionally designated
Wilderness area becomes protected "as an *enduring* resource of wilderness"
(Wilderness Act of 1964, 16 U.S.C. § 1131a). The key to this presumption of
permanence is found in how any changes in boundaries or protection are decided. This the Congress reserved for itself. All decisions to alter the boundary
of a Wilderness area, to weaken the basic protections the Act provides, or to
declassify an area must be a congressional action (Wilderness Act of 1964,
16 U.S.C. § 1132e). Any of these steps would require passing a new act of
Congress. Most recently, Congress altered a Wilderness boundary by just 31
acres—but it took a law to do so (Mount Naomi Wilderness Boundary Adjustment Act, 2003).

    Passing an act of Congress was purposely designed by the Founding
Fathers to be difficult—as the eight-year effort to enact the Wilderness Act
demonstrated. The difficulty in gaining enactment is the reason for requiring
that any change in a Wilderness area must be accomplished through a new
act of Congress. It is this shifting of the burden of proof to those that would
alter a Wilderness that underlies the Act's intention to preserve "an enduring
resource of wilderness....for the permanent good of the whole people" (Wilderness Act of 1964, 16 U.S.C. § 1131a and title).

How the Wilderness System Was To Be Built

In the 40 years since the Wilderness Act became law, Congress has passed well
over 100 new Wilderness laws, adding acreage and areas to the National Wilderness Preservation System. Once a new area is designated, it continues to be
managed by the same federal agency originally charged with its administration.
Also, regardless of laws previously affecting its management, each new area
is to be managed so as to preserve its "wilderness character," as described in
Zahniser's ideal concept of Wilderness (Wilderness Act of 1964, 16 U.S.C. §
1133b). As of January, 2004, the National Wilderness Preservation System
totals 105.7 million acres (42.7 million hectares) embracing over 660 units of
federal lands in 44 states and Puerto Rico.

    The growth of the Wilderness System since 1964 reversed a historic trend.
From the administrative designation of the first wilderness area in 1924 until
congressional enactment of the Wilderness Act, just 14.6 million acres were

protected expressly for wilderness values—all by administrative, not statutory, designation. This total grew little after 1939. In the 40-year period since 1964, however, more than seven times as much natural land has been preserved, all under the protection of *statutory* law. In considering the growth of the National Wilderness Preservation System, three points stand out:

(1) **The crucial policy change brought about with enactment of the Wilderness Act** *was replacement of administrative decision making with legislative decision making.*

In the 1940s and 1950s, experience taught conservation organizations that protection promised in administrative decisions could easily be abandoned. In fact, significant portions of areas administratively designated in the 1920s and 1930s were altered by later administrative decisions to make resources—usually timber—commercially available. (Gilligan, 1954)

Given their goal of protecting wilderness in perpetuity, many activists lost faith in administrative decisions that could be changed by the stroke of a pen. Writing in 1939, the head of the Izaak Walton League expressed a growing disillusionment: "There is no assurance that any [wilderness area], or all of them, might not be abolished as they were created—by administrative decree. They exist by sufferance and administrative policy—not by law" (Reid, 1939). Some might interpret this historic change from administrative to legislative decision making as a turn away from professional policymaking by agency experts toward more political processes. In reality, however, administrative decisions can be just as political.

All lands under congressional consideration for designation are federally owned, and as such are the common heritage of all Americans. However, the legislative process of Congress gives additional weight to the views of the congressional delegations from the state and vicinity where a proposed Wilderness area is located. Members of Congress routinely defer to those who represent the local area, just as they would expect deference on matters affecting their own states. Thus, successful designation of additional federal lands as Wilderness reflects a combination of national support leavened with a significant emphasis on local interests, usually necessitating compromise.

Those advocating additional areas must work through a legislative process, which inherently offers great leverage to those who would slow or oppose passage of a new bill. In conceiving and drafting the 1964 Act, wilderness advocates seemed fully aware of the amount of work new legislation would require. They also saw it as a better alternative to the perceived nondurability of administrative protections.

(2)   The politics of Wilderness protection was and is *bipartisan*.

The Wilderness Act was originally championed in the Senate by a liberal Democrat and in the House of Representatives by a conservative Republican. Continuing this bipartisanship, democratic leaders who worked to extend Wilderness designation to additional lands have included Democrats such as Reps. Morris K. Udall (D–AZ), Rep. John F. Seiberling (D–OH), Sen. Frank Church (D–ID) and Sen. Dale Bumpers (D–AR). Republican leaders who worked to add designations have included leaders such as Sens. Thomas Kuchel (R–CA), James L. Buckley (R–NY), and Dan Evans (R–WA).

With the 1964 Wilderness Act in place, the largest increment to the National Wilderness Preservation System (66.3 million acres) came during the administration of a Democrat— President Jimmy Carter. President Carter championed and signed the historic Alaska National Interest Lands Conservation Act of 1980. Republican presidents, however, have signed almost three-quarters of the laws adding areas to the Wilderness System. Of Republican presidents, President Ronald Reagan signed the most bills (43) giving Wilderness status to some 10.6 million acres in 31 states.

This pattern of bipartisan support and the focal role of the local congressional delegations continue to shape the growth of the Wilderness System. In 2002, President George W. Bush signed four Wilderness laws. The largest designated nearly 452 thousand acres in part of Nevada near Las Vegas and was the result of a legislative package worked out between Sen. Harry Reid (D–NV), Sen. John Ensign (R–NV), and conservative Congressman Jim Gibbons (R–NV).

(3)   The *work of citizen conservation organizations* has also been a significant driver behind the growth of the National Wilderness Preservation System.

As discussed earlier, a central concern of members of Congress and industry representatives who were opposed to the original Wilderness Bill was that new designations or boundary changes could only be made through an act of Congress. But in Zahniser's initial design of the designation process, as found in the version of the bill passed by the Senate in 1961, and again in 1963, a somewhat different process was specified. An area recommended by the President for designation would become a new wilderness area, unless within a set time period, Congress "vetoed" it by passing a resolution of disapproval. Ultimately, the chairman of the committee handling the bill in the House of Representatives insisted that a new act of Congress would be required for any additions to the system.

What was viewed by wilderness legislation advocates at the time as a defeat became, in fact, a key to the growth of the Wilderness System. In 1968,

Stewart Brandborg, who succeeded Zahniser as executive director of The Wilderness Society, concluded:

> [the committee chairman's] "blocking effort," as we saw it at the time, has turned out to be a great liberating force in the conservation movement. The Wilderness Law, as it was passed, has opened the way for a far more effective conservation movement, in which people in local areas must be involved in a series of drives for preservation of the wilderness they know.

Sen. Frank Church acknowledged the positive impact of limiting designations to congressional actions in a 1972 conversation with Sen. Gordon Allott who had led Wilderness Bill opponents:

> I recall I was not persuaded at that time that this was the necessary way of handling new additions to the wilderness [system], but from what I have seen since, I think you were quite right. I am glad the act contains this provision because it enables us now to exercise an oversight that we otherwise might well have relinquished to executive discretion alone. (Sen. Frank Church, *Preservation of Wilderness Areas*, 1972, p. 65)

In expanding the National Wilderness Preservation System, Congress has not limited itself to agency and presidential proposals. Proposals prepared by grassroots citizen groups have earned considerable credibility with Congress, often becoming the basis for expanding agency proposals. Congress has seemed to serve as a "court of appeals" to which citizen groups may turn to challenge agency recommendations at times when they may view them as inadequate or based on policies harmful to Wilderness preservation.

As the legislative process is exercised, neither prodesignation nor antidesignation groups have seemed to have any particular advantage in approaching Congress. Either may argue for or against new Wilderness legislation in an attempt to influence a congressional decision. Also, federal land management agencies themselves have considerable influence with Congress. For all the criticisms leveled at Congress, its processes seem well-attuned for weighing and sorting among competing visions and proposals, and rendering decisions that are fundamentally political, but for the most part seemingly nonpartisan.

As Congress has acted on Wilderness designation bills over the past four decades, it has often significantly expanded proposed Wilderness areas beyond the boundaries recommended by the agencies. This process would not have been possible if the only option were for Congress to either accept or veto a presidential recommendation.

Growth of the Wilderness System

The 1964 law set off a hectic pace of agency studies, each including a local public hearing. The requirement for public involvement was an innovation occurring long before the National Environmental Policy Act of 1969, as well as other reforms in planning processes for public lands. It gave citizens a greater right to be heard in federal land management decisions.

Beginning in 1968, Congress began acting on presidential recommendations and passing laws designating new Wilderness areas. As Congress considered these initial recommendations, it had to resolve all manner of complexities, such as how to deal with old roads within a potential Wilderness area, or how to treat pre-existing nonconforming uses and structures. A steady pace of Wilderness designation bills was passed and signed, and they were not limited to areas the Act had originally specified for study.

Designating National Forest Roadless Areas

Even as the initial Wilderness designation laws were being proposed and passed, citizen groups realized that nothing in the Act limited Congress from designating new Wilderness on National Forests beyond the limited five million acres of National Forest "primitive areas" originally specified for study. Favorite roadless tracts viewed as threatened by logging, road building, or other activities could be brought directly to the attention of local congressional representatives.

In an effort to better influence the designation process, the Forest Service initiated the first of two national inventories of roadless areas in 1972—the Roadless Area Review and Evaluation inventories (RARE). Some 60 million acres of National Forest roadless lands were identified through these inventories. None of these lands had been required for study by the Wilderness Act. Though the agency sought to sort between areas to be recommended for Wilderness designation and those to be opened for development, more than 30 years after the first RARE inventory began, considerable controversy remains over the fate of National Forest roadless areas. At the end of his administration, President William J. Clinton issued the Roadless Area Conservation Rule to protect roadless National Forest lands. The future of the "roadless rule" remains uncertain. It has been challenged through numerous lawsuits, and the George W. Bush administration exempted some areas that were to be protected under the Clinton Rule. For example, in early 2004, all roadless National Forest lands in Alaska were exempted.

In the early 1970s, a Forest Service interpretation of the Wilderness Act led to a view that virtually no lands in the eastern half of the United States could qualify as Wilderness because they had a history of prior human development, such as logging and roads (Roth, 1988). Wilderness advocacy organizations challenged this Forest Service interpretation. There was concern that this interpretation might limit designation of more Wilderness areas not only in the East but also in many western valleys where there was evidence of prior human settlement. In compromise, the Forest Service advocated a new "separate-but-equal" system for the East where new designations could be less "pure." This compromise conception would require securing congressional agreement to a new and limiting interpretation of Zahniser's definition of Wilderness as found in the Wilderness Act. Sen. Frank Church, a long-standing advocate of Wilderness, expressed concern to the Chief of the Forest Service that adoption of a "separate-but-equal" philosophy regarding Wilderness in the East would

> be saying, in effect, that you can't include a comparable area in the West in the wilderness system. That is the precise effect of your approach, because you will have redefined section 2(c) [of the Wilderness Act]. (*Eastern Wilderness Areas Hearing*, 1973, p. 31)

This "purity issue" was put to rest in 1975 when President Gerald R. Ford signed the Eastern Wilderness Areas Act designating many new Wilderness areas across the East, South, and Midwest, without altering the Wilderness Act definition. This law reaffirmed the intention of the Wilderness Act; that is, that there was to be one *national* Wilderness System for which the same practical criteria apply—East and West.

Designating BLM Roadless Lands

When the Wilderness Act was being considered by Congress, it was viewed as politically impractical to consider including lands administered by the Bureau of Land Management (BLM). BLM manages tens of millions of acres of lands qualifying as roadless. At that time, however, the agency had no administrative category equivalent to the National Forest "primitive areas," such as was used by the Forest Service in the 1930s and 1940s. When the Wilderness Act was being debated in Congress, to have required an inventory of all BLM roadless lands for potential Wilderness designation was not politically feasible. The result of not considering BLM lands represented a gap in uniformly considering federal lands for Wilderness designation. As political conditions shifted, however, and as it was reforming many of the numerous laws that had grown up around BLM's huge land holdings, Congress included provisions extending the Wilderness review process in the Wilderness Act to BLM-administered roadless lands in 1976 (Federal Land Policy and Management Act of 1976). A subsequent inventory of roadless BLM lands led to a selection of areas for congressional consideration. Some 6.5 million acres of these lands have since been designated by Congress and are now administered under the provisions of the Wilderness Act.

Designating Wilderness on a Grand Scale in Alaska

In the second half of the 1970s, Wilderness protection focused on the future of the vast federal lands in Alaska. Conservation groups argued that before more federal lands were transferred to the State of Alaska or were otherwise opened to development, attention had to be given to protecting "national interest lands," such as potential national parks, wildlife refuges, wilderness, and wild rivers. President Jimmy Carter took office with a stated commitment to the goal of preserving some of the Alaskan federal lands. Conservation groups made their positions known through lobbying and media campaigns. The outcome was the Alaska National Interest Lands Conservation Act that established more national parks, refuges, wilderness, and wild rivers than any single law in U.S. history. This law more than doubled the size of the Wilderness System, adding 56.3 million acres. Included was the nation's largest unbroken expanse of statutorily protected Wilderness, 13 million acres in a unit combining most of the Gates of the Arctic National Park and Noatak National Preserve.

Wilderness and "Release Language"

During the Carter Administration, the federal courts found that the second Forest Service roadless area inventory process (RAREII), completed in 1979, did not adequately consider the site-specific wilderness values of each roadless area before proposing that many of these areas be opened for development. An injunction to stop development led industry groups to demand that bills designating new Wilderness areas on National Forests should specify that roadless areas not designated were to be "released" from further designation consideration until the next rounds of forest management plan revisions were completed—ten to twenty years later. This resulted in a large number of new Wilderness designation laws which also included "release language" for those roadless areas not included as new designations (Roth, 1988). In 1984 alone, President Ronald Reagan signed laws designating eight million acres of new National Forest Wilderness in 22 states combined with release language.

Current Status and Management
of the Wilderness System

Public Support

One measure of the status of the National Wilderness Preservation System is the degree to which it seems supported by the American public. As Congress built the Wilderness System over the last four decades to its present makeup and size, public support has seemed to remain strong. This support has been reflected by both national- and state-level surveys of public opinion. (More detailed coverage of public opinion surveys is provided in Chapters 7 and 8.) Across these public opinion surveys, results have been relatively consistent in indicating public support, whether the surveys were sponsored by the media, advocacy groups, or the federal government. For example, based on sampling results from the National Survey on Recreation and the Environment, support for protecting more Wilderness has remained high over the last several years. In 2000–2001 data, the NSRE found:

- 70 percent of Americans 16 years of age or older favored designating more of the federal lands in their own states as Wilderness, while just 12 percent were opposed.

- Percentages supporting more designations did not differ significantly between regions of the country, nor between urban and rural residents.

- Three-quarters of Hispanic voters favored protecting more Wilderness areas in their own states, while 7 percent were opposed. (Scott, 2003)

A second measure of the status of the Wilderness System is apparent congressional support. Through numerous actions, some noted earlier, Congress has engaged in the ongoing expansion of the National Wilderness Preservation System. This expansion has continued even through periods of varying interest among administration officials, agency leaders, or key congressional leaders. As a result:

- Today, 4.7 percent of all land in all ownerships in the United States, including Alaska, has been protected under the Wilderness Act.

- Looking only at the lower 48 states, 2.5 percent of all land in all ownerships is designated as Wilderness.

- Congress has frequently acted to add area to individual Wilderness areas. For example, the Ventana Wilderness Area in California began as an administratively designated primitive area of 54,857 acres in 1931 and has since been designated and expanded four times to comprise a 239,688-acre Wilderness area today.

- In a legislative process that inherently gives added weight to each state's own congressional delegation, there have been new designations in most states. In most of these states, sponsorship has been bipartisan.

Agencies continue to recommend to Congress additional Wilderness as they take periodic stock through comprehensive management planning of the lands they are charged to administer. Grassroots citizen groups continue to submit new Wilderness proposals through their congressional delegations as well. Citizen proposals led to congressional additions of Wilderness in Alabama, Oregon, and Colorado in 2000 (signed by President Bill Clinton), and additions in Colorado, South Dakota, California, and Nevada in 2002 (signed by President George W. Bush).

Management

Management to Preserve Wilderness Character

The Wilderness Act's goal of preserving the "wilderness character" of selected federal lands for future generations requires more than a congressional decision to designate the areas. It also takes a great deal of management attention by the federal agencies charged with their administration. As George Marshall (1969) wrote: "At the same time that wilderness boundaries are being established and protected by Acts of Congress, attention must be given to the quality of wilderness within these boundaries, or we may be preserving empty shells."

The Wilderness Act sets out one overarching directive for Wilderness administration, regardless of which agency is involved:

> Except as otherwise provided in this Act, each agency administering any area designated as wilderness shall be responsible for preserving the wilderness character of the area and *shall so administer such area for such other purposes for which it may have been established as also to preserve its wilderness character.* (Wilderness Act of 1964, 16 U.S.C. § 1133b, emphasis added)

Zahniser linked this fundamental directive to preserve wilderness character to the ideal definition of Wilderness. Otherwise, the directive would have had no practical function in the Act (Scott, 2002). As Zahniser testified, the ideal definition makes plain "the character of lands with which the bill deals" and functions to give meaning to the Act's directive that administrators preserve "wilderness character."

As the Wilderness System has grown in size, it has also grown in geographical and ecological diversity. The popularity of Wilderness for recreational activities such as backpacking, wildlife viewing, and fishing poses complex challenges for the four federal agencies as they strive to preserve wilderness character across the System's diversity and provide recreational access. To help meet these and other challenges, Rep. Bruce Vento (D–MN), proposed to establish two new institutions: one to promote research and another to train agency personnel for the management of Wilderness. Representative Vento's ideas were the basis for administrative establishment in 1993 of the Aldo Leopold Wilderness Research Institute and the Arthur Carhart National Wilderness Training Center—both headquartered in Missoula, Montana. These institutions have given an emphasis to professional Wilderness management that otherwise would not likely have occurred.

The "Minimum Requirement" Process

Management usually requires the use of tools and equipment, and sometimes ecosystem disturbing activities. Limitations on the types of equipment and uses within Wilderness areas is central to the protections intended by the Wilderness Act. A subsection of the Act captioned Prohibition of Certain Uses (Wilderness Act of 1964, 16 U.S.C. § 1133c) carefully distinguishes prohibited uses, such as commercial enterprises and permanent roads. While there may be exceptions, only under very limited circumstances is equipment, such as chainsaws, motorized equipment, and vehicles, considered necessary. The limitation on agency discretion to select appropriate means and equipment in management of Wilderness was phrased by Zahniser's as follows:

> *[E]xcept as necessary to meet minimum requirements for the administration of the area for the purpose of this Act* (including measures required in emergencies involving the health and safety of persons within the area), there shall be no temporary road, no use of motor vehicles, motorized equipment or motorboats, no landing of aircraft, no other form of mechanical transport, and no structure or installation within any such area. (Wilderness Act of 1964, 16 U.S.C. § 1133c, emphasis added)

This language instituted a two-part test for determining exceptions for normally prohibited equipment and activities by agency personnel. The first test is whether the proposed exceptional activity is judged *necessary*; the second test is selection of the means by which the excepted activity would be the *minimum* required to achieve the intended purpose. Sen. Frank Church, a leader in enacting the Wilderness Act, explained the rationale for this provision:

> We intend to permit the managing agencies a reasonable and necessary latitude in such activities within wilderness where the purpose is to protect the wilderness, its resources and the public visitors within the area—all of which are consistent with "the purpose of the Act." The issue is not whether necessary management facilities and activities are prohibited; they are not—the test is whether they are in fact necessary. (*Preservation of Wilderness Areas*, 1972, pp. 61–62)

The Carhart Wilderness Training Center provides a detailed Minimum Requirement Decision Guide, including instructions and worksheets for a minimum requirements analysis (http://www.wilderness.net/index.cfm?fuse=MRDG).

"Purity" and Nondegradation of Wilderness

Taken together, the directive to preserve wilderness character and the stipulation of "minimum requirements" resulted in a mandate for Wilderness managers. This mandate is often referred to as a *"nondegradation directive."* Congress may designate lands that are not totally natural; that is, lands with some fading imprints of human activities, including nonconforming uses. In effect, whatever an area's past history of human use, once a Wilderness area has been designated, the goal in its management is to move it toward the ideal concept of Wilderness; that is, guided by the ideal where "the earth and its community of life are untrammeled by man." The "nondegradation" concept means management so that all designated areas are to the greatest extent possible moving toward what the etymology of the word "wilderness" suggests: *self-willed lands* (Foreman, 2004).

Congress reinforced the nondegradation idea since passage of the Wilderness Act in its numerous actions to add new areas to the National Wilderness Preservation System. There are many examples where these congressional actions dealt with areas where there was evidence of past human uses and sometimes even development. The lead sponsor of the Act as it passed, Sen. Clinton Anderson (D–NM), urged designation of areas where there was evidence of old roads: "Nature probably will re-cover such a small mark and as long as most of the values are there for wilderness status, the area should be preserved" (*San Gabriel, Washakie, and Mount Jefferson Wilderness Areas*, 1968, p. 178). In 1969, Rep. Morris Udall (D–AZ) successfully urged designation of the Desolation Wilderness in California, even though there existed in the area two small and somewhat inconspicuous dams. Rep. Udall argued:

> No one really wants manmade reservoirs within the national wilderness system. An attempt to build a new reservoir within the national wilderness system would be vigorously opposed. Yet the fact is that scores of similar small reservoirs are already in the system. They were already in existence at the time of passage of the Wilderness Act in 1964 .
>
> It would be nice to have our national wilderness system absolutely pure and completely free of any sign of the hand of man. But the fact is that we are getting a late start in this business of preserving America's wilderness....Whether some prior existing imperfection — something less than absolute purity — is to be accepted... should be determined by whether its inclusion will significantly contribute to the implementation of this national policy of wilderness preservation or whether its omission will significantly obstruct this policy. (*Cong. Rec.*, 91st Cong., 1st sess., 24 September 1969, p. 26909).

A Single, Integrated Wilderness System

As stated earlier, designation of a Wilderness area does not change the agency which has jurisdiction for management of the land. This was a deliberate choice made early in drafting the legislation. It was recognized that multiple jurisdictions were likely the only politically viable approach to creating a Wilderness System. However, this approach creates the obvious need to harmonize policies, as well as day-to-day management, across the responsible agencies. With each agency having its own history, policies and culture, it was seen as entirely possible that different approaches to management and different interpretations of "wilderness character" could emerge.

Zahniser, his advisors, and the original congressional sponsors of the Wilderness Act worked to create some mechanism to promote a unified wilderness system. As first introduced in 1956, the Wilderness Bill provided for a National Wilderness Preservation Council. That council was to include the heads of the wilderness management agencies, together with the chairman and ranking minority party member of the House and Senate committees with land management jurisdiction, six citizen members "known to be informed regarding, and interested in the preservation of wilderness," and the Secretary of the Smithsonian Institution, who was to serve as secretary and maintain the council headquarters (Section 4 of the Senate bill as introduced, S. 4013, 84th Congress, 2d session, 7 June 1956). It was to be "a nonexclusive clearinghouse for exchange of information among the agencies administering areas within the System." However, because of lack of agency, stakeholder and political agreement, sponsors of the Wilderness Bill dropped the idea of a council in 1959. The concept that emerged to replace it, and that was ultimately enacted, was to retain each management agency's jurisdiction over its designated lands but to impose one consistent management mandate for all Wilderness areas regardless of agency jurisdiction.

A Recent Assessment of the Status of Management of the National Wilderness Preservation System

As the Wilderness Act was implemented and the Wilderness System grew in the early years after 1964, it did indeed seem that differences in interpretations and policies among the agencies regarding management of the Wilderness System were emerging. In some instances, contiguous Wilderness areas would be administered by two or three different agencies, each with a somewhat different philosophy and approach to management. While some differences such as permitting hunting were intentional, the overall management or stewardship mandate of the Act is supposed to be identical across agencies. The Act says each agency is to "so administer such area for such other purposes for which it may have been established as also to preserve its wilderness character"

(Wilderness Act of 1964, 16 U.S.C. § 1133b). Preservation of Wilderness character was intended to supercede any other inconsistent agency purposes and to constrain those uses and actions that would conflict with the wilderness preservation mandate.

Increasing recognition of the need for consistency and a growing list of management issues shared across agencies led to the realization of need for interagency review of how the Wilderness System was being administered. This growing realization resulted in an invitation from the four federal wilderness agencies to the Pinchot Institute for Conservation to convene a panel of external experts to review the first 35 years of Wilderness System management. The ultimate aim was to have the Panel make recommendations for the System's future management. The resulting Wilderness Stewardship Panel was chaired by Dr. Perry J. Brown, Dean of the School of Forestry and Conservation at the University of Montana in Missoula. In its September 2001 report, the "Brown Panel" observed that "the National Wilderness Preservation System is more important to the American people than ever before." The Panel's fundamental recommendation was to build

> an integrated, collaborative system across the two departments and four wilderness agencies [The Forest Service is in the Department of Agriculture; the other three agencies are in the Department of the Interior]. To manage the Wilderness as a system means that each area is part of a whole, no matter which agency administers it. It means that all Wilderness [areas] are subject to a common set of guidelines, and thus requires that such guidelines be developed. (Brown, 2001)

The Brown Panel proposed the following eight principles:

- Adherence to the Wilderness Act is a fundamental principle for wilderness stewardship.

- Preservation of wilderness character is a guiding idea of the Wilderness Act.

- U.S. Wilderness is to be treated as a system.

- Wilderness areas are special places and are to be treated as special.

- Stewardship should be science-informed, logically planned, and publicly transparent.

- Nondegradation of wilderness should guide stewardship.

- Recognizing the wild in wilderness distinguishes it from most other land classes.

- Accountability is basic to sound stewardship.

With an aim to increase the probability that the Wilderness System would be sustained, the Brown Panel recommended accelerating the completion of required management plans for each Wilderness area to help guide stewardship and assure evaluation and accountability. The Panel emphasized that the ultimate responsibility lies at a political level, with the Secretaries of the Departments of Agriculture and of the Interior. The Panel recommended that their organizational structure be revised so that consistent management would be the rule across all agencies.

Today, the senior wilderness experts in the Washington, DC, headquarters of each of the four federal agencies meet together as the Wilderness Policy Council, with a major focus of their discussion being to work toward this vision of a single, integrated Wilderness System. While more effort will certainly be needed, it is fair to say that the Brown Panel has helped sensitize agency officials and outside organizations to the importance of this integrated approach, grounded in the mandates of the Wilderness Act.

Wilderness Management in a Larger, Evolving Context

As the social, economic, and ecological landscapes in this country evolve and grow more complex, so too does the context within which the Wilderness System exists, is influenced, and must be managed. For example, growing awareness and science-based understanding of ecological processes and conditions in Wilderness bring with it new challenges. One result of this growing awareness is greater recognition of invasive, non-native plant and animal species in Wilderness areas. A primary question arising in management is how far the agencies should go, if at all, in their removal of invasives and in the restoration of natural conditions. But nature is not static, of course, and this makes the definition of natural conditions complex. Phenomena, such as climate change, makes sorting man-caused change from natural ecological progression highly challenging. Growing sophistication in the ecological sciences could tempt us to undertake well-intentioned management actions that may be in conflict with the fundamental idea of Wilderness as a place which is self-regulating.

Early framers of wilderness legislation, such as Howard Zahniser, cautioned that well-intentioned manipulation of Wilderness could pose a serious threat to the wilderness concept itself. Growing ability to carry out such manipulations could lead to rationalization of certain management actions that may well be in conflict with the philosophy of "protecting areas at their boundaries and trying to let natural forces operate within the wilderness untrammeled by man." As the ideal, Zahniser said, Wilderness areas "should be managed so as to be left unmanaged" without human intervention or manipulation. "With regard to areas of wilderness we should be guardians, not gardeners" (Zahniser, 1963).

Such ideals are noble, yet the modern-day dilemma is that Wilderness areas are not islands protected from influences outside their congressionally designated boundaries. For example, other public lands adjacent to Wilderness areas typically are not managed in ways that would assure protection of ecological conditions within area boundaries. Such other public lands are often vital corridors and habitat for wildlife species that move across a larger territory, including the interiors of Wilderness areas. As another example, Wilderness is a scenic resource for large numbers of people who view it from nearby roads, developed recreation sites or the increasing number of nearby homes. People's perception of the quality of the natural scenery provided by Wilderness, however, can be influenced by the uses and appearance of surrounding lands.

There has been congressional and other concern that buffer zones might be established to control uses of lands surrounding Wilderness. This concern has led to routine additions of language to acts to establish new areas that prohibit such buffer zones. Typical is this language from a 1984 law designating areas in Washington State:

> Congress does not intend that designation of wilderness areas in the State of Washington lead to the creation of protective perimeters or buffer zones around each wilderness areas. The fact that nonwilderness activities or uses can be seen or heard from areas within a wilderness shall not, of itself, preclude such activities or uses up to the boundary of the wilderness area. (Section 9, Washington State Wilderness Act of 1984, Pub. L. No. 98-339, 98 Stat. 30)

If these outside influences can imperil the Wilderness but explicit buffer zones are not allowed, then it is important that Congress specify, as it very often has, that Wilderness boundaries should reach to the edge of present roads and development. For example, when Congress altered the boundary recommended for the High Uinta Wilderness in Utah the congressional committee explained

> The Forest Service's recommended wilderness boundary on the north slope of the range was adjusted to incorporate lower elevation lands in key areas. According to Forest Service and other wildlife data these additions comprise some of the finest elk, moose, and other wildlife habitat in the entire Uinta range. They also include some of the most popular horseback and hiking access trails into the wilderness and will further act as a buffer to keep vehicles and other development removed form [*sic*] the fragile high country that forms the core of the Uinta Range. (H.R. Rep. No. 98-1019, 1984, pp. 4–5)

There are many more examples of the growing complexities of Wilderness management than can be detailed here—and the list is very likely to grow. These growing complexities and challenges will make sound, science-based management and policy even more important in the future (Hendee & Dawson, 2002).

Conclusion

Overall, in 2004, the year of the 40th anniversary of the Wilderness Act of 1964, it appears that the Wilderness Act has had significant effects:

- The United States now has a national system of diverse protected wildlands—diverse ecologically and geographically, diverse in size, and diverse in the mix of compatible human uses.

- The Wilderness System is protected by law, not by administrative sufferance, thus giving it greater permanence.

- The Wilderness System continues to grow, propelled by strong public support nationally and in the states involved.

- Despite inevitable controversies surrounding most Wilderness designation proposals, elected legislators continue to expand the Wilderness System.

- Because of the Wilderness Act, a significant portion of the federal estate has been preserved in natural condition in perpetuity. In Howard Zahniser's words, "The wilderness that has come to us from the eternity of the past, we have the boldness to project into the eternity of the future." (*Wilderness Preservation System Hearings,* 1964, p. 1205)

Tens of millions of acres of roadless federal lands remain suitable for designation as Wilderness. It is likely that more of this roadless acreage will be added to the Wilderness System over coming decades. How much will be added at whose bidding is a question that can only be answered as the future unfolds. Designation decisions are made by Congress, responding to proposals coming in many different ways from many different interests. Just as Congress was far from finished in its building of the National Park System when that system's 40th anniversary came, so too is the building of the Wilderness System far from finished today. One perspective, still relevant today, was offered by U.S. Supreme Court Justice William O. Douglas, writing soon after the Wilderness Act became law forty years ago:

Today we look backward to a time when there was more wilderness than the people of America needed. Today we look forward (and only a matter of a few years) to a time when all the wilderness now existing will not be enough. (Douglas, 1965)

Literature Cited

Alaska National Interest Lands Conservation Act, Pub. L. No. 96-487, 94 Stat. 2371, 16 U.S.C. § 3101 et seq. (1980).

Brandborg, S.M. (1968). Executive Director's Report to the Council, 1966–1967. Wilderness Society Papers, Western History Department, Denver Public Library, Box 2, Denver, Colorado.

Brown, P. L. (2001). *Ensuring the stewardship of the National Wilderness Preservation System: A report to the USDA Forest Service, Bureau of Land Management, US Fish and Wildlife Service, National Park Service, U.S. Geological Survey.* Retrieved April 26, 2004, from http://pinchot.org/publications/policy_reports/wilderness_report.pdf

Congressional Record, 85th Cong, 1st sess., 11 February 1957, p. 1906.

Congressional Record, 86th Cong, 2d sess., 2 July 1960, p. 14454

Congressional Record, 91st Cong., 1st sess., 24 September 1969, p. 26909

Cordell, H.K., Tarrant, M.A., and Green, G.T. (2003). *International Journal of Wilderness, 9*(2), 27–32.

Designating Certain National Forest System Lands in the State of Utah for Inclusion in the National Wilderness Preservation System to Release Other Forest Lands for Multiple Use Management, and for other Purposes, H.R. Rep. No. 98-1019, Pt. 1, 98th Cong., 2d sess., September 13, 1984, pp. 4–5

Douglas, W.O. (1965). Introduction. In H. Manning, *The wild Cascades: Forgotten parkland* (pp. 14–15). San Francisco, CA: Sierra Club.

Eastern Wilderness Areas: Hearing before the Subcommittee on Public Lands, Committee on Interior and Insular Affairs on S. 316, Senate, 93d Cong., 1st sess., February 21, 1973: 31 (testimony of Sen. Frank Church)

Federal Land Policy and Management Act of 1976, sec. 603, 43 U.S.C. § 1782.

Foreman, D. (2004). *Rewilding North America: A vision for conservation in the 21st century.* Washington, DC: Island Press.

Gilligan, J.P. (1954). The contradiction of Wilderness preservation in a democracy. In *Proceedings, 1954 Annual Meeting, Society of American Foresters* (pp. 119–122). Reprinted in *The Living Wilderness 20* (52, Spring-Summer 1955), 25–29.

Harvey, M. (2005). *Wilderness forever: Howard Zahniser and the path to the Wilderness Act.* Seattle, WA: University of Washington Press.

Hendee, J.C. and Dawson, C.P. (2002). *Wilderness management: Stewardship and protection of resources and values* (3rd ed., p. 640). Golden, CO: WILD Foundation and Fulcrum Publishing.

Light, P.C. (2000). *Government's greatest achievements of the past half century.* The Brookings Institution. Retrieved on March 5, 2004, from http://www.brook.edu/comm/reformwatch/rw02.htm

Marshall, G. (1969). Introduction. In M.E. McCloskey and J.P. Gilligan (Eds.), *Wilderness and the quality of life* (pp. 13–15). San Francisco, CA: Sierra Club.

Marshall, R. (1936). Maintenance of Wilderness Areas. In *Proceedings*, 30th Convention of the International Association of Game, Fish and Conservation Commissioners, August 31–September 1, 1936. Grand Rapids, Michigan.

Mount Naomi Wilderness Boundary Adjustment Act, Pub. L. No. 108-95, 117 Stat. 1165 (2003).

National Environmental Policy Act of 1969, 42 U.S.C. § 4321 et seq. (1970).

National Wilderness Preservation Act: Hearings before the Committee on Interior and Insular Affairs, Senate, 88th Cong., 1st sess., February 28 and March 1, 1963, p. 68 (supplementary statement of Howard Zahniser)

Preservation of Wilderness Areas: Hearing before the Subcommittee on Public Lands, Committee on Interior and Insular Affairs on S. 2453 and Related Wilderness Bills, Senate, 92d Cong., 2d sess., May 5, 1972, p. 1, 61–62, 65 (testimony of Sens. Gordon Allott and Frank Church)

Reid, K.A. (1939). Let Them Alone! *Outdoor America, 5*(1), 6.

Roth, D.M. (1988). *The Wilderness movement and the National Forests*. College Station, TX: Intaglio Press.

San Gabriel, Washakie, and Mount Jefferson Wilderness Areas: Hearings before the Senate Subcommittee on Public Lands, Committee on Interior and Insular Affairs, 90th Cong., 2d sess., February 19–20, 1968, p. 178

Scott, D.W. (2002). "Untrammeled," "Wilderness Character," and the Challenges of Managing Wilderness. *Wild Earth, 11*(3-4), 72–79.

Scott, D.W. (2003). *A mandate to protect America's wilderness: A comprehensive review of recent public opinion research*. Washington, DC: Campaign for America's Wilderness. Retrieved March 5, 2004, from http://www.leaveitwild. org/reports/polling_report.pdf

Trustees for Conservation. (1956, June 5). [pamphlet]. San Francisco, CA: Author.

Washington State Wilderness Act of 1984, Pub. L. No. 98-339, 98 Stat. 30

Wilderness Act of 1964, 16 U.S.C. § 1131 et seq. Retrieved November 10, 2004, from http://uscode.house.gov/search/criteria.php

Wilderness Act of 1964, Pub. L. No. 88-577. Retrieved November 10, 2004, from the Wilderness Network at http://www.wilderness.net/index.cfm?fuse=NWPS &sec=legisAct

Wilderness Preservation System: Hearings before the House Subcommittee on Public Lands, Committee on Interior and Insular Affairs, 88th Cong., 2d sess., April 27–30, May 1, 1964, p. 1205. (testimony of Howard Zahniser)

Zahniser, H. (1963). Guardians, not gardeners [editorial]. *The Living Wilderness*, Spring/Summer, 1.

Chapter 4
An Organizing Framework for Wilderness Values

John C. Bergstrom
Russell Professor of Public Policy and
Professor, Department of Agricultural and Applied Economics
University of Georgia, Athens, Georgia

J. M. Bowker
Research Social Scientist
USDA Forest Service, Athens, Georgia

H. Ken Cordell
Senior Research Scientist and Project Leader
USDA Forest Service, Athens, Georgia

Authors' Note: The authors gratefully acknowledge the extensive contributions of participants in the National Wilderness Values Workshop held in Washington, DC, June 2000, toward the development of this framework.

Scientists, philosophers, poets, and politicians have defined wilderness in various physical, biological, and metaphysical terms. Following a metaphysical line of thought, wilderness has been described as a subjective "idea" in the mind of the beholder (Oelschlaeger, 1991). The Wilderness Act uses many physical and biological terms to define statutory wilderness as a land area "without permanent improvements or human habitation....which generally appears to have been affected primarily by the forces of nature" and "has at least five thousand acres of land or is of sufficient size as to make practicable its preservation and use in an unimpaired condition" (Wilderness Institute, 2004). Thus, according to the Wilderness Act, statutory wilderness is clearly a physical place and not just a metaphysical idea.

Capturing both the physical and metaphysical perspectives, Aplet (1999) defines wilderness as "a place where an idea is clearly expressed: the idea of wilderness." The subjective idea of wilderness is also reflected in the language of The Wilderness Act which indicates that wilderness is a place "retaining its primeval character and influence" where "man himself is a visitor who does not remain" and which has "outstanding opportunities for solitude or a primitive and unconfined type of recreation" (Wilderness Network, 2004).

In this chapter, we are concerned with identifying the types of values wilderness provides as a place and as an idea. When referring to Wilderness in this chapter, we mean statutory or official Wilderness with a big "W" as defined by The Wilderness Act. Included are all the separate federal areas across the country that have been officially designated by Congress as Wilderness areas within the National Wilderness Preservation System (NWPS). This chapter begins by presenting a general organizing framework to identify and inventory the values of designated Wilderness. The framework combines the ecological model of ecosystem structure, functions, and services with scientific and philosophical concepts of value. In subsequent sections, different types of Wilderness values are discussed in more detail. Connections among Wilderness values and concluding comments are offered in the final section.

Wilderness Value Accounts, Attributes, Functions, and Services

In June 2000, a national wilderness values workshop was held in Washington, DC. A primary objective of this workshop was to develop a cross-disciplinary framework for understanding and organizing the values of Wilderness and the various dimensions of these values. Figure 4.1 summarizes the results of workshop discussions and deliberations between ecologists, economists, sociologists, social psychologists, philosophers, wilderness educators, planners, and policymakers. The framework accounts for the following dimensions of relevance to identifying, assessing, and measuring Wilderness values: value accounts, Wilderness attributes, Wilderness functions, Wilderness services, and Wilderness values.

Figure 4.1 An organizing framework for Wilderness values

Basic Functional Connections	Measurement Accounts or Categories	Examples of Measures or Indicators
	Social	Developmental/Health Value Social Identity Value Spiritual Value
Wilderness Values	Economic	Active Use Value Passive Use Value Economic Impacts
	Ecologic	Human Life Support Value Animal and Plant Life Support Value
	Ethical	Instrumental Value Intrinsic Value
Wilderness Services	Animal and Plant Habitat Carbon Sequestration Subsistence Living Cultural Preservation Historic Preservation Scientific Discovery Educational Development Personal Physical Health and Growth Personal Emotional Health and Growth Personal Spiritual Health and Growth Community Health and Quality of Life	
Wilderness Functions	Preservation of Natural and Wild Places Recreational and Experiential Setting Ecosystem and Biodiversity Preserve	
Wilderness Attributes	Geographic Geologic Hydrologic Atmospheric Biologic Naturalness Wildness Constructed	

Value Accounts

Four primary accounts for categorizing Wilderness values, but not in a mutually exclusive manner, are the social, economic, ecologic, and ethical accounts or categories (see Figure 4.1). The social account includes a broad array of anthropocentric values and impacts of Wilderness on individuals and communities not measured in dollar terms. The economic account includes anthropocentric values and impacts of Wilderness on individuals and communities measured in dollar terms. The ecologic account includes biophysical concepts and measures of Wilderness ecosystem health and biodiversity. The ethical account includes philosophical concepts of values and impacts related to fairness, justness, and goodness.

Wilderness Attributes

As mentioned previously, wilderness is both an idea and a place. As a place given special status, Wilderness areas have particular observable attributes or characteristics. These attributes, which are objectively measurable, include geographic area, location, topography, geologic composition, hydrologic composition, climate, atmosphere, fauna, and flora. One of the first steps toward assessing Wilderness values is to inventory the attributes of Wilderness. As indicated earlier, this inventory applies specifically to the attributes of statutory Wilderness designated by Congress as areas within the National Wilderness Preservation System. This inventory can occur at different scales including assessing the attributes of an individual designated Wilderness area, all designated Wilderness areas in a region, or all designated Wilderness in the United States. Various attributes of the current National Wilderness Preservation System are discussed in Chapters 5 and 6.

Wilderness Functions

The objectively measurable attributes of Wilderness areas, such as flora and fauna, water storage and flow, and geographic features, support a number of major functions. These functions or fundamental purposes include preservation of natural and wild places, provision of recreational and experiential settings, and preservation of ecosystem health and biodiversity.

The Wilderness Act clearly recognizes preservation of natural and wild places as one of the functions or fundamental purposes of Wilderness areas. The Act, for example, indicates that a Wilderness area is a place of "primeval character and influence" which is protected and managed "so as to preserve its natural conditions." In the context of the Wilderness Act, natural conditions or naturalness refers to the presence of plants, animals, and physical landscape features in ecosystems that are not being manipulated by humans. In an analysis of the nature of *wildness*, Aplet (1999) explains the degree of wildness in a place is a function of naturalness and "freedom from control." Aplet argues that Wilderness is a place with a high degree of wildness where high levels of both naturalness and freedom from human management can be observed and experienced. Thus, a unique function or fundamental purpose of Wilderness, as recognized by most authors, is that it preserves high levels of both naturalness and freedom from human interference or control (Aplet, 1999; Godfrey-Smith, 1979; Hammond, 1985; see also Chapters 5 and 6).

The Wilderness Act also clearly recognizes the function of Wilderness as a setting for recreational and other human experiences. The Act, for example, states that Wilderness is a place with "outstanding opportunities for solitude or a primitive and unconfined type of recreation." The experience of "solitude" referred to in the Act may or may not be tied to recreational activities. A solitude experience, for example, may be an outcome of a course or program in personal development or therapy involving visits to a Wilderness area. The function of Wilderness as an experiential setting is also indicated in The Wilderness Act passage stating that Wilderness areas "may also contain ecological, geological, or other features of scientific, educational, scenic, or historical value." The unique recreational opportunities and therapeutic, scientific, educational, scenic, historical, and cultural experiences supported by Wilderness have been addressed by a number of authors (Aplet, 1999; Godfrey-Smith, 1979; Hammond, 1985; Morton, 1999; Oelschlaeger, 1991; Rolston, 1985; see also Chapters 7, 8, 9, 10 and 12).

In recent years, designation of areas as Wilderness in order to preserve their ecosystem health and biodiversity has gained more attention. The Wilderness Act does not explicitly recognize this function, but it is alluded to in the passage indicating that Wilderness is an area of undeveloped federal land which retains its primeval character and influence and which is protected and managed so as to preserve its natural conditions. The ecological function of Wilderness areas includes preservation of healthy, functioning ecosystems and the support of native biodiversity. Preservation of healthy ecosystems, including perhaps entire ecosystems within the boundaries of a designated Wilderness area, can provide a storehouse of opportunity for scientific observation of a variety of plants and animals and components of regional and even global chemical cycles, such as hydrologic, carbon, and oxygen cycles (Morton, 1999; Noss, 1996; Rolston, 1985; see also Chapters 11 and 12).

Wilderness Services

Wilderness services flow to individual nonhuman and human agents and to communities alike. These services are a result of the functions of Wilderness areas as ecosystem preserves and experiential settings, which are in turn the result of the extant attributes of Wilderness. For example, the function of Wilderness areas to provide *recreational and experiential settings* supports services such as personal leisure associated with on-site recreational activities and personal healing associated with on-site therapeutic activities.

Wilderness areas also provide a setting where people can contemplate the inspirational qualities of nature and may experience "spiritual revival, moral regeneration, and aesthetic delight" (Godfrey-Smith, 1979; Rolston, 1985). The presence of Wilderness may also contribute to the overall social well-being and quality of life in human communities through recreational, therapeutic, religious, or spiritual activities. The quantity and quality of personal physical, emotional, or spiritual growth; community well-being; and quality of life supported by recreational or therapeutic activities are influenced by the attributes of Wilderness areas where the activities take place.

The function of preserving natural and wild places complements the recreational function of Wilderness. Wilderness areas, for example, provide primitive camping opportunities where one can see and experience wildlands as they once were before westward expansion from the populated East Coast (Hammond, 1985; Morton, 1999; Rolston, 1985). Wilderness recreational experiences characterized by high degrees of both naturalness and freedom from human control also complement the function of providing a setting for personal physical, emotional, and spiritual growth. Wilderness can also provide unique opportunities for scientific discovery and educational development as a natural, outdoor classroom (Aplet, 1999; Godfrey-Smith, 1979; Morton, 1999; Rolston, 1985; Russell, Hendee & Cooke, 1998). In some areas of the United States, such as Alaska, Wilderness may also support subsistence living for Native American populations, and by so doing help preserve Native American cultures.

The function of Wilderness to preserve ecosystem health and biodiversity complements its other two functions, discussed earlier, in the provision of many of the services listed in Table 4.1. For example, preservation of ecosystem health and biodiversity greatly enhances the use of Wilderness as a natural outdoor laboratory and classroom. As well, preservation of ecosystem health and biodiversity may contribute to personal physical, emotional, and spiritual growth through nature-based medicines and personal satisfaction gained from contemplating the existence of well-functioning and biologically diverse ecosystems. Healthy ecosystems also complement the function of preservation of natural and wild places to directly serve nonhuman biological agents through the provision of animal and plant habitat.

As a component of regional and global chemical cycles, Wilderness areas contribute to ecological services such as carbon sequestration. Such ecological services have the potential to affect living organisms over broad geographic and temporal scales. For example, to the extent that carbon sequestration helps to regulate global climate, the carbon stored in or released from Wilderness areas may contribute to both regional and global life support in the short- and long-run (Costanza & Daly, 1992; Costanza et al., 1997; England, 2000). Values supported by these wilderness services are introduced in the next section.

Wilderness Values

Wilderness areas are part of the natural capital of a region or landscape (Morton, 1999). Natural capital can be defined as an asset composed of objectively measurable attributes, such as flora, fauna and geologic features. These attributes interact to provide major functions, such as chemical cycling. The major functions of natural capital provide asset services to people and all other living organisms, such as oxygen to breathe and water to drink. Like other forms of capital assets (e.g., financial, constructed, human capital), if the attributes and functions of the capital asset are protected and maintained, asset services can be provided on a sustainable basis, unless the service involves depletion of a fixed stock (e.g., crude oil extraction). In the case of Wilderness areas, most natural capital services are derived from renewable resources and therefore are in the nature of sustainable asset flows (Bergstrom & Loomis, 1999; Costanza & Daly, 1992; England, 2000; Morton, 1999).

Natural capital services provide individuals and society with a broad array of benefits. Human, animal, and plant health benefits, for example, are often cited as major reasons for protecting and maintaining ecological services, such as chemical cycling, which are dependent upon natural capital (Costanza et al., 1997; Daly & Cobb, 1994; England, 2000). As a special form of natural capital, the attributes and functions of designated Wilderness areas as defined by the Wilderness Act provide the services illustrated in Figure 4.1. The services from Wilderness provide values which can be organized into the four accounts or categories shown in Figure 4.1; that is, social, economic, ecologic, and ethical.

As illustrated in Figure 4.1, each of the four value accounts can be linked to specific types of value measures or indicators. These measures or indicators originate from different scientific disciplines, each of which has developed its own sets of theories and scientific methods. Under the social account, as discussed in Chapters 7 and 8 of this book, psychologists, sociologists, and anthropologists have developed social concepts of use and nonuse values and quantitative and qualitative ways of accounting for these values. Under the economic account, as discussed in Chapters 9 and 10 of this book, economists have developed economic concepts of use and nonuse values and economic impacts means of measuring these values in dollar terms. Under the ecologic account, and discussed in Chapter 11 of this book, ecologists and other biological scientists include human life support indicators and animal and plant life support indicators. Under the ethical account, as discussed in Chapter 12 of this book, philosophers include instrumental values and intrinsic values.

The Wilderness value accounts shown in Table 4.1 are not necessarily mutually exclusive as more than one discipline may have a perspective on the most appropriate measure or method for assessing the value of Wilderness. For example, consider the concept of existence value. Existence value for, say, an endangered bird species may be broadly defined as the value ascribed to its continued existence whether or not people are able to see, photograph, or otherwise directly interact with it. The existence value of the bird species, as defined broadly here, could be taken into account under each of the four value accounts shown in Figure 4.1.

Under the social account, the bird's continued existence may provide specific psychological or sociological values to particular individuals or cultures that cannot be quantified in monetary terms. Under the economic account, existence value of the bird species is a specific type of passive use value and could be defined in monetary terms (e.g., willingness-to-pay) to reflect the value an individual places on continued existence of the bird beyond economic values associated with active use in the present or future (e.g., present or future birdwatching activities). Under the ecologic account, continued existence of the bird may be an important indicator of overall ecosystem health and biodiversity needed to support both human and nonhuman life.

Under the ethical account, continued existence of the bird would have both instrumental and intrinsic values. An example of an instrumental value is the value of the bird as an input into generating happiness in a person who enjoys viewing the bird in the field or in pictures. Instrumental values obviously overlap with social and economic values. Intrinsic values of the bird include values of the bird beyond human active or passive use. That is, philosophically, the intrinsic value of the bird is the value that exists even in the absence of people.

In summary, Table 4.1 provides an organizing framework that recognizes the linkages between Wilderness attributes, functions, services, and values. Wilderness attributes support functions, Wilderness functions support services, and Wilderness services support Wilderness values. However, while Table 4.1 implies a linear relationship, the contributions of attributes, functions, and services of Wilderness to specific types of values, such as existence value, are inseparable.

Literature Cited

Aplet, G.H. (1999). On the nature of wildness: Exploring what wilderness really protects. *Denver University Law Review*, *76*, 347–367.

Bergstrom, J.C. and Loomis, J.B. (1999). Economic dimensions of ecosystem management. In H.K. Cordell and J.C. Bergtrom (Eds.), *Integrating social sciences with ecosystem management* (pp. 181–193). Champaign, IL: Sagamore Publishing.

Costanza, R. and Daly, H.E. (1992). Natural capital and sustainable development. *Conservation Biology*, *6*, 37–46.

Constanza, R., d'Arge, R., de Groot, R., Farber, S., et al. (1997). The value of world's ecosystem services and natural capital. *Nature*, *387*, 253–260.

Daly, H.E. and Cobb, J., Jr. (1994). *For the common good*. Boston, MA: Beacon Press.

England, R.W. (2000). Natural capital and the theory of economic growth. *Ecological Economics*, *34*, 425–431.

Godfrey-Smith, W. (1979). The value of wilderness. *Environmental Ethics*, Winter, 309–319.

Hammond, J.L. (1985). Wilderness and heritage values. *Environmental Ethics*, Summer, 165–170.

Morton, P. (1999). The economic benefits of wilderness: Theory and practice. *Denver University Law Review*, *76*, 465–518.

Noss, R.F. (1996). Soul of the wilderness. *International Journal of Wilderness*, August, 3–8.

Oelschlaeger, M. (1991). *The idea of wilderness: From prehistory to the age of ecology*. New Haven, CT: Yale University Press.

Rolston, H. (1985). Valuing Wildlands. *Environmental Ethics*, Spring, 23–48.

Russell, K., Hendee, J.C., and Cooke, S. (1998). Social and economic benefits of a U.S. wilderness experience program for youth-at-risk in the Federal Job Corps. *International Journal of Wilderness*, December, 2–8.

Wilderness Institute. (2004). *Wilderness legislation: The Wilderness Act of 1964*. Retrieved May 5, 2004, from http://www.wilderness.net/index.cfm?fuse=NW PS&sec=legisAct

Chapter 5
The Human Context and Natural Character of Wilderness Lands

H. Ken Cordell
Senior Research Scientist and Project Leader
USDA Forest Service, Athens, Georgia

Danielle Murphy
Research Coordinator, Department of Agricultural and Applied Economics
University of Georgia, Athens, Georgia

Kurt Riitters
Research Scientist
USDA Forest Service, Research Triangle Park, North Carolina

J. E. Harvard III
former University of Georgia employee

This chapter describes the lands that make up the National Wilderness Preservation System (NWPS). The first section includes statistics on trends in designations since the creation of the NWPS and describes the current size of the System in total land area and number of areas across the country. Also included are descriptions of the prevalence of NWPS lands by states and regions of the country and for each of the four federal land management agencies responsible for their management. The second section describes the human context of Wilderness lands; that is, their location relative to human population centers, other land uses, and roads. A third section summarizes three key natural features of Wilderness—elevation, precipitation, and ecosystem types—represented in the System.

Data to describe the NWPS were obtained from a number of major sources. These include the Wilderness Information Network, the U.S. Geological Survey (USGS), the Bureau of Census, the USDA Natural Resources Conservation Service, and the USDA Forest Service. To calculate acreage, area, and the spatial distribution of Wilderness lands, and to track trends by year of their designation, data were obtained from the Wilderness Information Network (Wilderness Institute, 2003). Data describing the uses of land across the country were obtained from the National Resources Inventory (USDA, 2001). Data for describing the relationship between roads and Wilderness were obtained through the National Land Cover Database (Vogelmann et al., 2001; Vogelmann, Sohl & Howard, 1998). Much of the descriptive data summarized here are reported by Census region or by Census division within regions (Figure 5.1). Alaska is reported separately from the West region where data availability permits. Alaska is officially in the West Census region, but that state is so geographically separated and different from other western states that it is treated as a separate region. Throughout this chapter, and as in preceding chapters, Wilderness is capitalized to distinguish lands officially designated by Congress as areas within the NWPS.

Trends in Designations and Current Size of the NWPS

The first lands designated as units of the National Wilderness Preservation System in 1964 included 54 areas the legislation identified as totaling 9.1 million acres, but later determined to be 11.4 million acres. Today, after numerous new designations over the four decades since passage of the original Act, the NWPS is made up of 662 units that total 105,678,911 acres (as of January 2004; see Table 5.1, page 60). This is nearly a twelve-fold increase over the original System land area (Wilderness Institute, 2003). The total area of Wilderness to date is 4.7 percent of the land area of the United States, including Alaska.

Alaska alone accounts for almost 55 percent of the total area of the NWPS (Campaign for America's Wilderness, 2002). And, as noted in Chapter 3, the System continues to grow. Eighteen new areas were designated in November 2002 alone, adding 452,530 acres. As well, legislation was under way to make further additions in 2004 (Wilderness Institute, 2003).

System Designation Trends

Figures 5.2 through 5.4 (pages 61–63) show the changes in total acreage and number of Wilderness areas over time in the East, West, and Alaska regions. The Mississippi River is used to distinguish between the East and West regions. The five periods used to show trends include the first year of the system, 1964, and the subsequent periods of 1965–1974, 1975–1984, 1985–1994, and 1995–2003.

Figure 5.2 (page 61) shows the number of acres (millions) designated in the East and West in the contiguous United States from 1964 to 2003. Comparison of the number of acres added between these two regions emphasizes the significantly greater amount of federal land in the West which has met the definition presented in the Wilderness Act. The areas originally comprising the

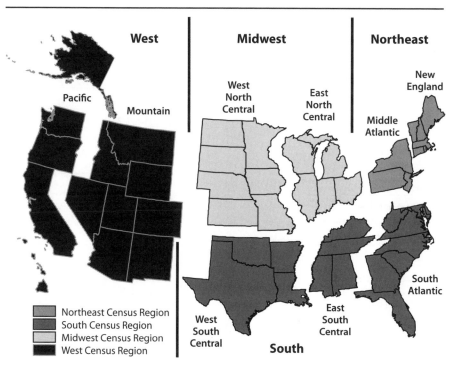

Source: Map created using the states shape file provided by Environmental Systems Research Institute (ESRI), 1999

Figure 5.1 Census regions and divisions of the United States

NWPS included mostly mountainous National Forest land in the West, much of which had been administratively designated for protection as primitive or wilderness areas by the Forest Service decades earlier. In 1964 only 36 thousand acres were designated Wilderness in the East. But, as significant additions have occurred across the years to include lands representing alpine tundra, shortgrass prairie, swamp, and ocean strand, a greater representation of eastern ecosystems types has also been added (Carter, 1992).

In the following ten years, 1965 to 1974, more acres were designated in the East, a total of 390 thousand. In the West during this same period, 1.9 million acres were added. From 1975 to 1984, highly active legislation added areas and acreage throughout the United States. In the East during this period, some 2.3 million acres were added. This included some major additions resulting from the Eastern Wilderness Areas Act of 1975 (EWAA). In the West, 16.8 million

Table 5.1 Number of Wilderness areas and acres by census region, managing agency, and in Alaska, 2004

Census Region	Areas	Acres	Percentage of National Total
Alaska	48	57,509,859	54.4
Forest Service	19	5,753,336	5.4
Fish & Wildlife Service	21	18,676,912	17.7
National Park Service	8	33,079,611	31.3
West	438	43,856,229	41.5
Bureau of Land Management	159	6,512,227	6.2
Forest Service	239	27,059,553	25.6
Fish & Wildlife Service	15	1,461,047	1.4
National Park Service	25	8,823,402	8.4
Midwest	48	1,354,061	1.3
Forest Service	33	1,070,237	1.0
Fish & Wildlife Service	12	57,742	0.1
National Park Service	3	226,082	0.2
South	109	2,753,038	2.6
Forest Service	84	796,966	0.8
Fish & Wildlife Service	18	470,280	0.5
National Park Service	7	1,485,792	1.4
Northeast	19	205,724	0.2
Forest Service	13	183,384	0.2
Fish & Wildlife Service	5	20,977	0.0
National Park Service	1	1,363	0.0
National Total	662	105,678,911	100.0

Source: Wilderness Institute, 2003

acres were added between 1975 and 1984. Between 1985 and 1994, 280 thousand acres were added in the East. In the West there was another round of sizeable designations adding 13.2 million acres. From 1995 through 2003, designation continued, adding 20 thousand acres in the East and 1.4 million acres in the West. Again, the large difference in acreage reflects the relative abundance of federal lands in each region.

Alaska seems to hold a special place in people's minds with regard to wildness. In 1879 John Muir remarked, "To the lover of pure wildness Alaska is one of the most wonderful countries in the world" (Nash, 1982). It was not until 1980, however, that substantial acreage in Alaska was added to the NWPS. Figure 5.3 (page 62) shows the number of acres designated Wilderness in Alaska over the three time periods: 1965–1974, 1975–1984, and 1985–1994. No Alaskan lands were designated with the first Wilderness legislation in 1964, and none has been added of late; that is, between the years 1995 and 2003. It

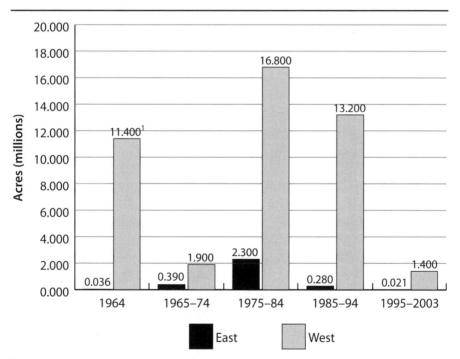

[1] The Wilderness Act requires that agencies validate the acreage of any areas designated by Congress. The validation that occurred after passage of the Wilderness Act later showed that the acreage for the 54 original areas designated actually totaled 11.4 million acres, rather than the estimated of 9.1 million.

Source: Wilderness Institute, 2003

Figure 5.2 Number of acres designated as Wilderness in the East and West regions of the contiguous United States between 1964 and 2003 (excluding Alaska)

was during the decade from 1965 to 1974 that the first designations were made in Alaska, totaling just 90 thousand acres. In the next ten years, however, very significant additions were legislated, totaling 57.2 million acres—more than half the total area of the Wilderness System as it exists today. This was a result, as noted in Chapter 3, of the Alaska National Interest Lands Conservation Act of 1980 (Wilderness Institute, 2003). The most recent Wilderness designations in Alaska between 1985 and 1994 consisted of 280 thousand acres.

Figure 5.4 shows the number of individual Wilderness areas designated in the East, West and Alaska from 1964 to 2003. The number of areas designated generally follows the same trend as the number of acres designated. In 1964 there were 3 areas designated in the East and 51 in the West. From 1965 to 1974, 12 areas were designated in the East, 21 in the West. During this period as well, 6 areas were added in Alaska.

The highest number of Wilderness areas designated among the time periods for a single region was during the period 1975 to 1984 in the West region. During these years, 229 areas were designated in the West, 82 in the East, and

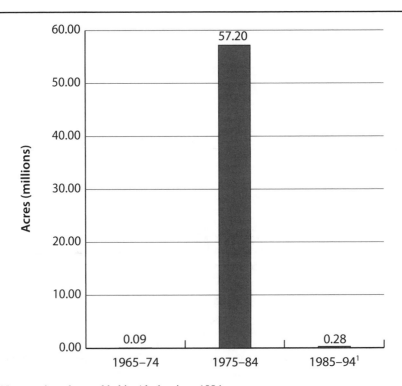

[1] No acres have been added in Alaska since 1994.

Source: Wilderness Institute, 2003

Figure 5.3 Number of acres designated Wilderness in Alaska, 1965 through 1994

37 in Alaska. During the next decade, 1985 to 1994, 35 areas were added in the East, and 144 areas were added in the West. The last additions made to the NWPS in Alaska (5 areas) were legislated between 1985 and 1994. From 1995 to now, only 4 areas have been added in the East while 33 areas were added in the West. Although relatively few areas have been designated in Alaska, by far that state has the greatest total acreage of designated Wilderness. The average size per designated Wilderness area in Alaska is 1.2 million acres. In the West the average size is considerably less at around 94 thousand acres. In the East, it is only 22 thousand acres (Wilderness Institute, 2003).

Size, Regions, and Management Agencies

Table 5.2 (page 64) shows Wilderness areas as a percentage of total U.S. land area and as a percentage of total federal land area. Wilderness makes up almost 16 percent of all land in Alaska. Of federally owned land in Alaska, 26 percent is Wilderness. Relative to the other regions in the contiguous United States, the West Census region (excluding Alaska) has the largest percentage of its total land area (public plus private) designated Wilderness (5.8%). Of federal lands in the West region, just over 12 percent is Wilderness. The West Census

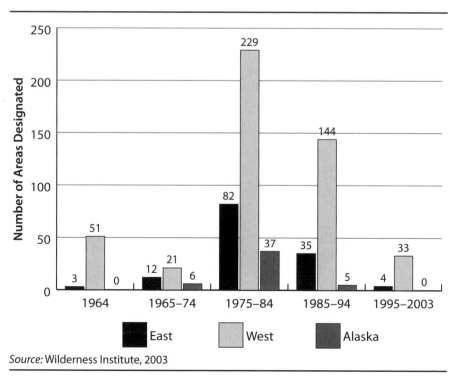

Source: Wilderness Institute, 2003

Figure 5.4 Number of Wilderness areas designated in the East, West, and Alaska between 1964 and 2003

region is followed, in order, by the South, Midwest, and Northeast regions in terms of percentage of total land area designated. In none of these three regions, however, is designated Wilderness a substantial percentage of land area. In the Northeast Census region, Wilderness is only 0.2 percent of total land area. Of all federally owned lands in the Northeast Census region, Wilderness comprises 8.3 percent. In the South, Wilderness is almost 0.5 percent of total land area, and 9.6 percent of federal lands in that region. In the Midwest, Wilderness is almost 0.3 percent of total land area and 5.7 percent of that region's federal lands.

The NWPS is managed by four federal land management agencies (see Table 5.1, page 60). These agencies include the Bureau of Land Management (BLM), which manages 6.5 million acres (2% of total BLM land, none is in Alaska). The NWPS is also managed by the USDA Forest Service which is responsible for 34.6 million acres (18% of all National Forest land). Almost 5.8 million acres of National Forest lands in Alaska are designated Wilderness. The U.S. Fish and Wildlife Service (FWS) manages 20.7 million acres of Wilderness (22% of that agency's total land area). Of the FWS designations, 18.7 million acres are in Alaska. The National Park Service (NPS) manages more Wilderness land than any of the other agencies, 44.2 million acres. Of the NPS lands in the lower 48 states, about 10.5 million acres has been designated. Almost 34 million acres of the National Park System land in Alaska is designated (Wilderness Institute, 2003). Figure 5.5 shows the proportion of Wilderness managed across all four managing agencies.

Table 5.1 also includes the number of Wilderness areas and acres of land area designated in each Census region and in Alaska. Fifty-eight percent of Wilderness in Alaska is managed by the National Park Service. Another 32 percent is managed by U.S. Fish and Wildlife Service. The remaining area of Wilderness is under the jurisdiction of the Forest Service. The West Census region contains over 41 percent of the total area of land in the NWPS and 438 of its 662 areas. This is two thirds of the Nation's total count of areas. The U.S.

Table 5.2 Percentage of total U.S. land base and percentage of land area designated as Wilderness by census region and for Alaska, 2004

Census Regions	Percentage of total land area	Percentage of Federal land area
Alaska	15.9	26.3
West	5.8	12.1
South	0.5	9.6
Midwest	0.3	5.7
Northeast	0.2	8.3

Sources: Total land area from U.S. Census Bureau, 2000; Wilderness land area from wilderness.net, November 2004

Forest Service manages 56 percent of the West's total land area designated as Wilderness, and about 59 percent of all of this region's designated areas. Following the Forest Service in terms of percentage of the West region's number of designated areas, but third in percentage of total land area designated, is the Bureau of Land Management. The Bureau manages 36 percent of the West region's Wilderness areas and just under 15 percent of its Wilderness land area. In descending order, the South has 2.8 million acres of designated Wilderness in 109 areas, the Midwest has over 1.3 million acres and 48 areas, and the Northeast region contains the least amount of Wilderness with a total of almost 205 thousand acres and 19 areas. Obviously, the average size of designated Wilderness areas in the West and in Alaska is much larger than in the other three regions to their east. Figure 5.5 shows the distribution of Wilderness management across all four managing agencies.

Table 5.3 (page 66) highlights the number of areas and acres in the ten states with the greatest total acreage of congressionally designated Wilderness (Wilderness Institute, 2003). As one might expect, the states with the greatest amount of designated land are Alaska, followed by nine other West region states. The nine western states in order of area within the System are: California, Arizona, Washington, Idaho, Montana, Colorado, Wyoming, Oregon, and Nevada. Together, Wilderness acreage in the top ten states comprises 93 percent of the NWPS. Total acreage of Wilderness among the ten states listed in Table 5.3 ranges from a high of 57.5 million in Alaska (15.4% of that state's total land area) to just over 2.1 million acres in Nevada. Of the "lower" 48 states, the state with the largest number of Wilderness areas is California, which has 130 areas. Wilderness in California makes up 13.8 percent of that state's total land area.

Average size of Wilderness areas varies considerably among the top ten states. For example, Idaho has the smallest number of Wilderness areas of the

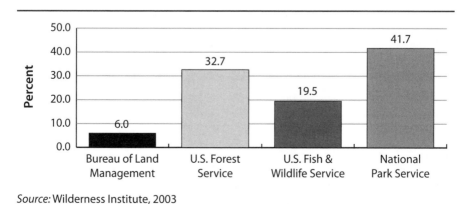

Source: Wilderness Institute, 2003

Figure 5.5 Percent of the National Wilderness Preservation System managed by each agency

ten top states listed in Table 5.3, but it ranks fifth in total land area designated. Average size of Wilderness areas in Idaho is approximately 574 thousand acres. The Frank Church River of No Return Wilderness in Idaho is one of the larger areas in the contiguous 48 states encompassing about 2.4 million acres. Nevada, on the other hand, has 42 designated areas statewide which total just over 2.1 million acres with an average area size of only 67 thousand acres, about one eighth the Idaho average. Six states do not have any designated Wilderness. They are Connecticut, Delaware, Iowa, Kansas, Maryland, and Rhode Island.

The Human Context of Wilderness

Ambient Population

The 2003 U.S. permanent resident population was estimated to be around 292 million. By 2020 the U.S. population is projected to be almost 325 million. Rising population and economic growth typically lead to increased land development and other intensive land uses. In the last few decades, land development has increasingly pushed into rural areas in regions such as the South, including forests and other areas previously dominated by natural processes (Cordell & Overdevest 2001; Wear, 2002). This spread of development and population onto rural lands often occurs near and sometimes adjacent to public lands, including lands designated as Wilderness. In turn, land development and associated human activities usually lead to disruptions of the natural functions of eco-

Table 5.3 Number of Wilderness areas and acres in the ten states having the greatest total acres, 2004

State	Areas	Acres	Percentage of national total acres
Alaska	48	57,509,859	54.4
California	130	13,975,535	13.2
Arizona	90	4,518,442	4.3
Washington	30	4,324,182	4.0
Idaho	7	4,015,061	3.8
Montana	15	3,442,416	3.3
Colorado	40	3,171,685	3.0
Wyoming	15	3,111,132	2.9
Oregon	40	2,258,238	2.1
Nevada	42	2,123,343	2.0
Total	**457**	**98,449,893**	**93.0**
National Total	**662**	**105,678,911**	

Source: Wilderness Institute, 2003

systems and sometimes can threaten their natural integrity and their ability to provide adequate life support to the plant and animal populations making up and inhabiting those ecosystems. In describing the National Wilderness Preservation System, it is important to include the spatial relationship of System lands with the uses and human habitation of surrounding lands. Because these surrounding lands do not have the same protection as designated Wilderness lands have, significant impacts are highly possible. Generally, the closer Wilderness is to developed, populated areas, the less autonomy they have and, therefore, the more vulnerable they are to outside, human influences. This section examines the spatial proximity of designated Wilderness to population centers of different sizes, roads, and nearby lands being used in different ways.

The first measure used for proximity of human habitation and activity to Wilderness examines how much of Wilderness System lands lay within 100 miles of populated areas of different sizes (Table 5.4). Population center sizes considered are: under 50,000, 50 to 100 thousand, 100 to 500 thousand, those 500 thousand to 1 million, and large cities of over 1 million.

This examination shows that most of the total land area designated as Wilderness lies within 100 miles of a population center of some size. In the contiguous 48 states, 93 percent of all designated Wilderness areas are within

Table 5.4 Number of areas and acres of Wilderness within 100 miles of population centers of selected sizes, by census region and in Alaska, 2004

Alaska	Areas	Acres	Midwest	Areas	Acres
0–50k	42	49,501,853	0–50k	44	1,344,387
50–100k	0	0	50–100k	17	988,837
100–500k	1	1,350,592	100–500k	9	51,737
500k–1 million	0	0	500k–1 million	1	12,945
over 1 million	0	0	over 1 million	0	0

West	Areas	Acres	Northeast	Areas	Acres
0–50k	409	42,503,512	0–50k	16	197,432
50–100k	250	24,049,945	50–100k	13	169,502
100–500k	240	16,525,460	100–500k	11	155,862
500k–1 million	54	3,817,420	500k–1 million	0	0
over 1 million	61	2,660,127	over 1 million	3	11,704

South	Areas	Acres
0–50k	106	2,752,137
50–100k	98	2,647,156
100–500k	67	2,040,936
500k–1 million	15	456,353
over 1 million	1	3,855

Sources: Cities and towns data from USGS, 2003; 2000 population data from U.S. Census Bureau, 2003; Wilderness data from Wilderness Institute, 2003

100 miles of at least one small to moderate size town with population under 50 thousand people. In Alaska 85 percent of all Wilderness areas are within 100 miles of a community of under 50 thousand. As the size of population centers is increased, however, the number of Wilderness areas within 100 miles decreases. Even at the upper extreme of population size—that is, population centers with greater than 1 million—there is at least one Wilderness area within 100 miles in the West, South, and Northeast. In terms of land area of designated Wilderness, across the country about 90 percent is within 100 miles of the smaller population centers of up to 50 thousand. Only 2.5 percent of total Wilderness land area is within 100 miles of the largest metropolitan centers; that is, those with a population of over 1 million.

The second measure of proximity of human habitation relative to the location of Wilderness is an examination of the number of people living within 25, 50, 100, 200, and 400 miles, whether urban or rural. Population enumeration for this second measure was at a fine scale; that is, census block group level. The data source is the 2000 Census of Population (Geolytics, Inc., 2001).

The entire population of the United States as of the 2000 Census, 282 million people, lives within 400 miles of one or more Wilderness areas (Table 5.5). About 70 percent of this national population lives within 100 miles of a Wilderness area. Loosely translated, this means that over 195 million persons live within a two-hour drive of one or more areas of the NWPS. Almost 41 percent live within 50 miles, roughly a one-hour drive, and nearly 17 percent are within 25 miles. Population within 25 miles accounts for around 47.5 million people, which is approximately 2.23 acres of wilderness per person living within 25 miles.

Uses of Nearby Non-Wilderness Land

Generally, as human population increases and spreads further from metropolitan areas into rural areas, there is greater influence on natural lands, including nearby

---

Table 5.5 Number and percentage of population of people living within 25, 50, 100, 200, and 400 miles of Wilderness, 2004

Distance from Wilderness	Population	Percent of Population
25 miles	47,495,997	16.8
50 miles	114,497,257	40.6
100 miles	195,745,452	69.4
200 miles	262,151,985	93.0
400 miles	281,918,792	100.0

Sources: Geolytics (2001). Note: Census Tract group 22075LA Plaquemines Parish, tract number 22075050100 was not available, therefore 3,025 people were not included; Wilderness data from Wilderness Institute (2003)

forest, range, wetlands, and other lands with natural cover. Some of these impacted natural lands are designated Wilderness (Sarkar, 1999). Not only are the physical and biological characteristics of natural lands altered as human activities increase but often their ecological health is diminished as well (Sanderson et al., 2002). Negative effects can include loss of biodiversity, air pollution, deforestation, and withdrawal of water (Kilic, Senol & Evrendilek, 2003).

The nature of the land use–ecosystem health relationship depends, of course, on the intensity and type of interaction occurring between humans and their external environment (Sanderson et al., 2002). Even though humans are not permitted to live in or substantially alter Wilderness areas, increasing numbers of people nearby, along with their activities, can effect the ecological health of Wilderness. Examples of such activities include expanding development (both commercial and residential), greater withdrawal of ground and surface water, and many other forms of human consumption and alteration of nearby natural lands. At the same time human activity may be damaging to ecological health, protected Wilderness lands typically provide substantial positive benefits and improved quality of life for the same nearby human settlements. An example is the role Wilderness plays in supplying clean, potable water. Another is the scenic beauty of wild lands as a pleasing backdrop for nearby rural or resort communities. For Wilderness and its management, surrounding human activities and uses of land are a highly important context that can have both positive and negative sides.

Land use in North America over the past four centuries, especially over the last century, has drastically reduced the amount and changed the look and function of rural land. One clear example of land use as a change agent is the growth of intensive agriculture (Turner & Rabalais, 2003). Cropping, use of fertilizers and pesticides, and depletion of soils has had many effects—one of which is lowering the quality of water. Turner and Rabalais conducted a study to examine the link between intensive land use and water quality in the Mississippi River Basin. They found that 44 percent of the rivers that they surveyed in the 15 Mississippi River Basin states were impacted as a result of conversions from natural to intensive uses, such as agricultural and industrial development. Such transformations of natural lands, along with extensive areas used for intensive agriculture can also lead to habitat fragmentation and destruction. Agricultural land use over the past 30 years is responsible for changes in the rates of nitrogen fixation and phosphorus accumulation in soils, soil erosion, and runoff causing nutrient loading in waterways like the Mississippi River (Sanderson et al., 2002).

Land uses in the United States have been classified by the USDA Natural Resources Conservation Service and inventoried through that agency's ongoing National Resources Inventory System (NRI; USDA, 2001). The 1997 county-level NRI data were used to calculate percentage of total county land area being used as cropland, developed (urban and other built-up), forest and water uses. These land uses are depicted in relation to the locations of designated Wilderness areas in Plates 1 through 4 (see Appendix). Plates 1 through 4 are further divided by region to make map images easier to interpret.

Almost all counties of the United States have some percentage of land area devoted to cropland use (see Plate 1). Percentages of crop land range from nearly zero to almost 94 percent across the counties of the country. Most of the land in the country used for cropping and other agriculture generally is in the Midwest, Great Lakes states, and the Mississippi River valley. In the West, the counties with the greatest percentages of total land area in crops lie in eastern Colorado, northern Montana, southeastern Washington, parts of Idaho, and central California. In all of these states, some cropland lies close or adjacent to designated Wilderness. Adjacency of croplands to Wilderness is especially noticeable in north central Montana and central California. In the Midwest, South, and Northeast there is relatively little land area designated as Wilderness. In part, this is because little natural land existed in these regions after passage of the Wilderness Act that would meet the criteria for designation. From western North Dakota to Chicago and western Ohio, down the Mississippi valley and southwest from Indiana to northern Texas, vast stretches of land are in crops. The small amount of Wilderness in these states (except for northern Minnesota) translates to very little cropland adjacent to Wilderness lands. In comparison with some areas of the West, no eastern states have large areas of designated Wilderness near croplands. Relative to other eastern States, however, Vermont and northern Virginia have greater amounts of designated Wilderness in counties near or within those heavily used for crops.

Developed land is more prominent in the East and along the Great Lakes, including the Minneapolis–St. Paul metropolitan area and eastern Texas (see Plate 2). Percentages of total land area that is developed across the country's counties range from near zero in counties made up from public land to well over 90 percent in several metropolitan counties. While less pervasive among counties in the West, relative to counties in the Midwest and East, there are nonetheless a number of areas that are heavily developed in that region. Included are western Washington, coastal California, southwestern Arizona and cities from Denver, Colorado, to Spokane, Washington. As one might expect, the majority of Wilderness lands are in areas that are not highly developed. In the West, the exceptions are southern California and Arizona, central Colorado, northwestern Oregon and northwestern Washington, and a few other scattered urban areas, such as in the Salt Lake City area. In the Midwest, very few Wilderness areas lie close to or within the more developed counties. The South and Northeast are much more highly developed. Wilderness in southern Florida, the southern Appalachians, northern Virginia, and northern New Hampshire are in close proximity to developed land uses, relative to the rest of the East.

Plate 3 shows percentages of total county area under water across the United States. Water area percentages range from nearly zero in many of the arid western counties to almost 70 percent in some coastal and riverine areas of the country. In the West, greater areas of water cover are found in northwestern Wyoming, northern Idaho, coastal Washington, and north central and coastal California. In these western areas, almost all counties with relatively high water cover have Wilderness. In the South, a region of relatively high precipitation, the Mississippi River area, Gulf of Mexico counties, and Atlantic coast counties have the highest proportion of county land area covered by water. Still, there is little association between high water coverage and Wilderness in this region. In the Midwest, central Minnesota, central North Dakota, eastern and northeastern Wisconsin, and in a few other areas in that region, relatively high water area percentages are found. Only modest association between the location of Wilderness areas and the higher water concentrations in this region exist with the exception of the Boundary Waters Canoe area of northern Minnesota. In the Northeast, coastal and north central Maine, northeastern New York and coastal counties in other New England states have relatively high water coverage. Because most of the Wilderness acreage in this region is inland in Vermont and New Hampshire, there again is only modest association between the location of Wilderness and water area.

Forest lands, almost all of which are managed for tree crops, water, and wildlife, are much more compatible with the management and protection of Wilderness values than more intensive land uses. The map of forest land shows that most forest land is located in the eastern half of the United States (see Plate 4). Of the Wilderness areas in the East, most lie within areas that are 27.5 to 95 percent forested. In the West, relative to other states in that region, most forest land counties are in the coastal states of Washington, Oregon, and California, and also in northern Idaho, northwestern Montana, central Colorado, northern New Mexico and northeastern Arizona. Vast stretches of Wilderness lie in these forested zones, especially in western Washington, Oregon, and California. But it is evident by comparing Plates 3 and 4 that most designated land in the West is relatively arid with sparse forest cover. In contrast, except for the Everglades in southern Florida, almost all Wilderness in the East is in heavily forested counties. This is especially true for southern Georgia, the southern Appalachians, and the New England states.

Proximity to Major Roads and Rivers

One of the most intensive and irreversible uses of land is development of roads. As with other intensive land uses, roads have many impacts on the natural appearance and functioning of nearby lands (Forman et al., 2002). Because roads provide transportation, they bring people, activities, vehicles, and equipment close to and, at times, even into the borders of Wilderness. The existence of roads can sometimes stimulate building additional roads and other development in lands adjacent to Wilderness. Examples are building of primary and secondary homes and development of resorts. Thus, the location of roads is a highly significant spatial context for Wilderness. This is especially the case for major roads, such as interstate highways, which carry large volumes of traffic into the proximity of public lands. Examples of activities stimulated by roads include extraction of raw materials (e.g., minerals), waste disposal, off-highway vehicle driving, and many other uses (Sanderson et al., 2002). In addition to roads, rivers also provide transportation for people and for their activities. As is the case for major roads, the transportation provided by rivers can have substantial effects on uses of land near Wilderness. Obviously, nearby roads and navigable rivers in part determine how much interior use Wilderness areas receive.

To assess the distribution of Wilderness areas relative to roads and rivers, GIS software was used to overlay Wilderness boundaries on digital maps containing major roads and rivers to see their spatial coincidence (see Plates 5–9, Appendix). Interstate map data were obtained from the *National Atlas of the United States* (USGS, 1999). But, as is often the case for Alaska, comparable roads data for that state were not available. River map data were available for all states, including Alaska, and show the location of the country's 56 largest rivers (ESRI, 1999).

Because of the broad-scale coverage of the roads and river data, Alaska and each of the four Census regions covering the 48 contiguous states were mapped separately. These maps show the location of Wilderness areas in relation to major interstates and rivers. Boundaries for the states making up each Census region are also shown. Wilderness areas are green, interstates black, and rivers blue.

In Alaska (Plate 5, showing only rivers),Wilderness areas are large and highly significant portions of the landscape. The major rivers in Alaska (e.g., the Yukon and Kuskokwim) tend to flow from southeast to northwest. These major rivers are for the most part distant from Wilderness areas and do not seem to play a large role in providing human access to this state's designated areas. Wilderness areas do serve as watersheds and thus act in part as the sources of water for those rivers. There are only a few major highways in Alaska, mostly in and emanating from the Anchorage area. These are not shown on the map.

In the West Census region (i.e., states west of a line drawn south from the western border of North Dakota to the western border of Texas), there are a number of major rivers. Examples are the Colorado flowing southwest to the Gulf of California and the Columbia/Snake River System flowing west into the Pacific (see Plate 6). The Colorado River begins in northern Colorado and moves southwest to end in the Gulf of California. It is approximately 1,500 miles long and passes through numerous canyons along its path, including the Grand Canyon in northern Arizona. The Columbia/Snake River System is a fast-flowing river coming from southeastern British Columbia in Canada passing through the state of Washington to empty into the Pacific Ocean. This river system rises in Canada and Wyoming and passes through Idaho. It is about 1,150 miles in length and serves as migration routes for a number of species of anadromous fish, including salmon. The reach of these and other western rivers inland from the Pacific, Gulf of California, and Gulf of Mexico includes many thousands of miles across multiple states. The headwaters for most western rivers lie, in part, in designated Wilderness.

Because rivers are crossed many times by highways and interstates, they provide a considerable amount of upstream and downstream access to the Wilderness areas of the West, as well as to other close-by public lands. There are 10 different Interstate highways in the 11 western states (see Plate 6). They run north-south and east-west and often pass close to, and in some cases between designated Wilderness areas. In areas where Interstates pass near Wilderness, physical access to these designated areas is significantly easier to larger numbers of people. Interstates in the West and in all U.S. regions, connect countless state, county, and local roads giving access to state and federal public lands throughout the West. At the same time, travelers using these highways benefit from visual access and scenic vistas made up in part and sometimes entirely from these highly protected lands. An example subregion where Interstate highways run close to and through Wilderness areas is the Sierra Nevada Mountain area in eastern California. Another is Interstate 70 running west from Denver into western Utah.

The portion of the South region lying east of the Mississippi River, has many more Wilderness areas than are found in the Northeast (cf. Plates 7 and 9, Appendix). As well, the South has significant stretches of major rivers and highways. In Texas, the Rio Grande and the Brazos flow in a southeasterly direction into the Gulf of Mexico. Further North, the Missouri and Ohio Rivers flow generally south to form the Mississippi, the largest river in the country. The Mississippi flows through the South to empty into the Gulf of Mexico where it forms the boundary between Louisiana and Mississippi. The Mississippi is almost 2,340 miles in length and has its origins in northwestern Minnesota. This river serves as a major national transportation artery, especially when combined with its major tributaries, the Missouri and Ohio Rivers. Combined, these three rivers stretch almost 3,400 miles, but they generally do not link people and their activities to designated Wilderness.

There are 14 major interstate highway routes throughout the South, all of which are linked to a considerable number of connector routes and three-digit local loops (see Plate 7, Appendix). From Interstate 95, which connects Florida with the Northeast, to Interstate 25, which begins in New Mexico and extends to the north into the foothills of the Rockies, the north-south system of interstate highways carry enormous traffic loads. The north-south interstates east of Texas often pass close to and sometimes through national forests, national parks, and other public lands. Some of these public lands have been designated as Wilderness areas. Unlike the West, the East has much less public land to act as a buffer between highways and designated Wilderness. In fact, unlike the West, very few designated Wilderness areas in the East can be considered remote. Thus, because the interstate highways of the East carry large numbers of travelers and are often located near or nearly next to Wilderness, they play a significant role in providing access to designated Wilderness. A good example is Interstate 81 from Dandridge, Tennessee, through the Southern Appalachian Mountains northeast through Shenandoah National Park in central and northern Virginia, to within 70 miles west of Washington, DC.

In the Midwest and the Northeast Census regions (Plates 8 and 9 respectively) there are relatively few designated Wilderness areas. In areal size, the Boundary Waters Canoe Area in the extreme north of Minnesota, and the areas designated Wilderness in New Hampshire and Vermont are exceptions. Much of the Wilderness in New Hampshire and Vermont lies close to Interstate 93. Unlike the Wilderness in these states, the Boundary Waters Canoe Area is relatively remote and uninfluenced by traffic on either major rivers or on interstate highways.

Pervasiveness of Roads Near Wilderness

In 2001, the contiguous states of the United States contained approximately 3.9 million miles of public roads. Over 990 thousand of these road miles were classified as nonlocal rural roads (U.S. Department of Transportation [USDT], 2002). The ecological change brought about by roads is easily seen within a few feet of roadsides, but their impacts can extend out several miles. Building and using roads can alter water drainage patterns, modify habitats, disrupt wildlife movements, introduce exotic species, modify microclimates and the chemical environment, increase noise levels, and provide direct human access. Roads also contribute to development impacts by facilitating commercial and residential building and further extending the road network itself (Riitters & Wickham, 2003). Generally, the more pervasive the road systems in any given area, the more impacts they are likely to have on adjacent and nearby lands.

This section examines the spatial pervasiveness of roads in relation to the locations of Wilderness areas. There are three measures used to examine pervasiveness. The first measure looks from Wilderness boundaries outward to examine average miles of roads and railroads at different distances from Wilderness boundaries. The second measure looks from the nearest road at different distances back toward designated Wilderness to examine total acres and proportion of protected Wilderness within those distances by Census region. The third measure is the mapped relationship between the location of lands with different densities of roads and the location of Wilderness areas. Density of roads is measured as the proportion of equal size units of land having one or more roads.

The first measure is average miles of roads at three distances from Wilderness boundaries. This first measure was estimated for the lower 48 and for each region of the country. (Alaska is not included because comparable road data are not available for that state.) Table 5.6 summarizes these estimates. The original source of these data was Geographic Data Technology (2002). From 0 to 3 miles of area boundaries, the highest average miles of road per designated area is in the West with 220 miles. Next highest is the South with 152 miles per Wilderness area. Average miles of road per area is highest in the West in part because area size in this region is much larger than area size in the other regions. The national average miles of road per area from 0 to 3 miles of area boundaries is approximately 198 miles. It is important to note that there are some historic roads within Wilderness boundaries. For the most part, these roads predated passage of the Wilderness legislation designating an area. After designation, however, mechanical transportation on these preexisting roads is prohibited.

The average miles of road per Wilderness area increased at the greater distance of between 3 and 6 miles from area boundaries. In the West, slightly over 300 miles of road are found within these distances, about 278 are found in areas of the South, and just over 260 miles of road per area in the Northeast region. Estimates of miles of road per Wilderness area are even closer among regions at distances within 6 to 9 miles. The national average is just over 392 miles per Wilderness area between these distances. Highest is the South at about 414 miles per area, next is the Northeast with about 400 miles per area, and least is the Midwest with about 330 miles per area. At these longer distances, the

Table 5.6 Average miles of roads, highways, and railroads per Wilderness area by distance from area boundary and by census region, 2004

	Average Miles per Wilderness Area		
Census Region	0–3 miles	3–6 miles	6–9 miles
West	219.8	303.9	393.0
South	151.7	277.5	413.6
Midwest	135.6	227.7	331.6
Northeast	120.8	261.4	400.9
National (lower 48 only)	198.0	292.1	392.4

Note: Land area within 3, 3–6, and 6–9 miles out from Wilderness boundaries vary by size of Wilderness area. Thus large areas may be associated with greater average road mileage.

Sources: Geographic Data Technology, 2002; Wilderness land area from wilderness.net, November 2004

much more prevalent road systems of the South and Northeast become evident. Third in average miles of road per area is the West with 393 miles per area. Obviously, roads near Wilderness are important in describing the context within which the ecosystems represented by Wilderness areas must function, and they are important to understanding a very significant aspect of the context for Wilderness management and protection decisions.

The second measure of the pervasiveness of roads is acreage of designated Wilderness within different distances from the nearest road. Examined is area in acres and percent of total land area designated Wilderness that is 0.02, 0.23, and 3.2 miles from the nearest road. These distances were selected to correspond with distances used in the primary literature source on which this spatial analysis was based (Riitters & Wickham, 2003). Riitters and Wickham conducted their research to look at the proportion of total and forest land area in the United States located within nine different distances of the nearest road. As one might expect, they found that as distance from the nearest road increases, there is an increase in proportion of total land area included (both forest and nonforest). Their estimated proportions increased rapidly at the shorter distances, but then leveled off at around 800 meters (approximately 0.5 mile). Compared with total land area, forest land was slightly more remote, but followed a similar trend line. The difference in total land area and forest area varied only by 2 percent at each distance.

Like the analysis of forest land area near roads, area of designated Wilderness was computed by Census region for the same three distances from nearest road (i.e., 0.02 mi., 0.23 mi., and 3.2 mi.) that were used by Riitters and Wickham (2003). Results are presented in Table 5.7. Like the forest land analysis, the Wilderness distance-to-area analysis was based on maps gridded at 30 meters and distances were based on the diagonal of a 30-meter grid cell, which is 42.4 meters. So each distance is a multiple of 42.4 meters. The shorter two of the three distances were used in this and in the original study because at these distances the distance-to-area relationship changed rapidly. These three selected distances were used to examine a conservative, medium, and liberal measure of potential impact from roads.

On average, across the four Census regions, quite small areas of Wilderness lay within the nearest distance of 0.02 miles. As well, at approximately one quarter of a mile (0.23 mi.), a distance at which road traffic is usually out of sight, but easily heard, less than 10 percent of designated land area is included. At this distance, the least land area and percentage of total Wilderness acres are in the West, where roads are less prevalent and where there is significantly more other federal land as a buffer. In the South, almost 10 percent of all designated Wilderness is within 0.23 miles of the nearest road. At 3.2 miles, a distance just over the Recreation Opportunity Spectrum distance for the primitive class of unroaded wildlands (More, Bulmer, Henzel & Mates,

2003), considerably more of National Wilderness Preservation System lands are included. The largest percentage is in the Northeast, at almost 64 percent, nearly two thirds of that region's Wilderness. Next in order is the South at almost 54 percent. The West is lowest at 39 percent. From these estimates across the three distances, it seems that Wilderness in the South is at greatest exposure from road impacts. Next in exposure is the Midwest, followed by the Northeast and West.

Plate 10 (see Appendix) maps the spatial distribution of grid cells across the United States containing one or more roads. To create this map, the United States was divided into 140,000 squares, each square being approximately 7.5 square kilometers. Each of these squares was then further divided into 62,500 subcells, each being 30 square meters in size. A detailed road map was overlayed and each 30-square-meter cell that contained a road was scored. The percentage of 30-square-meter cells containing a road was calculated (Riitters & Wickham, 2003; Wear, Pye & Riiters, 2004).

As evident from the map in Plate 10, most of the Wilderness in the West is in areas of relatively low road density (i.e., buffered from roads by other lands of low or zero road density). Exceptions in the West region are the Salt Lake

Table 5.7 Total percentage of Wilderness acres within 0.02 miles (141 ft), 0.23 miles (1,253 ft), and 3.2 miles (16,980 ft) of the nearest road, by census region (excluding Alaska), 2004

Census Region Distance to nearest road	Acres	Proportion of total area
West	Region Total 43,519,489	
0.02 miles	136,294	0.3
0.23 miles	2,084,581	4.8
3.20 miles	17,057,393	39.2
South	Region Total 2,752,198	
0.02 miles	18,194	0.7
0.23 miles	271,852	9.9
3.20 miles	1,477,281	53.7
Midwest	Region Total 1,344,652	
0.02 miles	6,913	0.5
0.23 miles	107,516	8.0
3.20 miles	625,064	46.5
Northeast	Region Total 204,900	
0.02 miles	647	0.3
0.23 miles	11,425	5.6
3.20 miles	130,630	63.8

Sources: Distance to roads from Riitters and Wickham, 2003; Wilderness land area from wilderness.net, November 2004

City, Utah; Denver, Colorado; Albuquerque, New Mexico; Phoenix, Arizona; coastal California; the Klamath area of southern and central Oregon; and the Seattle, Washington, areas. In the South, Wilderness is found in areas with road densities greater than in the West. Examples are the Miami, Florida; Little Rock, Arkansas; the southern Appalachians of north Georgia; western North Carolina; southwestern Virginia; and the Charleston, South Carolina, areas. In the Northeast, nearly all Wilderness areas reside in moderate to heavy road-density areas with little buffering. Greater density of roads indicates greater fragmentation of the landscape and the natural systems making up the landscape. The functioning and appearance of these fragmented landscapes can be dramatically altered as roads expand in number, density, and width (Riitters & Wickham 2003). Further treatment of road density as a natural land fragmentation factor will be provided in Chapter 11.

The Natural Character of Wilderness

Thus far the National Wilderness Preservation System has been described in terms of its size, the number of people living in nearby communities, surrounding land uses, and the network of transportation systems in the local area. This section examines some of the natural characteristics of the System's protected lands. First, the range of elevation of the lands included within the NWPS are described. Next precipitation amounts over the areas in the NWPS are shown. Following, at a macroscale, the ecosystems represented in the Wilderness System are inventoried at the Division level of the ecoregion classification system. The system widely known as the *Bailey system* was adopted for this analysis (Bailey, 1995).

Over the years, Congressional designations have protected some ecosystems better than others. For example, high-elevation lands, sometimes above tree line, are generally better represented in the NWPS. These lands typically are less roaded and have had little detectable human disturbance. Nevertheless, the NWPS includes a wide variety of natural land forms and habitats. The natural character of these protected lands differs greatly across the country. Some areas are extremely remote, expansive, and unmodified cool climate lands, like the 8.7-million-acre Wrangell–St. Elias Wilderness in Alaska. Others are much smaller, warmer, nearer to sea level, and closer to places heavily inhabited by humans, such as the five-acre Pelican Island Wilderness in Florida. Protection of natural character is more difficult in the areas that lay in close proximity to large urban areas. These areas are often heavily influenced by nearby human land uses (Cole, 2000). Following is an overview of three of the natural characters of Wilderness: elevation, precipitation, and broad-scale ecosystem classification.

Wilderness at Different Elevations

Elevation is an important characteristic of natural lands because it is closely associated with, and over time has played a large role in, determining the distribution of species of native animals or plants. A good example is that of the northern spotted owl, whose native habitat occurs at lower elevations in the Pacific Northwest (Noss, 1996). This species was federally listed as threatened in 1990 (Forsman, n.d.). Because much of the designated Wilderness in the Pacific Northwest has been at higher elevations, there tend to be significantly fewer spotted owl locations within Wilderness than in the managed forests of that same region. In general, the more diverse the elevation and other natural characteristics of the Wilderness System, the greater its contributions toward sustaining a variety of native species.

To examine the diversity of elevations represented by the current inventory of areas within the NWPS in the 48 contiguous states, a digital elevation map was used to identify the range of elevations within each Wilderness area. This digital elevation map is a giant grid of cells where each cell measures about 85 meters a side. Across the Wilderness System, this map indicates that elevations range from 262 feet below sea level to approximately 14,370 feet. Elevations across the landscape within each cell were averaged and rounded to the nearest 10 meters. Then, for each Wilderness area, the number of square meters of land area falling within each of the resulting 444 10-meter elevation classes was calculated. Ultimately, to facilitate presentation in a table for this chapter, these 444 elevation classes were aggregated into seven classes as follows: less than 0, 0–99, 100–499, 500–2,499, 2,500–4,999, 5,000–9,999, and 10,000 feet and over. To correct for coarseness in the estimation procedure used, the amount of Wilderness area was summed across each of these seven elevation ranges for each Wilderness area and then divided by the sum across ranges to obtain an estimate of percentage of area within each range for each Wilderness area. The resulting elevation percentages were then multiplied by the known land area of each Wilderness area to get an adjusted estimate of number of acres by elevation class that would sum to the true acreage of Wilderness, area by area and within the NWPS. The number of designated Wilderness acres was summed across elevation ranges for each of the nine census division of the United States as well. Results are shown in Table 5.8 (all elevation ranges; see page 80) and in Figure 5.6 (which focuses only on the highest two elevation ranges; see page 81).

Table 5.8 shows acres and percentage of the total area estimated for the seven elevation ranges for the contiguous 48 states. (Comparable data were not available for Alaska.) Focusing on the 21.5 million acres of designated Wilderness in the 48 contiguous states that lie under 5,000 feet in elevation, one can see that just over 17 million acres, approximately 80 percent, is in the West Census region, mostly in the Pacific West. Slightly over half of the acres

Table 5.8 Acres and the proportion (%) of Wilderness system total area by elevation ranges and by census division of the contiguous 48 states

Census Division	Number of acres in elevation range							Total acreage
	<0 feet	0–99 feet	100–499 feet	500–2,499 feet	2,500–4,999 feet	5,000–9,999 feet	>9,999 feet	
West—Pacific	166,553 (0.01)	91,929 (0.00)	284,875 (0.01)	4,159,823 (0.20)	7,594,485 (0.36)	7,605,439 (0.36)	1,041,387 (0.05)	20,944,491 (0.44)
West—Mountain	0 (0.00)	0 (0.00)	21,381 (0.00)	2,359,155 (0.11)	2,574,016 (0.12)	12,967,006 (0.58)	4,279,866 (0.19)	22,201,424 (0.47)
Midwest—West North Central	0 (0.00)	0 (0.00)	7,957 (0.01)	915,033 (0.90)	79,746 (0.08)	9,558 (0.01)	0 (0.00)	1,012,294 (0.02)
Midwest—East North Central	0 (0.00)	0 (0.00)	6,957 (0.02)	325,136 (0.98)	0 (0.00)	0 (0.00)	0 (0.00)	332,093 (0.01)
South—South Atlantic	0 (0.00)	1,571,060 (0.67)	317,457 (0.14)	158,745 (0.07)	283,264 (0.12)	10,124 (0.00)	0 (0.00)	2,340,650 (0.05)
South—West South Central	0 (0.00)	8,965 (0.03)	57,616 (0.21)	165,243 (0.59)	4,073 (0.01)	43,226 (0.15)	0 (0.00)	279,123 (0.01)
South—East South Central	0 (0.00)	8,961 (0.07)	1,722 (0.01)	85,283 (0.66)	33,760 (0.26)	0 (0.00)	0 (0.00)	129,726 (0.00)
Northeast—New England	0 (0.00)	5,902 (0.03)	3,909 (0.02)	90,571 (0.49)	82,780 (0.45)	1,003 (0.01)	0 (0.00)	184,165 (0.00)
Northeast—Middle Atlantic	0 (0.00)	8,044 (0.39)	3,660 (0.18)	8,663 (0.43)	0 (0.00)	0 (0.00)	0 (0.00)	20,367 (0.00)
National Total	166,553	1,694,861	705,534	8,267,652	10,652,124	20,636,356	5,321,253	47,444,333

Source: USGS, 1993

under 5,000 feet in the West are at between 2,500 and 4,999 feet. Very little lies under 500 feet above sea level. Outside the West, the greatest acres and percentages are in the South, mostly in the South Atlantic states from West Virginia to Florida. The Florida Everglades, the Okefenokee Swamp, and areas in the southern Appalachians make up most of that designated land. Of the designated land in the South, 58 percent is under 99 feet in elevation. Nearly 12 percent of the designated Wilderness in the South is between 2,500 and 4,999 feet. Most of the Wilderness designated in the Midwest lies between 500 and 4,999 feet. Of designated Wilderness in the Northeast, about 58 percent is under 2,500 feet in elevation, while most of that (about 90%) is between 500 and 2,499 feet.

Figure 5.6 focuses on designated Wilderness lands at or above 5,000 feet elevation. Shown are percentages of the NWPS between 5,000 and 9,999 and above 10,000 feet by Census division and nationally. As mentioned earlier, a substantial portion of the Wilderness System is at the higher elevations. Nationally, there are almost 26 million acres over 5,000 feet, making up approximately 55 percent of the total Wilderness area in the lower 48 states. Most of this high elevation Wilderness is in the West Census region. At elevations between 5,000 and 9,999 feet in this region, there are over 20 million acres.

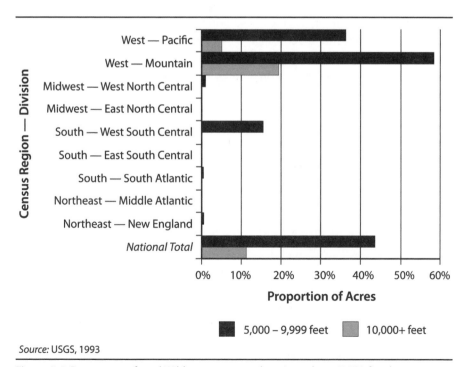

Source: USGS, 1993

Figure 5.6 Percentage of total Wilderness area at elevations above 5,000 feet by census division and nationally

Even at the very highest elevations, at or beyond 10,000 feet, there are almost 5.3 million acres of western Wilderness. In the Pacific West, over one third of Wilderness lands are between 5,000 and 9,999 feet; about 5 percent are at 10,000 or more feet. In the Mountain West, almost 60 percent of Wilderness lands are between 5,000 and 9,999 feet, another 19 percent are at elevations of 10,000 feet and above. Just under 10,000 acres of the Midwest Wilderness is over 5,000 feet in elevation, and none is above 10,000 feet. Around 47 thousand designated acres in the South are above 5,000 feet, mostly in the West South Central states. In the Northeast, only about 1,000 acres lie above 5,000 feet. In no region other than the West is there any representation of landscapes above 10,000 feet.

Precipitation Over Wilderness

Precipitation data in inches per year were obtained from the *National Atlas of the United States* (USGS, 1999) for the 48 contiguous states. Alaska was not included because comparable precipitation data are not available for that state. Ranges in rainfall amounts were identified using GIS software to spatially outline overall land area within each precipitation range. Following this step, boundary shape images of Wilderness areas were overlain onto the spatially outlined precipitation ranges in each census region. A precipitation range was assigned to each Wilderness area based on the area's geographic midpoint. Precipitation ranges included 0–15, 16–30, 31–40, 41–60, 61–90, and 100 or more inches per year. The estimates of areas and acres are not additive. If a Wilderness area midpoint lays on a break between precipitation ranges, it was double counted.

In the West there were over 30 percent of area and 146 areas designated Wilderness within the driest precipitation range of 0–15 inches annually (Table 5.9). Unlike the other three regions, Wilderness in the West is spread across all levels of annual precipitation, including some areas receiving over 100 inches. Because much of the West is arid to semiarid, just over 70 percent of the designated land in the West receives less than 41 inches, just over 50 percent receives under 31 inches, and 30 percent receives less than 16 inches. In the Midwest, all areas receive at least 16 inches and none more than 60 inches. Most of the Wilderness in the Midwest receives between 16 and 30 inches. In the South, much more rainfall is intercepted per acre of Wilderness. Most of the System acres in the South receive between 41 and 60 inches. A similar precipitation pattern is found for Wilderness in the Northeast. Nationally, about two thirds of the Wilderness in the lower 48 states receives between 0 and 40 inches of precipitation per year. About 28 percent of this Wilderness receives under 16 inches. Natural attributes, such as amount of precipitation, contribute enormously to determining the plant and animal species making up protected Wilderness ecosystems.

Ecosystems Represented

Every acre designated as Wilderness protects a number of aspects of natural systems. This is true whether that acre (or those thousands of acres) is in high mountain desert in Arizona, in natural wetlands in the Florida Everglades, or in native grasslands in South Dakota. All protected acres contribute to sustaining native ecosystems. A related goal of many organizations and individuals in their support of Wilderness is preservation of biodiversity across ecosystems. Lands protected across a range of elevations, precipitation, and other natural attributes contribute to this goal. By protecting a range of ecosystems, the sustainability of ecological and evolutionary processes, the maintenance of species diversity, and the encouragement of native species in natural patterns of abundance and distribution are all enhanced (Noss, 1996).

Table 5.9 Number of areas and percentage of acres of Wilderness by precipitation amounts per year and by census region (excluding Alaska), 2004

| **West** | | | | **Midwest** | | |
Precipitation (inches)	Areas	Percent of acres		Precipitation (inches)	Areas	Percent of acres
0–15	146	30.2		0–15	0	0.0
16–30	127	20.0		16–30	10	77.7
31–40	76	20.1		31–40	15	13.0
41–60	75	16.8		41–60	17	9.4
61–90	37	7.5		61–90	0	0.0
100+	20	5.5		100+	0	0.0

| **South** | | | | **Northeast** | | |
Precipitation (inches)	Areas	Percent of acres		Precipitation (inches)	Areas	Percent of acres
0–15	0	0.0		0–15	0	0.0
16–30	1	1.7		16–30	0	0.0
31–40	10	1.1		31–40	0	0.0
41–60	79	87.4		41–60	14	74.4
61–90	22	9.8		61–90	4	25.6
100+	0	0.0		100+	0	0.0

| **National** | | |
Precipitation (inches)	Areas	Percent of acres
0–15	146	27.6
16–30	138	20.3
31–40	101	18.7
41–60	185	20.9
61–90	63	7.5
100+	20	5.0

Sources: Annual precipitation shapefile from Daly and Taylor, 2000; Wilderness land area from wilderness.net, November 2004

The NWPS preserves lands with a variety of natural attributes that may otherwise be lost to human uses and development of land. In 1990, more than half of current Wilderness areas protected one or more federal- or state-listed species classified as threatened and/or endangered (Cordell & Reed, 1990). But, protection of listed species is only one aspect representative of nature. It falls short of adequately describing the full range of diversity of natural systems. Typically, *biological diversity* is thought of as diversity and balance of genes, species, and other elements making up an ecosystem (Sarkar, 1999). Noss (1990) argued only very large Wilderness areas can support broad-scale level biodiversity that is full spectrum. He pointed out that only 2 percent of the 261 Bailey-Kuchler ecosystem types in the United States and Puerto Rico are represented in Wilderness areas of 1 million hectares or more. And, all of these are in Alaska (Noss, 1990). Only 19 percent of all the ecosystem types are represented in units of at least 100,000 hectares.

An alternative to viewing diversity as a large-area phenomena is to take the perspective that diversity also pertains to representation of different natural ecosystems regardless of scale. While this system-of-systems approach may not account for some important species or natural functions, this approach can enhance understanding of how broadly and to what degree the diversity of ecosystems has been retained for the future. U.S. Forest Service ecologist Robert Bailey (1995) and others have produced a widely accepted system for differentiating ecosystems from regional to local scales. In that work, land areas are classified into domains, divisions, provinces, and sections. The resulting groupings reflect similarities in ecological processes, vegetation, climate, and groups of species (Stein, 2001). They aid in inventorying landscape diversity across all biological gradients (e.g., elevation, aspect, latitude) and the species that respond to those gradients (Noss, 1990). The broadest scale of ecological regions are domains, which are primarily based on climate. The four domains in the Bailey system are the Polar, Humid Temperate, Dry, and Humid Tropical domains. The Polar domain ecosystems are located at higher latitudes and are controlled by arctic and polar air flows. In the middle latitudes, the Humid Temperate domain climate is regulated by both polar and tropical air masses. The Dry domain is defined by the absence of water. The Humid Tropical domain is found at low latitudes and controlled by equatorial and tropical air masses. Domains are broken down into divisions that are subdivided into provinces based on vegetational macrofeatures. The smallest ecosystem level is the section. Sections are defined by more refined climactic differences. For this chapter, description of ecosystems represented within the NWPS is limited to the division level.

Table 5.10 shows the number of acres in total for the United States, acres protected as Wilderness, and percentage of total area protected for each Bailey's domain and division by Census region in the lower 48 states and in Alaska.

Table 5.10 Area in acres (thousands) and percentage of ecoregional division total area by ecoregional division and by Census region (Alaska shown separately)

	Alaska (W)	West	Midwest	South	Northeast	Total Acres Protected by Wilderness	Total Acres in the United States	Percent Protected by Wilderness
100 Polar Domain						**43,494**	**332,736**	**13.07**
120 Tundra Div.	2,577	0	0	0	0	2,577	57,344	4.49
M120 Tundra Regime Mtns	26,655	0	0	0	0	26,655	103,104	25.85
130 Subarctic Div.	2,129	0	0	0	0	2,129	54,272	3.92
M130 Subarctic Regime Mtns	12,133	0	0	0	0	12,133	118,016	10.28
200 Humid Temperate Domain						**29,230**	**1,035,264**	**2.82**
210 Warm Continental Div.	0	0	1,399	0	20	1,419	94,272	1.51
M210 Warm Continental Regime Mtns	0	0	0	0	164	164	27,904	0.59
220 Hot Continental Div.	0	0	117	68	12	197	239,680	0.08
M220 Hot Continental Regime Mtns	0	0	0	581	0	581	47,680	1.22
230 Subtropical Div.	0	0	1	742	0	743	263,104	0.28
M230 Subtropical Regime Mtns	0	0	0	49	0	49	5,632	0.86
240 Marine Div.	0	56	0	0	0	56	9,536	0.59
M240 Marine Regime Mtns	13,922	5,181	0	0	0	19,103	75,072	25.45
250 Prairie Div.	0	0	0	2	0	2	190,912	<0.01
260 Mediterranean Div.	0	259	0	2	0	259	21,824	1.19
M260 Mediterranean Regime Mtns	0	6,656	0	0	0	6,656	59,648	11.16
300 Dry Domain						**30,871**	**919,872**	**3.36**
310 Tropical/Subtropical Steppe Div.	0	1,221	0	10	0	1,230	162,432	0.76
M313 Tropical/Subtropical Regime Mtns	0	1,292	0	22	0	1,314	32,128	4.09
320 Tropical/Subtropical Desert Div.	0	10,469	0	22	0	10,491	110,656	9.48
330 Temperate Steppe Div.	0	412	118	0	0	531	271,808	0.20
M330 Temperate Steppe Regime Mtns	0	14,696	10	0	0	14,696	144,576	10.16
340 Temperate Desert Div.	0	1,990	0	0	0	1,990	170,368	1.17
M340 Temperate Desert Regime Mtns	0	620	0	0	0	620	27,904	2.22
400 Humid Tropical Domain						**1,447**	**7,360**	**19.67**
410 Savanna Div.	0	0	0	1,447	0	1,447	7,360	19.67

Sources: Bailey, 1995; Bailey, McNab, Avers, and King, 1994

(Protected ecosystem details at scales finer than division level appear in Chapter 11.) The last column in Table 5.10 is especially important to understanding representation because it shows the percentage of total land area by ecosystem type included in the NWPS.

The results in Table 5.10 show the greatest number of divisions (11) found in any single region is in the West. Next are 8 divisions found in the South Census region. Represented by Alaskan Wilderness are 5 divisions, the same number as found in the Midwest region. In the Northeast region there are only 3 divisions represented. Across the country, the greatest percentage of any single domain represented by Wilderness is the Humid Tropical domain at almost 20 percent, mainly represented by the Everglades National Wildlife Refuge in south Florida. Next is the other extreme of climate, the Polar domain represented by various designations in Alaska totaling just over 13 percent of the tundra and subartic divisions. Just over 3 percent of the steppe and desert divisions of the Dry domain are represented and under 3 percent of the Humid Temperate domain of the Midwest and South are represented. As noted when describing elevations of Wilderness lands, much of the preserved Wilderness is classified as mountain ecosystems (roughly ¾). Almost 12 percent is classified as desert in the Dry domain.

Plates 11 and 12 (see Appendix) show the geographic distribution of Wilderness lands relative to the location of the Bailey's ecosystem domains and divisions, respectively for the four Census regions of the 48 contiguous states and Alaska. Plate 11 shows that the Temperate Prairie (at less than 0.01%), Temperate Continental (a band stretching from northern Arkansas to southern Michigan and New York at just over 0.25%), and Temperate Subtropical (from coastal Louisiana to the tristate area of Kentucky, Missouri, and Arkansas) are poorly represented in terms of percent land area of each ecosystem type. Much greater representation, because of the history of federal lands and the designation process noted in Chapter 3 are the dry, mountainous, interior lands of the West and the marine ecosystems of the Pacific Coast. Vast stretches of the tundra, subartic, and marine mountains of Alaska have been designated as shown in Plate 12.

Conclusion

Since passage of the Wilderness Act in 1964, a large number of areas and acres have been added to the National Wilderness Preservation System. Most of the original and added lands are at higher elevations or are otherwise not highly accessible. Thus, they historically have not been occupied or utilized in substantial ways, or at all. Increasingly, however, lands once remote with highly limited accessibility can be reached. This chapter has shown how closely associated many of the areas in the NWPS are with human habitation and activity. As a growing population distributes itself further and further onto the rural landscape, as the mileage and distribution of roads rises, and as utilization and development of rural lands expands, wildlands, especially designated Wilderness, will become of greater uniqueness. While the diversity of ecosystem types represented by the 662 areas in the NWPS is highly varied, it does not represent the full spectrum of ecosystem types once found in this country very well. Prairie, for example, has long since been devoted to agricultural and developed uses. It is highly unlikely that appreciable representation of prairie ecosystems will ever come about because these lands are solidly committed for long-term agricultural, commercial, and residential uses. There are, however, still natural lands in this country representative of other ecosystem types. Many of these lands are roadless, and many of them exhibit a relatively high degree of wildness (as Chapter 6 describes). These lands, and those already designated will surely become ever more rare in the face of the steady development trend in the United States. As they become more and more scarce, they will likely become even more valued. Chapters 7 through 12 explore the multiple values of Wilderness as a unique and ever more scarce resource.

Literature Cited

Alaska National Interest Lands Conservation Act of 1980, Pub. L. No. 96-487, 94 Stat. 2371, 16 U.S.C. § 3101 et seq. (1980).

Bailey, R.G. (1995). *Description of the ecoregions of the United States* (2nd ed.; Misc. Pub. 1391). Washington, DC: USDA Forest Service.

Bailey, R.G., McNab, W.H., Avers, P.E., and King, T. (1994). *Ecoregions and subecoregions of the United States*. Washington, DC: USDA Forest Service. Retrieved September 17, 2003, from http://www.fs.fed.us/institute/ftp/maps

Campaign for America's Wilderness. (2002). *America's wilderness heritage in crisis: Our vanishing wild landscape*. Washington, DC: Campaign for America's Wilderness.

Carter, L.E. (1992). Wilderness and its role in preservation of biodiversity: The need for a shift in emphasis. *Australian Zoologist, 28*(1-4), 28–36.

Cole, D.V. (2000). Paradox of the primevil: Ecological restoration in wilderness. *Ecological Restoration, 18*(2), 77–86.

Cordell, H.K. and Overdevest, C. (2001). *Footprints on the land* (pp. 113–144). Champaign, IL: Sagamore Publishing.

Cordell, H.K. and Reed, P.C. (1990). Untrammeled by Man: Preserving diversity through wilderness. In P.C. Reed (Ed.), *Preparing to manage wilderness in the 21st century: Proceedings of the conference* (pp. 30–33; GTR SE-66). Asheville, NC: USDA Forest Service, Southeastern Forest Experiment Station.

Daly, C. and Taylor, G. (2000) United States average annual precipitation, 1961–1990. In U.S. Department of the Interior, *National atlas of the United States*. Retrieved September 17, 2003, from http://nationalatlas.gov/prismm.html

Eastern Wilderness Areas Act of 1975, Pub. L. No. 93-622, 88 Stat. 2096; 16 U.S.C. § 1132 nt (1975).

Environmental Systems Research Institute, Inc. [ESRI]. (1999). ArcView GIS (Version 3.2) [Computer software]. Redlands, CA: ESRI.

Forman, R.T.T., Sperling, D., Bissonette, J.A., Clevanger, A.P., Cutshell, C.D., Dale, V.H. et al. (2002). *Road ecology: Science and solutions*. Washington, DC: Island Press.

Forsman, E.D. (n.d.). Northern spotted owl. USDA Forest Service, Pacific Northwest Research Station. Retrieved September 23, 2003, from http://biology.usgs.gov/s+t/SNT/noframe/pn172.htm

Geographic Data Technology. (2002). *Dynamap/2000 user manual*. Lebanon, NH: Geographic Data Technology, Inc.

Geolytics, Inc. (2001). *Census CD® 2000 Blocks* (Release 1.1) [Computer software]. East Brunswick, NJ: Geolytics, Inc.

Kilic, S., Senol, S., and Evrendilek, F. (2003). Evaluation of land use potential and suitability of ecosystems in Antakya for reforestation, recreation, arable farming and residence. *Turkish Journal of Agriculture & Forestry, 27*(1), 15–22.

More, T.A., Bulmer, S., Henzel, L., and Mates, A.E. (2003). *Extending the Recreation Opportunity Spectrum to non-federal islands in the Northeast: An implementation guide* (GTR NE-309). Newton Square, PA: USDA Forest Service, Northeastern Research Station.

Nash, R. (1982). *Wilderness and the American mind* (3rd ed.). New Haven, CT: Yale University Press.

Noss, R.F. (1990). What can wilderness do for biodiversity? In P.C. Reed (Ed.), *Preparing to manage wilderness in the 21st century: Proceedings of the conference* (pp. 49–61; GTR SE-66). Asheville, NC: USDA Forest Service, Southeastern Forest Experiment Station.

Noss, R.F. (1996). Soul of the wilderness: Biodiversity, ecological integrity, and wilderness. *International Journal of Wilderness, 2*(2), 3–8.

Riitters, K.H, and Wickham, J.D. (2003). How far to the nearest road? *Frontiers in Ecology and the Environment, 1*(3), 125–129.

Sanderson, E.W, Jaiteh, M., Levy, M., Redford, K.H., Wannebo, A.V., and Woolmer, G. (2002). The human footprint and the last of the wild. *BioScience*, 52(10), 891–904.

Sarkar, S. (1999). Wilderness preservation and biodiversity conservation: Keeping divergent goals distinct. *Bioscience, 49*(5), 450.

Stein, B.A. (2001). A fragile cornucopia: Assessing the status of U.S. biodiversity. *Environment, 43*(7), 11–22.

Turner, R.E. and Rabalais, N.N. (2003). Linking landscape and water quality in the Mississippi River Basin for 200 years. *BioScience, 53*(6), 563–573.

U.S. Census Bureau. (2000). No. 336. Total and federally owned land by state, 2000. In U.S. Census Bureau (2002), *Statistical abstract of the United States* (p. 211). Retrieved September 17, 2003, from http://www.census.gov/prod/2003pubs/02statab/geo.pdf

U.S. Census Bureau. (2003). *Population estimates, 2000.* Retrieved on September 17, 2003, from http://www.census.gov/popest/estimates.php

U.S. Department of Agriculture, Forest Service, Inventory and Monitoring Institute. (2003). Map data. Retrieved September 17, 2003, from http://www.fs.fed.us/institute/ftp/maps/na_regns.shp.zip

U.S. Department of Agriculture, Natural Resources Conservation Service. (2001). *1997 national resources inventory* (rev. December 2000) [CD-ROM, Version 1]. Washington, DC: Author.

U.S. Department of Transportation, Federal Highway Administration. (2002). *Highway statistics 2001* (as published). Retrieved September 17, 2003, from http://www.fhwa.dot.gov/ohim/hs01/aspublished

U.S. Geological Survey. (1993). *Digital elevation models—Data users guide 5.* Reston, VA: Author.

U.S. Geological Survey. (1999). Major roads of the United States. In U.S. Department of Interior, *National atlas of the United States.* Retrieved on September 17, 2003, from http://nationalatlas.gov/roadsm.html

U.S. Geological Survey. (2003). *Map layer info.* Retrieved September 17, 2003, from http://www.nationalatlas.gov/mld/citiesx.html

Vogelmann, J.E., Howard, S.M., Yang, L., Larson, C.R., Wylie, B.K., and Van Driel, N. (2001). Completion of the 1990s national land cover data set for the conterminous United States from Landsat Thematic Mapper data and ancillary data sources. *Photogrammetric Engineering & Remote Sensing, 67,* 650–662.

Vogelmann, J.E., Sohl, T., and Howard, S.M. (1998). Regional characterization of land cover using multiple sources of data. *Photogrammetric Engineering & Remote Sensing, 64,* 45–57.

Wear, D.N. (2002). Land use. In D.N. Wear and J.G. Greis (Eds.), *Southern forest resource assessment* (pp. 153–173; GTR SRS-53). Asheville, NC: USDA Forest Service, Southern Research Station.

Wear, D., Pye, J., and Riitters, K. (2004). Defining conservation priorities using fragmentation forecasts. Retrieved May 20, 2005, from http://www.ecologyandsociety.org/vol9/iss5/art4/

Wilderness Institute. (2003). *Wilderness Information Network, National Wilderness Preservation System database.* Retrieved on September 19, 2003, from http://www.wilderness.net

Chapter 6
Wilderness Attributes and the State of the National Wilderness Preservation System

Gregory H. Aplet
Senior Forest Scientist
The Wilderness Society, Denver, Colorado

Mark Wilbert
GIS Analyst, Center for Landscape Analysis
The Wilderness Society, Seattle, Washington

Pete Morton
Senior Resource Economist
The Wilderness Society, Denver, Colorado

In 1936, one year after the founding of The Wilderness Society, Robert Marshall and Althea Dobbins (1936) published a landmark paper documenting the extent of remaining roadless lands in the conterminous United States. They identified 48 forested roadless areas in the contiguous United States larger than 300,000 acres and 29 desert roadless areas over 500,000 acres. While they acknowledged that few of these areas were large enough to qualify as roadless in "a pioneering sense," Marshall and Dobbins nevertheless identified almost 90 million acres of potential wilderness in the lower 48 states alone. Since then, there have been several other attempts to document the condition of America's wilderness (Kendeigh et al., 1950/1951; Strittholt, Staus & White, 2000; USDA Forest Service, 1979). Similar efforts to quantify wilderness have been undertaken elsewhere in the world (Carver, Evans & Fritz, 2002; Lesslie & Maslen,1995; Sanderson et al., 2002).

While each of these approaches is somewhat different, they all share a common foundation—they seek to describe the condition of the land by evaluating measurable qualities of the land itself. These qualities, or "attributes" in the parlance of Chapter 4, are the most tangible descriptors of wilderness and provide the basis for more involved discussions of wilderness values.

This chapter further explores dimensions of the context within which the National Wilderness Preservation System resides. Like Chapter 5, recently available spatial data describing Wilderness lands and other lands across the country are employed to develop this context. An index of "wildness" is constructed from spatial data to describe and compare designated Wilderness and other lands. While some of the data sources are the same as those in Chapter 5, other sources have been added as well. This chapter's treatment of population, land use, development, and other land status data that were employed in Chapter 5 takes these measures further in that the focus is on indexing them to provide an overview of the "wildness" character of Wilderness and other lands.

Wildness: The Essence of Wilderness

Over the past several years, The Wilderness Society has conducted an investigation into the nature and distribution of wilderness attributes (e.g., Aplet, 1999; Aplet, Thomson & Wilbert, 2000). Surveying a century of wilderness literature, Aplet and colleagues concluded that "wildness" is the essence of wilderness, and it is composed of two essential qualities—naturalness and freedom from human control. Naturalness refers to the degree to which the land retains its primitive character, and freedom refers to the degree to which land functions without the influence of people. Other writers (Cole, 2000; Landres, Brunson & Merigliano, 2000/2001) prefer to use the term "wildness" in place of freedom, but they agree that the concept of wilderness incorporates both naturalness and freedom from control. Gudmundsen uses the term *autonomy* to express this quality of freedom (see Chapter 12).

The dualistic nature of wildness can be illustrated with a simple figure. Figure 6.1 represents landscapes in the two-dimensional space created by freedom and naturalness. In this conception, wildness increases in two directions, from the controlled to the "self-willed" along a gradient of freedom, and from the artificial to the primitive along a gradient of naturalness. Where freedom and naturalness are highest is wilderness. Land can possess any combination of freedom and naturalness, and a greater or lesser degree of wildness.

To place a landscape in this two-dimensional "wildness space" requires measuring attributes of the land. Again, through survey of the literature, The Wilderness Society has determined that the essential attributes that determine naturalness are the degree to which the land retains its primeval composition, the degree to which land remains free of artificial structures, and the degree of its purity or lack of pollution (Aplet, Thomson & Wilbert, 2000). The attributes that confer freedom from human control are the ability of the land to provide opportunities for solitude, the remoteness from roads and mechanical conveyance, and the degree to which ecological processes function unhindered by humans.

The rest of this chapter explains in greater detail the derivation of these attributes and some of the spatial indicators available to measure them. It then explain how these data were used to map the distribution of a wildness index

The Wildness Continuum

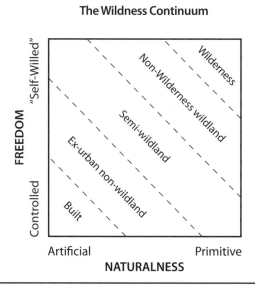

Figure 6.1 The continuum of wildness as a function of both naturalness and freedom from human control

across the landscape. Finally, the significance of the findings is interpreted for the current National Wilderness Preservation System and the future of Wilderness preservation.

Wilderness Attributes: A Basis for an Inquiry into Values

In Chapter 4, wilderness attributes were described as "observable...objectively measurable" characteristics of wilderness, including topography, geological composition, flora, and fauna. They note, "One of the first steps toward assessing Wilderness values is to inventory Wilderness attributes." This section describes the attributes measured in an effort to characterize the state of the National Wilderness Preservation System.

Natural Composition

Composition, the relative abundance of genes, species, plant communities, and other components of ecosystems, is one of the defining characteristics of ecosystems! It helps identify the degree to which modern ecosystems have retained their primitive or primeval character and is one of the defining characteristics of wildness. Poet Gary Snyder (1990) writes, "In ecology, we speak of 'wild systems.' When an ecosystem is fully functioning, all the members are present at the assembly. To speak of wilderness is to speak of wholeness." An ecosystem that has lost its native species or has been invaded by nonnative species has been altered in a fundamental way. In general, this chapter recognizes the most natural ecosystems as those that have retained their full complement of native species and harbor no exotics.

Unaltered Structure

Ecosystem structure refers to the spatial arrangement of the components of ecosystems. This can refer to the gross-scale features of geomorphology, the arrangement of vegetation patches, or the arrangement and spacing of trees in a forest stand. The degree to which ecosystem components retain their historical arrangement contributes to the naturalness of the system.

As with natural composition, the standard against which alteration should be judged is the condition of the ecosystem prior to disturbance by modern technological society, begun in North American 300–400 years ago. As has

---

[1] Assemblages of genes, species, and so forth are often referred to as *biodiversity* (UNEP, 1992); however, others (e.g., Crow, Haney & Waller, 1994; Franklin, 1988) have argued that biodiversity should also include structural and functional components, which this chapter does not include. Therefore, this chapter employs the narrower term *composition*.

been noted, pre-Columbian North America was a network of trails and settlements (Denevan, 1992/1998; Snyder, 1990). Some structures, such as the earthworks of the Southeast, were large by any standard. These structures were part of the historical ecosystem and considered by some as natural. Robert Marshall (1933/2002) recognized historical structures as entirely consistent with his view of wilderness: "Trails and temporary shelters, features such as were common long before the advent of the white race, are entirely permissible."

The Wilderness Act requires Wilderness to be "without permanent improvements or human habitation…with the imprint of man's work substantially unnoticeable." Robert Marshall's (1933/2002) definition stressed that "all roads, settlements, and power transportation are barred." Also, the conversion of natural forest into straight-rowed plantations alters ecosystem structure and diminishes naturalness. In an essay entitled "Wilderness," Aldo Leopold (1935/1991) lamented the "unnecessary outdoor geometry" of the plantation-dominated German countryside. The maintenance of unaltered structure has long been a litmus test of wilderness character and is the most familiar criterion for designation.

Purity (Lack of Pollution)

Wilderness carries with it an expectation of purity: clean water, fresh air, clean soil, and darkness at night. When air, streams, and the night sky are dirtied with coal-plant emissions, road dust, livestock feces and illuminated with industrial light, it diminishes the naturalness of the land and the experience it can provide. Poet Mark Strand (1996) made clear the relationship between pollution and wilderness when he wrote, "First we pollute the wilderness, then we pollute our minds with the belief that we've done the right thing. Then we pollute the wilderness more because we've lost our ability to see it. Soon the wilderness ceases to exist." Because of national laws, like the Clean Water Act and the Clean Air Act, which specifically mandate the prevention of significant deterioration of air quality in Wilderness areas, lack of pollution is one of the best-studied and best-documented attributes of wildness.

The Capacity to Provide Opportunities for Solitude

The "outstanding opportunities for solitude" afforded by wilderness have long been recognized as a key part of the "wilderness experience." Henry David Thoreau (1862/1982) enjoyed his opportunity to "walk ten, fifteen, twenty, any number of miles, commencing at my own door, without going by any house, without crossing a road except where the fox and mink do." Robert Marshall (1933/2002) required that wilderness have "no permanent inhabitants," and Sigurd Olson (1938/1998) exalted in "the ordinary phenomena of life in the open." The *2001 Draft Wilderness Stewardship Policy of the U.S. Fish and Wildlife Service* eloquently states

Wilderness solitude is a state of mind, a mental freedom that emerges from settings where visitors experience nature essentially free of the reminders of society, its inventions, and conventions. Privacy and isolation are important components, but solitude also is enhanced by the absence of other distractions, such as large groups, mechanization, unnatural noise, signs, and other modern artifacts… it is conducive to the psychological benefits associated with wilderness and one's free and independent response to nature. (U.S. Fish & Wildlife Service, 2001)

Solitude reflects freedom from human control because the more crowded the land is, the more it is being put to use. Such use can be passive (e.g., the simple act of occupancy), or it can be active (e.g., recreational use). The measurement of solitude, though, can be tricky. Crowding can be transient and does not require permanent occupancy. Also, solitude is an individual experience that is difficult to measure. Nevertheless, the ability of a place to provide uncrowded conditions is a measurable attribute of the land.

Remoteness

In Chapter 2 and in his recent book, *Driven Wild* (2002), about the founding of the modern wilderness movement, historian Paul Sutter argues that the very definition of wilderness arose as a response to the fanaticism with which America was constructing roads in the early 20th century:

The founding of the Wilderness Society was a crucial moment in the history of American environmental thought and politics not because it embodied a collective epiphany that wilderness was the ultimate expression of preservationist sentiment but because it involved the pragmatic act of giving a name to certain qualities that were disappearing from the landscape because of road building and the automobile.

Sutter sees roads as contributing to the control of the land and asserts, "Wilderness was as much about 'wildness,' the absence of human control, as it was about pristine ecological conditions."

Similarly, environmental historian Michael Cohen (1984) wrote that road construction is the first act of "trammeling" the wilderness. In his biography of John Muir, *The Pathless Way*, he wrote, "I am troubled by the term 'untrammeled.' At what point have we caught and trapped the wilderness? I would presume that a process of capturing or trapping begins when men try to 'open out routes' among the mountains." The very presence of a road diminishes the freedom of the land.

Remoteness from roads is clearly a time-honored measure of wildness. Aldo Leopold (1921) insisted that wilderness be "devoid of roads," and his son Starker's Commission on Wildlife Management in the National Parks considered the roadgrader to be "the most dangerous tool of all" (Leopold, Cain, Cottam, Gabrielson & Kimball, 1963/1998). Robert Marshall's (1933/2002) definition required wilderness to "possess no means of mechanical conveyance" in order that wilderness remain "free from mechanical sights and sounds and smells."

Uncontrolled Processes

The most free land is the least controlled land. With the invasion of new technologies that attended the recent settlement of North America, ancient ecological processes were radically altered in many parts of the country. Where once fires (whether lightning-caused or anthropogenic), floods and migrations marked the passage of the seasons, fire suppression, dams and extermination replaced them. If wilderness is to live up to one of its definitions, "self-willed land" (Turner, 1996), its historical ecological processes must be maintained.

The importance of uncontrolled processes to wilderness is amply noted in the literature. Wilderness has been described as a place where "a diversity of beings [flourish] according to their own sorts of order" (Turner, 1996) and "where nature prevails or might prevail given the passage of time...so long as active ecological succession, structural diversity, and naturalness are permitted" (Frome, 1997). Wilderness pioneer Arthur Carhart (1961) asserted, "[L]ands called 'wild' have retained the attribute of freedom. They have their own integrity intact. They have not been skinned, scraped, dug up, regimented and pounded into shapes and services desired and demanded by 'civilized' man." Robert Marshall (1933/2002), reflecting on the dynamics of forest succession, noted that "the wilderness is in constant flux." Even the Wilderness Act itself insists that wilderness "retain its primeval character and *influence*" (emphasis added).

The equation of uncontrolled processes with presettlement influences again raises the question of the role of indigenous people in landscape dynamics. Clearly, indigenous people have had tremendous influence on the character of the land in localized instances and may have altered the nature of ecosystems over broad areas through the use of fire and hunting practices (e.g., Denevan 1992/1998). Where this influence was intensive, we must view the land as under tight control and not free. However, where influence was extensive, aboriginal fire and hunting joined other sources of ignition and mortality, making it very difficult to distinguish between aboriginal control and "the will of the land." In this case, if only for practical purposes, we should consider extensive aboriginal influences to be part of the processes altered by the invasion of modern technological society.

Alteration of processes is probably the most difficult to measure of the six attributes that contribute to wildness. The science of historical ecology is just beginning to reveal the degree to which disturbance, hydrology, nutrient cycling, long-range migration, and other ecological processes have been changed over the past few centuries. And even when we know something about rates of change in specific locations, it is difficult to ascribe that information to the broader landscape. Nevertheless, progress has been made in mapping altered fire regimes, indices of watershed integrity, and other metrics that may allow us to quantify land's freedom from control of ecological processes.

Sources of Data and Approach to Indexing and Mapping Wildness

This section presents how the wildness attributes previously discussed were measured and combined into a measure of relative wildness at two scales: the contiguous United States and the regions of the East and the West. Though there are no hard and fast rules guiding how to apply these concepts, their application does require the selection of a consistent approach. In this case, the approach was to locate the best and finest scale spatial data available to represent each attribute (i.e., composition, structure, purity, solitude, remoteness, and uncontrolled processes). At the national scale, the land areas of the United States were divided into a matrix of just under 16 million cells, each approximately one kilometer square. Each of these cells was then assigned a value based on the data layer selected for each of the six attributes. Each attribute was represented with a value ranging between one and five. Some attributes (e.g., solitude) were derived from a single data set; others resulted from a combination of data sets (Table 6.1). The "wildness index" was then derived by summing the resulting six values for each cell. Spatial analysis and mapping was accomplished using the GRID module of Arc/Info GIS software. Although this wildness index suffers from many of the same shortcomings attending other indices (e.g., the addition of unlike units as though they were commensurate), it represents much of what contributes to the wildness of a place. The description of the data sources for each wildness attribute—natural composition, unaltered structure, purity, solitude, remoteness, and uncontrolled process—follow.

Natural Composition

Ecosystem composition can be measured a number of ways. Conceptually, one of the most straightforward is *species composition*. Ideally, data selected to measure species composition should provide information on the degree to which ecosystems retain the species typical of the area, and the degree to which exotic species have displaced natives. Unfortunately, such comparative data do not exist for the contiguous United States for both flora and fauna. Current vegetative species composition is available, however, in the form of the Seasonal Land Cover Regions (SLCR) satellite image classification conducted by the U.S. Geological Survey (USGS), which assigns surface vegetation to over 200 different classes of natural and exotic vegetation. Vegetative species data were combined with the urban classification data from a separate USGS Land Use and Land Cover data set. Each of the 16 million cells was then assigned one of five compositional classes, where a value of one is least natural and a value of five is most natural.

Unaltered Structure

Humans can alter ecosystem structure in a number of ways, from the construction of buildings, dams and roads to the planting of agricultural fields and the clearcutting of forests. An ideal data set would account for all these effects relative to historical conditions. Unfortunately, available data for the nation as a whole are limited to "built structures" and land use/land cover. Thus, the location of cities, towns, highways, dams, airstrips and agricultural land across

Table 6.1 Data sets used to represent wildness attributes

	Wildness Attribute					
GIS Data Layer	Natural Composition	Unaltered Structure	Purity	Solitude	Remoteness	Uncontrolled Process
Roads[1]		X			X	X
Population density[2]				X		
Land use[3]	X	X				
Populated places[4]		X				
Airports[5]		X				
Dams[6]		X				X
City lights at night[7]			X			
Superfund, nuclear reactor, and other EPA regulated sites[8]			X			

[1] National Highway Planning Network roads from the Federal Highway Administration, U.S. Department of Transportation (2004)
[2] Census tract population from the U.S. Census Bureau (1990)
[3] SLCR and USGS land use/land cover data from the U.S. Geological Survey (2004a, 2004d)
[4] Census populated places from the U.S. Census Bureau (1993)
[5] U.S. Geological Survey (1999; originally from the National Transportation Atlas)
[6] National Dams Inventory from the U.S. Army Corps of Engineers (1999)
[7] National Geophysical Data Center, U.S. Geological Survey (1995; originally from the Defense Mapping Agency, U.S. Department of Defense)
[8] U.S. Environmental Protection Agency (1996, 1997)

the country were mapped and assigned condition scores based on the nature of each cell and its surrounding cells. These scores were in turn assigned a scale value from one to five depending on where a cell score fell along a gradient of scores divided into five equal-interval ranges of structural scores. Final values range from one (most altered) to five (least altered).

Purity

Despite the abundance of data on pollution compiled for various locations, there exist very little spatial data describing the distribution of pollution across the entire country. The EPA maintains data recording the locations of Superfund sites, nuclear reactors, and other sites they regulate as sources of pollution. As well, an indication of light pollution is available in the image of "Earth at Night in 2000" for the United States (NASA, 2005). These data sets were combined, and cells were assigned a purity value from one (least pure) to five (most pure) based on their combined value.

Solitude

Ideally, the spatial representation of opportunity for solitude would display the probability of encountering other persons over a landscape. It would account not only for the presence of residents of the land but also for visitors as well. Unfortunately, there are no such data sets available for the contiguous United States. However, the U.S. Census Bureau keeps track of the distribution of the resident population across the country. Thus, solitude is represented with Census population density at the census tract level. The range of density values was divided into five equal-interval ranges then assigned solitude values ranging from one (lowest solitude) to five (highest solitude).

Remoteness

As a measure of an area's freedom from mechanical devices, remoteness is best represented by data describing the presence of the sights, sounds, and smells of a wide variety of devices, such as cars, bikes, lawn mowers, and airplanes. Such robust data are not available for the contiguous United States, so we represented remoteness with distance from highways as found in the National Highway Planning Network data set (U.S. Department of Transportation, 2002). Roads in the data set are also assigned to one of two categories to represent two different levels of use and, therefore, different potential impacts on remoteness. Remoteness was computed as the distance from a cell to the nearest road in each of these two categories. The scale value ranges from one (low remoteness) to five (high remoteness) depending on which of five equal-interval score ranges into which a cell value fell.

Uncontrolled Processes

Ecological processes are inherently difficult to measure. Mapping ecological processes is even more difficult, as it requires tying process measurements to particular places. Such data with national coverage are difficult to obtain, so we used hydrologic and landscape patch data as surrogates for ecological processes. One of the few data sets that suggest process impacts is the national inventory of dams available from the USGS. To account for changes in hydrologic function, the number of dams in major hydrologic units (watersheds) were evaluated.

To map terrestrial processes, we applied concepts developed by The Nature Conservancy (1998) that relate patch metrics (i.e., area, distance to edge, major axis) to landscape function. The approach assumes that ecological processes in larger, well-connected polygons of natural vegetation (delimited by major highways, agricultural lands and urban areas) are under less human control than in smaller, disconnected patches, regardless of whether those patches are themselves naturally fragmented. The hydrologic and patch data were combined and cells were assigned values ranging from one (most controlled) to five (least controlled).

Indexing

To construct the index and map of wildness (Plate 13, Appendix A), the values of the six attributes covered above were summed into an overall "wildness index." Because the index is the sum of six attribute values, each ranging from one to five, the wildness index ranges from a minimum value of 6 to a maximum value of 30. A unique color, ranging from purple through yellows and greens to blue was assigned to each index value and the spatial distribution of wildness values across the 16 million cells was displayed in the form of a map (Plate 13).

In addition to the map shown in Plate 13, distributions of wildness index values for various land classes (i.e., non-federal, federal non-wilderness, and Wilderness) were obtained by overlaying the wildness grid with ownership boundaries obtained from the *National Atlas of the United States* (U.S. Geological Survey, 2004b, 2004c), and extracting the index value and ownership class of each grid cell.

Throughout this analysis, it is important to keep in mind that the wildness index is just that—an index. It is not a direct measure of the wildness of land. It is highly subject to the types of data available and used to construct it, and it is subject to the range and scale of values in the underlying data. Our methods have yielded a range of values from 6 to 30, regardless of whether the landscape analyzed is in central Nevada or Central Park. Regardless of its limitations, however, the resulting index is a useful tool for exploring the relative wildness of landscapes.

Assessing Wildness

The national map (Plate 13) reveals a nation divided. Abundant precipitation, fertile soils, and a two-hundred-year head start on colonization have transformed the East into a heavily populated working landscape. The West, in contrast, with its mountains and infertile deserts, remains less settled and wild. The few fertile plains, such as Washington's Palouse wheatfields and the breadbaskets of California's Central Valley and Oregon's Willamette Valley join Seattle, Portland, the Bay Area, the South Coast, Phoenix, Salt Lake City, and Denver in an archipelago of development surrounded by a sea of wildness. In the East, the pattern is reversed. Minnesota's Boundary Waters, northern Maine, the Adirondacks, the central and southern Appalachians, Okefenokee Swamp, and the Everglades stand out from a sea of development.

Reflecting these differences in land use are differences in land ownership. Most federal land is located in the "Wild West." To explore the relationship between wildness and land ownership, distribution of wildness values for non-federal, federal non-Wilderness, and Wilderness were extracted and displayed (Figure 6.2). The figure shows that non-federal land is concentrated in the lower to middle portions of the range of wildness index values. The median wildness index for non-federal land is 17.0. In contrast, federal non-Wilderness land is concentrated at the wilder end of the spectrum. The median value of federal non-Wilderness land is 25.7 and the acreage increases as wildness increases. Reassuringly, Wilderness is concentrated on the wildest federal

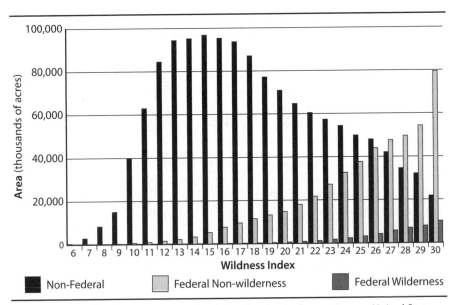

Figure 6.2 Distribution of wildness by land classification in the contiguous United States

lands. The 8.8 percent of federal lands in the lower 48 that is Wilderness has a median wildness of 27.2. Perhaps more unexpected is that Wilderness represents no more than 13 percent of the federal land in any wildness class, indicating that there is a lot of federal land, even in the wildest classes, that has not yet been designated Wilderness.

More interesting, though, is that Wilderness is distributed across almost every wildness class applying to federal land (Figure 6.2). Wilderness occurs from extremely wild places like Kanab Creek in Arizona and Pahute Peak in Nevada to relatively developed locales like the Great Swamp National Wildlife Refuge in New Jersey and the J. N. "Ding" Darling Wilderness off the coast of Florida (Tables 6.2 and 6.3). Such a range in average wildness indicates that Wilderness is not simply the wildest of the federal lands, rather, it is context dependent. Recall that some of the measures used in the index accounted for scores describing surrounding cells as well as scores for each individual cell. In this way, the wildness index recognizes Wilderness relative to its surroundings. If Wilderness represented only the wildest land in the federal system, it would be restricted to areas with an index of 30, but instead, it is found in almost every wildness class of federal land (Figure 6.3, p. 104). Wilderness areas, such as those found along the spine of the Appalachians or

Table 6.2 Wilderness areas with average Wildness of 30

Name	Agency	Acres
Alta Toquima Wilderness (NV)	FS	38,000
East Fork High Rock Canyon Wilderness (NV)	BLM	52,617
Gearhart Mountain Wilderness (OR)	FS	22,809
High Rock Canyon Wilderness (NV)	BLM	46,464
Kanab Creek Wilderness (AZ)	FS & BLM	70,460
Mount Trumbull Wilderness (AZ)	BLM	7,880
North Black Rock Range Wilderness (NV)	BLM	30,647
Pahute Peak Wilderness (NV)	BLM	56,890
Rawhide Mountains Wilderness (AZ)	BLM	38,470
South Jackson Mountains Wilderness (NV)	BLM	54,535

Table 6.3 Wilderness areas with average Wildness less than 15

Name	Agency	Acres
Brigantine Wilderness (NJ)	FWS	6,681
Congaree Swamp National Monument Wilderness (SC)	NPS	15,010
Great Swamp National Wildlife Refuge Wilderness (NJ)	FWS	3,660
J.N. "Ding" Darling Wilderness (FL)	FWS	2,619
Mount Olympus Wilderness (UT)	FS	15,300
Russian Wilderness (CA)	FS	12,000
Twin Peaks Wilderness (UT)	FS	11,396

adjacent to population centers of the West, may not have received the highest wildness values, but compared with all other lands of the lower 48, they are relatively wild which speaks to the reasoning underlying their designation.

The foregoing analysis makes clear the wide range of conditions over which Wilderness occurs. But the obvious differences between the East and the West seem to obscure the contribution of Wilderness designation to the protection of wildlands in each landscape. So little of the East appears wild that it is difficult to see the contribution of Wilderness designation to the protection of the wildest lands. Conversely, so much of the West is relatively wild that the importance of Wilderness is unclear. To facilitate a better understanding of the relative contribution of Wilderness designation to wildland conservation in the East and the West, the data were divided into two subsets, one including the states of Ohio, Kentucky, Tennessee, Mississippi, and other lands to the east, and another subset including the eleven western states (The Midwest was not examined). In each of these landscapes, the attribute "layers" were recalculated using only the range of values present in each region's landscape. The result is a map of the East that displays wildness in the East relative to just those lands in that region. This approach better highlights the wildness of lands of the East and the contribution of Wilderness designation to protect this wildness. The same is true for the West, except the result is that less of the lands in that region are highlighted as having a high degree of wildness character. Over the maps of each region, the outlines of existing Wilderness

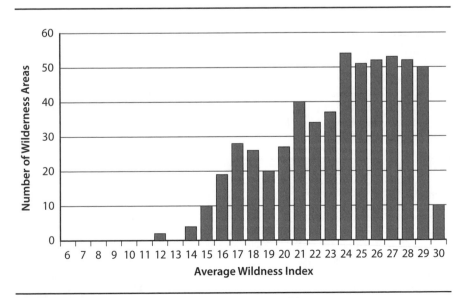

Figure 6.3 Distribution of wilderness units by average wildness

were superimposed to create Plates 14 and 15, allowing us to see Wilderness in a more realistic regional context.

In addition, the regional wildness data were subjected to the same breakdown of non-federal land, federal non-Wilderness, and Wilderness as used to create Figures 6.4 and 6.5. The differences between East and West regions are stark. In the East, land ownership is dominated by non-federal land (Figure 6.4). In this region, over 92 percent of the landscape is non-federal, and of the 8 percent of the landscape that is federal, only 7 percent of that federal land is Wilderness. That modest amount of Wilderness is concentrated near the wilder end of the spectrum relative to all other lands in the East. Most of the wildest of eastern lands are concentrated in the largely private landscape of northern Maine, and little of the wildest elsewhere is federal or designated Wilderness.

A very different picture emerges in the West. There, about 60 percent of the landscape is federal. These federal lands occur across all wildness classes, but federal lands dominate at the wildest end of the spectrum (Figure 6.5, p. 106). Unlike the East, Wilderness in the West is abundant across a wide range of wildness classes. This suggests that Congress has recognized Wilderness relative to its more immediate context, rather than relative to an imagined standard of purity. Significantly, as in the East, the amount of non-federal land exceeds the amount of Wilderness in the West across the full range of wildness values. Only in the wildest class does Wilderness exceed non-federal land, and there only by 7 percent.

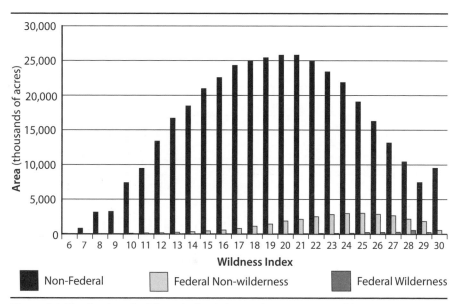

Figure 6.4 Distribution of wildness by land class in the eastern United States

One of the more revealing results of this analysis is how much non-Wilderness land is in the wildest land classes. Nationwide, as mentioned, no more than 13 percent of federal land in any one wildness class is designated Wilderness. To better understand this phenomenon, we further broke down federal land by administering agency and examined the distribution of wildness for Forest Service and BLM lands separately, nationwide (Figure 6.6 and 6.7). On national forests, Wilderness is concentrated on the wildest lands (Figure 6.6). As wildness increases, both the area of Wilderness and the proportion protected increase, such that in the wildest class (Wildness Index = 30), Wilderness represents almost one third of the national forest lands. Inventoried roadless areas (IRAs) follow a similar pattern, with almost as much acreage in IRAs as in Wilderness in the wildest classes (Figure 6.6).

On BLM lands, no agency-defined map of roadless areas exists, so Wilderness and Wilderness Study Areas were examined. Nationwide, less than three percent (i.e., 6,511,891 acres) of BLM's vast 270-million-acre holdings is designated Wilderness, despite the fact that our analysis identified over 58 million acres in the wildest class alone. Close examination of Figure 6.7 reveals that what has been designated is not concentrated in the wildest portions of the BLM's holdings. Wilderness Study Areas (WSAs), in contrast, are largely concentrated in the wildest classes, with WSAs making up 13 percent of total BLM land in the wildest class and less than seven percent of BLM land overall.

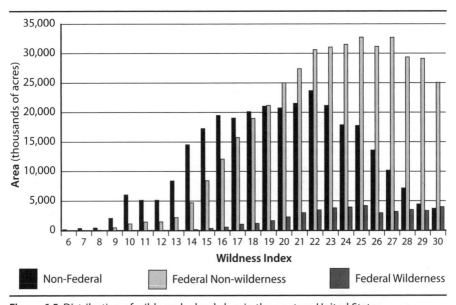

Figure 6.5 Distribution of wildness by land class in the western United States

Conclusion

Our analysis shows that the NWPS protects attributes of wildness and hence the Wilderness values discussed in this book. Nationwide, the median wildness

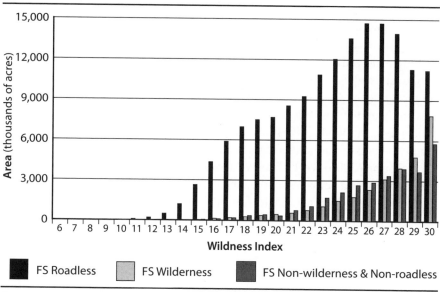

Figure 6.6 Distribution of wildness on national forests

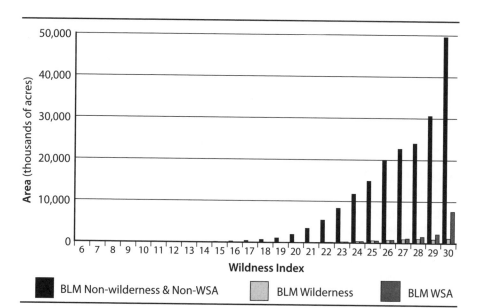

Figure 6.7 Distribution of wildness on Bureau of Land Management Lands

index for NWPS land is higher for Wilderness than for non-Wilderness federal land, and much higher than for non-federal land. Our results show that Wilderness occurs largely, but not exclusively, where attributes of wildness are highest.

The higher level of wildness for federal land in general, and the NWPS in particular, should not be surprising. Since the organization of the federal land systems around the turn of the last century, federal lands have been intentionally managed differently from the private landscape. Watershed protection, wildlife management, and the provision of outdoor recreation have resulted in public landscapes higher in wildness character than private ones. Our results (Figures 6.4 and 6.5) indicate that wildness is more abundant in the West, especially on the vast tracts of BLM land that have not yet been designated Wilderness. But wildness is found also to some degree throughout the country, mainly wherever public lands are found.

Morton (2000) writes that Wilderness makes positive contributions to the economy and helps offset the lack of Wilderness values on private land. The scarcity of Wilderness in the East makes the contribution of these wildest of public lands especially important. For example, Phillips (2000) has shown that proximity to Wilderness on the Green Mountain National Forest in Vermont positively affects the market value of private land. Ultimately, though, people value Wilderness not for its impact on jobs or recreational opportunities, but because they care about what it protects (e.g., clean air, clean water, wildlife habitat, and scenic beauty)—for now and for future generations—whether they ever get to see it or not (Cordell, Tarrant, McDonald & Bergstrom, 1998). Perhaps it is this expressed value of the land itself that explains how this country has been able to build a National Wilderness Preservation System exceeding 100 million acres and spanning the range from beloved "accidental wild spots" close to home to "vast expanses of virgin country" (Leopold, 1925). Little else seems to explain it.

Literature Cited

Aplet, G.H. (1999). On the nature of wildness: Exploring what wilderness really protects. *Denver University Law Review, 76,* 347–367.

Aplet, G., Thomson, J., and Wilbert, M. (2000). Indicators of wildness: Using attributes of the land to assess the context of wilderness. In S. McCool, D. Cole, W. Borrie, and J. O'Loughlin (Eds.), *Wilderness science in a time of change* (pp. 89–98; RMRS-P-15-Vol. 2). Ogden, UT: USDA Forest Service, Rocky Mountain Research Station.

Carhart, A.H. (1961). *Planning for America's wildlands: A handbook for land-use planners, managers and executives, committee and commission members, con-*

servation leaders, and all who face problems of wildland management. Harrisburg, PA: The Telegraph Press.

Carver, S., Evans, A., and Fritz, S. (2002). Wilderness attribute mapping in the United Kingdom. *International Journal of Wilderness, 8*(1), 24–29.

Cohen, M.P. (1984). *The pathless way: John Muir and American wilderness.* Madison, WI: University of Wisconsin Press.

Cole, D. (2000). Paradox of the primeval: Ecological restoration in wilderness. *Ecological Restoration, 18*(2), 77–86.

Cordell, H.K., Tarrant, M.A., McDonald, B.L., and Bergstrom, J.C. (1998). How the public views wilderness: More results from the USA Survey on Recreation and the Environment. *International Journal of Wilderness, 4*(3), 28–31.

Crow, T.R., Haney, A., and Waller, D.M. (1994). Report of the scientific roundtable on biological diversity convened by the Chequamegon and Nicolet National Forests (GTR-NC-166). St. Paul, MN: USDA Forest Service, North Central Forest Experiment Station.

Denevan, W. (1998). The pristine myth: The landscape of the Americas in 1492. In J. Baird Callicott and M.P. Nelson (Eds.), *The great new wilderness debate* (pp. 414–442). Athens, GA: University of Georgia Press. (Original work published 1992)

Franklin, J.F. (1988). Structural and functional diversity in temperate forests. In E.O. Wilson (Ed.), *Biodiversity* (pp. 166–175). Washington, DC: National Academy Press.

Frome, M. (1997). *Battle for the wilderness* (Rev. ed.). Salt Lake City, UT: University of Utah Press.

Kendeigh, S.C., Baldwin, H.I., Cahalane, V.H., Clarke, C.H.D., Cottam, C., Cottam, W.P., et al. (1950/1951). Nature sanctuaries in the United States and Canada: A preliminary inventory. *The Living Wilderness, 15*(35), 1–45.

Landres, P., Brunson, M., and Merigliano, L. (2000/2001). Naturalness and wildness: The dilemma and irony of ecological restoration in wilderness. *Wild Earth, 10*(4), 77–82.

Leopold, A. (1921). The wilderness and its place in forest recreational policy. *Journal of Forestry, 19*(7), 718–721.

Leopold, A. (1925). Wilderness as a form of land use. *The Journal of Land and Public Utility Economics, 1*, 398–404.

Leopold, A. (1991). Wilderness. In S. Flader and J.B. Callicott (Eds.), *The River of the Mother of God and other essays by Aldo Leopold* (pp. 226–229). Madison, WI: University of Wisconsin Press. (Original work published 1935)

Leopold, A.S., Cain, S.A., Cottam, C.M., Gabrielson, I.N., and Kimball, T.L. (1998). Wildlife management in the national parks. In J. Baird Callicott and M.P. Nelson (Eds.), *The great new wilderness debate* (pp. 103–119). Athens, GA: University of Georgia Press. (Original work published 1963)

Lesslie, R. and Maslen, M. (1995). *National wilderness inventory handbook of procedures, content, and usage* (2nd ed.). Canberra, Australia: Australian Heritage Commission, Australian Government Publishing Service.

Marshall, R. (2002). *The people's forests*. Iowa City, IA: University of Iowa Press. (Original work published 1933)

Marshall, R. and Dobbins, A. (1936). Largest roadless areas in United States. *The Living Wilderness*, November, 11–13.

Morton, P. (2000). Wildland economics: Theory and practice. In S. McCool, D. Cole, W. Borrie, and J. O'Loughlin (Eds.), *Wilderness science in a time of change* (pp. 238–250; RMRS-P-15-Vol. 2). Ogden, UT: USDA Forest Service, Rocky Mountain Research Station.

National Aeronautics and Space Administration. (2005). Earth's city lights. Retrieved January 20, 2005, from http://visibleearth.nasa.gov/view_rec.php?vev1id=5826

The Nature Conservancy. (1998). *Ecological processes at the ecoregional scale: Considerations for portfolio design: Guidelines for ecoregional team leaders from the stewardship expert team.* Unpublished draft manuscript.

Olson, S. (1998). Why wilderness? In J. Baird Callicott and M.P. Nelson (Eds.), *The great new wilderness debate* (pp. 97–102). Athens, GA: University of Georgia Press. (Original work published 1938)

Phillips, S. (2000). Windfalls for wilderness: Land protection and land value in the Green Mountains. In S. McCool, D. Cole, W. Borrie, and J. O'Loughlin (Eds.), *Wilderness science in a time of change* (pp. 258–267; RMRS-P-15-Vol. 2). Ogden, UT: USDA Forest Service, Rocky Mountain Research Station.

Sanderson, E., Jaiteh, M., Levy, M., Redford, K., Wannebo, A., and Woolmer, G. (2002). The human footprint and the last of the wild. *Bioscience, 52*, 891–904.

Snyder, G. (1990). *The practice of the wild*. New York, NY: North Point Press.

Strand, M. (1996). Untitled. In S. Trimble and T.T. Williams (Comps.), *Testimony: Writers of the West speak out on behalf of Utah wilderness*. Minneapolis, MN: Milkweed Editions.

Stritholt, J., Staus, M., and White, M.. (2000). *Importance of Bureau of Land Management roadless areas in the western USA*. Corvallis, OR: Conservation Biology Institute.

Sutter, P. (2002). *Driven wild: How the fight against automobiles launched the modern wilderness movement*. Seattle, WA: University of Washington Press.

Thoreau, H.D. (1982). Walking. In Carl Bode (Ed.), *The portable Thoreau* (pp. 592–630). New York, NY: Penguin Books. (Original work published 1862)

Turner, J. (1996). *The abstract wild*. Tucson, AZ: University of Arizona Press.

United Nations Environment Programme (UNEP). (1992). *Convention on biological diversity*. Retrieved April 2, 2004, from http://www.biodiv.org/convention/articles.asp

U.S. Army Corps of Engineers. (1999). *Corps national data sets: National inventory of dams.* Retrived August 18, 2004, from http://corpsgeo1.usace.army.mil/

U.S. Census Bureau. (1990). *1990 Census of the population and housing summary tape file 1* [CD-ROM]. Retrieved August 18, 2004, from http://factfinder.census.gov/metadoc/1990stf1td.pdf

U.S. Census Bureau. (1993). *TIGER/Line files, 1992.* Retrieved August 18, 2004, from http://www.census.gov/geo/www/tlmetadata/tl92meta.txt

U.S. Environmental Protection Agency. (1996). *Stability array (STAR) meterological stations for the conterminous United States.* Retrieved on August 18, 2004, from http://www.epa.gov/nsdi/projects/npl.htm

U.S. Environmental Protection Agency. (1997). *U.S. EPA-regulated facilities point locations from Enviofacts for the conterminous United States.* Retrieved on August 18, 2004, from http://www.epa.gov/nsdi/projects/nat_enviro.htm

USDA Forest Service. (1979). *Final RARE II environmental impact statement.* Washington, DC: USDA Forest Service.

U.S. Department of Transportation. (2002). *Highway statistics 2001.* Federal Highway Administration, Office of Highway Policy Information. Retrieved April 28, 2004, from http://www.fhwa.dot.gov/ohim/hs01/aspublished

U.S. Department of Transportation. (2004). *The national highway planning network.* Retrieved August 18, 2004, from http://www.fhwa.dot.gov/planning/nhpn

U.S. Fish and Wildlife Service. (2001). *2001 Draft wilderness stewardship policy pursuant to the Wilderness Act of 1964.* Retrieved April 27, 2004, from http://policy.fws.gov/library/01fr3708.pdf

U.S. Geological Survey. (1995). *Night-time lights of the world: 1994–1995.* Retrieved August 18, 2004, from http://dmsp.ngdc.noaa.gov/html/download_Night_time_lights_94-95.html

U.S. Geological Survey. (1999). *Airports: Map layer decsription file.* Retrieved August 18, 2004, from http://sun1.giac.montana.edu/gyadc/atlasmetadata/airports.html

U.S. Geological Survey. (2004a). *Global land cover characterization (version 1.2).* Retrieved August 18, 2004, from http://edcsns17.cr.usgs.gov/glcc/glcc_version1.html#North America

U.S. Geological Survey. (2004b). *National atlas of the United States: Federal lands.* Retrieved August 18, 2004, from http://edcftp.cr.usgs.gov/pub/data/nationalatlas/fedlanp020.tar.gz

U.S. Geological Survey. (2004c). *National atlas of the United States: NWPS lands.* Retrieved August 18, 2004, from http://edcftp.cr.usgs.gov/pub/data/nationalatlas/wildrnp020.tar.gz

U.S. Geological Survey. (2004d). *North American land cover characteristics.* Retrieved August 18, 2004, from http://www.nationalatlas.gov/metadata/landcvi020l.html

Chapter 7
The Social Value of Wilderness

Rudy M. Schuster
Faculty of Forest and Natural Resource Management
SUNY College of Environmental Science and Forestry, Syracuse, New York

Michael Tarrant
Associate Professor, Daniel B. Warnell School of Forest Resources
University of Georgia, Athens, Georgia

Alan Watson
Research Social Scientist
Aldo Leopold Wilderness Research Institute, Missoula, Montana

This chapter describes, in noneconomic terms, research evidence of the benefits that define the social values of federally designated Wilderness. The social values of Wilderness lie in the nature and importance of these benefits. These "noneconomic" benefits are viewed primarily from the perspectives of the disciplines of psychology, sociology, and anthropology (as briefly noted in Chapter 4). Examinations of Wilderness benefits in economic terms (i.e., from the perspective of economics) are presented in Chapters 9 and 10.

This chapter has four sections. The first section presents an overview of trends in what benefits Americans value most about Wilderness lands. A brief historical description is given of the evolution of what Americans have valued, going from the primarily utilitarian view of the past to the more holistic view of recent years. National Survey on Recreation and the Environment data (USDA Forest Service, 2004) is the principle source for describing trends in both use and nonuse benefits.

The second section of this chapter focuses on recent surveys of public opinions regarding the status of the National Wilderness Preservation System. The NSRE plus a variety of other recent public surveys conducted by government, private organizations, and academic institutions are used. The third and fourth sections of this chapter investigate the onsite benefits that Americans may accrue from actually spending time in Wilderness.

Underpinning this chapter's examination of benefits and values are two approaches recognized broadly in the fields of sociology, psychology, and anthropology—social construction and,goal directed. These approaches take a relatively holistic view of values and of how values are formed. The first approach is the *social construction approach*. Through this approach, meaning and value for Wilderness are created through historical, cultural, and political experiences over time. Specifically, it is the process by which "groups of people create shared meanings and understandings of a place and how those shared meanings, in turn, structure actions in and with respect to those places" (Williams, 2000, p. 78). "The labeling of a place or space as "wilderness"… carries with it the power to shape not only people's perceptions of that place, but [also] their behavioral attitudes towards it as well" (Bertolas, 1998, p. 100). Pressing a group to define the value of Wilderness provides insight into a culture's framework regarding land use and the benefits that underpin environmental values.

The second approach, the *goal-directed approach*, specifies a more utilitarian process through which Wilderness value is formed. Value formed this way "enables wilderness meanings and values of the landscape to be defined and managed in ways analogous to other, competing land uses (e.g., timber, water, grazing)" (Williams, 2000, p. 78). Thus, Wilderness is viewed as a collection of attributes that can be traded or consumed. The attributes considered are often specifically associated with the preferences of recreationists (i.e., onsite Wilderness users). The goal-directed approach may not always present a holistic view of Wilderness values. Recreationists represent a minority of the population who benefit from Wilderness. However, acknowledgment of both of these value construction processes creates a synergy of multiple social science methods, including quantitative and qualitative approaches, from the fields of psychology, sociology, anthropology, and economics.

Trends in Perceptions of Wilderness Benefits

A shift seems to have occurred in what benefits Americans value most about wilderness as a concept, and what is valued about the NWPS more specifically. In the early decades of European land settlement in this country, wilderness was viewed as something threatening, hostile, and of little (or no) worth. Most early settlers (particularly those of European descent) worked hard to clear and convert natural lands to domestic uses, usually in the name of progress and civilization (Nash, 1982). As these same lands later became valued primarily for large-scale commercial uses (including timber, agriculture, mining, and water), a utilitarian perspective toward wild lands emerged. Over the past sixty or so years, however, this dominating utilitarian view has been slowly trending toward more of a natural land protection orientation (Tarrant & Hull, 2004). This chapter examines this emerging protection paradigm and presents the results of survey research that have addressed perceptions of the use and non-use benefits of the NWPS. Often, the total value of natural resources has been underestimated by not considering both use and nonuse values in decision making (Stevens, Benin & Larson, 1995).

As referenced in this chapter, use values of Wilderness are comprised of direct and indirect benefits. Nonuse values are derived from preserving lands in their pristine condition and include existence, bequest, option, and intrinsic benefits (Mountford & Kepler, 1999). Direct-use values derive from direct contact with Wilderness by those who are actually using it for such activities as recreation, grazing, and mining. Indirect-use values concern those Wilderness benefits that indirectly contribute to the well-being of humans through the protection of natural systems (e.g., provision of clean air and water). Existence values are the benefits humans perceive from simply knowing Wilderness exists, independent of any present or future on-site use of a designated area (e.g., spiritual and symbolic aspects of knowing Wilderness exists). Bequest value represents the value that people derive from maintaining Wilderness for use or nonuse benefits for future generations. Option values are preferences people have for reducing the risk of losing opportunities to benefit from or to use Wilderness in the future. Intrinsic values are the qualities that Wilderness possesses inherently, regardless of human knowledge or existence. Thus intrinsic values may or may not be recognized by humans.

Table 7.1 presents a list of thirteen use and nonuse Wilderness benefits and presents survey results to indicate how the public has rated the importance of these benefits over time. The period examined is from 1980 to 2000. While the first survey cited is not completely comparable with the latter two, its results do give some sense of trends since 1980. Survey respondents in that survey included individuals in 218 Colorado households in 1980 (Haas, Hermann & Walsh, 1986). The latter surveys included 1,900 households in a nationwide sample in 1995 (Cordell, Tarrant, McDonald & Bergstrom, 1998), and 5,000 households in a nationwide survey in 2000 (Cordell, Tarrant & Green, 2003).

Table 7.1 shows that, with the exception of tourism income, very few respondents in 2000 (less than 10%) rated any of the Wilderness benefits listed as "not important." The survey summaries shown in Table 7.1 suggest that Wilderness is becoming more important to people, as indicated by the higher proportions of respondents rating the listed Wilderness benefits as "very or extremely important" in 2000 as compared to 1980. In Table 7.1 also one can see that the greatest increases in percentages rating items as very to extremely important occurred for benefits related to ecological services, preserving ecosystems, and future option values. These results seem to point to a more fundamental shift in the ways that people value nature, away from the dominant social paradigm that emphasized economic growth,

Table 7.1 Trends in percentage of Americans 16 or older indicating level of importance and mean score[1] for each of 13 Wilderness benefits, 1980 ($n = 218$), 1995 ($n = 1,900$) and 2000 ($n = 5,000$)

Wilderness benefits	Very or extremely important			Not important			Mean score[1]		
	1980	1995	2000	1980	1995	2000	1980	1995	2000
Protecting air quality	77.2	78.0	92.3	5.5	2.6	0.6	1.85	1.79	1.52
Protecting water quality	87.1	78.9	93.1	3.2	1.7	0.6	1.61	1.77	1.53
Protection of wildlife habitat	79.3	78.6	87.8	2.8	2.6	0.6	1.85	1.81	1.62
For future generations	75.7	76.9	87.0	5.0	2.0	1.1	1.95	1.84	1.68
Protection for endangered species	70.7	73.7	82.7	4.1	4.9	1.8	2.01	1.92	1.74
Preserving ecosystems	65.6	66.5	80.0	6.4	7.0	1.6	2.13	2.14	1.82
Scenic beauty	70.2	59.7	74.0	3.7	5.4	1.8	2.05	2.18	1.98
Future option to visit	69.8	59.4	75.1	3.7	7.7	3.1	1.99	2.24	1.98
Just knowing it exists	58.7	56.1	74.6	10.6	6.4	2.2	2.44	2.23	1.98
Recreation opportunities	70.1	48.9	64.9	2.3	10.1	2.5	2.03	2.46	2.17
For scientific study	55.5	46.3	57.5	6.0	14.1	4.4	2.32	2.55	2.33
Providing spiritual inspiration	37.3	43.2	56.5	22.7	18.3	8.9	2.93	2.62	2.43
Income for tourism industry	23.4	22.8	29.7	24.8	41.1	17.6	3.26	3.33	3.12

[1] Importance scores ranged from "extremely important" = 1 to "not important" = 5
Sources: Cordell, Tarrant & Green, 2003; Haas, Hermann & Walsh, 1986

human dominance, and use of nature, and toward a new environmental paradigm that emphasized sustainable development, harmony with nature, and a balance of human and non-human uses and nonuses (e.g., Bliss, 2000; Steel & Lovrich, 1997; Tarrant, Cordell & Green, 2003; Xu & Bengston, 1997). Across the surveys at different time periods, ensuring clean air and water (i. e., indirect-use benefits), protecting wildlife habitat and endangered species (i.e., existence benefits), and future generations (i.e., bequest benefits) were consistently rated as the five most important benefits of Wilderness. Wilderness for science, tourism income, and spiritual inspiration were consistently rated as the least important benefits of Wilderness.

With the exception of on-site recreation use benefits (which showed somewhat of a decrease over the 20-year period from 1980 to 2000), there was very little difference in the relative importance of the thirteen benefits over time. We noted, however, that for several of the Wilderness benefits there was a slight decrease in importance from 1980 to 1995. This decrease was highest for recreation, science, and scenic beauty. One possible reason is that after the decade of the 1980s, in which few environmental laws were passed relative to the period from 1960 to 1980, public awareness of Wilderness and the natural environment may have been ebbing slightly.

Table 7.2 (p. 118) further elaborates on the social benefits of Wilderness by adding a different set of use and nonuse items. Data in Table 7.2 were collected in the 2003 version of the National Survey on Recreation and the Environment (NSRE). This added framework includes twelve new social benefit items: (a) Expression and Learning (i.e., educational, recreational, and artistic), (b) Growth (i.e., aesthetic, well-being, self-enlightenment, family/ social, character-building, and therapeutic), and (c) Societal Maintenance (i.e., scientific/research, cultural, and historical). The benefits in the Growth and the Expression and Learning domains are realized by actually spending time in Wilderness (i.e., direct benefits). The benefits in the Societal Maintenance domain can be realized without entering an actual Wilderness area (i.e., off-site or nonuse benefits). It should be noted that the artistic value of Wilderness might also be realized as an off-site benefit, such as in a case where an individual admires a photograph of Wilderness scenery.

A large majority of the American public either agrees or strongly agrees that all of the twelve benefits listed are important. The Expression and Learning domain illustrates that the American public values Wilderness as a place to educate our children and for adults to continue lifelong learning. It is also a source of artistic beauty that can be admired remotely and contributes to our lives outside of Wilderness. Americans also value Wilderness simply because it is an enjoyable place for recreation.

The Growth domain shows Americans strongly believe Wilderness can provide self-improvement qualities to citizens. People who have relationships

Table 7.2 Percentages of Americans 16 or older by level of agreement with benefit statement[1] and mean scores for 12 Wilderness benefits

Wilderness Benefit Statement	Benefit Class	Strongly or Moderately Agree	Neither Agree nor Disagree	Moderately and Strongly Disagree	Mean Score	Standard Deviation
Spending time in Wilderness:		*Expression & Learning*				
Provides an opportunity to study wildlife, plants, rocks, and minerals as they occur in nature	Educational	98.0	0.9	1.1	1.2	0.5
Allows people to have fun and enjoy outdoor recreation activities	Recreational	97.8	1.1	1.1	1.3	0.6
Provides unique and outstanding subjects for art, such as painting or photography	Artistic	95.9	2.3	1.8	1.4	0.6
		Growth				
Allows people to see and experience nature, such as wildflowers, wildlife, clear streams, or mountains.	Aesthetic	98.2	0.7	1.1	1.2	0.5
Helps people escape the stresses of everyday life	Well-being	95.7	1.4	2.9	1.3	0.7
Helps people meditate and reflect on how one's life is going	Self-enlightenment	92.3	4.1	3.6	1.5	0.8
Strengthens family bonds, values, and friendships	Family/social	90.3	5.7	4.0	1.6	0.8
Helps people learn skills beneficial in everyday life, such as leadership, overcoming challenges, and self-confidence	Character-building	86.9	6.9	6.2	1.7	0.9
Helps one recover from tragic life events or illness, such as death of a loved one, divorce, or depression	Therapeutic	80.6	10.7	8.7	1.9	1.0
Wilderness is important because:		*Societal Maintenance*				
It provides scientists an opportunity to study how nature works when not disturbed by humans.	Scientific	95.9	1.5	2.6	1.3	0.7
Nature and wild lands are important symbols of American culture	Cultural	90.6	4.2	5.2	1.5	0.9
It reminds us what it was like before European settlement	Historical	78.9	10.2	10.9	1.9	1.0

[1] Five-point scale: 1 = strongly agree, 2 = moderately agree, 3 = neither, 4 = moderately disagree, 5 = strongly disagree

Source: USDA Forest Service, 2005 (2003 National Survey on Recreation and the Environment)

with the individuals experiencing growth may also realize indirect benefits. Agreeing with the statements in this domain is agreeing with the assertion that Wilderness has therapeutic benefits and that people can experience a positive and meaningful change as a result of spending time there.

The Societal Maintenance domain shows that the American public seems to believe firmly that Wilderness contributes value to American society. Wilderness may be seen as a vital component of the social fabric that displays the character of American citizens and culture. Wilderness seems to be one path to the creation of, and continuation of, American heritage, history, and national identity. In addition, research is a useful conduit to receive benefits associated with other Wilderness values. Americans appear to agree that there is potential for Wilderness to teach lessons of successful coexistence with each other and with nature, and that beneficial information held in Wilderness may not be found elsewhere.

Public Opinion Surveys

Public opinion surveys help to define the value of Wilderness. When citing and interpreting public opinion surveys, care must be taken to avoid those with "push" bias. *Push polls* include those where the wording is leading and tends to encourage expression of opinions in agreement with the sponsor's position. In addition, care must be exercised with polls containing other high-profile environmental issues. Such design could result in association bias. Our coverage of selected polls is limited here to those *not* exhibiting push bias and those specific to the NWPS.

Three primary questions are covered by the polls reviewed in this section. Public response to these questions helps to indicate the value of Wilderness. The first addresses the amount of land now included in the NWPS, more specifically, whether there is enough land designated. The second investigates attitudes toward designating more federal land as Wilderness. The third asks about tradeoffs the American public is willing to make to have additional Wilderness. The nine different research institutions which conducted the polls summarized in this section used five different strata to investigate attitudinal differences among the American public. The most general stratum was national and care was taken to include studies which could be considered representative of the entire American adult population. At the next level, U.S. Census Bureau regions were used to stratify the American population by residence location (i.e., Northeast, Midwest, South, Mountain, and Pacific). Another level of stratification was to compare metropolitan versus rural residents. State level was the next stratification and finally, towns adjacent to the Green Mountain Forest were targeted as a local comparison with the general Vermont population concerning tradeoffs associated with increasing Wilderness designation in that Forest. Additional details of these polls and others can be found in a report compiled by the *Campaign for America's Wilderness* titled "A comprehensive review of recent public opinion research: A mandate to protect America's Wilderness" (Scott, 2003).

Not Enough Land Designated as Wilderness

The first question addressed in this section concerns awareness of, and support for, the amount of land currently in the NWPS. Based on a recent article by Cordell, Tarrant and Green (2003), Table 7.3 reports that while more people in 2000 (57.6%) than in 1994 (44.4%) were aware of the NWPS, this increase in awareness apparently has not translated into greater support for additional Wilderness acreage (Table 7.3). While a majority still supported more acreage for the NWPS in 2000 (51.6%), the percentage supporting additional acreage was somewhat less than in 1994. In 1994, 55.7 percent felt that there was currently not enough Wilderness under protection. The data from 2000 indicate that Whites, older people, and western residents were significantly more aware of the NWPS, but these groups also were significantly less likely to agree

Table 7.3 Percentage of Americans 16 or older indicating awareness of, and adequacy of size of, the National Wilderness Preservation System, 1994 and 2000[1]

Demographic Characteristic	Percent aware of NWPS 1994	Percent aware of NWPS 2000	Percent indicating size of NWPS is not enough 1994	Percent indicating size of NWPS is not enough 2000	Percent indicating size of NWPS is about right 1994	Percent indicating size of NWPS is about right 2000
Residence						
Metro resident	44.2	57.5	56.9	54.2	27.9	26.4
Rural resident	45.2	57.7	52.0	44.2	34.0	31.0
Region						
Eastern	42.7	56.0	56.3	53.4	28.0	26.2
Western	49.9	60.6	53.7	48.0	33.3	30.3
Age						
16–30	31.8	39.4	63.6	56.7	25.7	26.5
31–55	48.3	61.4	57.2	54.8	27.6	25.8
Over 55	57.1	69.9	38.3	38.5	39.4	33.3
Race						
White	45.5	61.3	56.4	52.4	28.7	27.9
Nonwhite	37.6	37.9	51.3	48.3	32.9	24.9
All Americans	44.4	57.6	55.7	51.6	29.3	27.6

[1] NSRE, 1994 (*N*=1,900) and 2000 (*N*=5,002). Questions: "Were you aware that Congress established the National Wilderness Preservation System?" and "Do you think the amount of land the Congress has designated as wilderness is not enough, about the right amount, or too much."

Source: USDA Forest Service, 2005

that we need more acreage in the NWPS than their non-White, younger, and eastern-resident counterparts.

One possible explanation for these findings is that the public viewpoint on Wilderness may be shifting somewhat from an emphasis on designation of additional land into the NWPS toward more concern for the stewardship and management of existing Wilderness lands (Hendee, Stankey & Lucas, 1990; Watson et al., 1999). Attitudes of residents in the western regions may be slightly less supportive of more designations because these regions are where the majority of currently designated Wilderness is located. The Congress has generally sought to balance between national interests and state and regional concerns in writing bills to expand the Wilderness System. However, while there are some differences between national and regional interests and some differences among demographics groups, overall there is consensus across the population that there is not enough Wilderness regardless of how the data are stratified.

Designating Additional Wilderness

The surveys summarized above looked at attitudes toward additional designations regardless of location. The question addressed here is how state residents feel about designating additional Wilderness in their own state. The first two of these surveys are summarized in Table 7.4. These studies asked residents of New Mexico and Nevada, respectively, if there is enough designated Wilderness in their home state. Results show residents expressing that there is "not enough;" that is, there is "too little" Wilderness in their states. Only 5 percent in New Mexico and 4 percent in Nevada indicated they felt there was too much designated land area in their respective states.

Table 7.4 Percentage of New Mexico and Nevada residents by attitudes toward the amount of Wilderness in their state

Attitude	New Mexico[1]	Nevada[2]
Too little/Not enough	57	56
About right	35	34
Too much	5	4
Not sure/Don't know	4	6

[1] Research & Polling, Inc., June 2002, $N=600$. Question: "Currently 2.2% of the land in New Mexico is set aside as Wilderness areas. Do you think New Mexico has too much Wilderness area, not enough Wilderness area, or the right amount of Wilderness area?"

[2] Mason-Dixon Polling & Research, October 2001, $N=625$. Question: "Currently 2.5% of the public land in Nevada is protected as Wilderness. Wilderness leaves areas open to hiking, camping, hunting, horseback riding, and livestock grazing, and prevents such activities as mining, oil and gas development, road building, and dirt bike or other off-road vehicle use. Do you think 2.5% is too much, too little, or about the right amount of Wilderness?"

Source: Scott, 2003

Table 7.5 summarizes NSRE data nationally and regionally regarding respondents own state. Overall, it shows that almost 70 percent of American citizens nationally support the designation of additional Wilderness in their state of residence. As noted in earlier chapters, six states currently have no designated Wilderness, making interpretation of this question different for these states. Table 7.5 stratifies the same NSRE data by Census region. A pattern similar to that seen nationally is presented in this table across the five different regions. Slightly higher percentages of residents in the Northeast, South, and Midwest favor more designation in their states relative to percentages for the Pacific and Mountain regions. Concerning these results, two general observations can be made. First, 48 percent in the West and 53 percent in the East indicated that there is "not enough" land designated for the NWPS generally. Across Census regions, larger percentages (62% to 75%) favor designating additional Wilderness in their state. Second, relatively small percentages of residents in any region oppose designating more federal lands in their state of residence as Wilderness, ranging from a low of just under 10 percent in the Northeast to a high of 21 percent in the Mountain region.

Five statewide studies have asked residents their attitude toward designation of additional Wilderness in their state (Table 7.6). Questions asked in Alaska, Vermont, California, and Idaho were worded to specifically address Wilderness additions. The question asked in North Dakota was slightly less direct and asked if Wilderness designation in that state was a "good idea." Except for Idaho, over 72 percent of residents polled favor designation of more Wilderness. Only 3 to 22 percent opposed more designation, except for Idaho in which 47 percent indicated they oppose more designation in their state.

Tables 7.7 and 7.8 ask about the amount of land designated as Wilderness specifically in the USDA National Forest System and in the Bureau of

Table 7.5 Percentage of Americans 16 or older nationally and by region by level of support for designating additional Wilderness on existing federal lands in their own state[1]

Attitude	Northeast	South	Midwest	Pacific	Mountain	National
Favor total	74.7	70.3	69.2	68.4	62.1	69.8
Strongly Favor	46.9	42.2	40.2	44.3	37.6	42.5
Somewhat Favor	27.8	28.2	29.0	24.1	24.5	27.3
Oppose total	9.6	11.1	12.0	13.7	21.2	12.4
Somewhat oppose	5.5	5.6	7.1	6.4	9.5	6.4
Strongly oppose	4.1	5.5	5.0	7.2	11.7	6.0
Neither	10.0	12.0	14.2	11.6	13.2	12.2
Don't know	5.7	6.6	4.6	6.3	3.6	5.6

[1] NSRE, 2000–2001 (*N*=10,382). Question: "How do you feel about designating more of the federal lands in your state as Wilderness? Would you say you strongly favor, somewhat favor, neither favor nor oppose, somewhat oppose, or strongly oppose this idea?"

Source: USDA Forest Service, 2005

Table 7.6 Percentage of population in five states by level of support for creating or managing *more* Wilderness or the existence of wilderness

Attitude	Alaska[1]	Vermont[2]	California[3]	Idaho[4]	North Dakota[5]
Favor/Support/Agree/Yes	73	73	72	44	87
Strongly Favor	40	27	52	25	0
Somewhat Favor	33	46	20	19	0
Oppose/Disagree/No	15	20	22	47	3
Somewhat oppose	10	17	10	20	0
Strongly oppose	5	3	12	27	0
Neither	12	7	0	0	7
Don't know	0	0	6	8	4

[1] Mail-in poll by Greg Brown, Environmental Science Department, Alaska Pacific University, July 1998 ($N=802$). Question: "There are many possible public uses of the Chugach National Forest. Please tell us whether you favor or oppose managing the Forest for the following uses." Level of favor and opposition for the use "wilderness" shown.

[2] University of Vermont Center for Rural Studies, February 2002, Statewide ($N=472$) voters. Question: "I am now going to read some statements to you. Please indicate whether you strongly agree, agree, neither agree nor disagree, disagree, or strongly disagree."

[3] Fairbank, Maslin, Maullin & Associates, August 25–30, 2001 ($N=901$). Question: "In general, would you support or oppose the government designating more land and rivers in California as protected Wilderness areas?"

[4] Davis, Hibbitts & McCraig, Inc., April 2002 ($N=500$). Question: "In general, would you strongly support, support, oppose, or strongly oppose Congress designating more federal land in Idaho as protected Wilderness?"

[5] Midwest Research Associates, November 1999 ($N=550$). Question: "As you know, wilderness is federal land designated to preserve its natural resources. Therefore, it contains no roads or development. However, it is open to activities such as livestock grazing, backpacking, horseback riding, and hunting on foot or horseback. Do you believe Wilderness areas are a good idea?"

Source: Scott, 2003

Table 7.7 American residents' attitude toward the amount of protected land in the USDA National Forest system

	Percent of Respondents[1]
Too little/Not enough	61
About right	24
Too much	8
Not sure/Don't know	7

[1] The Mellman Group poll, April 2001 ($N=1,000$) likely voters. Question: "Currently, 18% of the land in the United States' national forests is permanently protected from logging and other development. Do you think the U.S. has too much permanently protected areas in the national forests, not enough protected areas in national forests, or the right amount of permanently protected areas in national forests, or aren't you sure about that?"

Source: Scott, 2003

Land Management (BLM) system. The data in Table 7.7 reflect attitudes toward the current percentage of National Forest System lands (administered by the USDA Forest Service) that is preserved as Wilderness. The majority of Americans feel that the current percentage of the National Forest system designated as Wilderness is not enough (around 18% of the System is currently designated, see Chapter 5). The data in Table 7.8 tells us that the majority of Americans would favor a Presidential proposal to designate up to 40 percent (60 million acres) more of BLM's current land holdings as Wilderness.

Tradeoffs to Get More Wilderness

Tables 7.9, 7.10, and 7.11 highlight data from three different studies which asked about willingness to "trade-off" to gain Wilderness. From Table 7.9, it seems that at the national level voting American citizens are willing to accept higher costs for electricity, gasoline, and other consumer products to have more Wilderness lands designated and to have higher quality air over and near Wilderness. Voting citizens are also willing to support stricter environmental regulations to ensure air and scenic quality. Table 7.10 shows results from a Harris Interactive poll where nearly two thirds of respondents indicated willingness to accept higher gasoline prices to do more to protect Wilderness. In Table 7.11, focusing on state and local levels, Vermont residents indicated

---

Table 7.8 American residents' attitude toward protecting additional land in the Bureau of Land Management system

	Percent of Respondents[1]
Favor total	66
Strongly Favor	55
Somewhat Favor	11
Oppose total	18
Somewhat oppose	4
Strongly oppose	14
Don't know/No opinion	16

[1] The Mellman Group, April 2001 ($N=1,000$ likely voters). Question: "It has been proposed that President Clinton protect 60 million acres, or 40%, of BLM land in the Western states for wildlife habitat, nonmotorized recreation, and scientific research. Conservation groups say that we need to protect these lands from oil development and mining so we can leave them as a legacy for future generations. Some local politicians oppose this idea saying it locks up too much land and would cost jobs and that these lands should remain open to commercial development and off-road vehicle use. Would you favor or oppose the proposal that President Clinton protect these 60 million acres?" (If favor/oppose ask: "Do you feel that way strongly or not so strongly?")

Source: Scott, 2003

Table 7.9 Percent of Americans 16 or older by level of agreement with cleaning up air pollution obscuring Wilderness scenery, even if electricity or consumer product costs would increase

	Percent of Respondents[1]
Agree total	85.5
Strongly Agree	54.4
Agree	31.1
Disagree total	9.4
Disagree	5.1
Strongly Disagree	4.3
Neither	2.6
Don't know/Refused	2.6

[1] NSRE poll, 2000–2001 ($N=5,236$). Question: "Please indicate whether you strongly agree, agree, disagree or strongly disagree with the following statement: It has been documented that air pollution from power plants and industry obstructs views of Wilderness scenery. Companies should be required to clean up their air pollution, even if it meant you might pay more for electricity or consumer products."

Source: USDA Forest Service, 2005

Table 7.10 American residents' attitude toward protecting Wilderness even if it means gasoline prices would increase

	Percent of Respondents[1]
Favor	62
Oppose	33
Not Sure	5

[1] Time/CNN poll by Harris Interactive, April 2002 ($N=1,003$ adults). Question: "Protecting the environment sometimes involves costs and other kinds of sacrifices. Do you favor or oppose each of the following…Protecting Wilderness areas, even if it were to cause higher gas prices?"

Source: Scott, 2003

Table 7.11 Vermont residents' attitude toward protecting Wilderness even if it means decreasing snowmobile use

	Statewide Respondents[1]	Local Town Respondents
Agree	65	68
Disagree	33	26
Neither	5	6

[1] University of Vermont Center for Rural Studies poll, February 2002, statewide ($N=472$ voters; $N=112$ in towns in or adjacent to Green Mountain National Forest). Question: Respondents were asked whether they strongly agreed, agreed, neither agreed or disagreed, or strongly disagreed that "I would support the establishment of additional Wilderness areas on the Green Mountain National Forest, even it required the removal or re-routing of snowmobile trails?"

Source: Scott, 2003

willingness to trade away some snowmobile use or to redistribute snowmobile access on the Green Mountain National Forest in order to gain additional Wilderness.

There are only slight differences evident between the groups at the national, regional, state, and local levels based on survey results summarized in Tables 7.3 through 7.11. From these data one could observe that: (a) overall there is consensus across groups within the American population that there is not enough Wilderness, regardless of how the data are stratified; (b) residents support designating more Wilderness in their state of residence (Idaho being the least supportive of the states polled); (c) residents are willing to restrict or redistribute motorized access to recreation land to gain Wilderness; and importantly (d) Americans are willing to make unspecified monetary tradeoffs to gain additional Wilderness.

Wilderness Benefits, 1977–1985

Using some of the more familiar social value structures, the preceding sections of this chapter addressed what American citizens value about Wilderness. This section approaches the idea of value from a slightly different perspective, that is, by identifying the benefits of Wilderness recreation activities. One of the early thought leaders on the personal and social benefits of recreation and leisure was Beverly Driver. In the mid-1970s Driver pioneered the concept of managing recreation and leisure services to optimize the benefits to people from their participation in recreational activities. This approach to management is referred to as *benefits-based management* (BBM; Driver, 1990). After laying a foundation based on research and advocacy, Driver's BBM concepts have been widely integrated into the processes of planning and managing natural lands (Driver, 1976, 1990, 1996; Driver & Brown, 1975, 1983; Driver, Brown & Peterson, 1991).

Typical dictionaries define a benefit as "something that promotes or enhances well-being" (*The American Heritage Dictionary*, 1982). Accordingly, "an aspirin is a benefit to someone with a headache, and a wilderness is a benefit to a grizzly bear" (Driver, Nash & Haas, 1987, p. 295). This standard definitional approach looks at benefits as means to facilitate an improvement in one's condition, or at least a person's perception of condition improvement. However, this traditional view of benefits does not focus on *how* Wilderness might provide a benefit to humans, grizzly bears, or any other organisms. Driver expanded the concept of a benefit to include more focus on how a benefit is derived as "a specific advantageous condition, not the facilitator of such. Thus, the word *benefit* is used to denote a desirable change or state; it is a specific improved condition or state of an individual or a group of individuals, of a society, or even of nonhuman organisms" (Driver, Nash & Haas, 1987, p. 295). His conceptualization of benefit can also include the prevention of a worse state from happening.

According to expectancy theory (Atkinson & Birch, 1972; Fishbein & Ajzen, 1974; Lawler, 1973), people choose to participate in Wilderness-based recreational activities to receive specific benefits. The participant expects to produce certain valued beneficial outcomes by carefully choosing complementary outdoor settings and activities. Human behavior is goal oriented and directed toward fulfilling needs and achieving an expected level of satisfaction based on expectations. The benefits listed in Table 7.12 can motivate people to visit a Wilderness area or can be a beneficial outcome from spending time in Wilderness. For example, a parent might be motivated to take their children on a Wilderness backpacking trip to improve relationships among family

Table 7.12 Recreation experience preference (REP) scales making up the REP benefit domains

1. Enjoy nature
  a. Scenery
  b. General nature experience
	8. Family kinship[2]

	9. Introspection
	  a. Spiritual
	  b. Personal values

2. Physical fitness[2]	

3. Reduce tension
  a. Tension release
  b. Slow down mentally
  c. Escape role overloads
  d. Escape daily routine
	10. Be with considerate people[2]

	11. Achievement/Stimulation
	  a. Reinforcing self-confidence
	  b. Social recognition
	  c. Skill development
	  d. Competence testing
	  e. Seeking excitement

4. Escape noise and crowds
  a. Tranquility/Solitude
  b. Privacy
  c. Escape crowds
  d. Escape noise
	12. Physical rest[2]

	13. Teach/Lead others
	  a. Teaching/sharing skills
	  b. Leading others

5. Outdoor learning
  a. General learning
  b. Exploration
  c. Learn geography of the area
  d. Learn about nature
	14. Risk taking[2]

	15. Risk reduction
	  a. Risk moderation
	  b. Risk prevention

6. Share similar values
  a. Be with friends
  b. Be with people having similar values
	16. Meet new people
	  a. Meet new people
	  b. Observe new people

7. Independence
  a. Independence
  b. Autonomy
  c. Being in control	

[1] Table adapted from Driver, Nash, and Haas (1987)
[2] These domains have only one scale with the same title as the domain

members (i.e., family kinship). The value of family kinship motivates them to take a family trip to Wilderness with the expectation that spending time together in a natural setting would result in improved communication. According to Driver's conceptualization of a benefit, it is received if the condition of family communications improves or if going on the outing prevented communications from becoming worse.

Driver and his associates developed what have been termed Recreation Experience Preference (REP) items. These items represent the motivations for choosing settings and activities, as well as the benefits that are expected to ensue after participation. The REP items have been used in three ways: (a) to measure needs generated during everyday life that produce a desire to recreate (e.g., stress at work produces a need to escape); (b) as motivational factors driving engagement in recreation activities; and (c) to measure outcomes of recreation as benefits. Sixteen REP domains are listed in Table 7.12. Some of the domains have subcategories (also listed).

During the past 40 years, Driver and other have used the REP items to make a few simple, yet important points:

- People do not randomly engage in recreation; they have specific preferences for recreation activities and settings in which to partake in those activities.

- Choices for activities are based on personal needs generated during everyday life and desired benefits to be received from the experiences that fulfill those needs.

- People have expectations for what they will experience after choosing a recreation setting-activity pair.

- A specific setting only has the potential to produce a limited number of specific recreation opportunities. For example, an alpine mountain setting provides an opportunity for hiking and a river for rafting.

- Benefits are more likely to accrue when recreationist expectations for opportunities and settings are met.

- Land managers must be aware of the opportunities their settings can provide, the recreationists' expectations, and accurately inform recreationists of the opportunities available at a given recreation setting.

- And most important, the federal government provides recreation on Wilderness land as a service to the American public; providing opportunities for recreation is as important as other social services provided by the federal government (e.g., healthcare, the U.S. Postal

Service) because the benefits received from recreation are vital to the well-being of the American public.

Table 7.13 (p. 130) shows results from eight studies conducted between 1977 and 1987 in designated Wilderness areas. The table gives mean scores on a scale from one (most strongly adds to satisfaction) to nine (most strongly detracts from satisfaction) for sixteen of the REP domains using interview designs (i.e., REP Scales) developed by Driver and associates. Refer to Driver (1976) for a discussion of the development of these scales. At each Wilderness area a systematic sample of recreationists were asked to participate in the study after engaging in their chosen activity. Recreationists were asked to rate how much each type of experience domain would either add to or detract from their level of satisfaction with their visit to a particular area for their chosen activity. The footnote below Table 7.13 describes the nine-point scale used.

The REP scales were used as an indicator of desired and/or expected benefits from Wilderness-based recreation. When a Wilderness user indicated that a particular item would add to their satisfaction, they were indicating it would produce a valued state or condition and that the valued condition was a motivation for choosing Wilderness as a setting for recreation. For example, the REP domain Reduce Tensions has a grand mean of 2.2 for all eight domains. This score indicates that it would strongly add to satisfaction with a Wilderness experience. Thus, people are motivated to go to Wilderness areas to receive the benefit of reducing tensions created in everyday life. We see that Meeting New People has a grand mean of 5.1, indicating that meeting new people would neither add to nor detract from their Wilderness experience. From this we learn that people are not specifically seeking nor expecting to meet new friends in Wilderness, but meeting new people is okay when it does occur. Thus, Wilderness is valued as a place to reduce tension more so than as a place to meet people.

The following discussion focuses on the six most strongly sought and valued Wilderness benefits. The data in Table 7.13 indicate that the most strongly identified benefit people seek from spending time in Wilderness is the simple pleasure derived from viewing pleasing scenery and having direct contact with nature. Aesthetic value is nature that is pleasing to the eye (e.g., an eagle soaring, patterns on a sand dune, a murky swamp, the setting sun, shapes in irregular glacial till, the prowess of a cheetah). Many of these visually pleasing elements depend on natural conditions such as found in Wilderness. This includes the feeling that one gets from interacting with the environment. For example, an aesthetically pleasing feeling might result from climbing Mount Rainer, braving a violent electrical storm in the Wind River Range, or watching clouds while lying at the base of the Grand Canyon. Beauty is in the eye of the beholder and is the result of intimate contact with the environment producing sights, smells, and sounds. Wilderness is an environment that can provide innocent, pure, and pleasing images and feelings enjoyed by many humans. The

Table 7.13 Mean scores of responses to 16 recreation experience preference domains from surveys of visitors to specific Wilderness areas[1]

Benefit	Weminuche[2]	Maroon Bells[3]	Flattops[4]	Eagles Nest[5]	Rawah[6]	Linville Gorge[7]	Shining Rock[8]	Joyce Kilmer[9]	Grand Mean
Enjoy nature	1.5	1.5	1.5	1.5	1.7	1.5	1.6	1.4	1.5
Physical fitness	2.4	2.0	2.5	2.3	2.3	2.1	2.2	1.8	2.0
Reduce tensions	2.1	2.3	2.1	2.4	2.2	2.3	2.3	2.1	2.2
Escape	2.2	2.2	2.2	2.4	2.2	2.3	2.3	2.2	2.2
Outdoor learning	2.1	2.4	2.4	2.5	2.2	2.3	2.4	2.2	2.3
Sharing values	2.8	2.9	3.2	2.8	2.8	2.7	2.9	2.7	2.8
Independence	3.1	2.9	2.8	3.3	3.0	3.0	3.0	3.0	3.0
Family kinship	3.0	3.0	2.6	3.2	2.9	3.4	3.1	3.0	3.0
Spiritual	3.5	3.1	3.3	3.7	3.5	2.8	2.9	2.6	3.1
Considerate people	3.6	3.4	3.2	3.8	3.7	3.0	3.3	2.8	3.3
Achievement/Stimulation	3.9	3.1	3.4	4.0	3.9	2.9	3.1	3.0	3.4
Physical rest	3.8	4.3	2.5	3.9	3.9	3.2	3.3	3.4	3.5
Teach/Lead others	3.7	4.3	3.5	3.9	3.8	3.6	3.7	3.9	3.8
Risk taking	4.7	4.8	4.8	4.6	4.8	4.1	4.5	4.6	4.6
Risk reduction	4.8	4.7	4.7	4.7	4.8	4.7	4.7	4.7	4.7
Meet new people	5.6	5.3	5.5	5.5	5.8	4.6	4.5	4.5	5.1

[1] Ratings were made on the following nine-point response format. Adds to satisfaction: 1=most strongly, 2=strongly, 3=moderately, 4=a little; 5=neither adds or detracts; Detracts from satisfaction: 6=detracts a little, 7=moderately, 8=strongly, 9=most strongly.
[2] CO, N=313
[3] CO, N=268
[4] CO, N=135
[5] CO, N=271
[6] CO, N=212
[7] NC, N=249
[8] NC, N=297
[9] NC, N=80

Source: Driver, Nash & Haas, 1987

aesthetics of Wilderness can be long-lasting and provide stability for people forced to cope with an unstable world. One principal of protection of Wilderness is that it can provide its beauty across generations.

The value selected as second strongest is improved physical fitness associated with the rigors of being in Wilderness. Many activities such as hiking along a steep trail, carrying a heavy backpack, climbing a harrowing peak, or paddling a raft down river include physical exertion that is uncommon in most people's daily lives. In addition, the physical environment in Wilderness may be perceived as more pure than the physical environment in an urban setting. Physical fitness may be attributed to something as simple as breathing clean air.

The third and fourth values most strongly adding to satisfactions are similar in that they address recovering from stress directly attributable to everyday life. Wilderness can be an escape from the everyday routine and the stress of multiple social roles. For example, role stress occurs when one person has several responsibilities, such as being a professional engineer, mother, wife, daughter, member of a local civic organization, and soccer coach. Wilderness can also be the opposite of many of the stressful physical attributes of urbanized society. Escape from the noise and crowds produced in developed areas and seeking a place to experience solitude and privacy to engage in desirable social interactions can be very important to some people. The pressures of society can be removed and social situations can be simpler in a Wilderness setting. Daily routines in Wilderness are typically simplified and primary survival activities have different meanings. Examples are gathering firewood, boiling water to drink, and hiking to the next camp site. One has an opportunity to "get back to basics" and heal by focusing on simple, goal-oriented activities. Wilderness is considered by many to be a restorative environment.

The fifth strongest contributing benefit is associated with learning. Wilderness is a warehouse of educational opportunities about nature. Subjects such as geology, botany, zoology, and entomology rely in part upon observing living and nonliving things in undisturbed natural lands. Natural interactions between flora, fauna, and physical conditions can be observed in Wilderness or other protected lands. Teachers and researchers from elementary to graduate levels can use Wilderness settings as educational subject matter.

The sixth most strongly desired benefit from being in Wilderness is social sharing. Wilderness experiences can enhance existing friendships by providing a context for engaging in controlled social interaction in an environment with few distractions from other people. Because there are fewer distractions, their social interaction can be enhanced. As well, social bonding can be enhanced by shared participation in Wilderness activities. Sharing a unique or challenging nature experience can foster lasting relationships and affect positive social functioning.

Wilderness Benefits, 1985–Present

This section addresses both benefits and values to organized, facilitated groups, as well as benefits to individual, nonfacilitated users of Wilderness. Facilitated groups include organizations such as the National Outdoor Leadership School (NOLS), Outward Bound, and any other organization which takes groups into Wilderness for personal growth. Ewert and McAvoy (1999) reported that there were over 700 organizations offering Wilderness programs designed to facilitate personal growth in 1999. They reported further that this number has been growing at a rate of approximately 15 percent per year in recent years. Not included in the facilitated-use category are commercial outfitting organizations. Nonfacilitated users include individuals and parties who visit Wilderness as private users and organize and supply their own trip. Typically these users are families or small groups of friends. The distinction between facilitated and nonfacilitated is illustrated in the following example. A group of eight friends call each other on the phone and self-plan a backpacking trip to the Bridger Wilderness in Wyoming. This would be considered a nonfacilitated trip. If that same group of eight friends enrolled in a NOLS backpacking course to the Bridger Wilderness, that would be considered a facilitated trip. The defining factors for this facilitated trip are that there is a leader (i.e., facilitator or teacher); the course has a curriculum; the curriculum is designed to produce specific personal growth outcomes and meet learning objectives; and the trip is structured, planned, and supplied by NOLS.

Table 7.14 Taxonomy of personal benefits from visiting wilderness, updated to reflect current research[1]

1. Developmental
  a. Self-concept/self-identity
  b. Skill development
    i. Outdoor skills
    ii. Adventure
	6. Educational
	  a. Nature learning
	  b. Environmental ethic
	  c. Environmental stewardship

2. Therapeutic/mental health	7. Spiritual

3. Physical health	8. Aesthetic/creative
	  a. Nature appreciation
	  b. Aesthetic appreciation

4. Self-sufficiency, independence
  a. Self-reliance
  b. Primitive living	

5. Social identity
  a. Family kinship
  b. Group cohesion
  c. Social recognition	

[1] Adapted from Roggenbuck and Driver, 2000

The eight research projects listed in Table 7.14 used the same REP items in different Wilderness areas, allowing comparisons between studies and areas. While much of the more current research uses this same benefits structure as a foundation (i.e., as developed by Driver), it often relies on different theories, measurement instruments, and methods from sociology and/or psychology. As well, many of the more recent studies have targeted specific populations including persons with disabilities, all-women groups, behavioral therapy groups, youth-at-risk, psychiatric treatment groups, and family therapy groups. Pervious benefits research involving the REP items typically used post-trip surveys asking respondents to recall their experience. Current methods attempt to understand the entire recreation experience as it unfolds, beginning with the planning phase and tracking through the on-site experience and recollection phases. Also, qualitative research methods have become increasingly popular as an addition to quantitative methods. These variations in methods and populations studied make it more difficult to compare findings across studies than was the case with the studies cited in Table 7.13. However, by focusing at a general level of benefits, some comparisons can be made.

Table 7.14 is an updated structure of recreation benefits that is based both on the original REP items and on more current research. Tables 7.15 (pp. 134–135) and 7.16 (p. 136) provide summaries of research that has addressed some of the domains of this benefit structure, covering both facilitated and non-facilitated Wilderness visits. The three more prominent Wilderness benefit domains that have been studied since 1987 are developmental, therapeutic and mental health, and social identity. Self-esteem, self-concept, and self-efficacy were the most frequently identified benefits among the projects within the developmental domain. These concepts refer to knowledge that the individual holds about themselves and includes perception of performance, appearance, and abilities. It is believed that these beliefs enhance judgment, decision making, and social functioning. Facing and overcoming challenges during Wilderness experiences have been found to increase self-efficacy. An increased perception of one's general efficacy to produce desirable outcomes when faced with difficult situations leads to increased performance in the work place and within the family unit. This logic is supported by the increases of general recreation skill, competency, personal growth, increased problem-solving ability, and general feelings of personal growth.

Learning group and personal skills are believed to be a result of the person-environment interaction. Because a Wilderness environment cannot be easily changed, attention must be shifted inward as one seeks to maintain a balanced person-environment relationship. The theory suggests that one must align oneself with the environment to cope with emerging situations. Many outdoor programs (aimed at personal growth) depend on challenging conditions as often faced in Wilderness. Experiencing stress sufficiently above one's personal

skill level to produce fear, physical challenge, or emotional challenge can promote personal growth by challenging the individual and allowing successful
problem solving. Coping with Wilderness conditions can prompt the individual
to overcome psychological barriers that can be reinforced by urban environments. Overcoming these barriers is viewed as preparation for confronting
the unfamiliar and unexpected (Scherl, 1989).

Some rather tangible results have been observed within the therapeutic
and mental health domain. For example, research has indicated that there is
value to disadvantaged youth in Wilderness experiences in terms of increased
school attendance, job retention, and reduction of problem behaviors. As well,
studies of disadvantaged youth who have participated in Wilderness backpacking programs designed to promote citizenship and job retention have

Table 7.15 Summary of research addressing benefits derived from participation in facilitated wilderness experiences (continued next page)

Population	Benefit Received	Reference
	Developmental	
Twelfth-grade students, Camping and hiking	Increased self-esteem, self-concept	Gillett, Thomas, Skok & McLaughlin, 1991
Persons with disabilities integrated with others	Positive attitude change; Recreation skill development; Increased social relationships, willingness to take risks, self-efficacy; For people with disabilities skills transferred to rest of life; People without disabilities increased tolerance for people with disabilities	McAvoy, Lais, Anderson & Schleien, 1995; Anderson, Schleien, McAvoy, Lais & Seligman, 1997
All-women wilderness trip	Increased self-efficacy, empowerment, problem solving, connection to others, mental clarity	Pohl & Borrie, 2000
Hearing-impaired individuals, ten-day ski trip	Increased self-esteem	Luckner, 1989
Patients with schizo-phrenia and related disorders, wilderness therapy program[1]	Increased self-efficacy, self-esteem; Decrease in general symptoms; Decreased hospital readmission	Kelly, Coursey & Selby, 1997; Pawlowski, Holme & Hafner, 1993
Parents and youth at risk child, three-day wilder-ness family trip after child was on a 21-day wilderness therapy course	Increased self-concept among adoles-cents on 21-day component. *Post 21-day trip:* Increased normal family functioning; Decreased parental-reported problem behavior, delinquency, reported police and court contacts for children	Bandoroff, Huffaker & McNally, 1994

[1] hiking, climbing, canoeing, caving, biking

benefitted in other ways (Russell, Hendee & Cooke, 1998). Some of these other ways include promoting a sense of community, fostering efforts to help achieve communal goals, and teaching respect for other members of the community. Wilderness experiences can reduce inhibitions in communication with peers and promote effective communication with authority figures. Russell, Hendee, and Cooke (1998) found that disadvantaged youth hired by the Federal Job Corps were more likely to retain their jobs if they had participated in a Wilderness-based education program. Specifically, a 36 percent reduction in termination rates was found for participants versus those who had not participated.

There also appears to be crossover between the therapeutic/mental health and developmental domains. Increasing physical and mental fitness, which

Table 7.15 Summary of research addressing benefits derived from participation in facilitated wilderness experiences

Population	Benefit Received	Reference
Therapeutic & Mental Health		
Outward Bound course, NOLS course, Student Conservation Association	Increased interest in school, physical and mental fitness, commitment to environment; Positive behavioral changes; Life-changing events	Kellert, 1999
Youth at risk, backpacking program	Increased self-esteem, motivation, job retention, sense of community, effort to achieve communal goals, respect for other members of the community; Promotion of effective communication with authority figures	Russell, Hendee & Cooke, 1998
Juvenile offenders, adventure-based therapy	Decreased conduct-disordered behavior and drug use; Decreased depression, obsessive compulsive behavior, disorganized thinking, manic excitement, anxiety; Increased openness to other forms of treatment	Gillis & Simpson, 1991
Adolescents with severe mental health issues[2], ten-week treatment program, 4–5 day wilderness trips	Decrease in behavior difficulties; Increase in school attendance	Crisp, 1998
Behaviorally disordered adolescents	Increased cooperative behavior	Sachs & Miller, 1992
Social Identity		
Outward Bound course	Improved group orientation, organization, group cohesion, interdependency, problem solving	Ewert & Heywood, 1991

[2] physical and psychological abuse, mental illness, substance abuse, school refusal

is categorized as a therapeutic affect, also can contribute to improved self-image. The values of positive self-image, community, respect for peers, respect for authority, goal setting, achievement, and positive family relations, as can be fostered through Wilderness experiences, are not only important to an

Table 7.16 Summary of research addressing benefits derived from participation in nonfacilitated wilderness experiences

Population	Benefit Received	Reference
	Developmental	
Nine-day outdoor challenge program	Increased connections with nature and biological self	Talbot & Kaplan, 1986
Extended river rafting trip on the Colorado River	Increased personal growth, renewal of self, competency, self-awareness, communion with nature, understanding of biological relation with nature	Arnould & Price, 1993
Okefenokee (swamp) Wilderness users, Georgia	Increased connection with nature and biological self; Strong sense of time-lessness (lack of concern for watches)	Borrie, 1995
Canoeists, Juniper Prairie Wilderness, Florida	Learned to overcome frustrating situations; Increased way-finding ability, ability to face the unknown, general recreation skills	Patterson, Williams, Watson & Roggenbuck, 1998
Extended trip on Colorado River, and Nine-day challenge trip	General acquisition of skills	Arnould & Price, 1993; Talbot & Kaplan, 1986
	Therapeutic & Mental Health	
Nine-day challenge trip	Increased physical renewal, mental renewal, relaxation, feeling of being alive	Talbot & Kaplan, 1986
Wilderness vacationers	Increased ability to focus attention	Hartig, Mang & Evans, 1991
	Social Identity	
Extended trip on Colorado River, and Juniper Prairie Wilderness	Gained acceptance by other members of the group; Increased family bonding (when family was present); Increased feeling of communion with friends, family, and strangers	Arnould & Price, 1993; Patterson, Williams, Watson & Roggenbuck, 1998
All-women group, Boundary Waters Canoe Area	Increased group trust, emotional support, sharing of common life changes, spiritual growth, and noncompetitive atmosphere	Fredrickson & Anderson, 1999
Okefenokee, and Nine-day challenge trip	Increased commitment to conservation of nature, knowledge of nature	Borrie, 1995; Talbot & Kaplan, 1986

individual but also to American society generally. In addition, any individual, regardless of advantaged or disadvantaged status, can realize these values.

Fostering social identity can have three immediate positive associations including family, friends, and functioning in the work place. First, the research cited here found that families who engaged in Wilderness activities together experienced improved bonds and communication among members. This was especially true for families previously troubled by problem youth. But the same values of improved communication and bonding were identified for relationships among friends who experienced Wilderness together. In addition, people learn to have greater trust of other people as a result of engaging in Wilderness activities together. Wilderness experiences help to improve existing and foster new friendships. Other outcomes of a Wilderness experience are improved functioning within the group and fostering cooperation to achieve a common goal.

Another set of benefits accruing from Wilderness experiences is improved abilities to function within a group, organize a group, work toward common goals, trust fellow group members, and maintain positive relationships with group members. All of these are qualities highly valued in the work place. It seems that Wilderness can provide a number of social benefits equivalent to a number of government subsidized social services.

Conclusion

This chapter was organized to describe research on the social benefits and value of federally designated Wilderness. Emphasized were trends in Wilderness values over time, surveys concerning different types of Wilderness values, results from a variety of public opinion surveys, and theory and research regarding the recreation and personal growth benefits of Wilderness. The ultimate payoff of this research is the opportunity to apply it in the management of the NWPS. A list of seven opportunities as identified by Driver, Nash, and Haas (1987) follows:

Improve Resource Allocation Decisions. Benefits information can be used to make cost-benefit analyses that go beyond economic terms. Benefits data, however, whatever the academic disciplinary basis, will hopefully allow managers to avoid making decisions overweighted by short-term gains that could result in undesirable long-term effects.

Promote Optimal Management. Understanding expectations and desired benefits of Wilderness use can help managers to establish clearer management objectives and methods for monitoring conditions in Wilderness. Management can be directed at maximizing the benefits from the public land for the good of all citizens (both Wilderness users and off-site beneficiaries).

Identify Substitutes. Better understanding of benefits can distinguish those unique to Wilderness and those that can be obtained from other sources. This can ease the burden on existing Wilderness lands by directing users to alternative locations.

Facilitate Additional Research. The research conducted thus far is intended to function as a building block to generate hypotheses and obtain more insightful data. Benefits data can also function in concert with other forms of Wilderness-value research as a means of cross-validation.

Enhance Voter Sovereignty. Information on the benefits of Wilderness should facilitate more rational consumer and voter behavior with respect to Wilderness use and protection.

Advance Professions. Knowledge is necessary to advance any profession. Professionals in land management, policy, planning, advocacy, and valuation need benefit data to grow and legitimize their function.

Promote a Wilderness Philosophy. Wilderness philosophy is founded upon values and the belief that there are benefits from preserving Wilderness. Benefits data provide a defensible foundation for a wildness philosophy that can be used to advocate for better stewardship of the Wilderness System.

The social values described in this chapter can be viewed as noncompeting and nonconsumptive (Rolston, 1985). A beneficial educational experience, for example, does not necessarily interfere with a character-building experience. Likewise, physical health benefits are seldom impacted by scientific observations occurring in Wilderness. Realizing social benefits such as these in Wilderness is largely sustainable in that it does not disrupt ecological functioning and integrity. One can enjoy the benefit of a spiritual experience or gain therapeutic value without disturbing the soils or habitats that Wilderness designation was intended to sustain. At the same time, sustaining the integrity of ecosystems in Wilderness better assures a future flow of bequest, option, and existence values.

Social values can also complement one another. For example, protected natural habitats are often essential for the continued existence of nationally significant species. Thus, Wilderness can directly contribute to maintaining some of the important symbols of American culture, such as the bald eagle. Nature photographers find artistic and aesthetic value in photographing eagles as well as other animals. Thus, while providing ecological value, Wilderness can at the same time enhance opportunities for social benefits. In addition, multiple social benefits can be attained simultaneously, such as learning about nature, gaining esthetic appreciation, and promoting family stability concurrently.

The social research results presented in this and in the chapters to follow provide a framework of benefits and values that help one see a larger picture of the importance of the National Wilderness Preservation System than could be seen from any single disciplinary perspective. In the chapter that follows differences in values between different groups within our society are explored and discussed. Following that are two chapters that examine many of the same values explored in this chapter, but examined from the perspective of economics. Following these chapters is an examination of the ecological values of Wilderness, followed by an examination of ethical values, mainly intrinsic value as viewed through the eyes of a philosopher. There is little doubt that one will be left with a deeply seated impression of the importance of the NWPS upon reading the chapters to come.

Literature Cited

The American Heritage Dictionary (2nd ed.). (1982). Boston, MA: Houghton Mifflin Company.

Anderson, L., Schleien, S., McAvoy, L., Lais, G., and Seligman, D. (1997). Creating positive change through an integrated outdoor adventure program. *Therapeutic Recreation Journal, 31,* 214–229.

Arnould, E.J. and Price, L.L. (1993). River magic: Extraordinary experience and the extended service encounter. *Journal of Consumer Research, 20,* 24–45.

Atkinson, J. and Birch, D. (1972). *Motivation: The dynamics of action.* New York, NY: John Wiley and Sons.

Bandoroff, S., Huffaker, G., and McNally, M. (1994). Wilderness family therapy: An innovative treatment approach for problem youth. *Journal of Child and Family Studies, 2,* 175–191.

Bertolas, R.J. (1998). Crosscultural environmental perception of wilderness. *The Professional Geographer, 50*(1), 98112.

Bliss, J.C. (2000). Public perceptions of clearcutting. *Journal of Forestry, 98,* 4–9.

Borrie, W. (1995). *Measuring the multiple, deep, and unfolding aspects of the wilderness experience using the experience sampling method.* Unpublished doctoral dissertation, Virginia Polytechnic Institute and State University, Blacksburg, VA.

Cordell, H.K., Tarrant, M.A., and Green, G.T. (2003). Is the public viewpoint of wilderness changing? *International Journal of Wilderness Management, 9*(2), 23–28.

Cordell, H.K., Tarrant, M.A., McDonald, B.L., and Bergstrom, J.C. (1998). How the public views wilderness: More results from the USA survey on recreation and the environment. *International Journal of Wilderness, 4*(5), 28–31.

Crisp, S. (1998). International models of best practice in wilderness and adventure therapy. In C. M. Itin (Ed.), *Exploring the boundaries of adventure therapy: International perspectives* (pp. 56–74). Boulder, CO: Association for Experimental Education.

Driver, B.L. (1976). Toward a better understanding of the social benefits of outdoor recreation participation. In *Proceedings of the Southern States Recreation Re-*

search Applications Workshop (pp. 163–189; General Technical Report SE-9). Asheville, NC: USDA Forest Service, Southeastern Forest Experiment Station.

Driver, B.L. (1990). Focusing research on the benefits of leisure: Special issue. *Journal of Leisure Research, 22,* 93–98.

Driver, B.L. (1996). Benefits-driven management of natural areas. *Natural Areas Journal, 16,* 94–99.

Driver, B.L. and Brown, P. (1975). A sociopsychological definition of recreation demand with implications for recreation resource planning. In *Assessing demand for outdoor recreation* (pp. 62–88). Washington, DC: National Academy of Sciences.

Driver, B.L. and Brown, P. (1983). *Contributions of behavioral scientists to recreation resource management.* New York, NY: Plenum.

Driver, B.L., Brown, P., and Peterson, G. (Eds.). (1991). *Benefits of leisure.* State College, PA: Venture Publishing, Inc.

Driver, B.L., Nash, R., and Haas, G. (1987). Wilderness benefits: A state-of-knowledge review. In *National Wilderness Research Conference: Issues, state of knowledge, future directions* (General Technical Report INT-220). Ogden, UT: USDA Forest Service, Intermountain Research Station.

Ewert, A.W. and Heywood, J. (1991). Group development in the natural environment: Expectations, outcomes, and techniques. *Environment and Behavior, 23,* 592–615.

Ewert, A. and McAvoy, L. (1999). The effects of wilderness settings on organized groups: A state-of-knowledge paper. In S.F. McCool, D.N. Cole, W.T. Borrie, and J. O'Loughlin (Comps.), *Wilderness science in a time of change—Volume 3* (pp. 13–26; RMRS-P-15-Vol-3). Ogden, UT: USDA Forest Service, Rocky Mountain Research Station.

Fishbein, M. and Ajzen, I. (1974). Attitudes toward objects as predictors of single and multiple behavioral criteria. *Psychological Review, 81,* 59–74.

Fredrickson, L. and Anderson, D. (1999). A qualitative exploration of the wilderness experience as a source of spiritual inspiration. *Journal of Environmental Psychology, 19,* 21–39.

Gillett, D.P., Thomas, G.P., Skok, R.L., and McLaughlin, T.F. (1991). The effects of wilderness camping and hiking. *Journal of Environmental Education, 21,* 33–44.

Gillis, H. and Simpson, C. (1991). Project choices: Adventure-based residential drug treatment for court-referred youth. *Addictions and Offender Counseling, 12,* 12–27.

Haas, G.E., Hermann, E., and Walsh, R. (1986). Wilderness values. *Natural Areas Journal, 6*(2), 37–43.

Hartig, T., Mang, M., and Evans, G.W. (1991). Restorative effects of natural environment experiences. *Environment and Behavior, 23,* 3–26.

Hendee, J.C., Stankey, G.H., and Lucas, R.C. (1990). *Wilderness management.* Golden, CO: North American Press.

Kelly, M.P., Coursey, R.D., and Selby, P. M. (1997). Therapeutic adventures outdoors: A demonstration of benefits for people with mental illness. *Psychiatric Rehabilitation Journal, 20*(4), 61–73.

Lawler, E. (1973). *Motivations in work organizations.* Monterey, CA: Brooks/Cole Publishing Company.

Luckner, J.L. (1989). Effects of participation in an outdoor adventure education course on the self-concept of hearing-impaired individuals. *American Annals of Deaf, 135*(1), 45–49.

McAvoy, L., Lais, G., Anderson, L., and Schleien, S. (1995). Wilderness and persons with disabilities: A review or research and policy directions. *Trends, 23*(3), 50–64.

Mountford, H. and Kepler, J. H. (1999). Financing incentives for the protection of diversity. *The Science of the Total Environment, 240,* 133–144.

Nash, R. (1982). *Wilderness and the American mind* (3rd ed.). New Haven, CT: Yale University Press.

Patterson, M.E., Williams, D.R., Watson, A.E., and Roggenbuck, J.W. (1998). An hermeneutic approach to studying the nature of wilderness experiences. *Journal of Leisure Research, 3,* 423–452.

Pawlowski, M., Holme, G., and Hafner, R. (1993). Wilderness therapy for psychiatric disorder. *Mental Health in Australia, 5,* 8–14.

Pohl, S L. and Borrie, W.T. (2000). Women, wilderness, and everyday life: A documentation of the connection between wilderness recreation and women's everyday lives. *Journal of Leisure Research, 32,* 415–434.

Roggenbuck, J.W. and Driver, B.L. (2000). Benefits of nonfacilitated uses of wilderness. In S.F. McCool, D.N. Cole, W.T. Borrie, and J. O'Loughlin (Comps.), *Wilderness science in a time of change—Volume 3* (pp. 33–49; RMRS-P-15-Vol-3). Ogden, UT: USDA Forest Service, Rocky Mountain Research Station.

Rolston, H. (1985). Valuing wildlands. *Environmental Ethics, 7,* 23–48.

Russell, K., Hendee, J.C., and Cooke, S. (1998). Social and economic benefits of a U.S. wilderness experience program for youth-at-risk in the Federal Job Corps. *International Journal of Wilderness, 4*(3), 32–38.

Sachs, J.J. and Miller, S.R. (1992). The impact of wilderness experience on the social interactions and social expectations of behaviorally disordered adolescents. *Behavioral Disorders, 17,* 89–98.

Scherl, L.M. (1989). Self in wilderness: Understanding the psychological benefits of individual-wilderness interaction through self-control. *Leisure Sciences, 11,* 123–135.

Scott, D.W. (2003). *A comprehensive review of recent public opinion research: A mandate to protect America's wilderness.* Washington, DC: Campaign for America's Wilderness.

Steel, B.S. and Lovrich, N.P. (1997). An introduction to natural resource policy and the environment: Changing paradigms and values. In B.S. Steel (Ed.), *Public lands management in the West* (pp. 104–117). Westport, CT: Greenwood Publishing.

Stevens, T.H., Benin, S., and Larson, J.S. (1995). Public attitudes and economic values for wetland preservation in New England. *Wetlands, 15*(3), 226–231.

Talbot, J F. and Kaplan, S. (1986). Perspectives on wilderness: Re-examining the value of extended wilderness experiences. *Journal of Environmental Psychology, 6,* 177–188.

Tarrant, M.A., Cordell, H.K., and Green, G.T. (2003). The public values of forests scale. *Journal of Forestry, 101*(6), 24–30.

Tarrant, M.A. and Hull, R.B. (2004). Forest values and attitudes in the South: Past and future. In H.M. Rauscher and K. Johnsen (Eds.), *Southern forest science: Past, present, and future* (pp. 231–239; General Technical Report SRS-75). Asheville, NC: USDA Forest Service, Southern Research Station.

USDA Forest Service. (2004). National Survey on Recreation and the Environment. Retrieved August 18, 2004, from http://www.srs.fs.usda.gov/trends/Nsre/nsre2.html

USDA Forest Service. (2005). National Survey on Recreation and the Environment, 2000–2004 [Data Set SRS-4901]. Athens, GA: USDA Forest Service, Southern Research Station.

Watson, A., Cole, D., Friese, G.T., Linziger, M.L., Hendee, J.C., Landres, P., et al. (1999). Wilderness uses, users, values, and management. In H.K. Cordell (Ed.), *Outdoor recreation in American life* (pp. 377–402). Champaign, IL: Sagamore Publishing.

Williams, D.R. (2000). Personal and social meanings of wilderness: Constructing and contesting places in a global village. In A.E. Watson, G.H. Aplet, and J.C. Hendee (Comps.), *Personal, societal, and ecological values of wilderness: Sixth World Wilderness Congress—Volume II* (pp. 77–82; RMRS-P-14). Ogden, UT: USDA Forest Service, Rocky Mountain Research Station.

Xu, Z. and Bengston, D.N. (1997). Trends in National Forest values among forestry professionals, environmentalists, and the news media. *Society and Natural Resources, 10,* 43–59.

Chapter 8
Wilderness Value Differences by Immigration, Race/Ethnicity, Gender, and Socioeconomic Status

Cassandra Johnson
Research Social Scientist
USDA Forest Service, Athens, Georgia

J. M. Bowker
Research Social Scientist
USDA Forest Service, Athens, Georgia

H. Ken Cordell
Senior Research Scientist and Project Leader
USDA Forest Service, Athens, Georgia

John C. Bergstrom
Russell Professor of Public Policy and
Professor, Department of Agricultural and Applied Economics
University of Georgia, Athens, Georgia

For many Americans, protected wildlands are considered beneficial not only from a naturalistic, ecological perspective but also because they provide a foundation for democratic ideals. (Hammond, 1985; Turner, 1953). Frederick Jackson Turner, in his "frontier hypothesis," spoke passionately about how American democracy was possible because of the wildlands on the frontier. The 19th century wilderness champion, John Muir, went further, interpreting wilderness in sacred terms, wilderness as a "window opening into heaven, a mirror reflecting the Creator" (Nash, 1967, p. 125). Contemporarily, the National Wilderness Preservation System advocates present similar arguments, but with necessary attention to the legal and political issues surrounding its management and protection (Hammond, 1985; see also University of Denver, 1999).

Because most Americans' lifestyles are detached from direct contact with the land, some have begun to ask how relevant Wilderness is to the American public, particularly to ethnic and racial minorities concentrated mostly in urban areas. Notable from critics are questions about the relevancy of Wilderness to non-White ethnic and racial minorities, as well as to the poor, and in some cases, women. Writers such as Cronon (1996), DeLuca and Demo (2000), Callicott (1994/1995), Taylor (2000), and Merchant (2003) charge that the wilderness concept suffers from a cultural bias. (See also the collection of essays in Callicott & Nelson, 1998). They argue that both its conception and perpetuation are rooted in ideals specific to bourgeois, Anglo-American culture. Specifically, critics charge that protection of Wilderness reflects the interests of environmental enthusiasts who tend to be well-educated, White, male, and in the middle- to upper-income classes (DeLuca, 1999; Walker & Kiecolt, 1995); and that values attributed to Wilderness, especially values related to direct use, are held mostly by this "well-off" segment of our society. Indeed, on-site studies show Wilderness visitors are typically White, male, more likely to have attended college, and more likely to earn higher than average incomes (Ewert, 1998; Lucas, 1989; Parker & Winter, 1998; Roggenbuck, 1988; Watson, Williams, Roggenbuck & Daigle, 1992; Williams, Patterson, Roggenbuck & Watson, 1992; Winter, 1996).

If Wilderness and the values it represents are appreciated primarily by a relatively small, exclusive portion of the population, then the continued political support of such land designations may be weakening, and in the future may be less relevant, for example, to immigrants, native-born ethnic and racial minorities, or to the poor (Stankey, 2000). The question of Wilderness relevancy is important because the demographic changes (particularly ethnic and cultural diversity) that have occurred in recent decades, and those expected over the next half century are likely to impact natural resource use and management in the 21st century (Cordell, Green & Betz, 2002). Stankey (2000) addresses the likely impact of ethnic diversification on Wilderness in the United States:

My purpose in citing this ethnic change is to remind us of the need to be aware of new and different cultural conceptions of wilderness. This is not to suggest that people of other cultures and races are indifferent to or uninterested in wilderness. However, at its core, wilderness is a cultural construct, given meaning and importance within a particular cultural context; we need to be cognizant that as culture changes, so to will the use, meaning, value and political priority attached to it [Wilderness]. (p. 17)

Readers are no doubt familiar with the often cited figures from the U.S. Census concerning demographic changes in the population. Of the approximately 281.4 million Americans in 2000, 75.1% were White; 12.5% Hispanic (Hispanics may be any race); 12.3% Black; and 3.6% Asian (U.S. Census Bureau, 2000). In 2050, non-Hispanic Whites are predicted to comprise just barely over half (50.1%) the U.S. population, with the remainder consisting of Hispanics (24.4%); African Americans (14.6%); and Asians (8.0%). In addition to these ethnic/racial shifts, the population is also expected to increase substantially by 2050, with an increase of 48.8% over the 2000 U.S. population (U.S. Census Bureau, 2004).

Immigration and the relatively higher fertility rates of the largest immigrant groups (i.e., Hispanics and Asians) will contribute most significantly to total population growth in coming decades (Castles & Miller, 1998, p. 145; U.S. Department of Commerce, 1996, p. 15). This relatively rapid population increase has implications for the natural environment generally and for Wilderness in particular because of the inevitable increase in demand for natural resources associated with population increase (Beck, 1997; Ehrlich & Ehrlich, 1990; Pimentel, Giampietro & Bukkens, 1998).

In response to this predicted growth, environmental advocacy groups have petitioned for population stabilization by means of restricted immigration (Zuckerman, 1999). In 1998 the Sierra Club was criticized from both within and outside of the organization for considering a resolution that would call for limiting immigration as a means to stabilize the U.S. population (Zuckerman, 1999). Currently, the Sierra Club maintains an officially neutral position on immigration. The Wilderness Society's official position on population increase also calls for a reduction in immigration rates (Wilderness Society Population Policy, 1998).

In turn, immigrant rights groups have criticized environmental organizations and individuals advocating immigration control as being anti-immigrant, racist, and nativist (Simcox, 1997). The former maintain that those calling for immigration restrictions are more privileged in both sociodemographic and socioeconomic terms, compared to the groups for which population control is most advocated (Beck, 1997; Ehrlich & Ehrlich 1990).

Critiques suggesting Wilderness is less relevant to peripheral populations should be acknowledged, given the contrasting goals of a Wilderness agenda emphasizing resource preservation/population stabilization and current immigration policy. However, the arguments presented in this literature, for the most part, lack empirical backing. Relatively few scholars have actually compared Wilderness values by immigrant, ethnic/racial, gender, or socioeconomic status (SES), although there is a good deal more scholarship comparing Wilderness users by socioeconomic status and gender (Lucas, 1989; Pohl, Borrie & Patterson, 2000; Roggenbuck, 1988).

Hung's (2003) study of Chinese Canadians also reports that this group is much less inclined than White Canadians to visit wilderness. The relative lack of visitation is attributed in part to particular traits and notions the Chinese have traditionally assigned to wilderness-type areas; for instance, that civilized persons should avoid wilderness, that it is the realm of lower classes, and that wilderness is generally a fearful place.

The question we consider in this chapter is whether groups with relatively less privilege and power in U.S. society—immigrants, native-born ethnic/racial minorities, women, and persons of lower socioeconomic status—indicate less value for Wilderness than their counterparts. We compare Wilderness value indicators for the aforementioned groups. For instance, do women, compared to men, indicate a value for Wilderness visitation; or do they see a value in preserving Wilderness for future generations or believe Wilderness is intrinsically valuable, apart from benefits humans might derive from it?

Approach, Definitions, and Sources

The approach applied in this chapter is to combine published research and original data analysis to examine social variation in Wilderness valuation. As in previous and succeeding chapters, the premise here is that Wilderness is valued because it provides benefits. Thus, reference will frequently be made to the benefits of Wilderness, although it will be understood that the primary focus of this chapter and book is on the values of Wilderness.

Also consistent with other chapters in this book, three broad categories of natural resource and environmental benefits are referenced. These categories have been much discussed and refined by social scientists, philosophers, resource managers, and stakeholders over the last several decades. They include active use, passive use, and intrinsic benefits or values (Bergstrom & Loomis, 1999; Godfrey-Smith, 1979; Hammond, 1985; Hass, Herman & Walsh, 1986; Krutilla, 1967; Loomis & Richardson, 2000; Morton, 1999; Noss, 1996; Oelschlaeger, 1991; Randall & Stoll, 1983; Rolston, 1985; Watson & Landres, 1999).

Active use values[1] derive from direct contact or use of a natural resource. The first active use value typically discussed is on-site, current use value which refers to benefits derived from visiting a Wilderness area. The benefits typically referenced include on-site recreational, therapeutic, and spiritual benefits. On-site, future use values refer to benefits that would be derived from visiting a Wilderness area in the future. Similarly, these future benefits would include on-site recreational, therapeutic, and spiritual benefits. Off-site, current use value refers to benefits derived from enjoying a Wilderness area from afar in a nonconsumptive manner. For example, a person may enjoy seeing videos or a television program about Wilderness at home. Off-site environmental quality value refers to the general benefits people receive from cleaner air and water because of Wilderness. Off-site environmental quality value would include, for example, better health because the air and water from Wilderness are cleaner. Scientific and medicinal value refers to the benefits from Wilderness areas as "natural laboratories" and as reservoirs of biodiversity that can support both scientific and medicinal advancement.

Passive use values involve indirect use benefits from natural lands or the environment. These include option, bequest, and existence values. Option value refers to the benefits people perceive from maintaining an option to visit a Wilderness area in the future. From a monetary perspective, option value can be viewed as a type of "insurance premium" people would be willing to pay to ensure that Wilderness areas will be available to visit in the future. Intragenerational bequest value refers to the benefit of knowing that other people currently living are enjoying Wilderness areas. For example, a parent may derive enjoyment and thus benefit from the knowledge that a living child visits Wilderness areas. Intergenerational bequest value refers to benefits derived from knowing that future generations yet to be born will be able to enjoy Wilderness areas. For example, a person may derive enjoyment and thus benefit from the knowledge that a yet unborn grandchild or great grandchild will be able to visit Wilderness areas. Existence value refers to the benefits people perceive from the knowledge that Wilderness areas exist, independent of current use or potential future use by themselves or any other person.

Intrinsic value refers to the value of Wilderness areas unto themselves, along with their biotic and abiotic components. This value exists independent of human benefits and can be said to be inherent in the resource, present whether or not humans perceive it as such. Intrinsic value is the only Wilderness value referenced that is arguably not anthropocentric (see Chapter 12). However, as referenced in this chapter, our only measure of intrinsic value is to ask people

---

[1] Chapter 7 refers to these as direct use benefits. Chapter 7 also categorizes both passive use and intrinsic values as indirect benefits.

whether they agree such nonanthropocentric value exists and is important. Obviously, this is not a true measure of intrinsic value.

To examine whether social groups differ with regard to these three broad categories of values, Wilderness value indicators from the National Survey on Recreation and the Environment (NSRE; Cordell, Green, Leeworthy, Stephens, Fly & Betz, 2005) were analyzed by immigrant status, gender, race, and socio-economic status. As described in the preceding chapter, the NSRE is a national survey of persons 16 years of age and older. It is an in-the-home, random-digit-dialing telephone survey that focuses on outdoor recreation and environmental and public land management topics. One topic of focus in recent years has been Wilderness use and values. From within the constructs of this NSRE topic, ten questions or statements were selected to indicate active, passive, and intrinsic Wilderness values. Using demographic data also collected by the NSRE, comparative analyses were conducted to test whether different social groups responded to the ten questions about Wilderness values differently. The ten questions selected are listed in Table 8.1, along with identification of which of the three broad value categories and which specific value component each is meant to represent.

Logistical regression, a modeling procedure in statistics, was used to test for differences by immigrant versus native-born, male versus female, White versus non-White (i.e., Black, Latino, Asian), and socioeconomic status level. Separate models were run for each of the ten wilderness value items in Table 8.1 (see Johnson, Bowker, Bergstrom & Cordell, 2004, for a statistical presentation of results). Table 8.2 (p. 150) reports results of this analysis for the five questions representing the active values identified in Table 8.1. Table 8.3 (p. 151) reports results for the five items corresponding to passive and intrinsic values listed in Table 8.1. Both sets of results include sample means of the demographic variables and sample means for each Wilderness value variable.

Immigrant and Native-born

Based on the analysis of NSRE data described earlier, immigrant and native-born survey respondents were compared across the ten wilderness value items shown in Table 8.1. Results show immigrants were significantly less likely than native-born respondents to visit Wilderness (i.e., less likely to have an on-site, current use value). This is true regardless of the immigrant's race or ethnicity, gender, age, socioeconomic status, residence, or how long they have lived in the United States (i.e., acculturation). Immigrants were also significantly less likely to value an opportunity to visit Wilderness in the future (i.e., have an on-site future use value) or to see that Wilderness enhances off-site environmental quality. However, immigrants were significantly more likely to hold an off-site, current use value (e.g., view Wilderness images). In terms of passive use values, immigrants were significantly less likely to indicate that they held an option value for future Wilderness visits or to agree that Wilderness contains important intragenerational bequest or existence values.

To assess practical differences between immigrants and native-born respondents for each of the ten value indicators, the probability of a positive response for immigrants and U.S.-born respondents, respectively, were calculated. The probability of a foreign-born, Latino male, age 40 with post-secondary education, urban residence, and an acculturation score of five (i.e., five years in the United States) responding "yes" to the first value question in Table 8.1 is 0.17. A foreign-born Asian male with these characteristics would have a probability of having visited equaling 0.18. The probability of visitation for a native-born, White male with the same characteristics would be 0.62 (see

Table 8.1 Wilderness Value Indicators

Broad Wilderness Value Dimension and NSRE Question/Statement	Wilderness Value Component
Active Values	
1. Have you ever taken a trip to visit an area you knew for sure was one of the 626 designated Wilderness areas?	On-site, current use
2. Do you plan to visit a Wilderness area within the next year?	On-site, future use
3. I enjoy reading about and viewing pictures, videos, TV shows, and movies featuring Wilderness areas.	Off-site, current use
4. Wilderness areas are important to protect because they contribute to better local, national, and global air and water quality.	Off-site environmental quality
5. Wilderness areas are important because they help to preserve plant and animal species that could have important scientific or human health values, such as new medicines.	Scientific/medical
Passive Values	
6. Even if you do not plan on visiting a Wilderness area within the next year, would you want to visit one sometime in the future?	Option
7. I enjoy knowing that other people are currently able to visit Wilderness areas.	Intragenerational bequest
8. I enjoy knowing that future generations will be able to visit Wilderness areas.	Intergenerational bequest
9. I support protecting Wilderness just so they will always exist in their natural condition, even if no one were to ever visit or otherwise benefit from them.	Existence
Intrinsic Value	
10. I believe the trees, wildlife, free-flowing water, rock formations, and meadows that Wilderness protects have value themselves whether or not humans benefit from them.	Intrinsic

Table 8.2 Indicators comparing relative likelihoods of social groups saying "yes" to active use value components

Wilderness Value Item	On-site current use	On-site future use	Off-site current use	Off-site environmental quality	Scientific/medicinal
% of respondents answering "yes" to value item	41	76	92	96	95
Immigrant (v. native-born)[1] (% immigrant = 9)	less likely	less likely	more likely	less likely	nsd
Black (v. White) (% black = 12)	less likely	less likely	less likely	nsd	more likely
Latino (v. White) (% Latino = 15)	less likely	nsd	less likely	nsd	nsd
Asian (v. White) (% Asian = 3)	less likely	less likely	nsd	nsd	nsd
Female (v. Male) (% female = 53)	less likely	less likely	more likely	more likely	more likely
Age—Older (v. younger) (avg. = 43.13)	nsd	less likely	more likely	less likely	less likely
College (v. no college) (% college = 27)	more likely	more likely	more likely	nsd	less likely
Urban (v. Nonurban) (% urban dweller = 0.80)	nsd	nsd	nsd	nsd	more likely
Acculturation—More (v. less) (avg. years = 16.42)	more likely	more likely	nsd	more likely	nsd
Sample size	4,571	4,590	9,601	9,558	9,572

nsd = no significant difference
[1] The parenthetical group (e.g., "native born") is the group to which comparisons are made; for example, immigrants compared to native-born.

Table 8.3 Indicators comparing relative likelihoods of social groups saying "yes" to passive use and intrinsic value components

Wilderness Value Item	Option	Intragenerational Bequest	Intergenerational Bequest	Existence	Intrinsic
% respondents answering "yes" to value item[1]	95	96	98	96	95
Immigrant (v. native born)[1] (% immigrant = 9)	less likely	less likely	nsd	less likely	nsd
Black (v. White) (% Black = 12)	less likely	less likely	less likely	nsd	less likely
Latino (v. White) (% Latino = 15)	nsd	less likely	less likely	nsd	nsd
Asian (v. White) (% Asian = 3)	nsd	nsd	nsd	more likely	more likely
Female (v. male) (% female = 53)	nsd	more likely	nsd	more likely	more likely
Age—Older (v. younger) (avg. = 43.13)	less likely	nsd	less likely	less likely	nsd
College (v. no college) (% college = 27)	more likely	nsd	nsd	less likely	less likely
Urban (v. non-urban) (% urban dweller = 0.80)	nsd	nsd	nsd	more likely	nsd
Acculturation—More (v. less) (avg. years = 16.42)	more likely	more likely	more likely	more likely	nsd
Sample size	4,801	9,620	9,643	9,574	9,589

nsd = no significant difference

[1] The parenthetical group (e.g., "native born") is the group to which comparisons are made; for example, immigrants compared to native-born

Johnson, Bowker, Bergstrom & Cordell, 2004, for statistical modeling.) These findings show that for on-site, current use value, immigration status has both a large statistical and practical effect. Further, when the acculturation score increases to twenty years, the respective probability of visitation increases to 0.24 for a Latino male and 0.26 for an Asian male. This suggests that, over time, immigrants are more likely to develop on-site, current use values for Wilderness.

Similar to our results, Hung (2003) also found that the longer Chinese were in Canada or the more acculturated they were to Canadian society, the greater likelihood of them perceiving Wilderness similarly to White Canadians.

U.S.-Born Race/Ethnic Groups

Research shows U.S.-born African Americans are less likely than White Americans to engage in wildland-related recreation activities, one exception being fishing (Gramann, 1996). Other research on Wilderness perceptions shows non-Whites are less likely than Whites to be aware of the National Wilderness Preservation System (NWPS; Cordell, Tarrant & Green, 2003; Cordell, Tarrant, McDonald & Bergstrom, 1998).

Our current analysis of NSRE data showed African Americans were significantly less likely than White Americans to indicate a value for three of the five active use values—current on-site use, future on-site use, and current off-site use. But they were more likely than native-born Whites to value the scientific/medicinal values related to Wilderness. African Americans were also significantly less likely to respond positively to passive values associated with the option, intragenerational bequest, intergenerational bequest, or the intrinsic values of Wilderness.

Latinos born in the United States were less likely than Whites to agree that Wilderness is valuable for current on-site use or current off-site use benefits. They were also less likely to agree that Wilderness has either intragenerational or intergenerational bequest values. Similar to African Americans and Latinos, Asian Americans were less likely to indicate a value for current on-site use or future use. However, they were more likely to indicate existence and intrinsic values are important.

The probability of a "yes" response to the on-site, future use value question for a native-born Black female, age 30, of low socioeconomic status, and of urban residence, would be 0.65. The probability of a positive response to the same question from a native-born White female would be 0.86; for a Latina 0.80; and for an Asian American with similar sociodemographic characteristics 0.72.

The reasons for ethnic and racial differences in Wilderness values have not been fully explored. An earlier examination of constraints to Wilderness visitation from the NSRE showed Blacks were more likely than Whites to say they did not visit Wilderness because of structural constraints. These included travel-related expenses and lack of basic services in Wilderness (Johnson, Bowker & Cordell, 2001). African Americans and Latinos were also more likely to cite internal constraints related to feelings of discomfort in the wild, desire for outdoor recreation places with more people, and concern for personal safety in the wild.

Gender

The environmental literature provides conflicting findings on differences in environmental concern and activism by gender (Olli, Grendstad & Wollebaek, 2001). In some instances, ecofeminist writers claim that because women are inherently more nurturing than men, their environmental attitudes and practices are more humane and sustainable than those of men (Salleh, 1993). Along similar lines, Dietz, Kalof, and Stern (2002) propose that the greater tendency for altruistic values among women is linked to their higher levels of environmental concern. (See Merchant, 1995 for an ecofeminist explanation of gender differences in environmental concern and behavior.) However, Davidson and Freudenburg's (1996) examination of 85 studies related to gender and environmental risk showed few differences between the sexes with regard to environmental concern, although women showed greater concern for hazards closer to their homes.

As discussed earlier, most on-site studies show that men comprise the majority of Wilderness visitors (Lucas, 1989). In more recent years, however, the number of female Wilderness visitors has increased, with estimates ranging from 25 to 30 percent (Cordell et al., 1999, p. 378).

NSRE data show women were significantly less likely than men to attribute high importance to either a current or future on-site use value (Table 8.2). However, women were significantly more likely to agree that Wilderness provided important current off-site use, off-site environmental quality, and scientific/medicinal benefits. Women were also more likely to agree that Wilderness provided intragenerational, existence, and intrinsic values (Table 8.3). To examine practical differences between men and women for the various values listed in Table 8.1, the probability of a positive response indicating active use, passive use, and intrinsic values were calculated. The probability of a "yes" response to the current on-site use question for a Black rural-dwelling female, age 25, with low socioeconomic status would be 0.08. The probability of a "yes" response for a male with the same demographic attributes would be

0.11. The probability of a "yes" response for a White female, age 50, urban dwelling with high socioeconomic status would be 0.54. For a male with similar characteristics it would be 0.63.

The probability that an American-born female of Asian descent would agree to the statement about existence value would be 0.97. For Asian men, it would be 0.94. For Latinos, the probability of agreement would be 0.95 for women and 0.93 for males. Although there were significant gender differences for existence and intrinsic values, there was only minor variation in the probability of an "agree" response between males and females. Small differences of this kind are typical with large sample sizes.

Socioeconomic Status

The environmental movement generally and the Wilderness movement in particular have stressed natural resource preservation and wildlife protection since their inception. Because of this emphasis, critics charge that mainstream environmentalists exclude socioeconomic groups that have either little means or interest for experiencing nature in these terms (Taylor, 2000). Bullard (1990, 1996) maintains that poor people have focused more on environmentalism in terms of inequitable distribution of hazardous and toxic waste sites in lower-income and minority communities. This concern is usually identified with the environmental justice movement (Bryant, 1995; Mohai & Bryant, 1992). It is argued that lower socioeconomic status groups do not have the luxury of saving wildlife because they see themselves as being more "at risk" or endangered by various environmental threats.

As earlier noted, studies of on-site Wilderness visitation show that most visitors earn above average incomes and that a relatively high proportion have college degrees. Again, little data exist comparing Wilderness values by socioeconomic status. In one study, Williams, Patterson, Roggenbuck, and Watson (1992) examined symbolic and emotional attachment to four Wilderness areas in different parts of the country. Comparisons in attachment levels were made between different educational and income groups. Results showed lower income and education levels were associated with higher attachment to specific Wilderness areas. No significant differences were found by income or education for Wilderness attachment that was not geographically specific. As a possible explanation for these differences, the authors suggested attachment to specific wilderness places might develop through informal and more casual associations or interactions. More general attachment to Wilderness may arise through more formal means.

Table 8.2 shows results for socioeconomic status differences in Wilderness values. We use education level (i.e., postsecondary education) as a proxy for high socioeconomic status because years of education typically correlate positively with affluence. Results show that individuals with high socioeconomic status were more likely than those with low status to indicate current on-site, future on-site, current off-site, and option use values as important. Although higher socioeconomic status was associated with a greater likelihood of placing importance on these values, practical differences between those with high and low socioeconomic levels were minor. The probability of agreeing future use options were important was 0.98 for a 40 year-old, urban White male with a college degree. The probability of placing importance on future use options for someone with low socioeconomic status, but with otherwise the same demographic makeup was 0.97. Higher socioeconomic status respondents were less likely to indicate importance for scientific/medicinal, existence, or intrinsic values.

Discussion

This chapter is a contribution to greater inclusiveness of the views of peripheral groups (i.e., immigrants, ethnic/racial minorities, low socioeconomic status) into a discussion of Wilderness values. Critics of the National Wilderness Preservation System (NWPS) charge that Wilderness is of importance mainly to a very privileged segment of American Society, primarily middle- to upper-income, educated Whites. To some extent our findings as presented support this assertion, especially with regard to past or near-term on-site use of Wilderness areas. However, insofar as values derived from off-site and passive use benefits are concerned, there appears to be little practical value differences between U.S.-born Americans and immigrants, especially when one considers the mitigating effect of acculturation. The same can be said for differences between U.S.-born Whites and ethnic/racial minorities, females and males, or socioeconomic groups.

A number of economic studies have shown that even among the not-so-diverse users of Wilderness, the largest economic values come from off-site use and passive use benefits. Our results suggest something similar for both minorities and immigrants. The continuance of the NWPS will ultimately depend on popular political support from all voting Americans, and the varied perspectives they hold about Wilderness. If support for passive and intrinsic values are correctly assessed by our study, then political support for Wilderness may not diminish as appreciably in the future as some have speculated, even with the rapidly shifting American demography.

Literature Cited

Beck, R. (1997). Immigration-fueled U.S. population growth is "spoiler" in economic, social and environmental efforts. *Population and Environment: A Journal of Interdisciplinary Studies, 18*(5), 483–487.

Bergstrom, J.C. and Loomis, J.B. (1999). Economic dimensions of ecosystem management. In H.K. Cordell and J.C. Bergstrom (Eds.), *Integrating social sciences with ecosystem management* (pp. 181–193). Champaign, IL: Sagamore Publishing.

Bryant, B. (1995). *Environmental justice: Issues, policies, and solutions.* Washington, DC: Island Press.

Bullard, R.D. (1990). *Dumping in Dixie: Race, class, and environmental quality.* Boulder, CO: Westview Press.

Bullard, R.D. (1996). Environmental justice: It's more than waste facility siting. *Social Science Quarterly, 77,* 493–499.

Callicott, J.B. (1994/1995). A critique of and an alternative to the Wilderness idea. *Wild Earth,* Winter, 54–59.

Callicott, J.B. and Nelson, M.P. (1998). *The great new wilderness debate.* Athens, GA: The University of Georgia Press.

Castles, S.C. and Miller, M. J. (1998). *The age of migration: International population movements in the modern world* (2nd ed.). New York, NY: The Guilford Press.

Cordell, H.K., Betz, C.J., Bowker, J.M., English, D.B.K., Mou, S.H., Bergstrom, J.C., et al. (1999). *Outdoor recreation in American life: A national assessment of demand and supply trends.* Champaign, IL: Sagamore Publishing.

Cordell, H.K., Green, G.T., Leeworthy, V.R., Stephens, R., Fly, M.J., and Betz, C.J. (2005). United States of America: Outdoor recreation. In G. Cushman, A.J. Veal, and J. Zuzanek (Eds.), *Free time and leisure participation international perspectives* (pp. 245–264). Wallingford, Oxon, UK: CABI Publishing.

Cordell, H.K., Green, G.T., and Betz, C.J. (2002). Recreation and the environment as cultural dimensions in contemporary American society. *Leisure Sciences, 24*(1), 13–41.

Cordell, H.K., Tarrant, M.A., and Green, G.T. (2003). Is the public viewpoint of wilderness shifting? *International Journal of Wilderness, 9*(2), 27–32.

Cordell, H.K., Tarrant, M.A., McDonald, B.L., and Bergstrom, J.C. (1998). How the public views wilderness. *International Journal of Wilderness, 4*(3), 28–31.

Cronon, W. (1996). The trouble with Wilderness or, getting back to the wrong nature. *Environmental History, 1*(1), 7–28.

Davidson, D.J. and Freudenburg, W.R. (1996). Gender and environmental risk concerns: A review and analysis of available research. *Environmental Behavior, 28*(3), 302–339.

DeLuca, K. (1999). In the shadow of whiteness. In T. K. Nakayama and J. N. Martin (Eds.), *Whiteness: The construction of social identity* (pp. 217–246). Thousand Oaks, CA: Sage Publications.

DeLuca, K.M. and Demo, A.T. (2000). Imaging nature: Watkins, Yosemite, and the birth of environmentalism. *Critical Studies in Media Communication, 17*(3), 251–260.

Dietz, T., Kalof, L., and Stern, P. (2002). Gender, values, and environmentalism. *Social Science Quarterly, 75*(2), 245–269.

Ehrlich, P.R. and Ehrlich, A.H. (1990). *The population explosion.* New York, NY: Simon and Schuster.

Ewert, A.W. (1998). A comparison of urban-proximate and urban-distant wilderness users on selected variables. *Environmental Management, 22*(6), 927–935.

Godfrey-Smith, W. (1979). The value of Wilderness. *Environmental Ethics, 1*(4), 309–319.

Gramann, J.H. (1996). *Ethnicity, race, and outdoor recreation: A review of trends, policy, and research* (Misc. Paper R-96-1). Washington, DC: U.S. Army Corps of Engineers.

Haas, G.E., Hermann, E., and Walsh, R. (1986). Wilderness values. *Natural Areas Journal, 6*(2), 37–43.

Hammond, J.L. (1985). Wilderness and heritage values. *Environmental Ethics, 7,* 165–170.

Hung, K. (2003). Achieving cultural diversity in wilderness recreation: A study of the Chinese in Vancouver. Unpublished master's thesis. University of Waterloo, Ontario, Canada.

Johnson, C.Y., Bowker, J.M., and Cordell, H.K. (2001). Outdoor recreation constraints: An examination of race, gender, and rural dwelling. *Southern Rural Sociology, 17*(1), 111–133.

Johnson, C.Y., Bowker, J.M., Bergstrom, J., and Cordell, H.K. (2004). Wilderness values in America: Does immigrant status or ethnicity matter? *Society and Natural Resources, 17,* 611–628.

Johnson, C.Y., Bowker, J.M., and Cordell, H.K. (2001). Outdoor recreation constraints: An examination of race, gender, and rural dwelling. *Journal of Southern Rural Sociology, 17,* 111–133.

Krutilla, J.V. (1967). Conservation reconsidered. *American Economic Review, 57,* 777–786.

Loomis, J.B. and Richardson, R. (2000). *Economic values of protecting roadless areas in the United States.* Washington, DC: The Wilderness Society.

Lucas, R.C. (1989, Winter). A look at Wilderness use and users in transition. *Natural Resources Journal, 29,* 41–55.

Merchant, C. (1995). *Earthcare: Women and the environment.* New York, NY: Routledge.

Merchant, C. (2003, July). Shades of darkness: Race and environmental history. *Environmental History, 8*, 381–393.

Morton, P. (1999). The economic benefits of wilderness: Theory and practice. *Denver University Law Review, 76*(2), 465–518.

Mohai, P. and Bryant, B. (1992). Environmental racism: Reviewing the evidence. In B. Bryant and P. Mohai (Eds.), *Race and the incidence of environmental hazards: A time for discourse* (pp. 163–176). Boulder, CO: Westview Press.

Nash, R. (1967). *Wilderness and the American mind* (Rev. ed.). New Haven, CT: Yale University Press.

Noss, R. (1996). Soul of the wilderness: Biodiversity, ecological integrity and wilderness. *International Journal of Wilderness, 2*(2), 3–8.

Oelschlaeger, M. (1991). *The idea of wilderness: From prehistory to the age of ecology.* New Haven, CT: Yale University Press.

Olli, E., Grendstad, G., and Wollebaek, D. (2001). Correlates of environmental behaviors: Bringing back social context. *Environment and Behavior, 33*(2), 181–208.

Parker, J.D. and Winter, P.L. (1998). A case study of communication with Anglo and Hispanic wilderness visitors. Research brief. *Journal of Interpretation Research, 3*(1), 55–56.

Pimentel, D., Giampietro, M., and Bukkens, S.G.F. (1998). An optimum population for North and Latin America. *Population and Environment: A Journal of Interdisciplinary Studies, 20*(2),125–148.

Pohl, S.L., Borrie, W.T., and Patterson, M.E. (2000). Women, Wilderness and everyday life: A documentation of the connection between wilderness recreation and women's everyday lives. *Journal of Leisure Research, 32*(4), 415–434.

Randall, A. and Stoll, J.R. (1983). Existence value in a total economic value framework. In R. Rowe and L. Chestnut (Eds.), *Managing air quality and scenic resources at national parks and Wilderness areas* (pp. 265–274). Boulder, CO: Westview Press.

Roggenbuck, J.W. (1988). Wilderness use and user characteristics: Ending some misconceptions. *Western Wildlands,* Fall.

Rolston, H. (1985). Valuing wildlands. *Environmental Ethics, 7*(1), 23–48.

Salleh, A. (1993). Class, race, and gender discourse in the ecofeminism deep ecology debate. *Environmental Ethics, 15*(3), 225–244.

Stankey, G.H. (2000). *Future trends in society and technology: Implications for Wilderness research and management* (pp. 10-23; RMRS-P-15-Vol-1). Fort Collins, CO: USDA Forest Service, Rocky Mountain Research Station.

Simcox, D. (1997). Major predictors of immigration restrictionism: Operationalizing "nativism." *Population and Environment: A Journal of Interdisciplinary Studies, 19*(2), 129–143.

Taylor, D.E. (2000). The rise of the environmental justice paradigm: Injustice framing and the social construction of environmental discourses. *American Behavioral Scientist, 43*(4), 508–580.

Turner, F.J. (1953). *The frontier in American history.* New York, NY: Henry Holt and Company.

U.S. Census Bureau. (2000). Summary File 1. Table QT-P3. Race and Hispanic or Latino: 2000. Retrieved February 24, 2005, from http://quickfacts.census.gov/qfd/states/00000lk.html

U.S. Census Bureau. (2004). U.S. interim projections by age, sex, race, and Hispanic origin. Table 1a. Projected population of the United States, by race and Hispanic origin: 2000 to 2050. Retrieved February 24, 2005, from http://www.census.gov/ipc/www/usinterimproj

U.S. Department of Commerce, Bureau of the Census. (1996). Current population reports: Population projections of the United States by age, sex, race, and Hispanic origin: 1995–2050 (pp. 25–1130). Retrieved June 10, 2002, from http://www.census.gov/prod/1/pop/p25-1130

University of Denver. (1999). Symposium—Wilderness Act of 1964: Reflections, applications, and predictions. *Denver University Law Review, 76,* 2.

Walker, G.J. and Kiecolt, K.J. (1995). Social class and Wilderness use. *Leisure Sciences, 17,* 295–308.

Watson, A. and Landres, P. (1999). Changing Wilderness values. In H.K. Cordell (Ed.), *Outdoor recreation in American life: A national assessment of demand and supply trends* (pp. 384–388). Champaign, IL: Sagamore Publishing.

Watson, A.E., Williams, D.R., Roggenbuck, J.W., and Daigle, J.J. (1992). *Visitor characteristics and preferences for three national forest Wildernesses in the south* (Research Paper INT-455). Ogden, UT: USDA Forest Service, Intermountain Research Station.

Wilderness Society Population Policy. (1998). Retrieved June 10, 2002, from http://www.susps.org/ibq1998/discuss/twspolicy.html

Williams, D.R., Patterson, M.E., Roggenbuck, J.E., and Watson, A.E. (1992). Beyond the commodity metaphor: Examining emotional and symbolic attachment to place. *Leisure Sciences, 14,* 29–46.

Winter, P. (1996). San Gorgonio Wilderness visitor survey, summer and fall 1994. Unpublished research report, USDA Forest Service, Pacific Southwest Station, San Dimas Experimental Forest, Glendora, CA.

Zuckerman, B. (1999). The Sierra club immigration debate: National implications. *Population and Environment: A Journal of Interdisciplinary Studies, 20*(5), 401–412.

Chapter 9
The Net Economic Value of Wilderness

J. M. Bowker
Research Social Scientist
USDA Forest Service, Athens, Georgia

J. E. Harvard III
former University of Georgia employee

John C. Bergstrom
Russell Professor of Public Policy and
Professor, Department of Agriculture and Applied Economics
University of Georgia, Athens, Georgia

H. Ken Cordell
Senior Research Scientist and Project Leader
USDA Forest Service, Athens, Georgia

Donald B. K. English
Visitor Use Monitoring Program Manager
USDA Forest Service, Washington, DC

John B. Loomis
Professor, Department of Agricultural and Resource Economics
Colorado State University, Fort Collins, Colorado

Note: Senior authorship is shared among Bowker, Harvard, and Bergstrom.

The purpose of this chapter is to inventory and assess what is currently known about the economic or "dollar" values accruing to Americans from the National Wilderness Preservation System. This chapter identifies the benefits of Wilderness and the economic value of these benefits through an extensive review of published conceptual and empirical literature. It uses the definition of Wilderness provided by the Wilderness Act of 1964, which encompasses both the objective and subjective aspects of Wilderness (see Chapters 3 and 4). When this chapter refers to "Wilderness," the authors mean statutory or official Wilderness as defined by the Wilderness Act of 1964. The question that this chapter addresses is: "How much are the on-site recreation and passive use benefits of Wilderness worth to Americans?"

To assess the net economic value of Wilderness, this chapter presents an analysis of published research that has focused on the on-site recreation use benefits of Wilderness, and also research that has focused on the passive use benefits of Wilderness. From these analyses the authors estimate the total or aggregate net economic value of the recreation and passive use benefits of Wilderness.

A Taxonomy of Benefits and Values

Morton (1999) identified seven categories of benefits for defining the total economic value of Wilderness: on-site recreation, community, scientific, off-site, biodiversity conservation, ecological services, and passive use benefits (Figure 9.1). This section focuses on the on-site recreation and passive use benefits.

On-Site Recreation Benefits

On-site recreation benefits derive from consumptive and nonconsumptive activities in a Wilderness area. Among the types of activities in Wilderness from which people obtain these benefits are fishing, hunting, birdwatching, rafting, backpacking, hiking, and camping. Motorized activities are not permitted in Wilderness. Morton (1999) refers to on-site recreation or *in situ* Wilderness benefits as direct use benefits.

Passive Use Benefits

Passive use benefits, also called nonuse benefits (Freeman 1994, p. 145), are less tangible than the physical presence of a person being on-site and participating in a recreational activity (Figure 9.1). Krutilla (1967) is considered the originator of the concept of nonuse benefits of natural resources in general. However, his concept is easily adapted to Wilderness as a protected natural resource. For example, passive use benefits reflect the utility gained from knowing Wilderness is preserved, even if an individual does not visit or ever

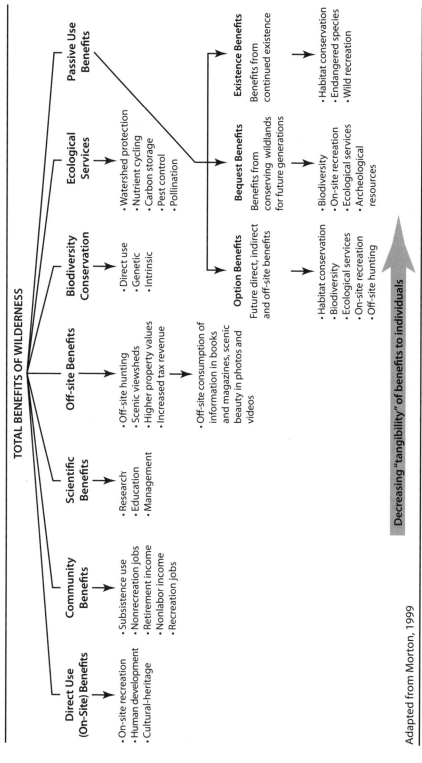

Adapted from Morton, 1999

Figure 9.1 The total economic benefits of wilderness

plan to visit the area. Hence, passive use benefits could be considered a form of off-site benefits. Passive use benefits for Wilderness consist of at least three components: (a) option benefits, (b) bequest benefits, and (c) existence benefits. Option benefits are received from current preservation, ensuring the opportunity to visit Wilderness areas in the future. Bequest benefits are gained from knowing that Wilderness will be available for use by one's heirs or future generations. Existence benefits derive from simply knowing Wilderness exists.

While there is some debate among economists over the precise definitions for the various components of passive use benefits, and perhaps even more debate as to the empirical measurement of the resulting economic values, most natural resource economists would agree with the concept of passive use benefits (Freeman, 1994, p. 141).

Other Benefits of Wilderness

Morton identifies five other benefits of Wilderness in addition to on-site recreation and passive use. They include community, scientific, off-site, biodiversity conservation, and ecological service benefits.

Community benefits include jobs and income created and supported through local spending by people who visit Wilderness for recreation. As well, there are other direct and indirect benefits realized by communities near Wilderness. For example, subsistence use of Wilderness lands for food, clothing, and shelter can be included as a community benefit (Morton, 1999). Rosenberger and English address the state of knowledge of community economic impacts of Wilderness recreation in Chapter 10. Tarrant and Schuster also address the idea of community benefits, but as a social value of Wilderness in noneconomic terms (see Chapter 7).

Morton identified three types of scientific benefits—research, education, and management (Morton, 1999). These benefits are also discussed from a social values perspective in Chapter 7. As a scientific benefit, Wilderness is recognized as a living laboratory and as a benchmark for evaluating the impacts of development elsewhere (Loomis & Richardson, 2000). These benefits from research are reflected in a sizeable number of scientific journal articles that use Wilderness as the research observation site. Educational benefits include development of Wilderness skills and clearing the mind for visualization and creative thinking (Morton, 1999). Wilderness areas can also act as templates for understanding and restoring natural forest ecosystems elsewhere. Thus, Wilderness provides examples of natural systems that can be observed in order to specify the makeup and functioning of various ecosystems when they are in pristine condition.

Wilderness provides habitat for fish, wildlife, and a wide variety of other wild species. However, the species depending on this habitat do not necessarily have to be enjoyed by visiting a Wilderness area. A golden eagle soaring beyond the boundary becomes an important off-site benefit for those lucky enough to see it. In many different ways, wildlife that depends on habitats within protected Wilderness may be viewed and enjoyed outside of its boundaries. Similarly, off-site benefits of Wilderness can include its contribution as natural and scenic views for the casual sightseer, as well as a backdrop for burgeoning resort and second home communities (McCloskey, 1990). "In both time and space, Wilderness benefits are not limited to visitors actually setting foot in Wilderness" (Morton, 1999).

Policymakers and scientists are becoming increasingly aware of the importance of conserving biodiversity. Biodiversity conservation is a growing consideration in Wilderness legislation and management in that it means helping preserve representations of ecosystems, species, and genetic diversity (Loomis & Richardson, 2000). Wilderness also plays a role in sustaining the ecological processes comprising our global life support system. Some ecological systems fostered in Wilderness include watershed protection, carbon storage, and natural pest control (Morton, 1999). Cordell, Murphy, Riitters and Harvard address the ecological values of Wilderness in more detail in Chapter 11. Gudmundsen and Loomis address the concept of intrinsic values that are separate from the economic and social values that humans place on Wilderness in Chapter 12.

Benefits-to-Value Linkage

The many benefits of Wilderness summarized here contribute to an individual's value for Wilderness attributes (e.g., wildness, geography), functions (e.g., preservation of wild places, recreational setting), and services (e.g., animal and plant habitat, cultural preservation; see Chapter 4). As with other goods and services, monetary measures pertaining to these benefits can be partitioned into two components: expenditures and consumer surplus. Expenditures are what an individual is required to pay to obtain a Wilderness benefit (Figure 9.2, Areas A, C, E, G and I, p. 166). Expenditures encompass things like travel expenses, gasoline used to visit a Wilderness, food, lodging, and public-use fees. Consumer surplus, or net economic value, is a measure of the value an individual receives from the same Wilderness benefit, above and beyond expenditures. In Figure 9.2, consumer surplus is represented by the amount of remaining area of the entire circle after the inner circle is subtracted (Areas B, D, F, H and J). Measured empirically, it may be more or less than actual expenditures.

Consider an example, adapted from Loomis (1993), of expenditures and consumer surplus for on-site recreation (Figure 9.3, p. 167). Assume an individual lives in Denver, Colorado. She enjoys visiting Indian Peaks Wilderness each summer and the expenditures for a one-day trip to Indian Peaks total $20. Also assume that for the first trip of the year to Indian Peaks, she would be willing to pay $30. This willingness to pay is her value for the trip to Indian Peaks. Having been there once, she values the second trip slightly less at $25. Subsequent trips provide less satisfaction, so she values the third trip at $20 and the fourth at $15. For the first two trips, she is willing to pay more than the trip costs. This difference is called consumer surplus, or net economic value. The value of the third trip equals its cost. Should she take the third trip, she would receive no additional consumer surplus. The fourth trip would cost more than the individual would receive in benefits, thus, she would likely take no more than three trips to Indian Peaks in a given year. Gross economic value, the sum of expenditures and consumer surplus, is $75 ($30 + $25 + $20). Expenditures for recreation at Indian Peaks equal $60 ($20 + $20 + $20). The net economic value received from either two ($10 + $5) or three ($10 + $5 + $0) visits is $15.

Passive use economic value can also be demonstrated. Consider the case where an individual knows about the Okefenokee Wilderness in southeastern Georgia. He enjoys envisioning the Okefenokee and its wild features, but does not intend to visit it in the future. Nevertheless, he derives personal pleasure from knowing that this Wilderness exists and will be protected. While he pays $25 annually to a fund supporting this Wilderness area, he would be willing to pay more, say $75, if he had to. As such, the net economic benefit this individual receives from knowing that the Okefenokee exists is $50 per year ($75 less $25).

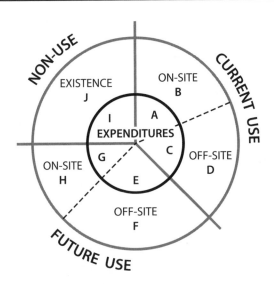

Adapted from Bergstrom, Stoll, Titre, and Wright, 1990

Figure 9.2 The total economic value of wilderness-based recreation

Review of Net Economic Value Research

As earlier stated, this chapter is based on a synthesis of a number of published studies of the economic value of on-site recreation and passive use benefits from Wilderness. Other benefits identified by Morton (1999) and briefly discussed, such as biodiversity conservation, also have positive benefits to people, but they are much more difficult to measure in monetary terms. Hence, few empirical studies have examined the economic value of these Wilderness benefits. The end result sought from this synthesis is an estimate of the nationwide economic value of the recreation and passive use benefits from the National Wilderness Preservation System.

On-Site Recreation Value Estimates

We identified fourteen published studies that estimated individual consumer surplus for on-site Wilderness recreation. All of these studies used either the travel cost method or contingent valuation method to estimate consumer surplus; that is, net economic value. The travel cost method estimates recreational visits to Wilderness based on actual travel behavior and associated actual expenditures. The contingent valuation method uses survey instruments to elicit an individual's stated willingness to pay for a recreation trip to a Wilderness area (Loomis & Walsh 1997).

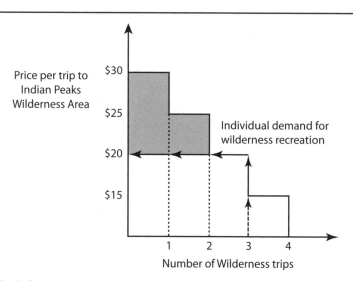

The shaded area represents consumer surplus. Arrows indicate the number of trips taken at $20 per trip.

Adapted from Loomis, 1993

Figure 9.3 Example of consumer surplus (or net economic value)

The fourteen studies yielded 31 estimates of net economic value. Of these 31 estimates, 27 are from Wilderness areas west of the Mississippi River. Thirteen of these 27 western area estimates are from California, Oregon, or Washington. One of the 31 estimates is from Alaska. The USDA Forest Service manages a majority of the Wilderness areas on which these studies focused. Sixty-nine of the 76 Wilderness areas (91%) in the literature are managed by the USDA Forest Service.[1]

Each observation represents the dollar value to an individual (i.e., net economic value or consumer surplus) for either a single-day or multiple-day trip to a given Wilderness (Table 9.1). All dollar values are base-year 2002, that is, deflated to equal the real purchasing power of a dollar in 2002 using the Consumer Price Index. The consumer surplus values per person per Wilder-

Table 9.1 Wilderness on-site recreation use empirical literature: Individual consumer surplus for single-day use and multiday use (2002 dollars)

Author	Year	State(s)	Single-Day Use Consumer Surplus	Multiday Use Consumer Surplus
Brown and Plummer	1981	OR & WA		4 estimates between $415 and $560
Smith and Kopp	1980	CA		$64
Walsh and Gilliam	1982	CO	$31	$185
Walsh et al.	1984	CO		$94
Leuschner et al.	1987	NC	$12	$16
Prince and Ahmed	1988	VA	$14	
Walsh et al.	1989	MN		$61
Barrick and Beazley	1990	WY		$16
Halstead et al.	1991	NH		$7
McCollum et al.	1990	9 USDA Forest Service regions	$22	8 estimates between $12 and $287
Hellerstein	1991	MN		$33
Englin and Shonkwiler	1995	WA		$27
Baker	1996	CA		6 estimates between $63 and $1,907
Richer and Christensen	1999	CA		$5

---

[1] Walsh, Loomis, and Gillman (1984) used "all" Wilderness in Colorado as the research setting. There are 41 Wilderness areas in Colorado, of which 36 are managed solely by the USDA Forest Service. Four other areas are managed in conjunction with the National Park Service, the U.S. Bureau of Land Management, or the U.S. Fish and Wildlife Service.

ness trip range from $4.64 to $287.22, with the median being $24.45. The consumer surplus per person per trip averaged across all studies done in the United States equals $61.47. With an average duration of 3.5 days per trip, average consumer surplus per person per day is $17.56. It should be noted that we excluded estimates from Brown and Plummer (1981) in our calculations. Their estimates were greater by two standard deviations from the average for all the reported studies (Table 9.1). Nothing was noted in their study to account for this large difference and therefore it was treated as an outlier.

Grouping the studies according to region, the average consumer surplus per person per trip for states west of the Mississippi River is $71.95, with a range of $4.64 to $287.22 and a median of $33.43. On a per-day basis, average consumer surplus per person per trip for western states is $20.56. For states east of the Mississippi, average consumer surplus per person per trip is $13.28. The values for the eastern United States range from $6.99 to $17.97, with the median being $13.87. On a per-day basis, average consumer surplus per person per trip for eastern states is $3.79. Only one study provided estimates for Alaskan Wilderness visits. McCollum, Peterson, Arnold, Markstrom, and Hellerstein (1990) estimated consumer surplus equal to $287.22 per person per trip. However, the average trip length was over 18 days, which equates to a per-day value of $15.38.

Grouping the studies according to trip length (single-day v. multiple-day trips), the average consumer surplus per person per trip for single-day use is $19.50. Consumer surplus values for single-day use range from $11.50 to $30.50, with the median at $17.99. Average consumer surplus per person per trip for multiday use equals $68.47. Multiday consumer surplus ranges from $4.64 to $287.22, with the median at $30.11.

Passive Use Value Estimates

Eight published studies which provided estimates of passive use values of Wilderness were identified (Table 9.2, p. 170). These studies used contingent valuation (Loomis & Walsh, 1997) to obtain either individual or household annual willingness to pay to protect Wilderness from various forms of development. The estimated values pertained to keeping the land managed as Wilderness, rather than letting it be developed. With the exception of one study on eastern Wilderness (Gilbert, Glass & More,1992), the body of empirical work has focused on western states and subsets of the National Wilderness Preservation System (NWPS) in those states. No studies pertaining to passive use values of Wilderness in Alaska were found.

It is difficult to compare results from studies of household willingness to pay (i.e., consumer surplus) for passive use of Wilderness. Each used a different sampling frame and base population. None that we could find attempted to measure the monetary value of passive use for the entire NWPS. Moreover, each study presented somewhat different development scenarios as alternatives to preservation of one or more particular Wilderness areas. Several studies presented multiple passive use values because more than one Wilderness area in different portions or combinations were presented to the survey respondents. In addition, some of the studies were more focused on methodological issues in the measurement of passive use value and thus did not provide actual estimates of the passive use economic value in such a way that they could defensibly be extrapolated for the whole country.

Although there is incongruence across the published literature, the authors opted to use an average across studies of the reported passive use value estimates as an initial approximation of household annual willingness to pay for Wilderness' protection. Because each reported study focused on a subset of NWPS areas, it seems reasonable to assume that each study represents a conservative estimated household passive use value for the whole NWPS. That is, if a household would pay $41 annually for passive use benefits of just the designated Wilderness areas in Colorado (Walsh, Loomis & Gillman, 1984), then it seems reasonable they would pay at least that much for the entire NWPS. This is especially defensible given that Wilderness area access is not an issue in order for passive use benefits to exist.

Estimates of annual household values of passive use benefits from the studies reported in Table 9.2 range from $20 to $861. All but the Keith, Fawson, and Johnson (1996) study in Utah reported annual household values of less than $100. Thus, that study was considered to be an outlier and was excluded. Averaging results of the remaining studies in Table 9.2 yielded a per household estimate of annual willingness to pay for passive use benefits from the NWPS of approximately $67 per year.

Table 9.2 Empirical literature, year, state, and annual household willingness to pay from study for passive use (2002 dollars)

Study	Year	State(s)	Annual Household Willingness to Pay (Consumer Surplus)
Walsh et al.	1984	CO	$72
Aiken	1985	CO	$98
Barrick and Beazley	1990	WY	$76 and $87
Pope and Jones	1990	UT	$80
Gilbert et al.	1992	Eastern U.S.	$19 and $21
Diamond et al.	1993	CO, ID, MT & WY	$38, $47, and $64
McFadden	1994	CO, ID, MT & WY	$61 and $96
Keith et al.	1996	UT	$861.03

Other Value Estimates

Although this chapter focuses only on the economic value of on-site recreation and passive use benefits, a brief summary of estimates of other Wilderness values as identified in Figure 9.1 is provided here. For example, the scientific values of Wilderness and roadless areas were studied by Loomis and Richardson (2000). They estimated that 422 journal articles had been based primarily on studies done in Wilderness. They used an estimate from Black (1996) to calculate the monetary value of the scientific contribution of these journal articles. Black estimated the economic value of one journal article to society as $12,000 per year. Using Black's approach, the 422 journal articles generate a potential value to society of $5.1 million annually (Loomis & Richardson, 2000).

We were unable to locate many quantitative indicators of Wilderness being the main focus of any educational programs. However, there are national organizations that foster educational benefits to people and use Wilderness as a backdrop for Wilderness Experience Programs (Friese, Hendee & Kinziger, 1998). These schools facilitate effective adaptation skills, problem solving, emotional development, and a greater awareness of and concern for Wilderness (see Chapter 7).

Very few researchers have attempted to estimate the economic value of Wilderness education programs to society. However, Russell, Hendee, and Cooke (1998) examined the economic benefits and costs of the Wilderness Discovery program designed for at-risk youth in the Federal Jobs Corps. They found statistical evidence suggesting a reduction in early terminations of Job Corps Center at-risk youth and a consequent increase in employability for students who participated in Wilderness Discovery. Their findings translated to a return in social benefits per student of $931 (inflated to 2002 dollars) for each $446 in program costs.

Wilderness (or proximity to Wilderness) may be considered a valuable amenity. Hedonic procedures exist allowing economists to estimate the contribution of amenities or other attributes to the overall value of a good or service (Freeman, 1994, p. 121). This procedure has been applied in real estate markets to value property attributes like air quality or proximity to amenities. Using an hedonic model, Phillips (2000) estimated that parcels of land in a town near Wilderness in the Green Mountain area of Vermont sold at prices 13 percent higher than comparable land in the area not proximal to Wilderness.

We found no literature addressing the economic value of ecological services or biodiversity conservation in Wilderness. However, we can draw some conclusions with roadless and other wild areas serving as a proxy for Wilderness. Costanza and colleagues (1997) estimated the benefits from temperate forests for climate regulation to be $35 per acre per year. Costanza and colleagues also estimated benefits from waste treatment services of $35 per acre per year from these same forests. Loomis and Richardson (2000), using Costanza and associates' values, estimated that these benefits from 42 million roadless acres are $980 million annually, or $23 per acre. Applying the per acre estimate to the 106 million acres of Wilderness, they calculated the ecological value of Wilderness in the United States to be $2.5 billion annually. Cordell, Murphy, Riitters, and Harvard address the ecological value of Wilderness from an overall ecosystem health and life-support perspective (see Chapter 11).

Aggregate Net Economic Value of Wilderness

Monetary estimates of the value of some of the benefits identified in Figure 9.1, including scientific, off-site, biodiversity, and ecological services, are still quite controversial and present considerable measurement challenges. Therefore, the chapter takes a conservative approach and includes only on-site recreation and passive use benefits in its calculations of the aggregate net economic value of the National Wilderness Preservation System (NWPS).

Net Economic Value for On-site Recreation

Calculation of the annual aggregate net economic value of on-site Wilderness recreation requires two key components: the average net economic value per person per trip and an estimate of the number of Wilderness trips.

In light of the very dispersed nature of Wilderness recreation, accurate estimation of on-site use is extremely costly. Of the four major federal land management agencies—USDA Forest Service, National Park Service, Bureau of Land Management, and Fish and Wildlife Service—the only visitation numbers consistently estimated are those maintained by the Forest Service for Wilderness areas within National Forests (Cole, 1996). A 1989 study of all Wilderness areas in the country identified that only 13 percent of Forest Service Wilderness areas had use estimates based on systematic counts at that time (McClaran & Cole, 1993).

Using a variety of on-site sources, Cole (1996) reported 16,988,000 recreation visitor days (RVDs) to all NWPS Wilderness in 1994. Loomis (1999), using Cole's data, estimated National Forest Wilderness visitation equal to 12,028,873 RVDs in 1993. Loomis (1999) estimated National Forest and National Park Wilderness visitation to equal 13,749,393 RVDs in 1993.

Cordell and Teasley (1998) use origin-based sampling to provide a different approach to Wilderness visitation estimation using the 1994–95 National Survey on Recreation and the Environment (NSRE). A household sample of persons across the United States was asked about their annual recreational trips consistent with Wilderness recreation. Depending on assumptions, the procedure they used led to an estimate of between 15.7 and 34.7 million trips per year to areas of the National Wilderness Preservation System. The authors indicated the most likely amount of trips to Wilderness was believed to lie somewhere between these lower- and upper-bound estimates.

Loomis and Richardson (2000) took a different approach. Their estimate of annual trips to Wilderness was based on an inventory of activities throughout the U.S. National Forest system, including roadless and backcountry areas. Using the ratio (106 million acres to 54 million acres) of Wilderness to "near Wilderness" lands in national forests (Loomis & Richardson, 2000), this equates to approximately 26.7 million visits per year—a likely upper bound for annual recreation use.

A more promising alternative and perhaps more scientifically based estimate of Wilderness visitation relies on the Forest Service's National Visitor Use Monitoring (NVUM) system. NVUM is a system designed to provide statistically reliable estimates of recreation visitation on national forests and national grasslands. Following a four-year cycle, recreational use on every national forest is surveyed. Wilderness is one of five strata in the sampling plan (English, Kocis, Zarnoch & Arnold, 2002). Wilderness visitation is estimated as recreation site visits for the entire National Forest System (Figure 9.4). A recreation visit is defined as "…one person entering and exiting a national

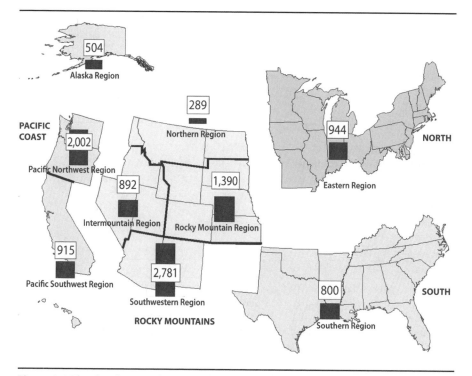

Figure 9.4 The distribution of Wilderness site visits in the National Forest System for the year 2001 (in thousands of visits)

forest, national grassland, or designated Wilderness area for the purpose of recreation" (English, Kocis, Zarnoch & Arnold, 2002). A site visit may be 10 minutes or 10 days. Annual visitation in 2001 to all National Forest Wilderness was estimated to be 10.5 million visits. Of these, 73 percent were single-day visits and 27 percent were multiple-day visits (Table 9.3). This ratio of day use to overnight use differs considerably from Cole's (1996) estimates for National Park Wilderness. He found that 26 percent of the visits were for single-day use and 74 percent for multiple-day use.

D.N. Cole (personal communication, 2003) estimated each agency's share of Wilderness visitation. He calculated that 82 percent of all Wilderness visitation is on National Forest lands, 15 percent on National Parks, 2.6 percent on U.S. Fish and Wildlife Service (FWS) lands, with the remaining 0.4 percent on areas managed by the U.S. Bureau of Land Management (BLM). Applying Cole's share estimates to National Park Wilderness and assuming that FWS and BLM ratios are similar to Forest Service NVUM estimates, the authors estimate that on-site recreation use for all NWPS areas is approximately 12.8 million visits per year (Table 9.4). This includes approximately 8.5 million single-day visits and 4.4 million multiple-day visits. Based on a sample average of trip length in days for multiple-day visits of just over 4 days, an estimated 18.2 million days were spent in Wilderness during multiple-day trips. Combining estimates of total days spent during single-day and multiple-day trips

Table 9.3 Percentages of single-day wilderness visits by Forest Service region

Forest Service Region	Percentage single-day visits (Forest Service only)
R1 Northern Rocky Mountain	55.8
R2 Rocky Mountain	85.9
R3 Rocky Mountain—Southwest	93.6
R4 Intermountain	84.0
R5 Pacific—Southwest	77.5
R6 Pacific—Northwest	62.6
R8 South	70.8
R9 North	29.8[1]
R10 Alaska	98.1[2]
Average	**73.1**

[1] Boundary Waters Canoe Area (BWCA) in Minnesota was one of the surveyed Forest Service sites for Region 9. BWCA is a remote wilderness requiring long travel times to reach, thus it is more likely that trip times will be long. This would explain why 30% of visitation in R9 is single-day use. As there are only two years of data, it remains to be seen if the BWCA will have a disproportionate effect on the visitation from R9. However, the two years of data is the best available.

[2] Most trips to Alaska are for a long duration. However, visitors have the opportunity to stay off-site and visit multiple sites during a multiday trip. Thus, there is a high percentage of single-day use.

leads to a total estimate of 26.6 million days of Wilderness use annually across all NWPS lands.

Combining the estimates of average per-person-per-trip consumer surplus reported in the studies summarized earlier and estimates of the total number of single-day trips to Wilderness, it is calculated that the annual net economic value of Wilderness single-day trips to be $163.8 million ($19.50 x 8.4 million). Following the same procedure for multiple-day trips to Wilderness, an estimate for annual net economic value of $301.3 million ($68.47 x 4.4 million) can be obtained. Taken together, the net economic value all recreation trips to the NWPS is estimated to be $465.1 million annually. For perspective, the product of annual trips and value per trip ($465.1 million) can be scaled by the number of acres in the NWPS (106 million) to obtain an estimate of annual per-acre average net value of recreation trips to Wilderness of $4.39 across the NWPS.

Net Economic Value for Passive Use

When estimating the aggregate annual passive use value for the NWPS, it is particularly important to identify the relevant population because the aggregate estimate is directly influenced by the size of the population selected. The passive use value studies reported earlier (Table 9.2, p. 170) are primarily based on household sampling. Therefore, one approach to estimating total passive use value is to aggregate across U.S. households. A conservative approach was chosen by following the average response rates for these studies which was approximately 50 percent. Thus, the authors aggregate passive use value across only 54.5 million households, one-half of the 109 million total households in the United States (U.S. Census Bureau, 2003). This conserva-

---

Table 9.4 Total site visits by agency and by single-day and multiday lengths of visit

Total National Wilderness Preservation System site visits	**12,825,610**
Forest Service (FS)	10,517,000
National Park Service (NPS)	1,923,841
Fish & Wildlife Service (FWS)	333,466
Bureau of Land Management (BLM)	51,302
Total single-day visits	8,458,490
Total multiday visits	4,367,120
Total FS, FWS and BLM visits	10,901,768
FS, FWS, and BLM single-day visits (73%)	7,958,291
FS, FWS, and BLM multiday visits (27%)	2,943,477
Total NPS site visits	1,923,841
NPS single-day visits (26%)	500,199
NPS multiday visits (74%)	1,423,643

Note: Any discrepancies in appropriate summation are due to rounding error.

tive procedure assumes that nonrespondent households from the studies reported earlier express no passive use value for Wilderness.

Aggregating the estimated average annual passive use value of $67 per household across 54.5 million households yields an aggregate estimate of passive use value for the entire NWPS of $3.7 billion per year. This is approximately $34.50 per acre annually. This calculated estimate demonstrates that the economic value derived from passive use exceeds the economic value derived from on-site recreation use by a ratio of nearly eight to one. These quantitative results indicating the relatively high value of passive use values compared to direct use values are consistent with the qualitative opinion survey results reported in Chapter 7.

Conclusion

Today's social and political climate increasingly leads to debates of whether certain publicly provided goods and services are "worth it" to taxpayers. The NWPS provides a multitude of benefits to the American population, some of which are indirect. These benefits lead to conceptually valid, albeit empirically elusive, estimates of the net economic value of Wilderness. While some people choose to visit Wilderness and obtain the direct benefits derived from on-site recreation, the majority do not. Nevertheless, numerous studies, including results discussed in this chapter and in Chapter 7, have shown that even for those with no intention of ever visiting the NWPS, benefits derived from off-site passive use are nontrivial and, in fact, considerably outweigh the value of recreation benefits.

Based on published literature, annual average individual consumer surplus for on-site Wilderness recreation is estimated to be $19.50 for day use and $68.47 for multiple-day trips. For passive use, annual average per-household consumer surplus is estimated to be $67. Combining these consumer surplus values and appropriately aggregating over the relevant populations yields an estimated annual net economic value for the NWPS of nearly $4.2 billion, or about $39 per acre per year. If one adds the per acre value of $23 for ecological services (Loomis & Richardson, 2000) another $2.4 billion of benefits could be considered.

For yet another perspective, annual flows of estimated economic values are often discounted to the present. This calculation of present value allows direct comparison of assets or projects with different annual flows of economic returns and possibly different project time horizons (Penson & Lins, 1980). Conservatively assuming a discount rate of 4 percent (as currently used by the USDA Forest Service federal agencies), assuming a constant population of on-site users and households deriving passive use benefits, and assuming constant nominal net economic values per household and per person per trip, the net present value of the NWPS across a 60-year time horizon is about $95 billion or, on average, about $900 per acre. Including the estimated value of ecological services would increase the estimated present value of the NWPS to almost $150 billion, or about $1,400 per acre.

Currently, there are millions of acres in the United States that are still wild or roadless, and do not yet have Wilderness designation. If more acres are added to the NWPS in the future, the aggregate net economic value to Americans of Wilderness in the system should be expected to grow. However, as demonstrated in a number of studies including Walsh, Loomis, and Gillman (1984) and Pope and Jones (1990), the value of additions to the System, while nonnegative, are likely less at the margin than the average values reported above. The Campaign for America's Wilderness (2003) estimates almost 319 million acres of remaining wild lands are unprotected by official Wilderness designation. Loomis and Richardson (2000) estimate that there are 42 million acres of roadless National Forest lands that could potentially qualify as designated Wilderness. According to their estimates, adding these roadless areas to the Wilderness roll could increase the aggregate net economic value of the NWPS by another $1.5 billion annually.

Literature Cited

Aiken, R. (1985). *Public benefits of environmental protection in Colorado.* Unpublished master's thesis, Colorado State University, Fort Collins, CO.

Baker, J.C. (1996). *A nested Poisson approach to ecosystem valuation: An application to backcountry hiking in California.* Unpublished master's thesis, University of Nevada, Reno, NV.

Barrick, K.A. and Beazley, R.I. (1990). Magnitude and distribution of option value for the Washakie Wilderness, Northwest Wyoming, U.S.A. *Environmental Management, 14*(Sept.), 367–380.

Bergstrom, J.C., Stoll, J.R., Titre, J.P., and Wright, V.L. (1990). Economic value of wetlands-based recreation. *Ecological Economics, 2,* 129–147.

Black, D. (1996). *Application of contingent valuation methodology to value a government public good.* Unpublished doctoral dissertation. Department of Economics, Colorado State University, Fort Collins, CO.

Brown, G. and Plummer, M. (1981). Recreation values, appendix a.5, final report, November 30, 1979. In J.H. Powel and G.K. Loth (Comps.), *An economic analysis of non-timber uses of forestland in the Pacific Northwest: Modules IIB, IIIB* (Final Report). Forest Policy Project, Vancouver, WA. (May 31): A.5-47.

Campaign for America's Wilderness. (2003). *A mandate to protect America's Wilderness: A comprehensive review of recent public opinion research.* Retrieved December 20, 2004, from http://www.leaveitwild.org/reports/polling_report.pdf

Cole, D.N. (1996). *Wilderness recreation use trends, 1965 through 1994* (INT-RP-488). Ogden, UT: USDA Forest Service, Intermountain Research Station.

Cordell, H.K. and Teasley, J. (1998). Recreation trips to Wilderness. *International Journal of Wilderness, 4*(1), 23–27.

Costanza, R., D'Arge, R., de Groot, R., Farber, S. Grasso, M., Hannon, B., et al. (1997). The value of the world's ecosystem services and natural capital. *Nature, 387,* 253–260.

Diamond, P.A., Hausman, J.A., Leonard, G.K., and Denning, M.A. (1993). Does contingent valuation measure preferences? Experimental evidence. In J.A. Hausman (Ed.), *Contingent valuation a critical assessment* (pp. 41–89). Amsterdam, NY: North-Holland.

Englin, J. and Shonkwiler, J. (1995). Estimating social welfare using count data models. *Review of Economics and Statistics, 77*(1), 105–112.

English, D.B.K., Kocis, S.M., Zarnoch, S.J., and Arnold, J.R. (2002). *Forest Service National Visitor Use Monitoring Process: Research method documentation* (GTR-SRS-57). Asheville, NC: USDA Forest Service, Southern Research Station.

Freeman, A.M., III. (1994). *The measurement of environmental and resource values: Theory and methods.* Washington, DC: Resources for the Future.

Friese, G., Hendee, J.C., and Kinziger, M. (1998). *The wilderness experience program industry in the United States: Characteristics and dynamics.* Unpublished manuscript, University of Idaho Wilderness Research Center at Moscow.

Gilbert, A., Glass, R., and More, R. (1992). Valuation of eastern wilderness: Extra-market measures of public support. In C. Payne, J. Bowker, and P. Reed (Comps.), *Economic value of wilderness* (pp. 57–70; GTR-SE-78). Athens, GA: USDA Forest Service, Southeastern Experiment Station.

Halstead, J., Lindsay, B.E., and Brown, C.M. (1991). Use of the TOBIT model in contingent valuation: experimental evidence from Pemigewasset Wilderness Area. *Journal of Environmental Management, 33,* 79–89.

Hellerstein, D.M. (1991). Using count data models in travel cost analysis with aggregate data. *American Journal of Agricultural Economics, 73*(3), 860–866.

Keith, J., Fawson, C., and Johnson, V. (1996). Preservation or use: A contingent valuation study of wilderness designation in Utah. *Ecological Economics, 18*(3), 207–214.

Krutilla, J. (1967). Conservation reconsidered. *The American Economic Review, 57,* 777–786.

Leuschner, W.A., Cook, P.S., Roggenbuck, J.W., and Oderwald, R.G. (1987). A comparative analysis for wilderness user fee policy. *Journal of Leisure Research, 19*(2), 101–114.

Loomis, J.B. (1993). *Integrated public lands management: Principles and applications to National Forests, Parks, Wildlife Refuges, and BLM Lands.* New York, NY: Columbia University Press.

Loomis, J.B. (1999). Do additional designations of wilderness result in increases in recreation use? *Society and Natural Resources, 12,* 481–491.

Loomis, J.B. and Richardson, R. (2000). *Economic values of protecting roadless areas in the United States.* Retrieved on February 1, 2005, from http://www.wilderness. org/Library/Roadless.cfm

Loomis, J.B. and Walsh, R.G. (1997). *Recreation economic decisions: Comparing benefits and costs* (2nd ed.). State College, PA: Venture Publishing, Inc.

McClaran, M.P. and Cole, D.N. (1993). *Pack-stock in wilderness: Use, impact, monitoring and management* (GTR-INT-301). Ogden, UT: USDA Forest Service, Intermountain Research Station.

McCloskey, M. (1990). Evolving perspectives on wilderness values: Putting wilderness values in order. In P.C. Reed (Comp), *Preparing to manage wilderness in the 21st century: Proceedings of the conference* (pp. 13–18; GTR-SE-66). Asheville, NC: USDA Forest Service, Southeastern Forest Experiment Station.

McCollum, D.W., Peterson, G.L., Arnold, J.R., Markstrom, D.C., and Hellerstein, D.M. (1990). *The net economic value of recreation on the National Forests: Twelve types of primary activity trips across nine Forest Service Regions* (RM-RP-289). Fort Collins, CO: USDA Forest Service, Rocky Mountain Forest and Range Experiment Station.

McFadden, D. (1994). Contingent valuation and social choice. *American Journal of Agricultural Economics, 76*(4), 689–708.

Morton, P. (1999). The economic benefits of wilderness: Theory and practice. *Denver Law Review, 76*(2), 465–518.

Penson, J.B. and Lins, D.A. (1980). *Agricultural finance: An introduction to micro and macro concepts.* Englewood Cliffs, NJ: Prentice Hall.

Phillips, S. (2000). Windfalls for wilderness: Land protection and land value in the Green Mountains. In S.F. McCool, D.N. Cole, W.T. Borrie, and J. O'Loughlin (Comps), *Wilderness science in a time of change-volume 2: Wilderness within the context of larger systems; 1999 May 23–27; Missoula MT.* (RMRS-P-15-VOL2). Ogden, UT: USDA Forest Service, Rocky Mountain Research Station.

Pope, C.A. and Jones, J. (1990). Value of wilderness designation in Utah. *Journal of Environmental Management, 30,* 157–174.

Prince, R. and Ahmed, E. (1988). Estimating individual recreation benefits under congestion and uncertainty. *Journal of Leisure Research, 20*(4), 61–76.

Richer, J.R. and Christensen, N.A. (1999). Appropriate fees for wilderness day use: Pricing decisions for recreation on public land. *Journal of Leisure Research, 31*(3), 269–280.

Russell, K., Hendee, J.C., and Cooke, S.C. (1998). Social and economic benefits of a wilderness experience program for youth at risk in Federal Job Corps. *International Journal of Wilderness, 4*(3), 32–38.

Smith, V.K. and Kopp, R. (1980). The spatial limits of the travel cost recreational demand model. *Land Economics, 56*(1), 64–72.

U.S. Census Bureau. (2003). *2000 Census.* Retrieved February 1, 2005, from http://www.census.gov

Walsh, R.G. and Gilliam, L.O. (1982). Benefits of wilderness expansion with excess demand for Indian Peaks. *Western Journal of Agricultural Economics, 7*(1), 1–12.

Walsh, R.G., Loomis, J.B., and Gillman, R.A. (1984). Valuing option, existence and bequest demands for wilderness. *Land Economics, 60,* 14–29.

Walsh, R.G., Peterson, G.L., and McKean, J.R. (1989). Distribution and efficiency effects of alternative recreation funding methods. *Journal of Leisure Research, 21*(4), 327–347.

Chapter 10
Impacts of Wilderness on Local Economic Development

Randall S. Rosenberger
Assistant Professor, Department of Forest Resources
Oregon State University, Corvallis, Oregon

Donald B. K. English
Visitor Use Monitoring Program Manager
USDA Forest Service, Washington, DC

As described in the Chapter 9, Morton (1999) identified seven categories of benefits comprising the total economic value of Wilderness: on-site recreation, community, scientific, off-site, biodiversity conservation, ecological services, and passive use benefits. Chapter 9 dealt with the economic value of on-site recreation and passive use benefits. This chapter will cover another of the seven categories—community benefits. Specifically, this chapter focuses on the effects of Wilderness on local and regional economies, in particular community-wide income, population, and employment levels. It presents a review of research regarding the role of Wilderness in the structure and function of local and regional economies. The chapter begins this review by discussing the structure and function of local economies as they pertain to land-use decisions, such as Wilderness designation. It then discusses available research evidence regarding how the existence of designated Wilderness in and near local areas affects the growth and stabililty of local economies. Another very good review of empirical evidence is provided by Rudzitis and Johnson (2000) in proceedings from the Wilderness Science in a Time of Change Conference held in Missoula, Montana, from May 23–27, 1999.

There are two primary arguments regarding the role of federally designated Wilderness on the well-being of local economies—one negative and one positive. Both of these arguments are being investigated within the scientific community; there is no general agreement on which is correct. The negative argument states that Wilderness designation suppresses economic growth and development (Power, 1996a). This negative view is based on two related assumptions:

1. Wilderness designation is criticized as prohibiting the ongoing expansion of an area's economic base by locking up natural resources that are central to local, basic industries. Thus, in that direct sense, Wilderness impoverishes an area and constrains its economic development.

2. Wilderness designation is criticized as being done primarily to provide free recreational opportunities to a relatively small number of primitive backcountry users. Thus, the gain to this tiny minority, given all the backcountry already available, is tiny, while the economic losses to the majority are substantial. So, the argument goes that this type of land management can only make the population collectively poorer. (Power, 1996a, p. 4)

For the most part, the empirical evidence reviewed for this chapter does not support these claims of economic suppression at a macrolevel. In specific instances the negative argument may very well be true, but in general it appears to be false. This does not mean, however, that the positive argument put forth by Wilderness advocates is generally correct. Thus, we must also investigate whether the proponents' position as summarized here is true:

Local economies with designated Wilderness near them have a comparative advantage over other local economies that are not near Wilderness. Distinct advantages of "Wilderness" economies over similar economies without Wilderness are their ability to keep pace with the general trends in the U.S. economy and provide residents with higher quality of life. Wilderness supplies amenities such as clean air, clean water, and untrammeled open space. These amenities draw people and service-sector jobs, thus fueling economic growth.

The burden of proof still remains as to whether Wilderness designation has a positive effect on the health and well-being of local economies. As this chapter reviews the empirical evidence on the effects of Wilderness on local economies, it will keep both the positive and negative economic arguments in mind.

Wilderness is a specific type of land use, as described previously. It is one primarily of limiting human uses in favor of preserving natural systems, processes, structures, and functions. These Wilderness functions, in turn, provide valued services. Some of these services emerge as social and economic benefits. However, at an aggregate level, the protection of natural areas as Wilderness may change and/or enhance the structure and function of local economies.

In evaluating the relationship between Wilderness and local economies, it is helpful to present a brief background on some concepts and terms related to economic structure and growth. The simplest characterization of an economy is to divide it into basic and nonbasic sectors. *Basic sectors* are those that respond to business forces and demands outside the local economy. These businesses export goods and services to other places, thereby bringing in outside money that is added to the flow of business within the local area. *Nonbasic sectors* are those that serve only the needs of the local area and depend on local conditions.

In traditional economic thought, having a large and diverse economic base is desirable. With a large and diverse base, the likelihood that all sources of the external demand for local products will suffer a simultaneous downturn is small. Thus, a diverse local base of industry provides greater stability for workers in the local community. A community that lacks a diverse economic base has no means of pulling itself out of a slump. If all demand for local products is local, a single event (e.g., flood, drought, fire) could eliminate all of them.

Most extractive industries are considered basic industries. Extractive industries usually produce raw materials (e.g., ore, timber, oil), although some level of initial processing may be done locally. The demand for these raw materials is directly linked to the demand for the final products. Almost always, the need for those final products comes from firms and households outside that local economy. With most of the demand coming from outside, typically there is not enough local demand in a small rural economy to support an extractive industry.

Although it occurs in a different way than with raw natural materials, recreation and tourism are typically considered basic industries. Economic activity is generated by the money visitors spend in the course of their recreation visit to a local area. Recreation visits are actually what is "exported," but in this case exportation means a visit into the local area by a tourist from outside. That part of the recreation and tourism industry economists consider as a basic industry is limited to business generated only by tourists from outside the local area. Implicitly, it is assumed that if the recreation and tourism opportunities these outside people visit were not available, they would spend their money similarly in some other location. However, it is at the same time assumed that local people would still spend the same amount of dollars in their local area, whether or not the particular opportunities they typically took advantage of were available. Thus, the recreation opportunities in the local area only generate "new" money and thus economic growth when it is derived from visitors from outside the local area (i.e., nonresidents).

To evaluate the full effect of money spent in a local area by nonresidents, one needs a model of how businesses and households purchase from one another and thus stimulate production of goods and services. For example, assume that nonresident visitors spend $50,000 in local restaurants in a year. This is a *direct* effect of tourism on the economy. Let's say that $20,000 of that $50,000 is paid in wages to restaurant workers and as profits to restaurant owners. Let's say further that $30,000 goes to purchase flour, vegetables, meats, and other foodstuffs and supplies that restaurants prepare into meals. If two thirds of the foodstuffs are purchased from farmers outside the region, then two thirds of that $30,000 (i.e., $20,000) "leaks" immediately out of the local economy without benefiting anyone inside it. However, the other $10,000 represents a first round *indirect* effect of tourism spending in the form of increased demand for local agricultural goods. These indirect effects are just one step removed from the direct spending by visitors. Local farmers, then, keep some of this $10,000 as income, but also must spend some of it to buy more seed and fertilizer to meet this level of demand. Whatever they purchase locally would be a second-round indirect effect.

Farmers, restaurant owners, and restaurant workers all have increased income stemming from visitor spending in restaurants. They and their households in turn will spend a portion of that income on goods and services produced locally, perhaps including clothing and yet more restaurant meals. This spending by local resident households has been *induced* by visitor spending and is rightly counted as part of the total effect of the spending by nonresident visitors.

The indirect and induced effects show how direct effects ripple through the local economy. A formal model of local economic structure allows us to estimate the total indirect and induced rippling effects for various types of direct effects. One type of model used in evaluating the role of recreation-related spending is an input-output (I-O) model, which is a linear mathematical characterization of the links between businesses and households. A detailed description of the mathematics of I-O models can be found in Miller and Blair (1985).

Economic Impacts of Visitor Spending

There is very little in the way of published literature that has examined the direct economic contribution from recreation in Wilderness areas. Keith and Fawson (1995) examined Wilderness recreation as a possible engine for economic growth in three rural Utah counties. Their study found that on average, visitors to four different Wilderness areas spent between $30 and $40 per person per day in businesses near the Wilderness areas. These spending amounts were $25 to $35 less per day than what was spent in association with visits to other types of recreation areas in Utah. As with most recreation visitors, the bulk of spending was for lodging (e.g., hotels, camping), food (e.g., groceries, restaurants), gasoline, recreation services, and gifts or souvenirs. The average number of days per visit varied across Wilderness areas studied from a low of 2.6 to a high of almost 4.5. Based on estimates of numbers of visits per Wilderness area overall, ranging from a few hundred to a high of about 7,000, Keith and Fawson (1995) estimated that Wilderness recreation accounted for between 0.5 percent and 1.5 percent of all expenditures in those three Utah counties. Their conclusion was that "expanding or contracting Wilderness areas in these counties would not be expected to increase or decrease the gross economic activity in the county by a significant amount" (p. 311).

In a study of out-of-state visitors to Montana, Moisey and Yuan (1992) examined the jobs and income generated by visitors engaging in three primary wildland activities: backpacking, angling, and nature study. Their data indicated that spending per person per day ranged from about $32 to $40. The average length of visit to Montana across visits where one of these three primary activities was the primary purpose for the visit was slightly less than eight days. It is important to note that this study did not specifically target visitors to Wilderness. All visitors to Montana who engaged in one or more of these three activities were included in the study.

The spending profiles identified in these two studies were used in estimating the job and income benefits of Wilderness recreation to Mono and Inyo counties in California (Richardson, 2002). The studies included visitation to all Wilderness located in these two counties, as well as to other natural areas that included Forest Service roadless areas, Bureau of Land Management Wilderness Study Areas, and several National Parks. Reported results indicated that visitation to this set of natural areas accounted for about 15 percent of all jobs in the two-county area, and about 12 percent of income earned by workers and business owners. Visitation to National Forest Wilderness made up about one fifth of the overall reported visitation, so that Wilderness could be expected to account for about the same proportion of overall economic activity.

A few other studies of visitor spending provided relevant information for identifying the spending patterns of Wilderness visitors. Most notably, Dr. Daniel Stynes at Michigan State University has developed spending profiles for visitors to several national parks which contain large amounts of Wilderness. Unfortunately, in all of these cases, the vast majority of park visitors do not visit the Wilderness portion of those parks. Thus, it is unlikely that these profiles are good representations of Wilderness visitors and their spending patterns during recreation visits to the parks. For this reason, we do not include those results here.

There is limited information regarding the economic impacts of Wilderness visitation. Therefore, we caution against extrapolating this information to the full spectrum of Wilderness areas. The average length of visit reported in the literature reviewed for this chapter was several days. Results from the Forest Service's ongoing National Visitor Use Monitoring program indicates that over 60 percent of visits to Forest Service Wilderness last less than 6 hours, and only about one quarter are over 24 hours (Figure 10.1; USDA Forest Service, 2002). Therefore, it appears that the studies reviewed were conducted in Wilderness areas where the proportions of overnight visitors were higher than normal. Since overnight visits entail significantly higher spending per day

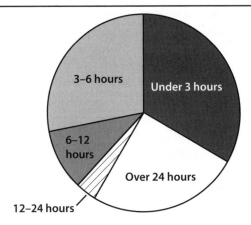

Source: USDA Forest Service (2000, 2001)

Figure 10.1 Distribution on Forest Service Wilderness visits by visit duration (in hours)

than do day visits, the overall average spending per visit would be noticeably lower than reported in the reviewed studies. However, it is important to note that spending patterns for Wilderness visitors are not more than, and are often less than, spending by other recreation visitors.

Ultimately, what limits the contribution of Wilderness to economic growth and development is relatively low levels of visitation, especially by nonlocal visitors. For Forest Service Wilderness, the current estimated number of recreation visits is about 12.7 million (USDA Forest Service, 2002). Slightly more than half (54%) of the total visits to Wilderness comes from people who live within 35 miles. These visitors would be considered local for economic impact analyses. The proportions of visitors who are local are greater in regions with high visitation (over 70% in the Southwestern Region) and smaller in regions with less Wilderness visitation (only about 20% of visits in the Northern Region are from locals). While there may be a few local economies in which Wilderness visitation plays a large role in overall economic structure, for most areas, the volume of nonlocal visitors and their spending is insufficient to have a major effect.

Trends in Rural Areas with Wilderness

Given that the majority of Wilderness visits are from local people and that Wilderness areas provide a variety of benefits to the local population (Morton, 1999), how are local areas where Wilderness is located doing relative to others where there is no Wilderness? If Wilderness enhances the economic growth of rural areas, then we should be able to observe greater economic well-being in counties which include or have nearby Wilderness (Lorah & Southwick, 2003). Power (1996b) notes there are five objective measures of economic growth: (1) increased dollar volume of business activity, (2) increased total income, (3) increased per capita income, (4) increased employment, and (5) increased population.

Employment in the United States has moved away from dependence on resource extraction and primary production (i.e., the "old economy") to one of services and information technology (i.e., the "new economy"). The service sector began to dominate the U.S. economy in 1976. However, resource extraction–dependent communities are typically located in rural areas. Figure 10.2 (p. 188) shows that in nonmetropolitan counties, the services sector did not dominate until 1982. These trends are a compelling force behind Power's (1996a, 1996b, 1996c) recommendation that public economic policy be guided by looking forward through trends that hint at what lies ahead, and not be guided by looking back through the "rearview mirror." A local economy that has historically been based on commodity export and resource extraction may not and perhaps sometimes should not continue on that basis. General economic trends are permeating all areas of the United States, rural as well as urban areas. Given these trends, rural areas that have protected natural lands, such as Wilderness, may have a comparative advantage over other rural areas that do not have these natural amenities

The primary question this chapter will try to answer is what role, if any, did Wilderness play in rural county transition from the "old economy" to the "new economy." Rasker (1994) identified three forces shaping the world economy in general, and the U.S. economy in particular:

> First, the industrial economy is becoming uncoupled from the primary products economy (i.e., raw materials). Many of the most valuable "products" in today's economy, like computer software and medical technology, require few raw materials. Second, within the industrial economy itself, employment has become uncoupled from production.

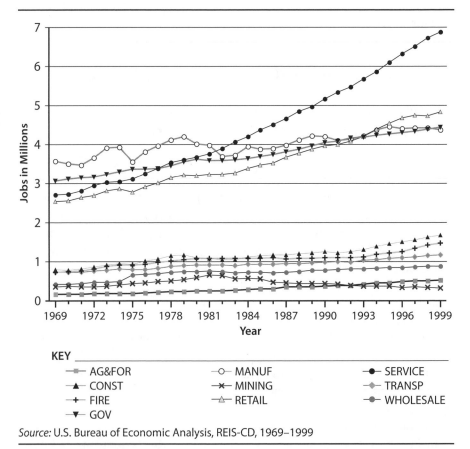

KEY

—■— AG&FOR	—○— MANUF	—●— SERVICE
—▲— CONST	—✕— MINING	—◆— TRANSP
—+— FIRE	—△— RETAIL	—●— WHOLESALE
—▼— GOV		

Source: U.S. Bureau of Economic Analysis, REIS-CD, 1969–1999

Figure 10.2 Total employment in nonmetropolitan counties by economic sector, 1969–1999

Manufacturing efficiency has decreased the demand for physical labor. Instead, human resources are increasingly applied in research, design, engineering, finance, marketing, and other "knowledge-based" or "value-added" applications. Third, capital has become "footloose"—money follows good ideas, no matter where they occur on the globe. (p. 37)

As the U.S. economy moves away from resource extraction and primary production, what will the future hold for rural economies whose past history was dominated by resource extraction and manufacturing?

Indications of a Wilderness-Related Advantage

Several studies have investigated the role of Wilderness in the transition of rural counties, especially in the western United States. We have appended more recent measures where appropriate and when data were available. Rudzitis (1996) found that rural counties near Wilderness areas and national parks in the Pacific Northwest were among the fastest growing in the nation (Table 10.1). As an example of potential growth rates, Rudzitis and Johansen (1989, 1991) calculated the percentage change in population for selected counties containing or very near Wilderness areas (Table 10.2, p. 190). In a recent study of the effect of Wilderness in the eastern United States, Rosenberger, English, and Sperow (2004a) also found evidence that counties with Wilderness grew at a faster pace (36%) than metropolitan counties (20%) or nonmetropolitan counties without Wilderness (25%) from 1969 to 2000.

It is not just population that is growing at a faster pace in counties that are near Wilderness resources. As Lorah and Southwick (2000) have shown, employment and income are also growing at faster rates in western counties with protected federal lands such as Wilderness, national parks, and national monuments (Table 10.3, p. 190). Evidence from the eastern United States was similar, with the per capita income growth rate (in constant dollars) being 77

Table 10.1 Percent change in county population, Pacific Northwest

Year	Metropolitan	All Nonmetropolitan	Nonmetropolitan, Wilderness	Nonmetropolitan, National Parks
1960–1970	17.1	4.3	12.8	24.6
1970–1980	10.6	14.3	31.4	34.2
1980–1990	11.6	3.9	24.0	26.0
1990–2000	17.3	8.7	18.3	13.4

Adapted and updated from Rudzitis (1996) as provided in Rudzitis and Johnson (2000)

percent and the employment growth rate being 75 percent from 1969 to 2000 for nonmetropolitan counties with Wilderness (both measures are greater than either their metropolitan or nonmetropolitan counties without Wilderness counterparts; Rosenberger, English & Sperow 2004a).

Lorah (2000) found a positive and statistically significant correspondence between the percent of land devoted to Wilderness protection and various economic development indicators that even exceeded the influence of nearby metropolitan counties (Table 10.4). This means that western rural counties with higher percentages of their land area designated as Wilderness grew faster than rural counties without Wilderness. The correspondence between protected natural areas and economic growth for western rural counties only becomes stronger if other types of protected areas (i.e., national parks, national monuments and Wilderness study areas) are taken into account (Lorah, 2000). Lorah and Southwick (2003) measured federal protected lands within a 50-mile buffer of county centers and showed similar results for correlations between the amount of protected federal lands generally and indicators of economic

Table 10.2 Percent change in population for sampled Wilderness counties

State	County	1970–1980	1980–1990	1990–2000
Arizona	Coconino	55.12	28.5	20.1
California	Lassen	28.96	26.6	22.1
California	Trinity	55.71	9.2	−0.3
Colorado	Eagle	77.64	65.3	87.9
Georgia	Charlton	29.27	15.6	20.6
Idaho	Valley	55.41	8.6	24.4
Missouri	Stone	57.11	22.6	49.6
Montana	Lake	31.89	10.2	26.6
New Mexico	Lincoln	45.46	11.0	59.3
Oregon	Deschutes	104.00	21.9	53.3
Wyoming	Teton	93.96	19.4	61.8

Adapted and updated from Rudzitis and Johansen (1989) and Rudzitis and Johansen (1991)

Table 10.3 Employment and income growth rates for western counties

Counties Containing:	Number of Counties	Employment Growth 1969–1997 (%)	Income Growth 1969–1997 (%)
No federal lands	13	63.5	755.9
Any federal lands	401	142.7	992.5
Federal multiple-use lands	172	115.6	864.5
Federal multiple-use lands and protected lands	230	163.3	1,089.7
More protected lands than multiple-use lands	13	197.3	1,109.2

Source: Lorah and Southwick (2000). Multiple-use lands are lands open to multiple uses whereas protected lands include Wilderness areas, national parks, and national monuments.

growth for nonmetropolitan western counties (Table 10.5). Similarly, Rosen-berger, English, and Sperow (2004a) found statistically significant and positive correlations between acres of Wilderness and population, employment and per capita income growth rates for nonmetropolitan counties in Appalachia (Table 10.6, p. 192). The *t* tests were also used to determine whether growth rates for nonmetropolitan counties with Wilderness versus those without Wilderness were statistically different. In all cases, counties with Wilderness had larger growth rates for population, employment and per capita income than counties without Wilderness in Appalachia (Table 10.6).

Another indicator that economic bases are shifting from dependence on resource extraction and primary production is a shift in sources of income from labor to nonlabor (Power 1996c). Nonlabor income consists of government transfer payments, retirement income, and income earned from past investments (i.e., dividends, interest and real estate [DIRE]). Power (1996c) estimated a cumulative growth impact of 23.5 percent on local economies from a 10 per-cent net in-migration of new residents.

Rasker (1994) noted that nonlabor income constituted 35 percent of the personal income in the Greater Yellowstone Ecosystem, which is more than two and one-half times greater than the income derived from mining, timber harvesting, and agriculture in that area combined. Lorah (2000) investigated

Table 10.4 Correlation of percentage of Wilderness in Western rural counties and their economic development indicators

	Employment Growth	Per Capita Income Growth	Total Income Growth	Population Growth
All rural counties (n = 113)	0.382	0.253	0.341	0.337
Rural counties not adjacent to metropolitan areas (n = 83)	0.443	0.289	0.406	0.453

Source: Lorah (2000); Results statistically significant at the 0.01 level or better.

Table 10.5 Correlation of percentage of Federal protected lands within a 50-mile buffer and economic growth, nonmetropolitan western counties

	Population Growth 1970–1990	Employment Growth 1969–1999	Income Growth 1969–1999	Per Capita Income Growth 1969–1999
Nonmetropolitan counties (n = 320)	0.24	0.26	0.26	0.22
Nonmetropolitan counties not adjacent to metropolitan counties (n = 111)	0.33	0.30	0.30	0.19

Source: Lorah and Southwick (2003); Results statistically significant at the 0.01 level or better.

the transition period for western rural counties as they shifted from extraction and primary production sources of income to nonlabor sources of income. The transition date was defined as the year nonlabor income exceeded extraction and agriculture as primary sources of income for rural counties. Lorah (2000) found three types of counties within his study period of 1969 to 1999: (a) a core group of rural counties that were already dominated by nonlabor income in 1969 and remained as such, (b) counties in transition from extraction to nonlabor sources of income, and (c) counties that remained dominated by extraction sources of income. Conducting a correlation analysis based on the date of transition and the percent of a county's land base in Wilderness showed that counties with Wilderness made a transition away from extraction dependence at an earlier date, and that the more Wilderness within a county the earlier the transition date (Table 10.7).

The empirical evidence discussed so far illustrates that economies near Wilderness are growing faster in several dimensions and that they transition away from raw materials and primary production sooner than other counties without Wilderness. The following section examines likely explanations for why counties with Wilderness seem to have a comparative economic advantage over counties without Wilderness.

Table 10.6 Correlation and *t* tests of economic development indicators between nonmetropolitan counties with and without Wilderness in the Appalachian Region

Correlation of Wilderness acres and:	Population Growth	Employment Growth	Per Capita Income Growth
All nonmetropolitan counties (n=366)	0.166	0.187	0.138
	t tests of average rates per:		
Nonmetropolitan counties without Wilderness (n=297)	34	76	74
Nonmetropolitan counties with Wilderness (n=69)	43	97	80
t statistic	1.49	1.96	1.58
Significance level	0.07	0.03	0.06

Source: Rosenberger, English and Sperow (2004a)

Table 10.7 Correlation of percentage of Wilderness in western rural counties and date of transition to nonlabor sources of income, 1969–1996

	Transition Date
All rural counties (n=113)	−0.348
Rural counties not adjacent to metropolitan areas (n=83)	−0.421

Source: Lorah (2000)

Wilderness and Migration

One likely explanation for greater growth in counties with Wilderness is called amenity migration. *Amenity migration* is the movement of people to areas of the country where there are significant natural amenities, often associated with public lands (Deller, Tsai, Marcouiller & English, 2001; Kusmin, Redman & Sears, 1996; Marcouiller & Deller, 1996; McGranahan, 1999; Vias, 1999). The uncoupling of the economy from heavy dependence on primary production industries and physical labor as a major source of employment has meant that both people and businesses can be more selective in where they choose to work and live than in the past (Rasker, 1994). What motivates people and businesses to migrate?

Rudzitis and Johnson (2000) provide a brief history of research and discussions concerning why people and businesses have begun to move in increasing numbers to rural areas. The traditional models and explanations for migration and growth failed to explain why rural areas were outpacing urban areas in job and income growth during the last three decades. Part of the explanation widely accepted is as identified previously; that is, the new economy enabled people to choose where they wanted to live. Dissatisfaction with urban life and associated crime, pollution, and crowding pushed people with the ability to move. Since World War II, amenities and other location-specific attributes have become important predictors of where displaced urban residents migrated. Not only did people move to warmer climates but also they sought out rural lifestyles and places near scenic landscapes (Rudzitis & Johnson, 2000; Vias, 1999). Highly trained and skilled people especially were able to take advantage of improved communications and to relocate to areas high in natural amenities (Beale & Johnson, 1998; English, Marcouiller & Cordell, 2000; McGranahan, 1999). Why was some of this relocation toward rural counties in general and counties having Wilderness areas in particular?

Part of the answer to this question is found in what people prefer and value. In-migration and willingness to stay in an area is found to be strongly tied to the benefits of environmental quality, diversity, and availability the area offers (Rudzitis, 1993). Thus, understanding the benefits people perceive they receive by living in a place is important in understanding their migration decisions. Schuster, Tarrant, and Watson (Chapter 7) provide evidence of the social benefits people perceive they receive by living near and using Wilderness. Bowker and colleagues (Chapter 9) provide evidence of the economic worth of the different benefits people associate with visiting areas with Wilderness. All of these benefits can be motives for moving to an area. In studies investigating why people had moved into counties with Wilderness areas (Rudzitis & Johansen, 1991; Rudzitis, 1996, 1999), both "push" and "pull" factors were identified. The push factors were those associated with dissatisfaction with one's previous place of residence, such as the pace of life, low environmental quality, high crime rate, and harsh climate (Table 10.8). The pull factors were those associated with the importance of various county attributes in drawing people to a new place of residence. Pull factors in counties with Wilderness areas included scenery, high environmental quality, pace of life, low crime rate, and moderate climate (Table 10.8). Employment opportunities were of relatively low importance in people's decisions to migrate. The most important factors affecting people's decisions to migrate were social and environmental amenities.

In fact, over 50 percent of the respondents to the Rudzitis and Johansen (1991) study stated that the presence of Wilderness near a place was an important reason why they moved there. Table 10.9 shows more results from Rudzitis and Johansen's (1991) national survey. A majority of respondents agreed that nearby Wilderness areas were important to the county and an important reason why they moved there or stayed in place, and disagreed that these areas should

Table 10.8 Dissatisfaction with previous location and importance of attributes of Wilderness county in decision to move (percent selecting)

	Push		Pull	
	Dissatisfied	Not Dissatisfied	Important	Not Important
Employment opportunity	16	67	30	56
Cost of living	14	64	14	58
Climate	22	57	47	28
Social services	7	85	10	69
Family access	11	76	19	64
Outdoor recreation	18	63	59	20
Crime rate	28	48	31	45
Scenery	20	62	72	13
Pace of life	31	47	62	18
Environmental quality	30	46	65	16

Source: Rudzitis (1999) as reported in Rudzitis and Johnson (2000)

Table 10.9 Percent agreeing or disagreeing with wilderness statement, national survey

Statement	Agree	Disagree	No Opinion
Nearby wilderness areas are important to county	81	10	9
Wilderness important reason why move or stay	53	26	22
There should be more access to wilderness	43	36	21
Additional wilderness should be designated nearby	39	35	26
Wilderness areas should be opened for mineral and energy development	22	65	13

Source: Rudzitis and Johansen (1991)

be opened for mineral and energy development. There was no consensus among respondents whether more access to Wilderness should be developed or whether additional Wilderness should be designated. A 1986 University of Utah study found that 78 percent of respondents agreed with the statement that Wilderness designation enhances the image of Utah as a tourist state, with about 13 percent disagreeing with this statement (Snyder, Fawson, Godfrey, Keith & Lileholm, 1995). In the same study, 25 percent of respondents agreed with the statement that Wilderness designation results in negative economic and social impacts to nearby communities, while the majority (55%) disagreed with the statement (Snyder, Fawson, Godfrey, Keith & Lileholm, 1995).

In another study, Johnson and Rasker (1995) surveyed local business owners within the Greater Yellowstone Ecosystem boundary. They had business owners rate several factors as to their importance for locating their businesses. Amongst the various factors business owners rated, scenic beauty and environmental quality ranked highest, with most economic factors ranking at the bottom of the list (Table 10.10). Amenity factors were identified as the most important factors in business location decisions over the traditional economic factors.

Table 10.10 Overall results regarding business location values by business owners in the Greater Yellowstone Ecosystem ($n = 43$)

	Mean Response (1 = Not Important; 5 = Very Important)	
	Overall Score	Overall Rank
Economic Values		
Overall tax structure	1.91	15
Cost of doing business	2.46	14
Proximity to the university	2.71	13
Qualitative Values		
Quality environment	4.41	2
Scenic beauty	4.47	1
Proximity to public lands	3.78	10
Community Values		
Overall community attributes	3.34	12
Low crime rate	3.95	9
Small-town atmosphere	4.08	5
Desire to live in a rural setting	4.21	4
Good place to raise a family	4.25	3
Recreational Values		
Recreation opportunity in general	4.21	6
Summer-based recreation	4.15	7
Winter-based recreation	3.69	11
Wildlife-based recreation	3.90	8

Source: Johnson and Rasker (1995)

A concern with in-migrants into a rural area is the effect it can have on existing residents. New ideas, competition for jobs and local resources (e.g., land, housing, commodities), and crowding are just some of the potentially negative aspects associated with growth and change from an outside influence (Rasker & Glick, 1994). Rudzitis and Johansen's (1989) survey of six western counties focused on long-term residents and new migrants (i.e., moved to the area within ten years of survey date). They found that both residents and new migrants shared much of the same attitudes toward development (Table 10.11). Both groups strongly supported protecting the natural environment and promoting recreation and tourism as local industries. Both groups of respondents agreed that the business district should be developed, perhaps to better attract tourists and their spending. A small proportion of both groups of respondents agreed that county officials should try to keep new factories out. This may mean that respondents wanted to keep their options open.

Thus, the traditional model of rural economies that posited commodity-based export industries as the primary driver of growth and well-being may be false (Tiebout, 1956). A competing argument is that people will choose to move to areas high in natural and social amenities if they are willing and able to do so. This is a major theme in Power's (1996b) work. This new line of reasoning states that people will move to an area if their demand for its qualities are greater than what is being supplied at their current location (Roback, 1982). Amenity-based nonexport industries may provide a significant foundation for rural economies. In fact, the U.S. Bureau of Economic Analysis has developed Tourism Satellite Accounts that measure the contributions of tourism to local economies. Recreation and tourism is not a separate industry in the traditional accounting of jobs and income in local economies, but instead crosses many of the existing accounting classifications. For example, some agricultural operations have included agritourism ventures, mining operations that offer tours, and multiuse management that includes guided hunting and fishing opportunities.

English, Marcouiller, and Cordell (2000) developed a method to identify tourism-dependent economies in rural areas and to measure jobs and income

Table 10.11 Attitudes toward development in six western counties (percent agreeing)

Should County Officials…	New Migrants	Residents
Keep environment in its natural state	90	85
Attract tourists and promote recreation	89	85
Develop the business district	82	82
Attract new residents to area	59	54
Keep new factories out	34	26

Source: Rudzitis and Johansen (1989)

derived from tourism. They showed that tourism-dependent counties had significantly higher per capita income levels in 1990 and higher per capita income increases from 1980 to 1990 than similar counties not dependent on tourism. These findings challenged the myth that tourism supplants high-paying extraction and production jobs with seasonal, low-paying service jobs. Lorah and Southwick (2003) confirmed this result by showing that per capita income grew fastest in the 50 nonmetropolitan counties with the highest levels of protected lands in the intermountain west of the United States. As well, Power (1996c) illustrated how services and other nonresource extraction jobs are more stable than the boom-and-bust cycle of the extractive industries.

Although English, Marcouiller, and Cordell (2000) found that tourism-dependent counties were less diverse than their counterparts, they also found that the diversity of tourism-dependent counties was on the rise. The housing sector in tourism-dependent counties was greater than in other rural counties, potentially illustrating the higher demand from in-migrants for location benefits such as nearness to natural areas including Wilderness. From 1980 to 1990, they found tourism-dependent counties to have higher growth rates in the number of housing units than in other rural counties. And they also found that the economies in tourism-dependent counties were growing at faster rates than in other rural counties. This finding agrees with previous research that there very well may be a comparative advantage in rural areas that offer high levels of natural amenities. As English, Marcouiller, and Cordell (2000) note:

> Dependence on recreation and tourism in rural areas is clearly tied to proximity to certain types of natural resources, including beaches, large lakes, forests, and mountainous terrain. In areas where these resources are owned by public agencies, recreation and tourism seem to be especially important parts of the rural economy. (p. 198)

Wilderness in Amenity Migration Models

Growth equilibrium modeling is one line of research that can help to better understand migration from urban areas into rural areas, and to simultaneously explain employment and population changes for a region. These types of models capture the direct and indirect linkages between population, employment, and other exogenous factors important in explaining migration patterns. In their early applications, growth equilibrium models were used to address the debate over whether people follow jobs or jobs follow people (Carlino & Mills, 1987). At the root of this debate is a simultaneity problem similar to the question of which came first, the chicken or the egg? Did migration of businesses into rural America create jobs that people followed? Or did people move and businesses follow them?

Beginning with Roback (1982), the equilibrium modeling strategy was used to identify the direct and indirect linkages between population and employment migration and amenity factors (Knapp & Graves, 1989). Roback's (1982) application investigated the linkages between crime rates and urban migration. More recent applications included migration linkages with natural amenities such as climate and topography (Carlino & Mills, 1987; Clark & Murphy, 1996; Kusmin, Redman & Sears, 1996), Wilderness areas in the western United States (Duffy-Deno 1998), natural amenities and recreation supply (Deller, Tsai, Marcouiller & English, 2001), and forested public land in the northern United Staes (Lewis, Hunt & Plantinga, 2002). There is significant evidence that the answer to the "chicken or the egg first" question is that jobs follow people in rural America (Rudzitis, 1996; Vias, 1999).

Growth equilibrium modeling assumes that households tend to migrate in order to maximize their individual benefits, or to minimize their travel costs for access to valued amenities. Households migrate in search of higher utility or well-being from the goods and services they purchase, and the location of their residence relative to workplace and spatially distributed amenities, including Wilderness. Several factors that can influence a household's decision to migrate include fiscal, local, and amenity factors (Figure 10.3). Fiscal factors

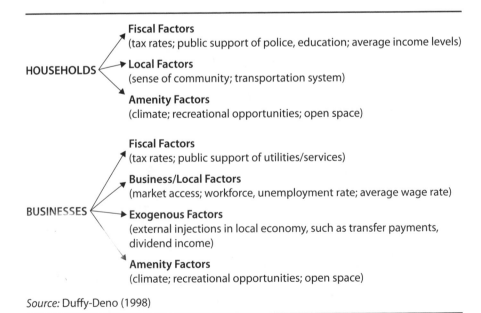

Source: Duffy-Deno (1998)

Figure 10.3 Factors associated with migration decisions, households, and businesses

that may affect household migration include lower per capita taxes, higher public expenditure on police and education, greater employment opportunities, and higher incomes. Local factors can include a strong sense of community and accessibility due to transportation infrastructure (e.g., highways, airports). Amenity factors that may affect household migration patterns include climate, topography, presence of open space and natural areas, recreation opportunities, and other quality of life factors such as lower crime rates and higher educational opportunities.

On the other side, growth equilibrium modeling assumes that businesses tend to migrate in order to minimize their costs and/or to maximize their individual benefits. Factors that influence business location decisions can be grouped into fiscal, business and local, amenity, and other exogenous characteristics of areas (Figure 10.3). Fiscal factors that may affect business migration patterns include various taxes and/or local incentive plans enticing businesses to locate in a specific locale. Business and local factors may include better access to markets, higher quantity and quality of local labor supply, lower labor costs, and lower utility costs. Amenity factors may include climate, access to natural and recreational areas, and landownership patterns. Other exogenous factors that may influence business location decisions include dividend income rates, local economic diversity, and other factors that can have multiplier effects on local economies.

The only published growth equilibrium modeling study that explicitly investigated the role of Wilderness was conducted by Duffy-Deno (1998). He looked at the geographic densities of population and employment in 1980 and 1990 for 250 nonmetropolitan counties in eight states in the intermountain west. He found no evidence that federal Wilderness was directly or indirectly associated with population density or employment density changes between 1980 and 1990 in the intermountain west. It is possible that the potential negative effects of Wilderness on employment in industries dependent on resource extraction (e.g., agriculture, mining) might be offset by the potential positive effects of Wilderness on employment in nonresource extractive industries (e.g., nature-based tourism). In a model that looked specifically at employment in resource extraction versus other nonfederal employment, he also found no empirical evidence that either type of employment sector was affected (positively or negatively) by the existence of Wilderness. As he concluded from his research: "…there is no statistical evidence of a negative relationship between federal Wilderness and county-level employment, [suggesting] that Wilderness designation may cause, on average, little aggregate economic harm to county economies" (1998, p. 133). In fact, other evidence suggests that Wilderness may enhance local economies that are not export, but are amenity-based (Deller, Tsai, Marcouiller & English, 2001; Lewis, Hunt & Plantinga, 2002; Rudzitis, 1996).

In a recent study, Rosenberger, English and Sperow (2004b) applied Duffy-Deno's (1998) growth equilibrium model to the Appalachian region of the eastern U.S. for the 1980 to 1990 period and 1990 to 2000 period. They looked at the geographic densities of population and employment for 374 nonmetropolitan counties of the 410-county, thirteen-state Appalachian region that extends from southern New York to northern Alabama. Unlike Duffy-Deno's (1998) results, they found that eastern Wilderness was positively and significantly associated with population densities in the 1980–1990 and 1990–2000 periods. Similar to Duffy-Deno (1998), they found no effect of Wilderness on employment densities in either the 1980–1990 or 1990–2000 period. No statistically significant effect on resource extraction employment density was found in both periods of analysis. Wilderness was significantly and positively associated with nonresource extractive employment for the 1980–1990 period, but not for the 1990–2000 period.

Conclusions/Discussion

This chapter reviewed the empirical evidence regarding the role Wilderness has played in determining the structure of rural economies. Generally, there are arguments indicating Wilderness enhances the structure and stability of nearby local economies, and there are arguments indicating Wilderness negatively effects the structure and stability of nearby local economies. Research has shown that having Wilderness within a county enhances the local economy somewhat by helping to capture recreation and tourism spending. However, the total volume of visitation to Wilderness and the associated spending by nonlocal visitors is usually insufficient to sustain any significant tourism industry by itself. Although the recreational use values for Wilderness are substantial for individual people (see Chapter 9), in aggregate, the number of Wilderness users is relatively small. These are reasons why the debate regarding the benefits of Wilderness preservation has shifted from direct-use to indirect-use, nonuse, and intrinsic values (Callicott & Nelson, 1998).

Economic growth in rural areas is increasingly being generated by the multiplier effects of consumer spending in the services and trades sectors. Growth triggered by a demand for export raw materials and commodities from rural industries is a thing of the past for much of rural America, although certain communities are still dependent upon resource-extraction and commodity production. Just as these export-based communities have a comparative advantage in being adjacent to resources of high-extraction value (e.g., timberlands, mineral deposits, water resources), so too are non–export-based communities at a comparative advantage due to their location near high natural amenity lands (e.g., Wilderness, beaches, publicly-owned natural areas).

The impacts on local economies from Wilderness protection are not universal and for any individual area may be positive, negative, or neutral. Mostly, the result depends on where the current structure of the community is and where that structure is trending. There are no discernible general patterns of negative effects. In fact, economic growth tends to be greater for nonmetropolitan counties that contain or are near publicly owned natural areas, including Wilderness. Counties that have Wilderness tend to have higher growth rates in population, income, and employment than their counterparts without Wilderness. This indicates that counties with Wilderness do have a comparative advantage over other nonmetropolitan counties across America.

However, tests that attempt to show a causal relationship between the designation of Wilderness and increases in economic growth usually fall short. Identifying a causal link is difficult given the multitude of factors potentially affecting economic growth in rural areas. The scientific evidence reviewed in this chapter suggests that Wilderness does not, in aggregate, negatively effect employment trends in either the eastern or western United States. No significant positive effect of Wilderness on population changes was found in the western United States for the 1980–1990 period, but a positive effect was found in both the 1980–1990 and 1990–2000 periods for eastern Wilderness. It seems that household decisions to migrate are significantly influenced by the quality of natural amenities (including Wilderness), among other things. Employment and business location decisions are, in turn, indirectly influenced by Wilderness as jobs follow people in the United States.

Literature Cited

Beale, C.L. and Johnson, K.M. (1998). The identification of recreational counties in nonmetropolitan areas of the U.S.A. *Population Research and Policy Review, 17,* 37–53.

Callicott, J.B. and Nelson, M.P. (Eds.). (1998). *The great new wilderness debate: An expansive collection of writings defining wilderness from John Muir to Gary Snyder.* Athens, GA: The University of Georgia Press.

Carlino, G.A. and Mills, E.S. (1987). The determinants of county growth. *Journal of Regional Science, 27*(1), 39–54.

Clark, D.E. and Murphy, C.A. (1996). Countywide employment and population growth: An analysis of the 1980s. *Journal of Regional Science, 36*(2), 235–256.

Deller, S.C., Tsai, T-H, Marcouiller, D.W., and English, D.B.K. (2001). The role of amenities and quality of life in rural economic growth. *American Journal of Agricultural Economics, 83*(2), 352–365.

Duffy-Deno, K.T. (1998). The effect of Federal wilderness on county growth in the Intermountain western United States. *Journal of Regional Science, 38*(1), 109–136.

English, D.B.K., Marcouiller, D.W., and Cordell, H.K. (2000). Tourism dependence in rural America: Estimates and effects. *Society & Natural Resources, 13*(3), 185–202.

Johnson, J.D. and Rasker, R. (1995). The role of economic and quality of life values in rural business location. *Journal of Rural Studies, 11*(4), 405–416.

Keith, J. and Fawson, C. (1995). Economic development in rural Utah: Is wilderness recreation the answer? *The Annals of Regional Science, 29,* 303–313.

Knapp, T.A. and Graves, P.E. (1989). On the role of amenities in models of migration and regional development. *Journal of Regional Science, 29*(1), 71–87.

Kusmin, L.D., Redman, J.M., and Sears, D.W. (1996). *Factors associated with rural economic growth: Lessons from the 1980s* (Tech. Bulletin 1850). Washington, DC: USDA Rural Economy Division, Economic Research Service.

Lewis, D.J., Hunt, G.L., and Plantinga, A.J. (2002). Public conservation land and employment growth in the Northern Forest Region. *Land Economics, 78*(2), 245–259.

Lorah, P. (2000). Population growth, economic security, and cultural change in wilderness counties. In S.F. McColl, D.N. Cole, W.T. Borrie, and J. O'Loughlin (Comps.), *Wilderness science in a time of change conference—Volume 2: Wilderness within the context of larger systems* (pp. 230–237). Ogden, UT: USDA Forest Service, Rocky Mountain Research Station.

Lorah, P. and Southwick, R. (2000). *Historical economic performance of Oregon and western counties associated with roadless and wilderness areas.* Retrieved August 5, 2004, from http://www.onrc.org/info/econstudy/onrceconstudy.pdf

Lorah, P. and Southwick, R. (2003). Environmental protection, population change, and economic development in the rural western United States. *Population and Environment, 24*(3), 255–272.

Marcouiller, D.W. and Deller, S.C. (1996). Natural resource stocks, flows, and regional economic change: Seeing the forest and the trees. *The Journal of Regional Analysis and Policy, 26*(2), 95–116.

McGranahan, D.A. (1999). *Natural amenities drive rural population change* (Agricultural Economic Report No. 781). Washington, DC: USDA Economic Research Service, Food and Rural Economics Division.

Miller, R.E. and Blair, P.D. (1985). *Input-output analysis: Foundations and extensions.* Englewood Cliffs, NJ: Prentice Hall.

Moisey, N. and Yuan, M.S. (1992). Economic significance and characteristics of select wildland-attracted visitors to Montana. In C. Payne, J.M. Bowker, and P.C. Reed (Comp), *The economic value of Wilderness* (General Technical Report SE-78). Asheville, NC: USDA Forest Service, Southeastern Forest Experiment Station.

Morton, P. (1999). The economic benefits of wilderness: Theory and practice. *Denver Law Review, 76*(2), 465–518.

Power, T.M. (1996a). Wilderness economics must look through the windshield, not the rearview mirror. *International Journal of Wilderness, 2*(1), 4–13.

Power, T.M. (1996b). *Environmental protection and economic well-being: The economic pursuit of quality* (2nd ed.). Armonk, NY: M.E. Sharpe.

Power, T.M. (1996c). *Lost landscapes and failed economies: The search for a value of place.* Washington, DC: Island Press.

Rasker, R. (1994). A new look at old vistas: The economic role of environmental quality in western public lands. *University of Colorado Law Review, 65*(2), 369–399.

Rasker, R. and Glick, D. (1994). Footloose entrepreneurs: Pioneers of the new west? *Illahee, 10*(1), 34–43.

Richardson, R.B. (2002). *The economic benefits of wildlands in the eastern Sierra Nevada region of California.* San Francisco, CA: The Wilderness Society.

Roback, J. (1982). Wages, rents, and the quality of life. *Journal of Political Economy, 90,* 1257–1278.

Rosenberger, R.S., English, D.B.K., and Sperow, M. (2004a). *Correlation tests, T-tests and trend analyses* (2nd Quarterly Progress Report; Cooperative Agreement #SRS-01-CA-11330144-397; SRS-4901). Athens, GA: USDA Forest Service, Southern Research Station.

Rosenberger, R.S., English, D.B.K., and Sperow, M. (2004b). *Growth Equilibrium Modeling of Wilderness Effects in Appalachia* (3rd Quarterly Progress Report; Cooperative Agreement #SRS-01-CA-11330144-397; SRS-4901). Athens, GA: USDA Forest Service, Southern Research Station.

Rudzitis, G. (1993). Nonmetropolitan geography: Migration, sense of place, and the American west. *Urban Geography, 14*(6), 574–484.

Rudzitis, G. (1996). *Wilderness and the changing American West.* New York, NY: John Wiley & Sons.

Rudzitis, G. (1999). Amenities increasingly draw people to the rural west. *Rural Development Perspectives, 14*(2), 9–13.

Rudzitis, G. and Johansen, H.E. (1989). Migration into western wilderness counties: Causes and consequences. *Western Wildlands, 15*(1), 19–23.

Rudzitis, G. and Johansen, H.E. (1991). How important is wilderness? Results from a United States survey. *Environmental Management, 15*(2), 227–233.

Rudzitis, G. and Johnson, R. (2000). The impact of wilderness and other wildlands on local economies and regional development trends. In S.F. McCool, D.N. Cole, W.T. Borrie, and J. O'Loughlin (Comps.), *Wilderness science in a time of change conference—Volume 2: Wilderness within the context of larger systems* (pp. 14–26). Ogden, UT: USDA Forest Service, Rocky Mountain Research Station.

Snyder, D.L., Fawson, C., Godfrey, E.B., Keith, J.E., and Lilieholm, R.J. (1995). *Wilderness designation in Utah: Issues and potential economic impacts* (Research Report 151). Logan, UT: Utah State University, Utah Agricultural Experiment Station.

Tiebout, C.M. (1956). Exports and regional economic growth. *Journal of Political Economy, 64*(2), 160–169.

USDA Forest Service. (2002). *National and regional project results: 2002 National Forest Visitor Use Report.* Retrieved February 1, 2005, from http://www.fs.fed.us/recreation/programs/nvum/

USDA Forest Service. (2001). *National and regional project results: FY2001 National Forest Visitor Use Report.* Retrieved February 1, 2005, from http://www.fs.fed.us/recreation/programs/nvum/

USDA Forest Service. (2000). *National and regional project results: CY2000 National Forest Visitor Use Report.* Retrieved February 1, 2005, from http://www.fs.fed.us/recreation/programs/nvum/

Vias, A.C. (1999). Jobs follow people in the rural Rocky Mountain west. *Rural Development Perspectives, 14*(2), 14–23.

Chapter 11
The Natural Ecological Value of Wilderness

H. Ken Cordell

Senior Research Scientist and Project Leader
USDA Forest Service, Athens, Georgia

Danielle Murphy

Research Coordinator, Department of Agricultural and Applied Economics
University of Georgia, Athens, Georgia

Kurt Riitters

Research Scientist
USDA Forest Service, Research Triangle Park, North Carolina

J. E. Harvard III

former University of Georgia employee

Authors' Note: Deepest appreciation is extended to Peter Landres of the Leopold Wilderness Research Institute for initial ideas for approach, data, and analysis and for a thorough and very helpful review of this chapter.

> *The most important characteristic of an organism is that capacity
> for self-renewal known as health. There are two organisms whose
> processes of self-renewal have been subjected to human interfer-
> ence and control. One of these is man himself. The other is land.*
> —Aldo Leopold, 1949

In Chapters 7 through 10 of this book, we examined the social and economic benefits or values from Wilderness. In this chapter, we attempt to examine the natural ecological values of Wilderness. We define ecological value generally as the level of benefits that the space, water, minerals, biota, and all other factors that make up natural ecosystems provide to support native life forms. Ecological values can accrue to both humans and nonhumans alike. To humans, these benefits typically are bestowed externally as cleaner air and water. To nonhuman species, these ecological benefits are usually much more direct and on-site. Ecosystems contribute their greatest ecological value when they are in their most natural state. In their most natural state, they are at their peak of natural health and provide their greatest level of native life support. Native life support is the ecological value of Wilderness. Cole (2000) has argued that ecological value is directly and positively correlated with degree of natural-ness. We will argue that such measurements of naturalness as we can devise or discover are our best shot at demonstrating whether Wilderness has greater ecological value than non-Wilderness lands.

Naturalness and Wildness

The Wilderness Act was put into place to protect selected wildlands in the United States from human disturbance. Landres, Morgan, and Swanson (1999) defined "natural condition" or naturalness as the relative lack of human distur-bance. Haney, Wilbert, De Grood, Lee, and Thomson (1999, p. 1) stated that "the wilderness system is often promoted as a means to safeguard (natural) ecological attributes no longer found on, or at great risk within, extensively managed lands." Thus, the most significant attribute of Wilderness is its nat-uralness. In addition to protection of the naturalness of designated lands, the Wilderness Act also identified maintenance of "wildness" as a purpose. Cole (2001) and Turner (1996) pointed out that the concept of "untrammeled" means just this, wildness. Wildness means freedom from human manipulation of any kind, including freedom from restoration of what we understand to have been "original" natural conditions. The operative idea behind the concept of wild-ness is that of granting designated lands freedom or autonomy from modern human interference. Thus, natural condition, or naturalness, is an ecological con-dition, and wildness is status relative to modern human control or manipulation. Granting wildness eventually leads to greater "naturalness" of historically disturbed lands—or at least as much naturalness as an area can attain given modern broad-scale external influences, such as nonpoint source pollutants, altered distribution of species, and global climate change (Landres, Morgan & Swanson, 1999).

In the early part of this chapter, a modest sampling of the voluminous literature pertaining to the interrelated ecology concepts of ecosystems, ecosystem health, and naturalness is summarized. However, the richness of this literature and of the theories in ecology and other natural sciences applicable to assessing the ecological health and condition of Wilderness far outstrip the availability of data explicitly describing Wilderness lands. Our search for broad-scale data that would enable us to put into operation a set of meaningful indicators of the ecological health of the NWPS turned up very little. Thus, an important part of our effort in this chapter is to bring more attention to the need for better data so that the ecological conditions, benefits, and values of Wilderness can be better expressed and more fully understood.

The Field of Ecology and Ways of Looking at Ecosystems

Ecology

It is believed that a German biologist, Ernst Haeckel, first coined the term defining the emerging scientific field of "ecology" in 1866. Haeckel created the term from the root Greek words *oikos*, meaning "house," and *logos*, meaning "science." An early basis for this systems point of view is in the writings of James Hutton who described the earth as a total system (Hutton, 1788; Rapport, 2002). The companion term *ecosystem* seems first to have appeared in print in 1935 in an article by a British ecologist, Arthur Tansley. In that article, Tansley defined an ecosystem as "the whole system…including not only the organism complex but also the whole complex of physical factors forming what we call the experiment of the biome…. (1935, p. 299)." The term ecosystem was further defined by Raymond Lindermann in 1942 "as the system composed of physical-chemical-biological processes active within a space-time unit of any magnitude (p. 400)." This refinement enabled ecologists to apply their field to any scale of ecosystem, from landscape to prairie pothole.

In 1953, Eugene Odum published a key book, *The Fundamentals of Ecology*. His view of nature was a comprehensive one. It added the idea that ecosystems are dynamic systems (Chaffin, 1998) that include human activities as well as natural processes. He showed that ecology can include the study of systems as broad as watersheds and weather patterns. Odum helped to introduce a paradigm shift from a view of ecosystems as persistent, stable, balanced systems in equilibrium to a view of the natural world as dynamic and constantly changing. As the field has continued to evolve and mature, more emphasis has been given to recognition of spatial and temporal variability, of humans as part of ecosystem processes and functions, and of the importance of biodiversity in ecosystem functioning (Hobbs et al., 2004).

Recent writings have included more explicit study across a spectrum of ecosystems from heavily managed and human inhabited lands to autonomous natural lands and systems (Bertollo, 1998). As ecology has broadened its perspectives to include humans in the equation, there has emerged a greater need to clarify what is meant by the concept of ecosystem health applied to both managed and natural systems. Some ecologists in earlier decades outright rejected the notion of natural ecosystem health because some form of modern human influence seemed always to be present. Most ecologists now, however, recognize and have readily adopted the idea that ecosystem health is a valid perspective across the managed-to-natural spectrum. Our concern in this chapter is, of course, with those natural ecosystems thus far included within the National Wilderness Preservation System.

Linking Naturalness, Life-Sustaining Ecosystem Health, and the Ecological Value of Wilderness

Rapport (1989) asserted that a healthy ecosystem is one that has the ability to recover from minor disturbances and absorb stress. Costanza (1992) agreed that "an ecological system is healthy and free from *distress syndrome* if it is stable and sustainable — that is, if it is active and maintains its organization and autonomy over time, and if it is resilient to stress" (Costanza, 1992, p. 9). As the field of ecology has evolved, there has been increasing recognition that the definitions of ecosystem health from scientists, such as Rapport and Costanza, apply to both managed and natural ecosystems. Ecosystems exist at different spatial scales and on a continuum from highly managed to highly natural (Angermeier, 2000). Odum (1989) observed that the landscape is divided into developed, cultivated, and natural areas. He described a natural area as being "self-supporting" and "self-sustaining," and operating without energy or economic inputs from humans (i.e., autonomous). These natural areas include wildlands and provide the physiological necessities for supporting natural life. A healthy, natural life-support system is the environment, organisms, processes, and resources that interact to meet native life-sustaining needs (Odum, 1989).

In managed systems, there is explicit acknowledgment of the role of the human, as both inhabitant and manager. The health of managed ecosystems has been described as the set of conditions needing to exist where biotic and abiotic influences do not threaten management objectives (McIntire, 1988).

In natural systems, on the other hand, ecosystem health refers to the set of natural conditions needing to exist to support native life forms. It stands to reason that the more healthy the managed or natural systems, the better those systems are able to support the life forms within them.

The medical professions' view of human health is a useful analogy of the meaning of natural ecosystem health. Dahms and Geils (1997) described a key characteristic of human health as being that of homeostasis (i.e., system resistance to change). Homeostasis is one of the most common properties of highly complex open systems. A *homeostatic system* is one that maintains its structure and functions through a multiplicity of dynamic equilibriums rigorously controlled by interdependent regulation mechanisms. For the human body, a change measured against the standard of inherent condition and internal balances typically indicates a change in health. Like a human body has organs, ecosystems are dynamic communities of living organisms, plant, animal and other, bound by common energy pathways and nutrient cycles. Over time ecosystems can evolve, but in the short term, healthy systems exhibit the characteristic of homeostasis. They are resistant to change and work hard to maintain their inherent life support state (de Rosnay, 1997). Criteria for judging whether a natural system is healthy vary among scientific fields and individual scientists, but they typically include naturalness, normality, variability, diversity, stability, sustainability, vigor, organization, and resilience (Coates, Jones & Williams, 2002). As we see it, naturalness is the essential criteria from the list above.

Angermeier (2000) stated, "Naturalness is the foundation for…sustainable (natural) resource management (p. 379)." The health of natural resource systems lies their abilities to maintain optimum operating natural conditions (Kay, 1993). Karr and Dudley (1981) defined health as "…capacity of supporting and maintaining a balanced, integrated, adaptive community of organisms (that have) a species composition and functional organization comparable to that of the natural habitats of the region (Karr & Dudley, 1981, p. 56)." Ecosystems that are disturbed by human activity "usually exhibit reduced resistance to stress" (De Leo & Levin, 1997). Angermeier (2000) concluded that natural ecosystems seem less able to recover from anthropogenic changes than from natural disturbances.

Kolb, Wagner, and Covington (1994) asserted that healthy ecosystems can be distinguished by four qualitative attributes:

1. existence of the necessary physical environment, biotic resources, and trophic networks to support ecosystem integrity;

2. resistance and ability to recover from catastrophic change;

3. a functional equilibrium between supply and use of water, nutrients, light, and growing space for vegetation; and

4. a diversity of ages and vegetative structures that provide habitat for a variety of native species and ecosystem processes.

Another key concept in defining ecosystem health is biodiversity. Cole (2000) maintained that biodiversity "may be the most compelling reason to manage wilderness ecosystems (because it essentially defines)...naturalness (p. 83)" Christensen and colleagues (1996) stated there are three specific roles for biodiversity in ecosystem functioning: providing for essential processes, maintaining resistance to and recovery from disturbances, and adapting to long-term changes in environmental conditions. Biodiversity, or biological diversity, is the diversity of and in living nature. Biological diversity has been defined as "the variety and variability among living organisms and the ecological processes within which they occur." (Cordell & Reed, 1990, p. 32). Since 1986, the term *biodiversity* has achieved worldwide use among biologists, environmentalists, political leaders, and concerned citizens. Much of this has been driven by the growing concern over extinction of species. Another concern in biodiversity has been for the threats to the world's full range of functioning ecosystems (Davis, 1989).

We surmise, as did Cole (2000), that most ecological scientists and ecologically trained managers see naturalness as the ultimate goal for managing Wilderness. Naturalness is the ultimate "aim" of free functioning natural ecosystems. The more natural ecosystems are, such as those protected by Wilderness designation, the more healthy they are. The more healthy they are, the greater is their support of native life, and thus the greater their ecological value.

Measurement of Naturalness in Wilderness

In ecological literature, the term *natural* is commonly understood to mean a process, situation, or system free from modern human technological modification. Thus, naturalness is the way a system would function and the characteristics it would achieve in the absence of human intervention. By legal definition, Wilderness areas are natural areas where natural processes dominate and the natural landscape and habitats created by those natural processes are sustained without human intervention. This is not to say that external human activities do not influence Wilderness areas. They do. Even the most remote Wilderness area is effected by global climate change, pollutants, stratospheric ozone depletion and occasional human presence. Few would argue, however, that Wilderness areas, some of which are the last remnants of virgin forests or high alpine meadows, are more natural than a parking lot (Christensen et al., 1996). But, because no land, designated or not, is totally free from human influence, the challenge we face is to find and implement measures or indicators of relative naturalness enabling us to compare measures of naturalness between Wilderness and non-Wilderness ecosystems.

Literature Identifying Indicators of Ecosystem Health and Naturalness

When lands are modified, most ecologists would agree that they have less natural ecological integrity and ability to support natural life. But can this be measured? A number of scientists have provided ideas regarding the measurement of naturalness. A review of these ideas is useful not only to selecting feasible measures but also to setting up a discussion of needed data and measures to fill gaps in our knowledge.

Anderson (1991) proposed three indices of naturalness: the degree to which a system would change if humans were removed, the amount of energy supplied by technological humans to maintain the functioning of the system as it now exists, and the complement of native species in an area compared to the species in the area prior to settlement. Similarly, Angermeier (2000) proposed four criteria for assessing degrees of human alterations to natural ecosystems which include degree of change, degree of sustained control, spatial extent of change, and abruptness of change. Other examples of possible indicators of naturalness have been provided by Cole and Landres (1996). They listed geography, geologic composition, land forms, soils, hydrological character, elevation, water, and biologic distinctiveness as factors indicating naturalness. Other measures might include native species richness, proportion of extant species that are exotic, natural genetic diversity, degree of unbroken landscape, quality of air and water, the contribution to carbon sequestration, and/or absence of roads.

Bertello (1998) summarized a list of indicators of ecosystem health and naturalness as proposed by several authors. He included Odum, who in 1989 suggested energetics, nutrient cycling, community structure, and systems features as indicators of naturalness. Keddy, Lee, and Wisheu (1993) proposed diversity, guilds, exotics, rare species, plant biomass, and amphibian biomass. Rapport and colleagues (1998) suggested nutrients, productivity, abiotic zones, species diversity, genetic diversity, size distribution, biotic composition, and bioaccumulation of contaminants. Bertello (1998) cited a number of other authors who have suggested measures for monitoring and assessing ecosystem health and natural integrity. Some of the reoccurring parameters include measures of species richness, species composition, nutrient cycling and flow, productivity, and community structure.

Fu-liu and Shu (2000) provided a sampling and description of additional indicators to include the Index of Biotic Integrity (IBI) developed by Karr (1981; Karr, Fausch, Angermeier, Yant & Schlosser, 1986), and an overall system health index which incorporated vigor, organization, and resilience as proposed by Costanza (1992). Ulanowicz (1980, 1986) developed the index of network ascendency which incorporates species richness, niche specialization, developed cycling and feedback, and overall activity. Jorgensen (1995) suggested energy, structure, and ecological buffer capacity as indicators. Belaoussoff and Kevan (1998) demonstrated how norms of diversity and abundance could be used. They suggested characterizing ecosystem diversity-abundance relationships within ecological communities using lognormal distributions as they change under differing degrees of disturbance.

Selecting Feasible Naturalness Indicators

While the above indicators or measures all have scientific validity and broad applications to Wilderness, they are, for the most part, impractical because of high costs for primary data collection and very limited availability of secondary data. Very little consistently collected, sufficiently fine-scale, System-wide data were found to be available to address the suggestions from the above authors. This accepted, we turned to indirect surrogate measures as our remaining option (Coates, Jones & Williams, 2002).

A search was conducted for broad-scale data that would enable measurement of the selected indicators of naturalness and apparent ecological health. Desirable were data at a fine enough resolution to enable construction of an area-by-area database. Ideally this would include soils, water quality, air quality, vegetation, wildlife populations, and wildlife habitat. In limited instances, site-specific data are available, but mostly these data are the result of an individual scientist's research to study a specific organism, species, system, area, or issue. For example, Ryan (1990) studied lichens as a measure of air quality, but not across the System. Wetmore (1992) also studied lichens. Rollins, Thomas, and Morgan (2001) looked at changes in fire patterns in selected Wilderness areas and Bader (2000) examined the value of Wilderness habitat to grizzly bears. Because system-wide data were not generally available, the search expanded to looking for broad-scale data that cover all lands—Wilderness and other lands alike.

Limited broad-scale data are becoming available, but mostly at scales too coarse to enable distinguishing conditions specific to individual Wilderness areas (especially the smaller ones in the East). An example of a national database collected at too coarse a scale for our intended purposes is the National Resources Inventory (NRI), developed by the Natural Resources Conservation Service. These data are based on observable aerial units, which are samples of the total landscape, with sampling intensity meant to serve parameter estimation at state, regional, or national levels. Most other surface-measured, broad-scale data are inconsistently measured and do not provide consistent coverage across the NWPS. An example of inconsistently collected data is the Natural Heritage data. Natural Heritage data are independently generated by each state, using guidelines provided by NatureServe (NatureServe, 2003). Administration of these guidelines seems somewhat inconsistent across states. More promising in recent years has been amended satellite imagery, some available at 30-meter resolution. Amended data means that some other source is "overlaid" to enhance interpretation. Satellite data and the approaches used for processing the selected data for each of four selected naturalness indicators are forest fragmentation, natural land cover, distance from roads, and ecosystem representation.

Forest fragmentation is used to indicate the degree to which individual Wilderness areas and aggregates of geographically proximate Wilderness areas are intact, apparently not fragmented, and thus have retained inherent natural landscape integrity relative to other lands.

Natural land cover indicates the degree to which areas are under natural vegetative cover and thus have retained their natural landscape integrity relative to other lands).

Distance from roads is used to indicate the relative degree to which areas are insulated from roads, and thus are less likely to have been impacted by human activities and therefore have retained their inherent natural character relative to other lands.

Protecting not only the naturalness of individual areas from human activities but also a diversity of geographically spread natural areas goes even further toward sustaining life support on the earth. The greater the diversity of protected natural ecosystems, such as the 662 areas currently included in the National Wilderness Preservation System (NWPS), the greater will be the diversity of life forms protected. These 662 areas do not afford proportionate aerial representation of the range of ecosystem types to be found in the United States however. Thus, the fourth indicator of naturalness (across the System) is *ecosystem representation* defined as the diversity of ecosystems included in the NWPS, and thus within the confines of a region or subregion, that have protected broad-scale biodiversity and natural integrity, and thus diversity of species.

Background about the Data and Its Analytical Treatment

Forest Fragmentation

Forest fragmentation (or lack of it) is widely accepted as an important indicator of the capacity of natural forest ecosystems to sustain indigenous life. In the international Montreal Process, for example, fragmentation indicators are intended to show losses and degradation of large blocks of habitat that support native populations of flora and fauna (USDA Forest Service, n.d.). The assumption is that larger forest patches are more autonomous and better able to maintain natural disturbance regimes, resulting in more species, lower extinction rates, and greater genetic diversity for native interior forest species.

Fragmentation results in greater edge effect, potentially making forested areas more vulnerable to abiotic influences such as wind, and biotic influences such as exotic, early successional, and transient species (Debinski & Holt, 2000). Altered abiotic conditions can in turn influence ecosystem processes such as nutrient cycling (Debinski & Holt, 2000) through impacts on invertebrate species that are important in decomposition (Meffe & Carroll, 1997). When fragmentation results in smaller patches, large carnivores may be threatened by a reduction in available prey and exposure to human activities and hunting (Meffe & Carroll, 1997). Absence of fragmentation indicates that essential natural functions and processes are less likely to have been degraded or modified.

In this chapter, fragmentation within Wilderness areas is compared to fragmentation of all lands as a plausible indication that Wilderness designation protects areas from fragmentation and thus preserves natural ecological processes and habitats; that is, naturalness. There has been considerable recent work examining forest fragmentation at a national scale (Heilman, Strittholt, Slosser & Dellasala, 2002; Heinz Center, 2002; Riitters et al., 2002; Riitters, Wickham & Coulston, 2004). These studies generally indicate that while forest land is relatively well-connected over very large regions, fragmentation is so extensive that edge effects extending only 100 meters from forest edge potentially influence over half of all forest land. The largest reserves of core (i.e., intact or unfragmented) forest are found in areas not suited for agricultural or urban land uses, including many Wilderness Areas. Our examination of fragmentation in Wilderness relative to other lands is limited to eastern forests because the available data do not permit us to distinguish natural fragmentation from human induced fragmentation in western forests.

Following protocols described by Riitters and associates (2002), we evaluated forest fragmentation at two landscape scales and used three threshold levels to describe forest cover. The primary data source was the National Land Cover Data (NLCD), a national land-cover map at 30-meter pixel resolution that was developed from Thematic Mapper satellite imagery in 1992 (Vogelmann, Howard, Yang, Larson, Wylie & Van Driel, 2001). Briefly, each 0.09 hectare pixel of forest was classified according to the percentage forest cover in the surrounding neighborhood, for both 7 hectare (~17.5 acres) and 600 hectare (~1,400 acres) neighborhoods. For a given neighborhood size, we then applied threshold values of 60, 90, and 100 percent to label each pixel as dominant, interior, and core, respectively. A core forest pixel resides at the center of a completely forested neighborhood, while dominant and interior forest pixels reside in neighborhoods that are at least 60 and 90 percent forested, respectively. The level of fragmentation measured by these thresholds is seen as a plausible predictor of the plant and animal species present. For example, in the more fragmented dominant forest, there may be more edge or invasive species.

We then summarized the amount of forest that met the various criteria within, and outside Wilderness Areas. This was accomplished by overlaying boundary maps for all eastern Wilderness areas that contained forest land cover. Coastal Wilderness areas in the East were deleted to avoid including surface area outside of a Wilderness area along the coast that would appear as unforested (including water). The proportions of 30-meter (0.09 hectare) cells both within and outside of Wilderness as classified by the 60, 90 and 100 percent threshold levels, and for each window size (i.e., 7 hectare and 600 hectare) provided estimates for each Wilderness area of dominant, interior and core forest cover. Individual Wilderness area data were aggregated for the Eastern Region and proportions of total Wilderness acreage computed. A similar procedure was followed to compute proportions of total Eastern U.S. land area in dominant, interior, and core forest cover.

Natural Land Cover

Natural land cover is a relatively direct indication of naturalness as a condition of land (Jones et al., 2001). Natural land cover includes all land that is not developed, that is, not urban, not transportation, not agricultural (Cordell & Overdevest, 2001). Natural land is continually converted to developed uses. Between 1982 and 1997, three percent of natural range was converted to agriculture or developed uses and 11.7 million acres of natural forest cover was converted to developed uses (Cordell & Overdevest, 2001). In the eastern United States, most undeveloped natural land is in forest cover (Cordell & Overdevest, 2001). Over the past century there have been changes in forest cover that have raised concerns about carbon storage, biodiversity, water quality, nitrogen cycling, and the sustainability of forest resources. Land cover reflects ecosystem type, as well as past and current land use and management. Changes in cover caused by changes in land use have been accelerating over time as human technological ability has vastly increased. The effect of land cover change on climate can be seen throughout the United States. Agriculture has expanded and replaced grasslands in the Great Plains and Midwest. There has been a cooling effect in these areas demonstrated by a temperature change of more then one degree Fahrenheit. There has been a warming effect along the Atlantic Coast as croplands are replaced by forest and across the southwest where woodlands have replaced some desert (Roy, Hurtt, Weaver & Pacala 2003).

Land cover affects the concentrations of greenhouse gases, air and water quality, soil fertility, the capability of terrestrial and aquatic ecosystems to provide goods and services, local weather, the occurrence and spread of infectious disease, and species extinction (Stein, 2001) as well as other aspects of ecological health. The conversion of natural land to anthropogenic land uses affects the processes of water interception, infiltration, and runoff that effect flooding, water storage, and the quality of drinking water (Jones et al., 2001). Land use has significant effects on the quality of water in streams and groundwater. Basins with significant agricultural or urban development almost always contain higher than normal concentrations of nutrients and pesticides. Since 1991, USGS scientists with the National Water Quality Assessment Program have been collecting and analyzing data and information in more than 50 major river basins and aquifers across the Nation. Some of the highest levels of nitrogen and herbicides were found in streams and ground water in agricultural areas. Some of the highest levels of phosphorus and insecticides were collected from urban streams (USGS, 1999).

The data used to measure the natural land cover character of Wilderness for this chapter is referred to as National Land Cover Data 1992 (NLCD 92; Vogelmann et al., 2001). In addition to satellite imagery data, the NLCD 92 project used a variety of measures including topography, population census, agricultural statistics, soil characteristics, land cover maps, and wetlands data. The NLCD 92 scale resolution is 30 meters square, roughly the size of a baseball diamond. There are 21 land cover classes within the NLCD 92 that can be mapped consistently at 30 meters resolution across the United States. The data accessed for this analysis represented the number of square meters in each of the 21 NLCD land cover classes (e.g., water, barren land, shrubland, herbaceous upland natural/seminatural vegetation, wetlands, developed land, forested upland, non-natural woody, and herbaceous planted/cultivated). These 21 NLCD classes were subsequently aggregated into six broad cover classes, including five representing natural cover (i.e., water, grassland, wetland, forest, and shrubland). An additional non-natural land cover class including all other land cover classifications (e.g., agricultural, developed land) were combined to form a sixth class labeled "other."

Approximate total land area in each of these six land cover classes was calculated by overlaying GIS shape files for each of the designated areas in the NWPS with land cover classification boundaries. This step provided approximations because of inevitable incompatibilities in map data between different data sources. These approximate estimates of area in each of the land cover classes, for each Wilderness area, were divided by each area's total acreage to estimate the percentage of each Wilderness area in each land cover class. These percentages were used to recompute the number of acres in each class by multiplying each by the official acreage for each Wilderness area found at the Wilderness.net web site.

Distance from Roads

One of the leading contributors to habitat fragmentation and diminution of natural land cover is maintenance and expansion of the nation's road network. The United States was spanned by an extensive road network estimated in

2002 to include over 6.3 million kilometers of public roads of all types (U.S. Department of Transportation, 2002). For comparison, the U.S. Environmental Protection Agency (n.d.) estimated that there are only 5.3 million kilometers of streams and rivers in the country. Thus, roads exceed the linear expanse of streams in the United States by a substantial margin, and that margin is growing. Public road length, including interstates, principal and minor arterials, major and minor collectors, and local roads, grew by over 99,000 kilometers between 1993 to 2002. In some states there were especially large increases, such as Florida growing by 11,230 kilometers, Colorado by 12,210 kilometers, and Texas by 12,290 kilometers. In other states there were smaller increases, including Washington with 4,427 kilometers and Vermont with about a 200 kilometers increase (USDT, 1993, 2002).

Forman and Alexander (1998), Spellerberg (1998), Trombulak and Frissell (2000), and Forman and colleagues (2002) reviewed the ecological impacts of roads on terrestrial and aquatic systems. The distance from a road that is ecologically impacted is often referred to as the road ecological influence zone. Research indicates that road influence zones extend tens to hundreds of meters from roads, usually disrupting wildlife movement, modifying habitat, altering water drainage patterns, introducing exotic species, modifying microclimate and chemical environment, and increasing noise levels (Riitters & Wickham, 2003). The deleterious effects of road construction also include sedimentation from erosion, increased runoff and flow rates, and filling and draining of wetlands (MDNR, 2001). Roads are precursors to future impacts because they facilitate land development and further expansion of the road network itself (Riitters & Wickham, 2003).

Attention has recently focused more on the broad-scale impacts of roads at regional levels (e.g., Heilman, Strittholt, Slosser & Dellasala, 2002; National Research Council, 1997; Wickham et al., 1999; Wickham, O'Neill, Riitters, Smith, Wade & Jones, 2002). Nationally, using total highway length statistics for 1985 and assumptions concerning road density, spatial distribution of roads, traffic volumes, widths of road influence zones, and other factors, Forman (2000) estimated that 22 percent of the total land area of the country was at that time ecologically affected by roads. This was based on the assumption of a 100-meter influence zone near secondary roads, 305–365-meter influence zone near primary roads, and 810-meter zone near some urban roads. Based on the estimate that humans can drive to within one kilometer of 82 percent of all land in the United States, very little land area is untouched by the impact of roads and their uses. The presence of roads also influences potential impact from other sources as they open the way for future development (Riitters & Wickham, 2003).

The data used to calculate the proportion of Wilderness within 127 meters, 382 meters, 1,000 meters, and 5,000 meters from the nearest road were abstracted from an earlier study by Riitters and Wickham (2003). That original study examined the proportion of U.S. land that is close enough to a road such that is it likely to experience an ecological effect; that is, it is within the road influence zone. The 1992 NLCD land cover map (Vogelmann et al., 2001) and the national road map (GDT, 2002), which identified public roads ranging from interstate highways to four-wheel drive trails, were the basic sources used to assign a "road" land-cover classification to each 30-meter cell of land area in the United States. The GDT road map was also gridded into 30-meter cells in order to overlay it with the NLCD map. If an NLCD cell overlapped a road map cell then it was relabeled as a "road" cell, as opposed to another land cover class, such as forest. Distance to the nearest road cell was calculated for all grid cells. The resulting records for each Wilderness area in the country showed the proportion of land area within each of several discrete distances from the nearest road (including 127 m, 382 m, 1,000 m and 5,000 m). Data representing the proportion of Wilderness within the above distances from roads were aggregated for the East and West regions for comparison with the proportion of all land in the United States within these distances. In this study we examine the amount of Wilderness that is beyond each of the distances to the nearest road (e.g., How much Wilderness is more then 5,000 meters from the nearest road?).

Ecosystem Representation

Haney and associates (1999) stated that "wilderness might be expected to be sufficiently large or otherwise configured so as to contain all ecosystem structure, community types, or species representative of a bioregion (p. 2)." Organisms at the ecosystem level mediate flows of energy and materials and the mediation of these flows contributes to ecological health and life support. When organism diversity reaches low levels, such as those typically found in managed (i.e., modified) ecosystems, then the magnitude and stability of ecosystem functioning may be significantly altered (Naeem et al., 1999). To maintain biodiversity, it is desirable to preserve the integrity of entire natural landscapes (Dailey et al., 1997).

Ecosystems can be viewed at multiple scales, just as human communities can be viewed at different scales from the global to continental to local. They can be viewed at broad scales to include ecosystem regions (i.e., ecoregions), or they can be viewed at smaller scales, such as isolated canyon communities or puddles left after a rain. Whatever the scale, there is tremendous diversity of ecosystems across the United States and world. Although many ecosystem types have already been and currently are being altered by human land conversions in the United States, preserving representatives of the remaining diversity of ecosystems, as well as biodiversity within those ecosystems, is a primary goal of Wilderness protection.

Ecosystem identification typically begins with macroclimate as the most significant factor on earth determining the distribution of various life forms. As climate changes, so too does the distribution of mammals, fish, tree species, and all other forms of life. For example, Dymond, Carver, and Phillips (2003) found that low latitude and good climate are important determinants of species richness. The extant distribution of types of ecosystems across the United States is a direct result of evolving climate over tens of thousands of years. Most of this country's ecosystem types have been heavily transformed by human settlement and land uses in a matter of just two or three centuries, and mostly as a result of the last few decades. What remains of the untransformed ecosystems are essential to the continued existence of the diversity of life forms still found within these ecosystems. Thus, a focus on measuring ecosystem representation is one way to measure the biodiversity protection benefit of Wilderness. It is one dimension of the capacity of Wilderness to support natural life, as well as to provide ecological services to humans (Naeem et al., 1999; Risser, 1995). Noss (1990) acknowledged that Wilderness designation might be "the only opportunity to maintain the ecological gradients and mosaics that constitute native biodiversity at the landscape level."

Ecoregions have been defined by the World Wildlife Fund (2004) as

a large area of land or water that contains a geographically distinct assemblage of natural communities that
(a)   share a large majority of their species and ecological dynamics,
(b)   share similar environmental conditions, and
(c)   interact ecologically in ways that are critical for their long-term persistence.

Others have defined ecoregions as areas of ecological potential based on combinations of biophysical parameters such as climate and topography. Ecoregions transcend artificial human boundaries such as state lines or agency jurisdictions. We adopted the "Bailey system" for identifying ecosystems (Bailey, 2002). The system Bailey and his colleagues have developed and refined is meant to be comprehensive, across terrestrial and aquatic ecosystems. It is perhaps the best-known and most widely adopted ecosystem and ecoregional classification system (Bailey, 1995). This system for classifying ecological regions and subregions in the United States identifies domains, divisions, provinces, and sections. These groupings reflect similarities in climate, ecological processes, vegetation, and groups of species (Stein, 2001). The broadest scale of ecological regions are domains, which primarily reflect climate differences. The four Domains in the Bailey system are the Polar, Humid Temperate, Dry, and Humid Tropical. Polar Domain ecosystems are located at higher latitudes and are influenced mostly by arctic and polar air flows and include tundra and subarctic mountains. In the middle latitudes, the Humid Temperate Domain is regulated by both polar and tropical air masses. The Dry Domain is defined by the presence or absence of water and includes the deserts, steppes, high mountains, and dry coniferous forest division. The Humid Tropical Domain is found at low latitudes and controlled by equatorial and tropical air masses, such as the Everglades on southern tip of Florida. Domains are broken down into divisions that are subdivided into provinces based on vegetational macrofeatures (see the descriptive statistics on divisions in Chapter 5 of this book).

Spatial data representing area and boundaries by Bailey's ecoregion type (down to the province level) were accessed for this chapter using data from the USDA Forest Service. Within this database a narrative description and numeric code were provided for each ecological province. Wilderness boundary map data (Wilderness Institute, 2003) were overlaid onto mapped data of ecoregion boundaries in order to estimate land area within Wilderness boundaries representing each of Bailey's ecoregional provinces. For analysis, these overlays were visually mapped, as well as tabulated by computing percentages of total area within each ecological province protected by Wilderness.

Results

Fragmentation

The comparisons in Figures 11.1 and 11.2 indicate that eastern Wilderness forest land is less fragmented and thus in more natural condition than non-Wilderness

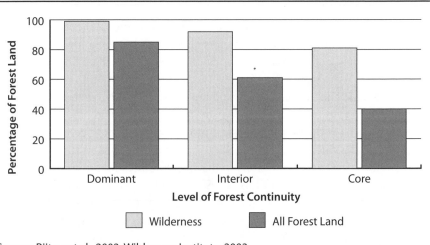

Sources: Riiters et al., 2002; Wilderness Institute, 2003

Figure 11.1 Percentages of forest land in Wilderness and all other forest land in the East by level of forest continuity at the 7-hectare landscape scale

forests. For both Wilderness and non-Wilderness forest lands, measured fragmentation is dependent on both landscape scale and fragmentation threshold. Figure 11.1 compares proportions of forest land at the 7-hectare landscape scale. Shown are percentages of eastern Wilderness forest land and all eastern forest land that are in dominant forest cover (60% or more), percentages classified as interior forest (90% or more), and percentages classified as core forest (i.e., all or 100% of 30m cells within the 7-ha landscape window are forested).

Much greater percentages of Wilderness relative to non-Wilderness forest at the more resolute 7-hectare landscape scale were found to exist across the three classes of forest continuity (i.e., dominant, interior, and core). Specifically, 99 percent of the Wilderness forest was classified as dominant, 92 percent was classified as interior, and 81 percent was classified as core (i.e., continuous) forest. The percentage of Wilderness forest not fragmented (i.e., core or continuous forest) is more than twice that of all other forest lands. This is an indication that unprotected forest lands are much more fragmented than Wilderness forest lands. Thus, Wilderness lands have retained much greater degrees of their natural integrity and connectivity.

Figure 11.2 compares percentages of eastern Wilderness forest land and all other eastern forest land that is classified as dominant, interior, and core forest at a much broader 600-hectare landscape scale. Measures of fragmentation at this scale tend to be much more sensitive to broken or discontinuous patterns of forest cover because the broader net that is cast is more sensitive to lands not forested. In other words, at this broader scale, one would expect greater incidence of nonforest plots of land relative to the location of any

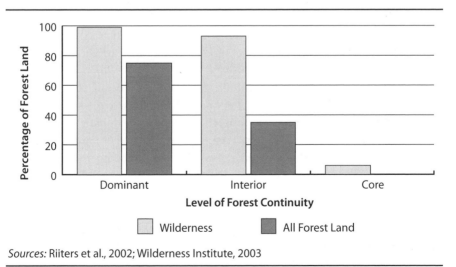

Sources: Riiters et al., 2002; Wilderness Institute, 2003

Figure 11.2 Percentages of forest land in Wilderness and all other forest land in the East by level of forest continuity at the 600-hectare landscape scale

single 30-meter cell. This greater sensitivity is evident when comparing bar heights for non-Wilderness forest between Figures 11.1 and 11.2. At this 600-hectare landscape scale, substantially smaller percentages of non-Wilderness forest lands met the dominant, interior, or core forest thresholds. At this broader scale as well, a much smaller percentage (only around 6%) of Wilderness forest was found to be core forest. At the 7-hectare scale, 40 percent of non-Wilderness eastern forest met the core forest threshold criteria. No non-Wilderness eastern forest met the threshold for being classified as core forest at the 600-hectare scale.

The results in Figure 11.2 comparing Wilderness and all other forest lands indicate even more strongly than the 7-hectare-scale results in Figure 11.1 that Wilderness designation leads to greater retention of naturalness; that is, forest continuity and habitat integrity. The decrease from 81 percent core forest in the 7-hectare-landscape in comparison to 6 percent core forest in the 600-hectare landscape demonstrates that this conclusion is scale-dependent. The broader the landscape net cast, the more likely is it that some fragmentation within or bordering Wilderness forests will be found.

Few Wilderness forests do not meet the dominant or interior forest thresholds, at either landscape scale. This is because Wilderness areas, themselves relatively unfragmented, tend more to be located within large tracts of public forest land with relatively little development. Among non-Wilderness forests, more fragmentation is apparent. Percentages of continuous non-Wilderness forest classed as either dominant, interior, or core are smaller than for Wilderness forest. At these lower percentages of continuous forest cover, it is much more likely that even small changes in forest cover will have a great impact on natural processes and species that depend on connected forest. Less then two percent of forested Wilderness land did not meet the dominant cover criteria. About 15 percent of all non-Wilderness forest land in the East was less than 60 percent forested at the 7-hectare landscape scale and about 25 percent of all forested land was less then 60 percent forested at the 600-hectare scale. Overall, these estimates of different levels of connected forests provide substantial evidence that forest land protected through Wilderness designation is less fragmented than other forest land in the East. Indeed, Wilderness areas appear to contain the only measurable remnants of core forest extending 1,000 or more hectares.

Land Cover

As described earlier, the U.S. Geological Service maintains data describing land area across the United States by various land cover types. These data represent pixels from satellite imagery classified by apparent dominant land cover. We aggregated the original 21 classes into six land cover types, five types of natural cover, plus a catchall sixth type representing all "Other" land uses (e.g., agricultural, urban lands). We use the term *natural* here to mean land area that is vegetated, under water, wetland, and similar undeveloped lands. We do not assume that the five cover types imply complete naturalness; rather, we assume undeveloped forest, wetlands, water area and shrubland is more natural and thus represents (in an indicator of) more naturalness than the Other land cover type. (We will refer to the undeveloped land categories as natural land cover.) Tables 11.1 through 11.4 (pp. 223–226) show for each U.S. Census Division the acres of land protected as Wilderness, percentage of Wilderness by land cover, total acres of all land, and percentage of all land by land cover class.

In the Northeast Census Region (Table 11.1), there are two divisions, the Middle Atlantic and New England. These divisions stretch from Pennsylvania to Maine. In the Middle Atlantic Division, there are a total of over 20 thousand acres of land in Wilderness. Over half of this land is forest, over one quarter is wetland, and nearly 18 percent is water. Compared with all land, Wilderness has much greater percentages in natural cover overall with over 95 percent falling within one of the five "natural" cover types. In contrast, over 30 percent of Middle Atlantic total area falls into the Other land cover class. Only about 12 percent

Table 11.1 Number of acres and percentages of Wilderness and of all land in each cover class[1] by division in the Northeast Census Region

Northeast Census Region	Total acres of Wilderness	Percentage of Wilderness in Census Division	Total acres of all lands	Percentage of all land in Census Division
Middle Atlantic	20,367		69,893,246	
Water	3,600	17.7	6,381,352	9.1
Forest	10,519	51.7	40,589,169	58.1
Wetland	5,286	26.0	1,706,202	2.4
Grassland	0	0.0	0	0.0
Shrubland	0	0.0	0	0.0
Other	962	4.7	21,216,523	30.4
New England	179,485		46,072,452	
Water	1,708	1.0	6,023,678	13.1
Forest	171,867	95.8	31,450,648	68.3
Wetland	3,104	1.7	2,150,126	4.7
Grassland	0	0.0	0	0.0
Shrubland	49	0.0	131,968	0.3
Other	2,757	1.5	6,316,032	13.7

[1] The Forest class combined the NLCD land cover classes Deciduous Forest, Evergreen Forest, and Mixed Forest. The Water category was created by combining Open Water and Perennial Ice/Snow. Wetlands included Woody Wetlands and Emergent Herbaceous Wetlands. Grasslands were represented by the NLCD category Grasslands/and Herbaceous and finally Shrublands equals Shrubland. The Other category includes all other classifications (e.g., agriculture and developed land).

Sources: Vogelmann et al., 2001; Wilderness Institute, 2003

is either water or wetlands. Although a relatively high proportion of all land is forested, it includes some planted forests and a great deal of managed area.

In the New England Division, over 98 percent of the land in the Wilderness System is in natural cover, mostly forest. Almost 96 percent of New England Wilderness is forested. Only 1.5 percent falls within the Other category, likely indicating human disturbance near Wilderness boundaries where the relative coarseness of the satellite imagery cannot discriminate well between land just inside and land just outside of a Wilderness boundary. Nearly 14 percent of non-Wilderness land in the New England Division falls into the Other land cover category. Over two thirds of all land is forested. These percentages indicate, as with the Middle Atlantic Division, that lands protected as Wilderness have substantially greater levels of natural land cover.

Table 11.2 Number of acres and percentages of Wilderness and of all land in each cover class[1] by division in the South Census Region

South Census Region	Total acres of Wilderness	Percentage of Wilderness in Census Division	Total acres of all lands	Percentage of all land in Census Division
South Atlantic	2,314,583		187,185,771	
Water	584,626	25.3	17,167,716	9.2
Forest	494,732	21.4	91,015,369	48.6
Wetland	1,122,204	48.5	24,206,769	12.9
Grassland	95,999	4.2	3,567,428	1.9
Shrubland	844	0.0	1,375,934	0.7
Other	16,176	0.7	49,852,555	26.6
East South Central	129,726		117,377,714	
Water	2,279	1.8	3,339,798	2.9
Forest	118,358	91.2	69,496,313	59.2
Wetland	4,997	3.9	6,580,470	5.6
Grassland	0	0.0	3,696	0.0
Shrubland	0	0.0	0	0.0
Other	4,091	3.2	37,957,437	32.3
West South Central	279,124		283,830,122	
Water	7,004	2.5	12,333,740	4.4
Forest	217,658	78.0	62,951,857	22.2
Wetland	8,720	3.1	13,769,070	4.9
Grassland	11,040	4.0	48,875,858	17.2
Shrubland	27,278	9.8	54,122,960	19.1
Other	7,426	2.7	91,776,637	32.3

[1] The Forest class combined the NLCD land cover classes Deciduous Forest, Evergreen Forest, and Mixed Forest. The Water category was created by combining Open Water and Perennial Ice/Snow. Wetlands included Woody Wetlands and Emergent Herbaceous Wetlands. Grasslands were represented by the NLCD category Grasslands/and Herbaceous and finally Shrublands equals Shrubland. The Other category includes all other classifications (e.g., agriculture and developed land).

Sources: Vogelmann et al., 2001; Wilderness Institute, 2003

There are around 2.7 million acres of federal lands protected as Wilderness in the South (Table 11.2). As with the Northeast Region, these protected lands among the divisions of the South are mostly in natural cover, ranging from just over 99 percent in the South Atlantic Division to just under 97 percent in the East South Central. In the East and West South Central Divisions, most of the cover in Wilderness is forest. In the South Atlantic, with such Wilderness Areas as the Everglades and Okefenokee Swamp, almost three quarters of the total area is either water or wetlands. Just over 21 percent is forest. In contrast, among all land in the South, much higher percentages are in the Other land use category. This includes nearly 27 percent in the South Atlantic and 32 percent in each of the other two Southern Divisions. These results indicate that in this region as well, Wilderness designation has, as expected, resulted in protection for much greater levels of natural land cover.

The Upper Midwest includes the East North Central and West North Central Divisions. These divisions together stretch from Ohio to Kansas to North Dakota. In the East North Central there are about 332 thousand acres of protected Wilderness (Table 11.3). In the West North Central, there are over one million acres of protected Wilderness, including the Boundary Waters Canoe Area in

Table 11.3 Number of acres and percentages of Wilderness and of all land in each cover class[1] by division in the Midwest Census Region

Midwest Census Region	Total acres of Wilderness	Percentage of Wilderness in Census Division	Total acres of all lands	Percentage of all land in Census Division
East North Central	332,093		187,009,685	
Water	17,646	5.3	31,563,555	16.9
Forest	209,282	63.0	46,974,048	25.1
Wetland	98,634	29.7	11,304,689	6.0
Grassland	668	0.2	1,354,051	0.7
Shrubland	0	0.0	14,207	0.0
Other	5,862	1.8	95,799,135	51.2
West North Central	1,012,294		333,016,281	
Water	148,759	14.7	8,319,855	2.5
Forest	625,152	61.8	36,170,273	10.9
Wetland	116,526	11.5	16,166,711	4.9
Grassland	74,296	7.3	85,562,607	25.7
Shrubland	9,077	0.9	3,586,058	1.1
Other	38,483	3.8	183,210,777	55.0

[1] The Forest class combined the NLCD land cover classes Deciduous Forest, Evergreen Forest, and Mixed Forest. The Water category was created by combining Open Water and Perennial Ice/Snow. Wetlands included Woody Wetlands and Emergent Herbaceous Wetlands. Grasslands were represented by the NLCD category Grasslands/and Herbaceous and finally Shrublands equals Shrubland. The Other category includes all other classifications (e.g., agriculture and developed land).

Sources: Vogelmann et al., 2001; Wilderness Institute, 2003

northern Minnesota. As with the other regions we have examined thus far, only small percentages of Wilderness acreage fall within the Other category of land cover. Again, these small percentages of seemingly disturbed and developed land uses are likely the result of the coarseness of the grid pattern laid across Wilderness and adjoining lands, making fine distinctions between them difficult. Over 61 percent of Wilderness lands in both of these Upper Midwest Divisions are forested. Five percent in the East North Central and nearly 15 percent in the West North Central are water. Nearly 30 percent in the East North Central and over 11 percent in the West North Central are wetlands. Over half of all land in these Upper Midwest Divisions are disturbed from their prehistoric natural conditions and are in use for human residency, commercial operations, transportation, or crop production. Only 11 percent in the West North Central and 25 percent in the East North Central is forested. In the West North Central, nearly 26 percent is in grassland cover, mostly grazed grassland.

Table 11.4 shows results for the vast West Census Region covering states from New Mexico to Washington (excluding Alaska because land cover data were not available at the time of this analysis). There are almost 33 million acres of Wilderness in these contiguous Western states. In the Mountain Divi-

Table 11.4 Number of acres and percentages of Wilderness and of all land in each cover class[1] by division in the West Census Region

West Census Region	Total acres of Wilderness	Percentage of Wilderness in Census Division	Total acres of all lands	Percentage of all land in Census Division
Mountain	15,569,924		552,510,837	
Water	136,467	0.9	5,021,370	0.9
Forest	6,713,845	43.1	107,953,105	19.5
Wetland	25,356	0.2	2,008,357	0.4
Grassland	2,085,987	13.4	145,231,555	26.3
Shrubland	5,109,633	32.8	226,916,346	41.1
Other	1,498,700	9.6	65,380,104	11.8
Pacific	17,231,941		213,355,725	
Water	191,484	1.1	9,520,746	4.5
Forest	5,865,577	34.0	76,410,972	35.8
Wetland	3,568	0.0	1,077,470	0.5
Grassland	835,450	4.9	21,990,654	10.3
Shrubland	8,480,386	49.2	67,930,205	31.8
Other	1,855,595	10.8	36,425,678	17.1

[1] The Forest class combined the NLCD land cover classes Deciduous Forest, Evergreen Forest, and Mixed Forest. The Water category was created by combining Open Water and Perennial Ice/Snow. Wetlands included Woody Wetlands and Emergent Herbaceous Wetlands. Grasslands were represented by the NLCD category Grasslands/and Herbaceous and finally Shrublands equals Shrubland. The Other category includes all other classifications (e.g., agriculture and developed land).

Sources: Vogelmann et al., 2001; Wilderness Institute, 2003

sion, stretching from the Mexican border to the Canadian border, over 43 percent of Wilderness is forested. In the Pacific Division, 34 percent is forested. Over 46 percent in the Mountain and over 54 percent in the Pacific Divisions are grasslands or shrublands. Around 10 percent in both Divisions fall into the Other category, indicating mostly the difficulty of distinguishing between disturbed/managed lands and natural covers, such as stretches of desert void of vegetation. Due to the vastness of the public lands in the West and Pacific Divisions, and because of the sparseness of the human population in many rural areas of these divisions, comparisons of natural cover between Wilderness and all land are not as distinctive. However, percentages of all land in the Other, more disturbed category are greater in both divisions than are the percentages in the more disturbed categories of cover in Wilderness land.

Figure 11.3 (p. 228) summarizes the percentages of Wilderness in land cover classes by Census Division. It visually illustrates that not only does Wilderness designation protect more of the naturalness character of land but also that over the last 40 years, it has preserved a diversity of land cover types. These range from the water and wetlands of the South Atlantic and the forests of the Northeast to the more arid grasslands and shrublands of the West.

Distance to Roads

Research has indicated that road influences can extend tens to hundreds of meters from the roads themselves, disrupting wildlife, water, and microclimate and raising noise levels (Forman et al., 2002). Such influences also can include sedimentation from eroding road banks and ditches, increased runoff, and destruction of wetlands (MDNR, 2001). In relation to the road distance data presented in Table 5.7 (p. 77), we have examined proportions of Wilderness acreage beyond different distances from roads, and thus the likelihood that road influences are more or less likely being exerted upon the naturalness of Wilderness. In Chapter 5, we provided estimates of acreage and proportion of Wilderness area within about 140 feet, within about 1,250 feet (about ¼ mile) and within about 17,000 feet of a road (a little over three miles) for each of the four major regions of the United States. Based on work by Riitters and Wickham (2003), this analysis was presented as one of the dimensions for characterizing the NWPS. We found that between about 70 (in the Northeast) and 44 percent (in the West) of designated Wilderness is within 3.2 miles (around 17,000 feet) from the nearest road (Table 5.7, p. 77). Road networks in the South, Northeast and Midwest, where much less public lands lie, are more densely developed and are rapidly increasing in length and coverage.

Figure 11.4 and Table 11.5 (page 229) show additional analyses of the proportions of Wilderness land in the East and West, and proportions of all land in the United States, that are more than 127, 382, 1,000, and 5,000 meters from the nearest road (excluding Alaska, for which fine-scale road data are

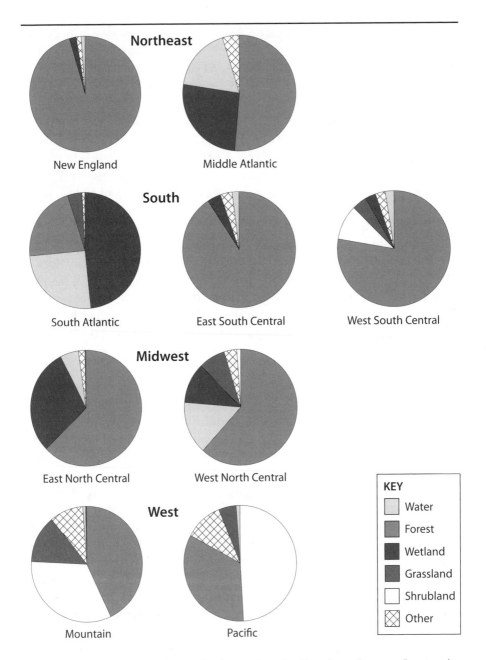

Note: The Forest class combined the NLCD land cover classes Decidous Forest, Evergreen Forest, and Mixed Forest. The Water category was created by combining Open Water and Perennial Ice/Snow. Wetlands included Woody Wetlands and Emergent Herbaceous Wetlands. Grasslands were represented by the NLCD category Grasslands/and Herbaceous and finally Shrublands equals Shrubland. The Other category includes all other classssifications (e.g., agriculture and developed land).

Figure 11.3 Percentages of Wilderness land in each land cover class by Census Division of the United States

not available). Distance of land from roads was calculated using broad-scale coverage of 30-meter grid cells. As one would expect of national coverage data, estimates of proportions of land area are subject to some error due to the coarseness of grid cells relative to Wilderness boundaries. However, from regional and national perspectives, 30-meter grid data are relatively fine scale and good indicators of overall road-land locations. The measure we sought was location of cells with roads relative to the location of cells with Wilderness, regardless of Wilderness boundary locations.

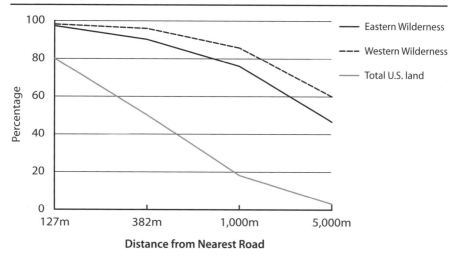

Sources: Riitters and Wickham, 2003; Wilderness Institute, 2003

Figure 11.4 Percentages of eastern and western Wilderness and of all U.S. land at four distances from the nearest road

Table 11.5 Percentages of Eastern and Western Wilderness lands and of all U.S. lands from nearest road at four distances[1]

Distance from the nearest road	Percentage of land in Eastern Wilderness	Percentage of land in Western Wilderness	Percentage of Total U.S. Land
>127 m	97.00	98.00	80.00
>382 m	90.00	95.00	50.00
>1,000 m	76.00	86.00	18.00
>5,000 m	47.00	60.00	3.00

[1] Measurements from grid cells containing Wilderness to those containing roads were taken on a diagonal with the diagonal of each 30 m cell being 42.2 m in length. Thus all of the distances in this study are multiples of 42.2 m. Some of these distances were rounded off (e.g., 1,060 m to 1,000 m; 5,176 m to 5,000 m).

Sources: Riitters and Wickham, 2003; Wilderness Institute, 2003

The delineation for East and West Regions in Figure 11.4 and Table 11.5 is the Mississippi river. Table 11.5 shows the percentages of land in Eastern and Western Wilderness and in the United States as a whole that are more than the four different distances shown from a road. In both the East and in the West, approximately 97 percent of Wilderness land area is more than 127 meters (a little over 400 feet) from a nearest road. Only about 80 percent of all U.S. land, however, was more than this relatively short distance from a road. In the East, 90 percent of designated Wilderness was more than 382 meters from the nearest road, and in the West, 95 percent was farther than 382 meters. These percentages are very high compared with only about 50 percent of total U.S. land area that is farther than this distance, about 1,275 feet. From these computations, it is clear that Wilderness designation results in smaller proportions of the protected land being relatively close to roads, and thus less under their influence.

Figure 11.4, a visual representation of the data in Table 11.5, shows that there are lower percentages of total U.S. land area than the percentages of Wilderness beyond all of the four distances from roads (i.e., 127 m, 382 m, 1,000 m, 5,000 m). Especially beyond the distances of 1,000 and 5,000 meters, the percentage of all U.S. land is much lower than the amount of Wilderness in both the East and the West. In fact, Figure 11.5 compares percentages of Wilderness in the East and West with percentages of all U.S. land that is beyond 5,000 meters of the nearest road. Of all U.S. land, only 3 percent is farther than 5,000 meters from a road. In contrast, 47 percent of Wilderness in the East and 60 percent of Wilderness in the West is beyond 5,000 meters of a road. As well, Figure 11.5 shows that greater percentages of Wilderness in the West, compared with the East, is beyond 5,000 meters. From the research reviewed earlier, one can interpret these results as indicating that Wilderness land is less under the influence of roads, and thus has likely retained more of its natural character than most other land in the United States.

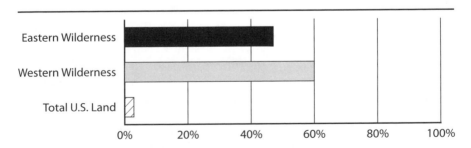

Source: Wilderness Institute, 2003; Riitters and Wickham, 2003

Figure 11.5 Percentage of land area beyond 5,000 meters of the nearest road

Ecosystem Diversity

Davis (1989) and many others have pointed out the importance of natural biodiversity for both current and future generations, and for the future of all life on this planet. One dimension of natural biodiversity is the extant and variety of ecosystems—the broader the diversity of natural ecosystems, the broader the diversity of natural habitats and life conditions supporting a broader diversity of native species and life forms. From high-mountain deserts in Arizona to wetlands, such as the Everglades of Florida, to the grasslands of South Dakota, a wide array of ecosystems have been included through designation of Wilderness areas. Because of the critical habitat Wilderness areas can sometimes protect, as of 1990 more than one half of current Wilderness areas protected one or more federal- or state-listed species classified then as threatened and/or endangered (Cordell & Reed, 1990). In this section, we cover the extent and diversity of ecosystems as classified by the Bailey system at the provincial scale.

Plates 16 through 19 (see Appendix) show the spatial distribution of Wilderness mapped across the United States using *Bailey's Province-level Ecosystem* classification system. Covered are the 48 contiguous states and Alaska. These figures are self-explanatory. In addition, Tables 11.6 through 11.9 show the total acres of Wilderness, total acres of all land, and percent of all land protected as Wilderness for all provinces in each of the Bailey's ecosystem domains. Table 11.6 covers the Tundra and Subarctic Divisions of the Polar Domain. The last column indicates the percentage of the total land area in each

Table 11.6 Acres in Wilderness, total acres in the United States, and percent of U.S. total in Wilderness by ecosystem domain and province: Polar Domain and its Provinces

Domain and Provinces	Total Acres Protected by Wilderness	Total Acres in the Domain	Percent Protected by Wilderness
Polar Domain	43,494,160	332,736,000	13.07
Arctic Tundra	0	12,224,000	0.00
Bering Tundra (Northern)	1,009,107	30,016,000	3.36
Bering Tundra (Southern)	1,568,146	15,104,000	10.38
Brooks Range Tundra–Polar Desert	19,452,783	65,024,000	29.92
Seward Peninsula Tundra–Meadow	0	13,184,000	0.00
Ahklun Mountains Tundra–Meadow	2,354,540	10,688,000	22.03
Aleutian Oceanic Meadow–Heath	4,847,465	14,208,000	34.12
Yukon Intermontane Plateaus Tayga	1,560,365	35,904,000	4.35
Coastal Trough Humid Tayga	0	10,048,000	0.00
Upper Yukon Tayga	0	8,320,000	0.00
Yukon Intermontane Plateaus Tayga–Meadow	1,796,597	35,200,000	5.10
Alaska Range Humid Tayga–Tundra–Meadow	10,298,473	39,040,000	26.38
Upper Yukon Tayga–Meadow	606,683	43,776,000	1.39

Sources: Bailey, 1995; U.S. Geological Survey et al., 1994; Wilderness Institute, 2003

province that has been designated Wilderness. In the Polar Domain, the best-represented provinces are the Aleutian Oceanic Meadow–Heath, Brooks Range Tundra–Polar Desert, Alaska Range Humid Tayga–Tundra, and Ahklun Mountains Tundra–Meadow provinces at 34, 30, 26, and 22 percent of total land area protected, respectively. Much smaller percentages of other provinces in the Polar Domain have been designated. Overall, just over 13 percent of the Polar Domain land area is within the National Wilderness Preservation System. The total area of this domain is just under 333 million acres.

Table 11.7 Acres in Wilderness, total acres in the United States, and percent of U.S. total in Wilderness by ecosystem domain and province: Humid Temperate Domain and its Provinces

Domain and Provinces	Total Acres Protected by Wilderness	Total Acres in the Domain	Percent Protected by Wilderness
Humid Temperate Domain	29,229,831	1,035,264,000	2.82
Laurentian Mixed Forest	1,418,825	94,272,000	1.51
Adirondack–New England Mixed Forest–Coniferous Forest–Alpine Meadow	163,736	27,904,000	0.59
Eastern Broadleaf Forest (Oceanic)	37,405	66,880,000	0.06
Eastern Broadleaf Forest (Continental)	159,224	172,800,000	0.09
Central Appalachian Broadleaf Forest–Coniferous Forest–Meadow	515,477	43,584,000	1.18
Ozark Broadleaf Forest–Meadow	65,698	4,096,000	1.60
Southeastern Mixed Forest	84,816	123,520,000	0.07
Outer Coastal Plain Mixed Forest	654,197	111,232,000	0.59
Lower Mississippi Riverine Forest	4,177	28,352,000	0.01
Ouachita Mixed Forest–Meadow	48,667	5,632,000	0.86
Pacific Lowland Mixed Forest	56,393	9,536,000	0.59
Cascade Mixed Forest–Coniferous Forest–Alpine Meadow	5,181,413	34,176,000	15.16
Pacific Coastal Mountains Forest–Meadow	10,068,353	25,600,000	39.33
Pacific Gulf Coastal Forest–Meadow	3,853,579	15,296,000	25.19
Prairie Parkland (Temporate)	0	139,648,000	0.00
Prairie Parkland (Subtropical)	2,277	51,264,000	0.00
California Coastal Chapparral Forest and Shrub	214,859	6,592,000	3.26
California Dry Steppe Province	0	12,288,000	0.00
California Coastal Steppe, Mixed Forest, and Redwood Forest	44,443	2,944,000	1.51
Sierran Steppe–Mixed Forest–Coniferous Forest–Alpine Meadow	5,276,431	43,712,000	12.07
California Coastal Range Open Woodland–Shrub–Coniferous Forest–Meadow	1,379,861	15,936,000	8.66

Sources: Bailey, 1995; U.S. Geological Survey et al., 1994; Wilderness Institute, 2003

Table 11.7 includes provinces in the Humid Temperate Domain, which ranges from prairie and continental to subtropical, marine, and Mediterranean climates. Best represented of the provinces within this Domain are the Pacific Coastal Mountains Forest–Meadow, Pacific Gulf Coastal Forest–Meadow, Cascade Mixed Forest–Coniferous Forest–Alpine Meadow, Sierran Steppe–Mixed Forest–Coniferous Forest–Alpine Meadow, and California Coastal Range Open Woodland–Shrub–Coniferous Forest–Meadow provinces. Under 3 percent of the total area of this domain of over one billion acres has been designated. This domain makes nearly one half of the overall land area of the United States.

Table 11.8 Acres in Wilderness, total acres in the United States, and percent of U.S. total in Wilderness by ecosystem domain and province: Dry Domain and its Provinces

Domain and Provinces	Total Acres Protected by Wilderness	Total Acres in the Domain	Percent Protected by Wilderness
Dry Domain	30,871,249	919,872,000	3.36
Great Plains Steppe and Shrub	9,536	11,264,000	0.08
Colorado Plateau Semi-Desert	1,187,966	48,192,000	2.47
Southwest Plateau and Plains Dry Steppe and Shrub	32,559	102,976,000	0.03
Arizona-New Mexico Mountains Semi-Desert–Open Woodland–Coniferous Forest–Alpine Meadow	1,313,602	32,128,000	4.09
Chihuahuan Semi-Desert	509,280	54,528,000	0.93
American Semi-Desert and Desert	9,981,523	56,128,000	17.78
Great Plains–Palouse Dry Steppe	518,590	186,048,000	0.28
Great Plains Steppe	12,006	85,760,000	0.01
Southern Rocky Mountain Steppe–Open Woodland–Coniferous Forest–Alpine Meadow	7,790,087	65,472,000	11.90
Middle Rocky Mountain Steppe–Coniferous Forest–Alpine Meadow	5,877,772	52,352,000	11.23
Northern Rocky Mountain Forest–Steppe–Coniferous Forest–Alpine Meadow	1,018,063	24,384,000	4.18
Black Hills Coniferous Forest	9,957	2,368,000	0.42
Intermountain Semi-Desert and Desert	1,028,430	68,544,000	1.50
Intermountain Semi-Desert	961,677	101,824,000	0.94
Nevada-Utah Mountains–Semi-Desert–Coniferous Forest–Alpine Meadow	620,200	27,904,000	2.22

Sources: Bailey, 1995; U.S. Geological Survey et al., 1994; Wilderness Institute, 2003

Table 11.8 includes provinces of the Dry Domain. Best represented of the provinces in this Domain are the American Semi-Desert and Desert, Southern Rocky Mountain Steppe, and the Middle Rocky Mountain Steppe-Coniferous Forest. Just under 3.4 percent of this domain is included within the Wilderness System. The total land area making up this domain is about 920 million acres. Together with the Temperate Domain, these two domains represent approximately 85 percent of the total U.S. land area.

Table 11.9 covers the Humid Tropical Domain, which is made up of only three provinces. The only one of these provinces represented within the National Wilderness Preservation System is the Everglades, totaling about 1.4 million acres. Not represented are ecosystems in Puerto Rico and Hawaii. The Everglades Wilderness, however, is nearly 20 percent of the Humid Tropical Domain's total of nearly 7.4 million acres.

Overall, of the 52 different provinces in the Bailey system covering ecosystems in the United States, only nine are not represented to some degree within the NWPS. The provinces within each domain that are best represented have been noted. Least represented are provinces in the East, the prairies of the Midwest, the tropical forests of Puerto Rico, and the Hawaiian Islands. Nevertheless, much of the diversity of ecosystems across the United States have been included—a diversity that represents many different natural ecosystems which provide essential support for native fauna and flora. For some provinces, however, the extent or area protected is small.

Data Gaps and Promising Programs

Overall, there appear to be considerable gaps in data needed to fully cover the many indicators recommended in the literature for describing and monitoring the health and naturalness of Wilderness. In this chapter, we have equated natural ecosystem health with naturalness as the necessary conditions for Wilderness to have ecological value. While we found a number of studies that

Table 11.9 Acres in Wilderness, total acres in the United States, and percent of U.S. total in Wilderness by ecosystem domain and province: Humid Tropical Domain and its Provinces

Domain and Provinces	Total Acres Protected by Wilderness	Total Acres in the Domain	Percent Protected by Wilderness
Humid Tropical Domain	1,447,381	7,360,000	19.67
Everglades	1,447,381	4,992,000	28.99
Puerto Rico	0	2,368,000	0.00
Hawaiian Islands	0	4,160,000	0.00

Sources: Bailey, 1995; U.S. Geological Survey et al., 1994; Wilderness Institute, 2003

focused on the ecological health of Wilderness, most were focused on specific areas, organisms, or issues. Few studies had taken a broad-scale approach, and limited broad-scale data were found for assessing the health and naturalness of the NWPS as a whole. As well, there is a general lack of essential synoptic data with assessments backed by field studies and appropriate analytical methods (Patil, Brooks, Myers, Rapport & Taillie, 2001). In reviewing ecological monitoring in Wilderness, Susan Bratton concluded, "…wilderness legislation has done little to encourage environmental monitoring. The sites which have extensive monitoring programs have them because of other legislation, or because of management histories which have little to do with the Wilderness Act" (Landres, 1995, p. 10). In this section of this chapter on ecological value, briefly presents some of the promising emerging programs that might help fill some of the data gaps in Wilderness monitoring. None of these programs were sufficiently developed by the time of analysis for this chapter for use as data sources.

Emerging Broad-Scale Data Sources

Broad-scale data providing coverage nationally and regionally are likely to be much more available in the future. These braod-scale data are increasingly resolute, enabling increasingly fine-grained examinations of Wilderness and other lands. Through mapping and other spatial analytics, changing land conditions can be monitored and emerging problems can be identified.

Gap Analysis Program (GAP)

GAP analysis is a systematic method for identifying the degree to which native animal species and natural communities are represented in any existing mix of conservation lands. The native species and communities not represented in the existing network of conservation lands constitute "gaps." GAP analysis was started in 1987 by Michael Scott and involved overlaying maps of land cover and species occurrence onto maps of protected areas using GIS technology. The resulting maps show areas of biological significance relative to protection status (USGS, 2004a). The purpose of GAP is to provide broad geographic information on the status of species, whether threatened, rare or not (Jennings & Scott, 1997). There is an aquatic component to GAP intended to focus on aquatic habitats and taxa, complementary to terrestrial gap analysis (USGS, 2004b). GAP "seeks to identify habitat types and species not adequately represented in the current network of biodiversity management areas" (Gap Analysis Program, 2000). Spatial distributions of GAP data with Wilderness boundary data enable assessment of the species makeup of Wilderness and identification of gaps perhaps needing management attention. Thus GAP represents a growing potential for assessing the ecological health and naturalness of Wilderness. Full data for every state of the United States is not yet available.

Natural Heritage Program

The NWPS can serve as a refuge for rare species and natural communities. Because rare species and communities are the focus of the Natural Heritage Program (NHP), its data also represent a potential for assessing Wilderness health. While the GAP includes all native species and natural land cover, the Natural Heritage Program analyzes only rare and endangered species and significant natural communities. The status of more than 30,000 species in the United States has been assessed by Natural Heritage scientists (Stein, 2001). The NHP's mission is to "develop, manage, and distribute authoritative information critical to the conservation of the world's biological diversity" (NatureServe, 2003). Like GAP, the NHP offers growing potential for monitoring the health and naturalness condition of Wilderness. Direct applicability at this time is limited because the methods used to gather and report data (and to complete analysis) vary from state to state. But the processes and comparability of the NHP data are improving and do offer potential for future monitoring of Wilderness.

Earth Observing System

Landres, Spildie, and Queen (2001) published a paper on the uses of GIS and broad-scale data for monitoring Wilderness, including the National Aeronautic and Space Administration's Earth Observation System satellite. As we have done in this chapter, these frequent, relatively high-resolution data, along with advancing systems of spatial analytic tools, are becoming ever more useful for monitoring Wilderness conditions. NASA's Earth Observing System provides "long-term, consistent measurements of many of the key physical characteristics of landscapes that can be used to identify shifts in variety and extent of natural system components. These data can provide overall assessments of both human-induced and natural disturbances, from local to global levels of resolution. Currently there are 24 measurements that include aspects of the atmosphere, land (e.g., land cover and land-use change, vegetation dynamics, fire occurrence), ocean, and cryosphere (e.g., land ice, snow cover; NASA 2004). These and other satellite data may be used in future studies.

Environmental Monitoring and Assessment Program (EMAP)

The U.S. Environmental Protection Agency (USEPA) has established the nationwide EMAP system (Landres, 1995). The objective of the EMAP program is to develop tools to monitor and assess the status of ecological resources in the United States and to "develop scientific understanding for translating environmental monitoring data from multiple spatial and temporal scales into assessments of current ecological conditions…" (USEPA, n.d.). This program employs indicators (as we have done in this chapter) to monitor the conditions of ecological resources, conduct large regional projects through multiagency monitoring, and guide monitoring with an improved understanding of eco-system integrity and dynamics. This research supports the National Environ-mental Monitoring Initiative of the Committee on Environment and Natural Resources. The National inventory includes the 34 national research and mon-itoring programs funded by the majority of the federal environmental moni-toring budget. These inventories include spatially continuous monitoring over large regions, including remote sensing, monitoring large regions using aerial sampling, and studies on particular research sites (USEPA, n.d.). The data gathered for this program includes many Wilderness sites (Landres, 1995).

NPS Inventory and Monitoring Program

The National Park Service's Inventory and Monitoring Program was developed to "provide monitoring data to detect long-term trends and...ecological con-sequences of environmental change" (Fettig & Thomas, 2004). Monitoring includes species occurrence and distribution, water resources and their chem-istry, air quality, meteorological conditions, soils, geologic features, and vegeta-tion. The NPS is cooperating with state geologic agencies to produce maps and assessments. The 270 National Parks are organized into 32 monitoring net-works. Key indicators, "vital signs," are monitored in each network to detect changes significant to the natural ecological health over time (NPS, 2003). The NPS has recently identified and prioritized potential vital signs related specifically for Wilderness conditions in the Southern Colorado Plateau Inven-tory and Monitoring Network (Fettig & Thomas, 2004). Such "vital signs" data is likely to be very important to monitoring ecological health and naturalness of at least NPS Wilderness in the future.

USGS–NPS Vegetation Mapping

One of the inventories in the NPS Inventory and Monitoring Program is veg-etation mapping. This work is being done cooperatively between the National Biological Survey and the National Park Service of the Department of Interior (NBS/NPS). The Vegetation Mapping Survey was developed to generate vegeta-tion maps for National Park units using a uniform, hierarchical classification system. Products include digital vegetation maps, digital meta data, textual descriptions, and keys to the vegetation classes (U.S. Geological Survey, 1994). Different parks currently are at different stages of completion. The classification standards may ultimately serve as models for detailed mapping of vegetation in Wilderness areas outside of the National Park System as well.

Air Quality Monitoring

Another measure for assessing natural qualities in Wilderness areas is air quality. The Clean Air Act mandates the "affirmative responsibility" to prevent dete-rioration of air quality in Class I areas (including Wilderness areas). Because of this mandate, systematic sampling protocols have been developed to monitor Air Quality Related Values (AQRVs) in Wilderness. Specific protocols have been developed for Pacific Northwest and California Wilderness (Landres, 1995). AQRVs include flora, fauna, soil, water, visibility, and odor (Holland-Sears, 1998). Over time, these data can be used in building a database of ecological attributes, and the sampling protocols used to monitor air quality across U.S. Wilderness areas.

National Hydrography Dataset

The National Hydrography Dataset (NHD) was created by integrating the USGS Digital Line Graph (DLG) hydrography data with drainage network information from the EPA Reach File Version 3 (RF3). The NHD is currently being used to study the value of water originating in Wilderness (Spildie, 2004). The NHD is a comprehensive set of digital spatial data containing coverages of surface water features such as lakes, ponds, streams, rivers, springs, and wells. These features are combined to from "reaches," which allow the user to link water-related data to the surface water drainage network. Linking data to the network enables display and analysis of data in upstream and downstream order (USGS, 2004c). There are several applications already available on the Internet (http://nhd.usgs.gov/applications.html). In future developments, data describing water quality can be linked to surface drainage systems for comparison of the quality of water flowing from Wilderness with quality of water flowing from urban and agricultural areas.

National Monitoring Protocol

The Aldo Leopold Wilderness Research Institute is collaboratively developing a National Monitoring Protocol for the four federal agencies that manage Wilderness. The protocol is based on the legislative definition of Wilderness and its attributes and centers on four qualities. These include untrammeled, undeveloped, outstanding opportunities for solitude, and naturalness. For each of these qualities, core indicators have been developed which can be practically and reliably monitored (Landres, 2004). At this point, data availability are the primary impediment to implementation of this work.

The Value of Water from Wilderness

Many of the areas protected by the NWPS are located in the headwaters of major drainages that provide water to downstream cities and metropolitan areas. The Value of Water from Wilderness project is under design by the Aldo Leopold Wilderness Research Institute for assessing the value of water coming from Wilderness and other protected areas. A pilot for this project is under way in the Fresno, California, area. This area was selected because it contains a metropolitan area with hydrographic connectivity to Wilderness (Spildie, 2004).

Other Contributing Studies

A number of other studies offer potential for improving our capacity to monitor and assess the ecological value of Wilderness. A few of these are described here.

Protecting Water Resources

The Trust for Public Land and the American Water Works Association (AWWA) recently released a report that provides scientific, economic, and public health linkages to protection of drinking water sources and recharge lands. The major conclusion was that protection of land is the only way to prevent contamination by nonpoint source pollutants. Protection provides greater groundwater services, cleaner water downstream, and less flooding and soil erosion (Ernst, 2004).

Montana Aquatics Study

A study that compared aquatic ecosystem health in watersheds containing Wilderness to those with no Wilderness protection found that the watersheds with more land protection were the healthier (Hitt & Frissell, 2000). They found that existence of Wilderness was a significant contributor to regional aquatic ecosystem conservation. Over 70 percent of the healthiest watersheds contained Wilderness, or were watersheds within Wilderness boundaries.

Southern Appalachian Wilderness Study

Haney and colleagues (1999) conducted a study which examined the ecological capacity of a multiunit Wilderness system in the Southern Appalachian region. They defined ecological capacity as ability to adequately protect a suite of designated natural attributes. This study provides an example of methods for assessing the ecological capacity of Wilderness in large-scale ecosystems, such as the Southern Appalachians.

Landscape Change and Ecological Resources

A study conducted by Jones and associates (2001) used satellite imagery and land cover data to assess landscape change in a large region over a 20-year period. The focus was on birds and nitrogen yield to assess the effects of land-scape change on ecosystem health in the mid-Atlantic region.

Eastern National Park Vegetation Mapping Project

The University of Georgia Center for Remote Sensing and Mapping Science has created databases and detailed vegetation maps of the Great Smoky Mountain National Park, the Everglade National Park, and other protected lands in Florida (Purdy, 2003). The primary focus is on the Great Smokey Mountains

National Park, an area of over 500,000 acres with 100 species of trees, more than 1,570 species of flowering plants, and another 4,000 nonflowering species. The resulting maps provide richness of detail accurate to within 15 feet (Purdy, 2003), and offers a model likely useful in the future to track natural and man-made disturbances to Wilderness and to measure naturalness.

Wilderness in Australia

Mackey, Lesslie, Lindenmayer, Nix, and Incoll (1998) studied designated Wilderness in Australia by overlaying National Wilderness Inventory (NWI) data with national-level data on threatened vertebrate animal species and plants. The NWI developed a set of indicators which measure and quantify the remoteness and naturalness of an area. This study found that high numbers of threatened species correlate with low Wilderness quality (i.e., remoteness and naturalness) with more threatened species in areas that have been heavily impacted by society.

Predicting Regional Biodiversity

Hansen, Waring, Phillips, Swenson, and Loehle (2003) integrated the use of traditional environmental variables, such as habitat type, with biophysical factors, such as climate, topography, and vegetation, to predict richness and abundance of bird, tree, and shrub species across the Pacific and Inland Northwest. The methods used integrate satellite data and computer simulation in ways that could be used nationally to predict and monitor biodiversity in Wilderness and non-Wilderness areas.

Summary

The Wilderness Act was passed to protect the naturalness of selected wildlands in the United States. In this chapter we focused on the idea that degree of naturalness is the key indicator of the life-sustaining health and ecological value of lands in the NWPS. We reasoned that the more natural are Wilderness lands, relative to other lands, the greater is their ecological value. The literature we reviewed supports this line of reasoning.

By legal definition, Wilderness areas are natural areas where natural processes dominate and the natural landscape is sustained without direct human intervention. In this chapter, we examined four measures that can be interpreted as indicators of naturalness. The objective was to examine whether Wilderness designation seems to be doing what it was meant to do; that is, prevent human activities so that it can provide self-determined natural life support. In today's society with its shifting values and viewpoints, knowing whether designation is actually protecting the essential natural character of Wilderness lands is an important question.

A wide range of potential measures of naturalness and ecosystem health have been identified in the literature. Unfortunately, data to support implementation of most of these measures is thus far quite limited. This accepted, we depended on four surrogate measures of naturalness including fragmentation, land cover, distance from roads, and ecosystem representation. Findings for each of these four measures are summarized briefly next.

Summary by Indicator

There has been considerable recent work examining ecosystem fragmentation, but little of it has examined types of ecosystems other than Eastern forests. For this reason, the analysis of fragmentation in Wilderness lands for this chapter, as compared to other lands, was limited to forests. Findings showed that overall there is substantial evidence that forest land protected through Wilderness designation is very little fragmented relative to other forest land in the East. We interpret this result as evidence that Wilderness forests are more natural and healthy, and thus have more ecological value than non-Wilderness forests.

Land cover is another indicator of the naturalness of land. Human activities alter land cover and can cause deterioration of the native life support services those lands provide. Results from an analysis of the level of undeveloped land cover in Wilderness indicates that Wilderness has been effective in protecting naturalness. This protection is especially prominent in the Northeast, South, and Midwest regions. Natural land cover was a little less helpful in assessing naturalness in the West region because in that region it is more difficult to distinguish between disturbed managed lands and "barren" natural land covers, such as stretches of desert void of vegetation. Nonetheless, Western Wilderness was shown to be considerably more natural than any other Western land compared.

Distance from roads was also used as an indicator of the naturalness of Wilderness. We examined the amount of Wilderness beyond specified distances from a nearest road. Generally, much greater percentages of Wilderness in both the East and West were beyond nearest roads as compared with percentages of all other lands in those regions. As well, more land in western Wilderness was beyond nearest roads than in eastern Wilderness. More land further from roads indicates that Wilderness is more natural, less subject to human disturbance, and of greater ecological value.

In addition to protection of species, genes, and other "microdiversity," protection of broad-scale biodiversity across the range of types of ecosystems in the United States is highly important. Ecoregions have been defined as relatively large units of land and water with distinct assemblages of natural communities and species and with boundaries that approximate the original extent of natural communities. We adopted the "Bailey system" of ecosystem classification (Bailey, 2002). The analysis of spatial data indicated that a wide range of ecosystem types has been protected under the Wilderness System. These include high-mountain deserts in Arizona, wetlands such as the Everglades of Florida, and grasslands such as in South Dakota. Overall, of the 52 different ecosystem types labeled in the Bailey system as provinces, only 9 are not represented to some degree within the NWPS. Least represented are provinces in the East, prairies of the Midwest, forests of Puerto Rico, and Hawaii's islands.

The four measures used to assess the naturalness of Wilderness showed clearly that designation distinguishes lands included from lands not included. This distinction shows up as an apparent higher level of naturalness and better ecological health. As such, Wilderness is better able to provide life support to native life forms. Wilderness is less fragmented, has greater amounts of vegetated land cover, and has greater proportions of area that are remote from roads. Generally, as well, Wilderness protects an important dimension of biodiversity; that is, ecosystem diversity. A considerable amount of research remains to be done to more fully understand the ecological value of Wilderness as a tool for assuring support for natural life. We are encouraged at the number of state and federal agencies, universities, and private groups with research and development programs aimed at improving monitoring of the condition and value of Wilderness, and other wildlands. It is our hope that these programs will quickly advance Wilderness assessment and monitoring capacities well beyond what is described in this chapter.

There are many pressures not only on unprotected wildlands, public and private, but also on Wilderness lands. These include fragmentation, road construction, off-road vehicle use, energy drilling, mining, urban growth and other human activities (Campaign for America's Wilderness, 2002). Designating Wilderness may be the last hope for protecting the health, naturalness, and ecological value of this country's wildlands. The assessment presented in this chapter indicates this to be the case.

Literature Cited

Anderson, J.E. (1991). A conceptual framework for evaluating and quantifying naturalness. *Conservation Biology, 5*(3), 347–352.

Angermeier, P.L. (2000). The natural imperative for biological conservation. *Conservation Biology, 14*(2), 373–381.

Bader, M. (2000). *Spatial needs of grizzly bears in the U.S. northern Rockies.* Missoula, MT: Alliance for the Wild Rockies.

Bailey, R.G. (1995). *Description of the ecoregions of the United States* (Misc. Pub. 1391). Washington, DC: USDA Forest Service.

Bailey, R.G. (2002). *Ecoregion-based design for sustainability.* New York, NY: Springer.

Belaoussoff, S. and Kevan, P.G. (1998). Toward an ecological approach for the assessment of ecosystem health. *Ecosystem Health, 4*(1), 4–8.

Bertollo, P. (1998). Assessing ecosystem health in governed landscapes: A framework for developing core indicators. *Ecosystem Health, 4*(1), 33–51.

Campaign for America's Wilderness. (2002). *America's wilderness heritage in crisis: Our vanishing wild landscape.* Washington, DC: Campaign for America's Wilderness.

Chaffin, T. (1998). *Whole-earth mentor: A conversation with Eugene P. Odum*—includes excerpt from Odum's "Ecology: A bridge between science and society" interview. Retrieved November 8, 2004, from http://www.findarticles.com/p/articles/mi_m1134/is_n8_v107/ai_21191216

Christensen, N.L., Bartuska, A.M., Brown, J.H., Carpenter, S., D'Antonio, C., Francis, R., et al. (1996). The report of the Ecological Society of America Committee on the Scientific Basis for Ecosystem Management. *Ecological Application, 6*(3), 665–691.

Coates, B., Jones, A.R., and Williams, R.J. (2002). Is "ecosystem health" a useful concept for coastal managers? *Coast to Coast, 55*–58.

Cole, D.N. (2000). Paradox of the primevil: Ecological restoration in wilderness. *Ecological Restoration, 18*(2), 77.

Cole, D.N. (2001). Management dilemmas that will shape Wilderness in the 21st century. *Journal of Forestry, 99*(1), 4–8.

Cole, D.N. and Landres, P.B. (1996). Threats to wilderness ecosystems: Impacts and research needs. *Ecological Applications, 6*(1), 168–184.

Cordell, H.K. and Overdevest, C. (2001). *Footprints on the land: An assessment of demographic trends and the future of natural lands inthe United States.* Champaign, IL: Sagamore Publishing.

Cordell, H.K. and Reed, P.C. (1990). Untrammeled by man: Preserving diversity through wilderness. In *Preparing to manage Wilderness in the 21st century,* Proceedings of the Conference (GTR SE-66; pp. 1–4). Athens, GA: USDA Forest Service, Southeastern Forest Experiment Station.

Costanza, R. (1992). Toward an operational definition of ecosystem health. In R. Costanza, B.G. Norton, and B.D. Haskell (Eds.), *Ecosystem health: New goals for environmental management* (pp. 239–256). Washington, DC: Island Press.

Dahms, C.W. and Geils, B.W. (Eds.). (1997). An assessment of forest ecosystem health in the Southwest (GTR RM-295). Fort Collins, CO: USDA Forest Service, Rocky Mountain Forest and Range Experiment Station.

Dailey, G.C., Alexander, S., Ehrlich, P.R., Goudler, L., Lubchenco, J., Matson, P.A., et al. (1997). Ecosystem services: Benefits supplied to human societies by natural ecosystems. *Issues in Ecology, 2.*

Davis, G.D. (1989). Preservation of natural diversity: The role of ecosystem representation with-in wilderness. In P.C. Reed, H.K. Cordell, and H.R. Freilich (Eds.),

Wilderness benchmark 1988: Proceedings of the National Wilderness Colloquium (GTR SE-51; pp. 76–82). Asheville, NC: USDA Forest Service, Southeastern Forest Experiment Station.

Debinski, D.M. and Holt, R.D. (2000). A survey and overview of habitat fragmentation experiments. *Conservation Ecology, 14*(2), 342–355.

De Leo, G.A. and Levin, S. (1997). The multifaceted aspects of ecosystem integrity [online]. *Conservation Ecology, 1*(1), 3. Retrieved November 9, 2004, from http://www.consecol.org/vol1/iss1/art3

de Rosnay, J. (1997). Homeostasis: Resistance to change. *Principia Cybernetica Web.* Retrieved November 9, 2004, from http://pcp.lanl.gov/HOMEOSTA.html

Dymond, C., Carver, S., and Phillips, O. (2003). Investigating the environmental cause of global wilderness and species richness distributions. In A. Watson and J. Sproull (Comp.), *Science and stewardship to protect and sustain wilderness values: Seventh world wilderness congress symposium* (RMRS-P-27; pp. 231–237). Fort Collins, CO: USDA Forest Service, Rocky Mountain Research Station.

Ernst, C. (2004). *Protecting the source: Land conservation and the future of America's drinking water.* Retrieved November 9, 2004, from http://www.wvnet.org/downloads/posted%20june102004/TPL_2004_protecting_the_source.pdf

Fettig, S.M. and Thomas, L. (2004, September). *Identifying potential signs for monitoring wilderness and wild land values* (#051407). Paper presented at the meeting of the Monitoring Science & Technology Symposium, Fort Collins, CO.

Forman, R.T.T. (2000). Estimate of the area affected ecologically by road system of the United States. *Conservation Biology, 14,* 31–35.

Forman, R.T.T. and Alexander, L.E. (1998). Roads and their major ecological effects. *Annual Review of Ecology and Systematics, 29,* 207–231.

Forman, R.T.T., Sperling, D., Bissonette, J.A., Clevenger, A.P., Cutshall, C.D., Dale, V.H. et al. (2002). *Road ecology: Science and solutions.* Washington, DC: Island Press.

Fu-liu, X. and Shu, T. (2000). On the study of ecosystem health: State of the art. *Journal of Environmental Sciences, 12*(1), 33.

Gap Analysis Program. (2000). *A handbook for conducting gap analysis.* Retrieved November 9, 2004, from http://www.gap.uidaho.edu/handbook

GDT (Geographic Data Technology). (2002). *Dynamap/2000 user manual.* Lebanon, NH: Geographic Data Technology.

Haney, J.C., Wilbert, M., De Grood, C., Lee, D.S., and Thomson, J. (1999). *Gauging the ecological capacity of Southern Appalachian reserves: Does wilderness matter?* Retrieved November 9, 2004, from http://www.wilderness.org/Library/Documents/upload/Gauging_the_Ecological_Capacity_of_Southern_Appalachian_Reserves.pdf

Hansen, A., Waring, R., Phillips, L., Swenson, J., and Loehle, C. (2003). *Using biophysical factors to predict regional biodiversity potential in the Pacific and inland Northwest.* Retrieved November 9, 2004, from http://www.homepage.montana.edu/~hansen/documents/downloadables/MSU_OSU_reportfinal.pdf

Heilman, G.E., Jr., Strittholt, J.R., Slosser, N.C., and Dellasala, D.A. (2002). Forest fragmentation of the conterminous United States: assessing forest intactness through road density and spatial characteristics. *BioScience, 52,* 411–422.

Heinz Center (The H. John Heinz III Center for Science, Economics and the Environment). (2002). *The state of the nation's ecosystems: Measuring the lands, waters, and living resources of the United States.* Cambridge, UK: Cambridge University Press.

Hitt, N.P. and Frissell, C. (2000). *An evaluation of wilderness and aquatic biointegrity in Western Montana.* Retrieved November 9, 2004, from http://www.wilderness.net/library/documents/Hitt_2_17.pdf

Hobbs, R.J., Arico, S., Aronson, J., Baron, J.S., Bridgewater, P., Cramer, V.A., et al. (2004). *Emerging ecosystems: Theoretical and management aspects of the new ecological world order.* Retrieved on November 5, 2004, from http://www.unesco.org/mab/EE/hobbs.pdf

Holland-Sears, A. (1998). *Air resource management plan: White River National Forest.* Retrieved February 14, 2005, from http://www.fs.fed.us/r6/aq/natarm/whiteriver.pdf

Hutton, J. (1788). *Theory of the earth; or an investigation of the laws observable in the composition, dissolution, and restoration of land upon the globe.* Retrieved February 14, 2005, from http://www.mala.bc.ca/~johnstoi/essays/Hutton.htm.

Jennings, M. and Scott, M.J. (1997). *Official description of the national Gap Analysis Program.* Retrieved on February 11, 2005, from http://www.gap.uidaho.edu/About/Overview/GapDescription/#Mission

Jones, K.B., Neale, A.C., Wade, T.G., Wickham, J.D., Cross, C.L., Edmonds, C.M. et al. (2001). The consequences of landscape change on ecological resources: An assessment of the United States Mid-Atlantic Region, 1973–1993. *Ecosystem Health, 7*(4), 229–242.

Jorgensen, S. (1995). The application of ecological indicators to assess the ecological condition of a lake. *Lakes and Reservoirs: Research and Management, 1,* 177–182.

Karr, J.R. (1981). Assessment of biotic integrity using fish communities. *Fisheries, 6,* 21–27.

Karr, J.R. and Dudley, D.R. (1981). Ecological perspectives in water quality goals. *Environmental Management, 5,* 55-68.

Karr, J.R., Fausch, K.D., Angermeier, P.L., Yant, P.R., and Schlosser, I.J. (1986). *Assessing biological integrity in running waters: A method and its rational* [M]. Champaign, IL: Illinois Natural History Survey, Special Publication 5.

Kay, J.J. (1993). On the nature of ecological integrity. In S. Woodley, J. Kay, and G. Fransis (Eds.), *Ecological integrity and the management of ecosystems* (pp. 201–213). Waterloo, ON: St. Lucie Press.

Keddy, P.A., Lee, H.T., and Wisheu, I.C. (1993). Choosing indicators of ecosystem integrity: Wetlands as a model system. In S. Woodley, J. Kay, and G. Fransis

(Eds.), *Ecological integrity and the management of ecosystems* (pp. 61–79). Delray Beach, FL: St. Lucie Press.

Kolb, T.E., Wagner, M.R., and Covington, W.W. (1994). Concepts of forest health: Utilitarian and ecosystem perspectives. *Journal of Forestry, 92*(7), 10–15.

Landres, P. (2004). Developing indicators to monitor the "outstanding opportunities" quality of Wilderness character. *International Journal of Wilderness, 10*(3), 8–11, 20.

Landres, P.B. (1995). The role of ecological monitoring in managing wilderness. *TRENDS/Wilderness Research, 32*(1), 10–13.

Landres, P. B., Morgan, P., and Swanson, F.J. (1999). Overview of the use of natural variability in managing ecological systems. *Ecological Applications, 9*(4), 1179–1188.

Landres, P., Spildie, D.R., and Queen, L.P. (2001). *GIS applications to wilderness management: potential uses and limitations* (GTR RMRS-80). Fort Collins, CO: USDA Forest Service, Rocky Mountain Research Station.

Leopold, A. (1949). *A Sand County almanac.* New York, NY: Oxford Press.

Lindermann, R.L. (1942). The trophic-dynamic aspect of ecology. *Ecology, 23,* 399–418.

Mackey, B.G., Lesslie, R.G., Lindenmayer, D.B., Nix, H.A., and Incoll, R.D. (1998). *The role of wilderness in nature conservation.* Retrieved November 12, 2004, from http://www.heritage.gov.au/anlr/code/pubs/rolewild.html

McIntire, T. (Ed.). (1988). *Forest health through silviculture and integrated pest management: A strategic plan.* Washington, DC: USDA Forest Service.

Meffe, G.K. and Carroll, C.R. (1997). *Principles in conservation biology* (2nd ed). Sunderland, MA: Sinauer Associates, Inc.

MDNR (Maryland Department of Natural Resources). (2001). *Maryland's greenprint program: Summary of methods to identify and evaluate Maryland's green infrastructure.* Retrieved November 12, 2004, from http://www.dnr.state.md.us/education/growfromhere/lesson4/greenprint/gpevaluation.pdf

Naeem, S., Chapin, F.S., Costanza, R., Ehrlich, P.R., Golley, F.B., Hooper, D.U. et al. (1999). *Biodiversity and ecosystem functioning: Maintaining natural life support processes.* Retrieved November 12, 2004, from http://www.epa.gov/watertrain/pdf/issue4.pdf

NASA. (2004). *The earth observing system: EOS program description.* Retrieved November 12, 2004, from http://eospso.gsfc.nasa.gov/eos_homepage/description.php

National Park Service, U.S. Department of the Interior (2003). *Park vital signs monitoring: A commitment to resource protection.* Retrieved November 12, 2004, from http://www.cnr.uidaho.edu/rrt496/Vital_signs_brochure.pdf

National Research Council. (1997). *Toward a sustainable future: Addressing the long-term effects of motor vehicle transportation on climate and ecology.* Washington, DC: National Academy Press.

NatureServe (2003). *About us.* Retrieved November 12, 2004, from http://www. natureserve.org/aboutus/index.jsp

Noss, R.F. (1990). What can wilderness do for biodiversity? In P.C. Reed (Ed.), *Preparing to manage wilderness in the 21st Century: Proceedings of the conference* (GTR SE-66; pp. 49-61). Asheville, NC: USDA Forest Service, Southeastern Forest Experiment Station.

Odum, E.P. (1989). *Ecology and our endangered life-support systems.* Sunderland, MA: Sinauer Associates, Inc.

Patil, G.P., Brooks, R.P., Myers, W.L. Rapport, D.J., and Taillie, C. (2001). Ecosystem health and its measurement at landscape scale: Toward the next generation of quantitative assessments. *Ecosystem Health, 7*(4), 307–316.

Purdy, J. (2003). Maps protect national treasures. *University of Georgia Research Magazine* [online]. Retrieved November 15, 2004, from http://www.ovpr.uga. edu/researchnews/fall2003/maps01.htm

Rapport, D.J. (1989). What constitutes ecosystem health? *Perspectives in Biology and Medicine, 33*(1), 120–132.

Rapport, D.J. (2002). The health of ecology and the ecology of health. *Human and Ecological Risk Assessment, 8*(1), 205–213.

Rapport, D.J., Costanza, R., Epstein, P. Gaudet, C., and Levins, R. (Eds.). (1998). *Ecosystem health.* Oxford, UK: Blackwell Science.

Riitters, K.R. and Wickham, J.D. (2003). How far to the nearest road? *Frontiers in Ecology and Environment, 1*(3), 125–129.

Riitters, K.H., Wickham, J.D., and Coulston, J.W. (2004). A preliminary assessment of Montreal process indicators of forest fragmentation for the United States. *Environmental Monitoring and Assessment, 91,* 257–276.

Riitters, K.H., Wickham, J.D., O'Neill, R.V., Jones, K.B., Smith, E.R., Coulston, J.W. et al. (2002). Fragmentation of continental United States forest. *Ecosystems, 5,* 815–822.

Risser, P.G. (1995). Biodiversity and ecosystem function. *Conservation Biology, 9,* 742–746.

Rollins, M.G., Thomas, W.S., and Morgan, P. (2001). Evaluating a century of fire patterns in two Rocky Mountain wilderness areas using digital fire atlases. *Canadian Journal of Forest Research, 31*(12), 2107–2123.

Roy, B.S., Hurtt, G.C., Weaver, C.P., and Pacala, S.W. (2003). Impact of historical land cover change on the July climate of the United States. *Journal of Geophysical Resouces-Atmosphere, 108*(D24).

Ryan, B.D. (1990). *Lichens and air quality in the emigrant wilderness, California: A baseline study.* Retrieved November 15, 2004, from http://airlichen.nacse.org/ airlichenPDF/Emigrant.pdf

Spellerberg, I.F. (1998).Ecological effects of roads and traffic: A literature review. *Global Ecology and Biogeography, 7,* 317–333.

Spildie, D. (2004). *The value of Wilderness water.* Aldo Leopold Wilderness Research Institute [online]. Retrieved on February 14, 2005, from http://leopold. wilderness.net/htopics/water_proj.htm.

Stein, B.A. (2001). A fragile cornucopia: Assessing the status of U.S. biodiversity. *Environment, 43*(7), 11–22.

Tansley, A. (1935). The use and abuse of vegetational concepts and terms. *Ecology, 16,* 284–307.

Trombulak, S.C. and Frissell, C.A. (2000). Review of ecological effects of roads on terrestrial and aquatic communities. *Conservation Biology, 14,* 18–30.

Turner, J. (1996). *The abstract wild.* Tucson, AZ: The University of Arizona Press.

Ulanowicz, R.E. (1986). *Growth and development: Ecosystems phenomenology.* New York, NY: Springer-Verlag.

Ulanowicz, R.E. (1980). An hypothesis on the development of natural communities. *Journal of Theoretical Biology, 85,* 223–245.

USDA Forest Service. (n.d.). *Ecosystem provinces.* Retrieved November 17, 2004, from http://www.fs.fed.us/colorimagemap/ecoreg1_provinces.html

USDT (U.S. Department of Transportation). (1993). *Federal Highway Administration, Highway Statistics 1993.* Retrieved February 14, 2005, from http://www.fhwa. dot.gov/ohim/hs93/Sec5.pdf

USDT (U.S. Department of Transportation). (2002). *Federal Highway Administration, Highway Statistics 2002.* Retrieved February 14, 2005, from http://www.fhwa. dot.gov/policy/ohim/hs02/xls/hm20.xls

USEPA (U.S. Environmental Protection Agency). (n.d.). *Environmental monitoring and assessment program (EMAP): About EMAP.* Retrieved November 15, 2004, from http://www.epa.gov/305b/2000report/chp2.pdf

USGS (U.S. Geological Survey). (1994). *USGS-NPS vegetation mapping program.* Retrieved February 14, 2005, from http://biology.usgs.gov/npsveg/classification/ index.html.

USGS (U.S. Geological Survey). (1999, May). *The quality of our nation's waters: Nutrients and pesticides—A summary* (USGS Fact Sheet 116-99). Retrieved February 14, 2005, from http://water.usgs.gov/pubs/fs/FS_116_99/

USGS (U.S. Geological Survey). (2004a). *GAP analysis program: GAP analysis in biodiversity.* Retrieved November 15, 2004, from http://www.gap.uidaho.edu/ About/Overview/IntroductionToGAShorter/default.htm

USGS (U.S. Geological Survey). (2004b). *GAP analysis program: Aquatic GAP.* Retrieved November 15, 2004, from http://www.gap.uidaho.edu/projects/Aquat- ic/default.htm

USGS (U.S. Geological Survey). (2004c). National hydrography dataset. Retrieved November 15, 2004, from http://nhd.usgs.gov/

U.S. Geological Survey, Bailey, R.G., McNab, W.H., Avers, P.E., and King, T. (1994). *Ecoregion and subecoregions of the United States.* Retrieved February 14, 2005, from http://www.fs.fed.us/institute/ecoregions/eco_download.html

Vogelmann, J.E., Howard, S.M., Yang, L., Larson, C.R., Wylie, B.K., and Van Driel, N. (2001). Completion of the 1990s national land cover data set for the conterminous United States from landsat thematic mapper data and ancillary data sources. *Photogrammetric Engineering and Remote Sensing, 67,* 650–652.

Vogelmann, J.E., Sohl T., and Howard, S.M. (1998). Regional characterization of land cover using multiple sources of data. *Photogrammetric Engineering and Remote Sensing, 64,* 45–57.

Wetmore, C.M. (1992). *Lichens and air quality in Hercules Glades Wilderness of Mark Twain* (National Forest. Final Report, contract #42-649). Rolla, MO: USDA Forest Service, Mark Twain National Forest.

Wickham, J.D., Jones, K.B., Riitters, K.H., O'Neill, R.V., Tankersley, R.D., Smith, E.R. et al. (1999). An integrated environmental assessment of the U.S. mid-Atlantic region. *Environmental Management, 24,* 553–560.

Wickham, J.D., O'Neill, R.V., Riitters, K.H., Smith, E., Wade, T., and Jones, K. (2002). Geographic targeting of increases in nutrient export due to future urbanization. *Ecological Applications, 12,* 93–106.

Wilderness Institute. (2003). *Wilderness information network, National Wilderness Preservation System database.* Retrieved November 16, 2004, from http://www. wilderness.net/index.cfm?fuse=NWPS&sec=advSearch

World Wildlife Fund. (2004). *Conservation science—Ecoregions.* Retrieved November 17, 2004, from http://www.worldwildlife.org/science/ecoregions.cfm

Chapter 12
Tracking the Intrinsic Value of Wilderness

Sandra Gudmundsen
Associate Professor, Department of Philosophy
Metropolitan State College of Denver, Denver, Colorado

John B. Loomis
Professor, Department of Agricultural and Resource Economics
Colorado State University, Fort Collins, Colorado

In conceptualizing the framework for the values of Wilderness for this book (see Chapter 4), there was agreement that intrinsic value had to be included as an essential dimension. At the first working group meeting in Washington, DC, Sandra Gudmundsen presented ideas on the meaning of intrinsic value and its application to a fuller understanding of the values of Wilderness. The participants in that early meeting all agreed that a philosopher's perspective of intrinsic value was needed and essential.

In the eyes of many, including some philosophers, "philosophy" is almost synonymous with "not practical." However, philosophy also means "deep thinking about things that really matter." Questions about things that really matter have answers that often determine practical choices. Answers will come from ideas about what exists, what they might mean, and how we might engage with them. For the purposes of this chapter, one of the "things that matter" is finding reasons to believe that wilderness is an entity, that it has integrity, and that it has intrinsic value. For this chapter, somewhat unlike the other chapters in this book, when the authors refer to wilderness, they are thinking about wild natural lands in general. Their comments and conclusions regarding intrinsic values, however, should be as applicable to the more specific case of officially designated Wilderness lands within the National Wilderness Preservation System (as discussed in Chapters 2 through 5).

The approach taken in this chapter is to attempt to identify what it is about wilderness that is valued, and what obligations we as humans have toward it. We understand that some sort of demonstration of the nature of wilderness and our duties toward it were expected. We also understand that some explanation was expected of how our lives might be enhanced if we seriously assumed obligations toward wilderness. In short, we as authors and educators understood that some sort of proof of intrinsic value was wanted. In philosophy, however, proving things is something of a holy grail. There is no universal agreement among philosophers as to whether any given set of objects (e.g., wildlife species, wilderness) has intrinsic value. And there is no universal agreement whether a duty or obligation exists toward those objects. Disagreements can be deep and persistent because it is impossible to provide empirical evidence that an object has intrinsic value. And even if we agree that an object has intrinsic value, and hence a duty toward it exists for us, a second source of disagreement is the inherent subjectivity of defining that duty. Different people can and will reach different conclusions about specific duties, even though they may all agree that existence of intrinsic value implies duties.

It is important to stress what this chapter can and cannot provide. We consider several logical and plausible arguments for the intrinsic value of wilderness. There is no intention, however, to declare any one of them superior or singularly right. We hope to show that there are common threads through all the arguments presented regarding the intrinsic value of wilderness. We readily admit there is a close connection between our own ideals and values and claims we may make about this intrinsic value. By the end of the chapter, it will be argued that individuals and society will be better off by taking seriously those obligations that arise from the intrinsic value of wilderness. In the two sections that follow, the authors review both the anthropocentric and nonanthropocentric ethics as bases for the intrinsic value of wilderness.

Anthropocentric Environmental Ethics

To explore the intrinsic value of something, one must first define what that something is. This definition must be quite apart from how we might make use of that something. Ideally, objective intrinsic value should be independent of human values and pleasures, or even knowledge of them for that matter. From a contemporary perspective, establishing that something is "objective" or inherently real means that it has value whether or not anyone ever perceives it. From a traditional moral philosophy perspective, however, intrinsic value exists only in humans. The reasoning behind this traditional view is that only human beings are capable of rational thought. Rationality has always been the basis for the most universally recognized intrinsic values: truth, beauty, and justice. These are intrinsic values because they are valued for their own sake. Rationality designates the intrinsic value of a being who can appreciate them. This leads us to the anthropocentric basis of environmental ethics.

Nonrational beings can be included in human-centered ethics. Instead of linking moral standing directly to rationality, a nonrational being can be seen as a valued instrument contributing to human well-being. There are four main categories of anthropocentric environmental ethics. These can be seen as four ways a nonrational being can have *instrumental* value for humans. These categories typically express a robust appreciation of nature, but they stop short of attributing intrinsic value to it.

Human Material Welfare

The first category contains theories that emphasize how nature promotes human material welfare. This category includes nature as a source of food, clothing, and shelter. Values in this category are closely related to the economic values of wilderness discussed in Chapters 9 and 10.

Human Excellence

The second category emphasizes how nature promotes human excellence. The focus is on human accomplishments (e.g., generation of new knowledge, cultural advancement, creation of new forms of aesthetic expression), rather than on the welfare of particular individuals. Nature preservation would be instrumentally valuable, according to these theories, because it is essential to human accomplishments, whether as inspiration, object of inquiry, or a precondition for living harmoniously. Such accomplishments may themselves be considered instrumentally valuable in other ethical theories, but in environmental ethics theory, they are considered intrinsically valuable (i.e., "in their own right"). The best known example of "human excellence" theories is virtue ethics from Passmore (1974). The strategy of virtue ethics is to condemn human actions that degrade, spoil, or destroy natural environments because they indicate inappropriate, less-than-virtuous human character. Values in the human excellence category are closely related to some of the social values of Wilderness discussed in Chapter 7.

Sociopolitical Ideals

The third category of anthropocentric environmental ethics emphasizes how sociopolitical ideals may be inspired by nature. In this category, the preservation of the natural environment is seen to exemplify or celebrate social ideals. For example, letting a wild river run free can symbolize various ideals of human action, such as autonomy or self-realization. Indeed, Sagoff (1988) has argued that respect for the autonomy of natural resources is essentially an affirmation of classical liberal democratic principles.

The same concept of equality that grounds the theory of democracy can be extended to nonhumans. To bestow this extension, we must show that animals and other living things are worthy of respect as fellow rights-bearers. In this extended sense of community, other living things would be entitled to rights and protection of those rights. Extension of rights removes any arbitrary distinctions regarding which species have rights. Every living thing becomes a member of the moral community. As members, they are entitled to political recognition. Such an extension would be more consistent with ideals of equality in a social democracy.

Spiritualism

The fourth category of anthropocentric environmental ethics emphasizes how nature promotes spiritualism. Here spiritualism concerns finding and accepting one's proper place in the universe. These theories are exemplified by Judeo-Christian stewardship ethics (Dobel, 1994), as well as by Native American spiritualism (LaDuke, 2000). More recent manifestations of spiritualism include ecofeminism (Merchant, 1990; Plumwood, 1991) and deep ecology (Naess, 1997). Some would not consider deep ecology to be anthropocentric. However, this view ignores the fact that the primary concern is with the human consequences of ecological destruction.

All of these four anthropocentric categories express important ways of valuing wilderness, ranging from an irreplaceable source of natural resources (e.g., wildlife species habitat) to a unique source of spiritual inspiration. All four share the assumption that the values of wilderness exist only in the context of human concerns. This anthropocentric view limits the intrinsic value of wilderness to perceptions of how it is of value to humans. Clearly the capacity of wilderness to inspire our more virtuous, noble, and spiritual attitudes is profound. Nonetheless, it is limited to what we as humans perceive as valuable. But is what humans can perceive the whole story of the intrinsic value of wilderness? This chapter will now explore the possibilities that there may be nonanthropocentric categories of intrinsic value.

Nonanthropocentric Environmental Ethics

Nonanthropocentric ethical theories try to identify a criteria other than rationality on which to base intrinsic values. In some ways, this is even more abstract and may involve a distinction between preserving individual members of a population and preserving the population or group as a whole. There are three categories of nonanthropocentric ethics identified next, together with the first principle proposed by each. In our view, it is pointless to approach this categorization with the intent of selecting a single best theory. Rather, each has a unique insight into the nature of nonrational intrinsic value.

Individualistic Nonanthropocentric Ethical Theory (Sentience Principle)

The first logical step away from the human-centered view of intrinsic value is the one that Jeremy Bentham (1996) suggested in early 1700s, specifically something is said to have intrinsic value if "it can suffer" or feel pain. Today we call that criteria *sentience*. When his criterion for moral considerability is used, the property of sentience becomes its defining principle. Replacing the criterion of rationality with sentience expands the number of beings entitled to respect and ethical consideration from being limited to human beings to including other animal species. But Bentham left nonsentient resources like rivers, rocks, and trees are outside the scope of moral considerability.

Biocentric Well-Being (Flourishing Principle)

The second logical step away from the human-centered view of intrinsic value asks a question. "Is it possible to be guilty of sentience chauvinism?" Limiting the extension of rights to just sentient creatures assumes that something can be harmed only if it can feel harm. But is this necessarily the case. For example, a tree is clearly "harmed" when it is cut down or killed, but most people don't believe that a tree feels that harm. Neither does the harm done to it refer to how cutting it down affects humans and sentient nonhumans. The harm done refers to the tree's death resulting from cutting it down, not to the loss of nonlumber resources or habitat. The flourishing principle makes it possible to say that the tree has intrinsic value even if it cannot experience harm or feel pain. Because it can be harmed, whether it "feels" it or not, the tree has intrinsic value. It has intrinsic value because it would otherwise flourish.

At this point, we have arrived at an individualistic kind of flourishing value in which the individual human, animal, or plant is recognized to have intrinsic value. The controversy which develops at this juncture in environmental ethics is not over the concept of flourishing, but rather over whether it is really the *individual's* flourishing or the flourishing of its *species* or *ecosystem* that has intrinsic value. Ultimately this controversy will bring nonanthropocentric theories back to the profound challenge of collectivism that confronts anthropocentric holism.

The flourishing principle holds that even if a thing cannot be said to have interests per se, it may nevertheless have *a good of its own*. A tree, for example, may be treated in such a way that its capacity for growth and reproduction is reduced or destroyed. This would amount to harming its *natural good*, even though it can't plausibly be said to have an interest in that good (Taylor, 1986). According to Taylor, all individual living beings qualify as moral subjects because they can all be benefited or harmed and consequently each has a good of its own. Significantly, Taylor denies that species are moral subjects with a good of their own because he regards "species" as a class name, and in his view, classes have no good of their own. For this reason, his view has been called *biocentric individualism*.

Holmes Rolston and others argue that ecological wholes, not specific individuals, are intrinsically valuable (Rolston, 1986, 1988). The difference between *holists* and *individualists* is this: according to holists, the good of a species or the good of an ecosystem or the good of the whole biotic community can "trump" the good of individual living beings. In other words, the value of the whole is greater than the sum of the parts: the systemic intrinsic value of the whole exceeds the net sum of the intrinsic values of the individuals, things and subsystems making up the whole system. In contrast, for individualists the good of each individual living thing must always be respected and so always "trumps."

Rolston's (1986, 1988) holistic approach traces back to Aldo Leopold's biocentric ethics in emphasizing the values of beauty, stability, and integrity and the products of the interrelationship and interaction of organisms and their environments (Leopold, 1949/1966). Rolston (1986, 1988) admits that what counts as beauty, stability, and integrity emerges from the interaction of the natural, objective world and rational concepts. But, he argues that the value of the ecosystem is not imposed on it—rather it is discovered already to be there. His works defend the claim that the value of the biotic whole has intrinsic value because the substantive, empirical content of the value is *in* nature and is located there independently of any human or otherwise valuing beings. Rolston's (1986, 1988) environmental ethics is the premiere example of *biotic holism* today.

Nonbiocentric Holism

The name of this category suggests the most radical departure from traditional ethics yet. In fact, it brings this chapter to the farthest margins of coherent environmental ethics. Prior to this point, the development of environmental ethics has followed the question, "On what grounds do we *limit* moral consideration (i.e., intrinsic value) to a particular entity?" At this point, the worry is not with limits, because all living things are included. Rather, now the question is whether we have engaged in "biochauvinism?" This new question leads us to our next principle of nonbiocentric holism—one that is best introduced by an example.

Consider that a stalactite is an organized collection of mineral compounds created by natural processes over time. If that organization is destroyed, whether by someone smashing it for fun or by mining, then it seems reasonable to say that the stalactite is no longer in the condition that is "good for it." When its chemical organization and structure are destroyed, the stalactite has been brought to a "bad" state relative to its own "good" (i.e., it has suffered a "wrong"). Biological organization may be more obvious and impressive because it refers to living things. But, it is ethically suspicious if we as living biological beings insist that an item's good must be defined in terms of biological organization.

If organization is the key to intrinsic value, then all natural entities are morally considerable, whether or not they are living things (Rolston, 1986, 1988). Rocks, fossils, mountains, rivers, waterfalls, stalactites, patterns of weathering on cliffs, glaciers, dunes, and lifeless planets would all be examples of natural beings that have intrinsic moral value. They have intrinsic moral value because they all exhibit sufficient organization and integration to be recognized as a whole that might not be sustained, but that might become nonexistent. This dimension, called *moral extensionism*, expands moral considerability to all things that exist (i.e., to all things that "are"). Moral extensionism seems to bring insight into the many kinds of spirituality that revere *creation*, creation in and of itself, regardless of what was created. Using this criterion, wilderness as a whole would have intrinsic value as a collection of self-organized natural phenomena.

The anthropocentric and nonanthropocentric theories sketched out here have taken us to the frontiers of what philosophy has to offer. Each of the theories presented provide useful insights into different possibilities for establishing the intrinsic value of wilderness. However, the last and broadest claim of intrinsic value arising from mere natural organization may not be the most practical place from which to introduce intrinsic value into the public policy arena. We need a more broadly appealing basis for introducing intrinsic value.

Another Look at the Values Map

Defining the intrinsic value of wilderness is indeed complex. Its definition cannot be accomplished by simply agreeing to look beyond radical equality of preferences and radical scientific objectivity. There are many approaches from anthropocentric and nonanthropocentric. Within the nonanthropocentric approach there are sentient and nonsentient bases, and within the nonsentient basis, there are group, individualistic, and holistic approaches. All of these, however, draw on the vocabulary and judgments of the traditional approaches which never looked beyond a rational being as the only moral subject and agent. None of these traditional, even in tag-team, can tell us for sure that other beings are intrinsically valuable because none can go beyond a human-centered perception of value.

Is there a way to reframe the debate without assuming a preferred approach, without begging the question? If there is, it will need to include both the claim that the intrinsic value of wilderness is an objective reality and the claim that different people have different values. Considering the practical distance even between those who want to *conserve* nature and those who want to *preserve* nature, this might look like an impossible task. Our earlier survey of alternative approaches, however, reminds us of two things. First, there are robust anthropocentric preservationist approaches available, some of which are amplified by radically critical approaches to social theory. Second, there are traditional, social and cultural values associated with wilderness which overlap and cut across positions—both popular and philosophical (see Chapter 7).

The next section argues that a constituency for wilderness might be available with a (1) *strategic retreat* from the search for intrinsic value in nonanthropocentric theories, (2) redirection of what philosophers call *the dialectic*, and (3) a scouting expedition into what Aldo Leopold called *the community* (Leopold, 1949/1966). We will find this a good place for reflection regarding the intrinsic value of wilderness.

A Strategic Retreat from Nonanthropocentric Approaches

No scientific line of reasoning has been successful in establishing intrinsic value beyond the diversity of human preferences. In rational forums from laboratories to seminar rooms to city hall auditoriums, the logical difficulty of defending moral consideration of things not able themselves to act "morally" infects discussion and leads to suspicions of bias and partisan agendas. Beginning from the need to justify preservation of species, Norton (2001) identified approaches for valuing species which we term a *strategic retreat* from nonanthropocentric perspectives.

First, one can argue that a species can or will fulfill an identifiable human demand and thus acquire value that recognizes its contribution to rational beings. Norton (2001) calls this approach *strong anthropocentrism*. A very different approach recognizes that a species or other things may transform human beings in valuable ways. For example, this transformation may include the potential of species to reform and enlighten human demands. Norton (2001) calls this approach to identifying value as *weak anthropocentrism.*

Norton's (2001) primary case for the preservation of species, and for prioritization when all endangered species cannot be saved, rests on *transformative values*. Such values would arise under weak anthropocentrism. Most of us operate daily on the assumption of transformative values, although such values are inevitably normative. Nonetheless, from the philosophical perspective, the concept of the transformative value of an endangered species only needs to show philosophically that the relationship of transformation does or can exist. It does not need to show that the relationship will produce a specific outcome. So although the concept of transformative value remains anthropocentric, since it depends ultimately on values recognized by human beings, it has the character of a consumer-demand value. It has the character of consumer demand because the individual purchaser makes his or her own idiosyncratic decision. For Norton (2001), endangered species represent universal transformative values because all persons may at some time engage in a relationship with them that can be transforming.

In the end, Norton (2001) rejected nonanthropocentric theories attributing intrinsic value to nonhuman individuals, species, and ecosystems as a guide for policy regarding species protection. His reasoning was, while individualistic, nonanthropocentric theories, like Taylor's (1986) biocentric individualism, might generate concern for some legendary, charismatic individual animals, they do not seem to accommodate a general compassion for the pain of various creatures across the phylogenetic scale. Furthermore, while individualistic concerns for rights or interests could be handled ad hoc, there is no reliable way to translate it into protection for *species* through time. Collectivist, non-anthropocentric theories, like Rolston's biotic holism however, carry considerable theoretical weaknesses and are not much better a solution. As Norton put it, no one has yet been able to establish that when an object, say *y*, possesses something, say *x*, that object *y* is inherently good by virtue of having *x*. For writing public policy, this is a fatal weakness since decisive policy arguments for preservation would almost never be made without a clear scientific basis.

In this book, the pure intrinsic value of wilderness is defined as the value of wilderness that would exist even in the absence of human preferences and values (Chapter 4). Thus, Norton's (2001) arguments for weak anthropocentrism and transformative values do not directly help to identify the pure intrinsic value of wilderness because these values ultimately depend on human preferences. The concept of transformative values, however, persuasively suggests that the retreat to anthropocentrism need not collapse merely into "strongly anthropocentric" instrumental values, such as the recreational use values discussed in Chapters 7 and 9.

First of all, Norton's (2001) argument indicates that wild places and species are symbols of American cultural heritage, and therefore are an important part of what we know about the intrinsic value of wilderness. Thus, weak anthropocentrism allows us to say that the destruction of wilderness is wrong for the same reason the destruction of a great work of art is wrong. In losing either, we lose the best example we have of a quality which we would not otherwise fully understand or better grasp (Sagoff, 1988). Second, Norton's (2001) argument directs our attention to the social character of the world in which transformative values are found. In fact, it is the allocation of scarce resources today that determines which transformative possibilities will exist in the future. No practical management of wilderness can occur in the absence of shared objectives and normative principles. If we cannot expect to arrive at a universally compelling claim about the intrinsic value of wilderness, we must give up the hope of persuading nonbelievers that such a value exists. But with Norton's (2001) strategy of weak anthropocentrism, we have reason to reconsider whether human needs and potentials might lead to greater recognition and genuine appreciation of the pure intrinsic value of wilderness.

Social Approaches to Establishing Intrinsic Value

The process by which private citizens deliberate together on issues of public concern with the aim of reaching collective agreement was called the *public sphere* by Habermas (1972). Because the public sphere is not controlled by external interests, or determined by particular power holders, the public sphere ideally promises democratic control and participation. A shared normative base toward wilderness is exactly what we are looking for in this book. When people deliberate on issues of public concern, decisions for action and/or legislation can emerge only if there is enough of a shared base from which to proceed.

In the course of asking how informed and intelligent discourse could fail to reach consensus in the public sphere, Habermas (1972) postulated three deep-seated interests underlying three types of objective and rigorous knowledge. The *technical interest* defines our instrumental relationship to nature. This is the cognitive interest which generates passion for the empirical-analytical sciences where the criteria for reliable knowledge is predictability, control, and successful manipulation of nature. In the wilderness context, it is probably wise to point out that there is nothing immoral about the technical interest; it is just one of three kinds of knowledge goals. The *practical interest* defines our social relationships with ourselves, others, and other cultures. The practical interest is sometimes called the *hermeneutic* interest, emphasizing the interpretive work of disciplines which pursue shared understanding, rather than "proof" to persuade others. The practical interest is also sometimes associated with intersubjectivity and communication, as well as the studies of culture, tradition, and exchange of ideas (Habermas, 1972).

The third kind of cognitive interest is the most controversial and provocative. It is the cognitive value which we think best defines inquiry into the intrinsic value of wilderness. The *emancipatory interest* motivates scientific study, but for a philosophical goal, namely, to live as an autonomous and responsible human being. Emancipatory interest is linked to the ability to reflect critically on one's own presuppositions with the aim of transcending constraints imposed from social, psychological, and contextual causes. This is the process of autonomous development wherein essential potentials are released from their constraints (Habermas, 1972). But autonomy is not license, and the world that awakens potentials exists prior to their actualization. Responsibility is essentially linked to autonomy in human development because success in being who one is, is being proud of it. Like Norton's (2001) concept of a transformative value, the concept of the emancipatory interest concerns normative claims about better and worse ways for human beings to live without making lists of specific commandments and prohibitions. Indeed, Habermas's (1972) overall goal was to determine the necessary conditions for enabling such lists to become policy within the public sphere. In his view, the possibility of a distinct kind of intellectual inquiry generated by distinctive *emancipatory* interest may have been the only solid justification for continued faith in democratic discourse in the public sphere. For this reason, the concept of the *emancipatory interest* differs from that of *transformative values* in its singularity, or its universal claim to define a value as absolutely fundamental to every rational being, namely, the value of autonomy and responsibility.

But the study of wilderness, wildness, and the relation of human societies to wilderness is, at its core, the study of self-formation, autonomy, and independence since wilderness is the practical or material embodiment of these values. In contrast, the majority of our world today is physically shaped by the aggressive sciences that have instrumental interests at their foundation. In this constructed world there is no aspect of autonomy because it is human plans and designs that define an object and its particular functions to be that object forever. If there were no more wilderness, would we still have a concept of autonomy, including a concept of our own autonomy? Or is the continued presence of areas still untamed, still without telephones or highways, still possibly threatening, and still "uncivilized" a necessary condition for the existence of the independent human spirit? It is this emancipatory power of wilderness that may provide a basis for an intrinsic value of wilderness.

The Ecological Community and Intrinsic Value

Leopold (1949/1966) begins Part IV of *A Sand County Almanac* with a reflection on the origins and purpose of ethics. For him, the extension of ethics is a process in ecological evolution. The sequences of this evolution are properly objects of both philosophical and ecological study. Ecologically, an ethic is a limitation on freedom of action in the struggle for existence. Philosophically, ethics implies limits that give that struggle meaning and purpose (Leopold, 1949/1966, p. 238). Leopold's insight is that the convergence between fact and value in the individual in its natural or civil world is the proper foundation of an ecological or holistic ethic. Whether as recognition or noncognitive response, whether to merely survive or to flourish or to progress, any individual, anywhere, proceeds as a member of a community.

> All ethics so far evolved rest upon a single premise: that the individual is a member of a community of interdependent parts. His instincts prompt him to compete for his place in the community, but his ethics prompt him also to cooperate, perhaps in order that there may be a place to compete for. (Leopold, 1949/1966, p. 239)

Was Leopold anthropomorphizing nonhuman individuals? Was he making use of the concepts we have to open doors to our perception of nonhuman communities? In his evolution from *Game Management* (1933/1986) to "The Upshot" in *A Sand County Almanac* (1949/1966), Leopold struggled with naming and classifying the biotic community, without violating its wildness. There likely will always be a struggle between the demand for scientific proof for existence claims and demand to go beyond the mere scientific exhibition of "facts." This is the age-old *human* struggle between being satisfied with knowing *how* it is and needing to know *why* it is (i.e., the ultimate reason for its being).

For Leopold, his "Land Ethic" in *A Sand County Almanac* was the third evolutionary advance in the historical development of human ethics. In his view, the first phase of ethics dealt with the relation between individuals. The second phase dealt with the relation between the individual and society. In the last nine years of his life, he argued that the third phase, the scientific one, should deal with the relation between the individual and the land. The land ethic would basically "enlarge" the boundaries of the community to include soils, waters, plants, and animals, or collectively, the land. Famously too, Leopold says:

> In short, a land ethic changes the role of *Homo sapiens* from conqueror of the land-community to plain member and citizen of it. It implies respect for his fellow-members, and also respect for the community as such. (Leopold, 1949/1966, p. 240)

Some may think that we are quoting Leopold here because it "knocks human beings down a peg." Rather, our motivation is that Leopold's (1949/1966) emphasis on ecological relationships is essential for understanding the value of wilderness. His crucial insight certainly begins with the idea that the biological whole in which a multitude of individuals live has priority. But, more importantly to the ethicist, it entails a notion of a community that contains a *plurality* of individuals who inevitably depend on, and are consequently limited by, the community. This is the idea of *holism,* equally applicable to ethics or ecology. Holism is the sense of the social integration of human and nonhuman nature. This sense of integration is generated by ecological science, the picture of human beings, plants, animals, soils, and waters "all interlocked in one humming community of cooperations and competitions, one biota" (Leopold, 1949/1966, p. 193). Holism is conceptual terrain where the noun "individual" changes positions with "environment" and "whole" far more rapidly than our rather outdated language of discrete individualism can bear.

Leopold's (1949/1966) biotic community is the conceptual foundation for seeing autonomy as an intrinsic value of nature. This has a parallel in ecology and economics with self-regulating ecosystems and economies. In nature, we may encounter a kind of living embodiment of the freedom to create our own selves through the unique experiences that chart our individual existence. In wilderness, we can meet an entity that grows first and tries to survive afterwards, much as humans' striving for autonomy generate some successes, and yet many failures. In the case we are urging, wilderness presents an unconditional affirmation of the value of *being*, *just in itself*, without regard for director, producer, or the weekly ratings. The basic need of radically free beings like ourselves in a world rapidly becoming more virtual than real is confirmation of the *value* of the autonomy we humans demand. This autonomy means less often freedom *from* invasions by others, and more often freedom *for* the actualization of possibilities recognized *with* others.

New Bearings, New Direction: Nonsentient, Nonconscious Autonomy

Prior to the late 18th century, no one thought that the differences between human beings had moral significance. Not until later did the idea emerge that each of us has an original way of being human and has his or her own "measure." Not until this idea emerged was the notion of diversity as an intrinsic value even thinkable. Since then, the idea has developed in two ways. On the one hand it has developed as the practical right for one to do as one wishes with their property. On the other hand, it has developed as a vague but sustaining ideal of moral authenticity. Today we are caught between the contradictory implications of these two opposing streams of thought. This is particularly so in matters concerning the natural world, on which we so intimately depend. We live with a hypercompetitive economic system that forces prioritization of selfish interests and threatens deadly catastrophe otherwise. At the same time, however, we remember ancestors and pioneers who clearly linked the life of the *new and the wild* to the pride and satisfaction with themselves as they *made themselves* to be. If we are to celebrate the authenticity of their independent wills and vision, we need to seriously consider the intrinsic value of the natural conditions that allowed for their actualization.

Political philosophy today is alive with debates issuing from the *politics of difference*. This contemporary line of thought is distanced from traditional classical liberal theory in much the same way as the intrinsic value of wilderness is distanced from traditional moral theory. Both reject the leveling, homogenizing effects of recognizing all people or beings in terms of how they are *the same*, or equal. The politics of difference demands that people be recognized in terms of their unique identity. It demands that understanding how one ought to live requires experiencing diversity and that no amount of marginalization by a dominant culture can truly extinguish the drive of the individual *to be*. Similarly, the ethics of biotic communities demand that ecological science be used to recognize their unique integrities. They demand understanding that how one ought to live requires experiencing at least the presence of their radical otherness. Further, it demands that in the case of wilderness, only global conformity and instrumental valuation can kill it.

Like the politics of difference, wilderness values depend on a rational belief that our world is a better place with than without diversity. Ecological science goes a long way in laying foundations for this belief. Only the philosopher, however, truly has the audacity to try to establish the legitimacy of such normative values in our cynical age. What we have taken as a reference point is the fact that in philosophical conversations, one compellingly noble concept emerges from all studies of diversity and value pluralism, that is, *autonomy*.

The universal ethic that the concept of autonomy inspires is relatively simple. If my autonomy, your autonomy, and the autonomy of other rational beings universally deserve moral consideration, then we are morally obligated to respect and defend one of the most autonomous *beings* of all, the wilderness. This is not capitulation to the anthropomorphism we repudiated at the outset. There is no claim here that wilderness is in any way like ourselves. Rather, the argument is that in a world without wilderness our ideas of independence and self-reliance are only unrealized capacities to acquire those virtues, not the actualization of them. Wilderness and wild things are the environmental conditions for the truly human being, provided that we pursue an active engagement with what does not take orders from us. The point is that the value of wilderness is transformative. Wilderness' intrinsic value exists only as long as we heed its claim to exist in our own striving to be.

It is extraordinarily risky to ask about the intrinsic value of wilderness in a forum charged primarily with practical policymaking. Measurable values and willingness to pay for them are public matters in the sense of being appropriately exposed to public observation and public scrutiny. Intrinsic values, by American definition, are not. Intrinsic values are private matters that are appropriately shielded from the public view, so the story goes, because their fragile bases cannot withstand critical inquiry. Intrinsic values, in other words, are understood as religious beliefs, faith-based positions, or worse, for the case we have made, preferences one happens to grow up with (or doesn't) depending on where, when, and to whom one was born.

Conclusion

This chapter argued that the intrinsic value of wilderness, while it may be subjectively held, is an essential value for every individual who aspires to self-determination and self-governance. However, this is not the only basis for an intrinsic value of wilderness. Justification for intrinsic value can be rooted in several principles. These include the flourishing principle of self-organization and of autonomy, both of which wilderness exemplifies. As well, justification for intrinsic value can be rooted in the principle of the emancipatory power of wilderness. It should clearly follow that to violate the intrinsic value of wilderness is to compromise the fundamental values legitimizing any possible demand for preference satisfaction at all. No demand is entitled to satisfaction, after all, unless it is true that all things begin equally with the *natural right* to freely become what they are destined to be on their own terms, and this includes wilderness.

Literature Cited

Bentham, D.J. (1996). An introduction to the principles of morals and legislation (J. H. Burns and H.L.A. Hart, Eds.), Oxford, UK: Blackwell Science. (Original work published 1789)

Dobel, P. (1994). The Judeo-Christian stewardship attitude toward nature. In L.P. Pojman (Ed.), *Environmnetal ethics: Readings in theory and Application* (pp. 20–24). Boston, MA: Jones and Bartlett.

Habermas, J. (1972). *Knowledge and human interests.* Boston, MA: Beacon Press.

LaDuke, W. (2000). Voices from white earth. In C. Anderson and L. Rundman (Eds.), *A forest of voices: Conversations in ecology* (2nd ed.; pp. 435–464). Mountain View, CA: McGraw-Hill.

Leopold, A. (1966). *A Sand County almanac.* New York, NY: Ballantine Books/ Oxford University Press. (Original work published in 1949)

Leopold, A. (1986). *Game management.* Madison, WI: University of Wisconsin Press. (Original work published in 1933)

Merchant, C. (1990). *The death of nature: Women, ecology, and the scientific revolution.* New York, NY: Harper.

Naess, A. (1997). Deep ecological movement: Some philosophical aspects. In R. Percival and D. Alevizatos (Eds.), *Law and the environment: A multidisciplinary reader.* Philadelphia, PA: Temple University Press.

Norton, B.G. (2001). *Why preserve natural variety?* Princeton, NJ: Princeton University Press.

Passmore, J. (1974). *Man's responsibility for nature.* New York, NY: Scribner's.

Plumwood, V. (1991). Nature, self, and gender: Feminism, environmental philosophy, and the critique of rationalism. *Hypatia, 6*(1), 3–27.

Rolston, H., III. (1986). *Philosophy gone wild.* Buffalo, NY: Prometheus Books.

Rolston, H., III. (1988). *Environmental ethics: Duties to and values in the natural world.* Philadelphia, PA: Temple University Press.

Sagoff, M. (1988). *The economy of the Earth.* Cambridge, MA: Cambridge University Press.

Chapter 13
The Multiple Values of Wilderness and the Future of the National Wilderness Preservation System

H. Ken Cordell
Senior Research Scientist and Project Leader
USDA Forest Service, Athens, Georgia

John C. Bergstrom
Russell Professor of Public Policy and
Professor, Department of Agricultural and Applied Economics
University of Georgia, Athens, Georgia

J. M. Bowker
Research Social Scientist
USDA Forest Service, Athens, Georgia

American society and its landscapes are changing dramatically. Then again, this country has always been a place of change. Both its population and landscapes are very different now than they were in the past, particularly when compared to the distant past. In that more distant past, even as early European settlement was occurring, there was an abundance of natural land—it seemed limitless. In more recent times, however, as there was greater realization that this country's natural resources have a limit, and as the abundance of undeveloped land diminished, some lands were put into state and federal land systems for conservation or reserve purposes (Carstensen, 1962). Some of the federal land systems established were quite remote and viewed as too far from human settlements to ever face development and raw material extraction pressures. By the dawn of the 20th century, however, it was becoming clear that no land was remote enough to escape human pressures and resource exploitation (see Chapter 2). By the middle years of the 20th century, a different vision was forming in some people's minds about the future of federal lands (see Chapter 3).

Toward the middle of the 20th century a number of visionary people had stepped up to push for a special status for some of this country's wildest federal lands. They saw to it that a National Wilderness Preservation System was created. This was truly a paradigm shift for America. In prior decades and centuries, wilderness had been viewed as the land beyond the frontier—land to be conquered and used to support livelihoods and amass wealth. With passage of the Wilderness Act, a new era for federal lands had emerged with ecological, scientific, and other nonconsumptive values taking on more importance than consumptive values derived from raw material extraction.

Being the dynamic country it is, change is still the most prominent characteristic of the United States. Significant change has occurred in just a few short years since passage of the 1964 Wilderness Act. For example, as of April 1, 1990, the country's population was just under 249 million. The latest Census indicated that total population had grown to over 281 million by 2000. By 2005, population has grown to nearly 295 million, a growth rate since 1990 of 1.3 percent annually (U.S. Census Bureau, 2004). As population has grown, it has spread over the nation's landscape. This growth has occurred not only in the already heavily populated Northeast and lower New England states but also in the Lower Great Lakes, South Atlantic, Florida, and Gulf Coast areas. As well, rapid population growth has occurred in east Texas, along the Front Range of Colorado, and in coastal California (Cordell, Bergstrom, Betz & Green, 2004). In many cases, rapid growth has extended up to the borders of public lands, including Wilderness.

But population growth is only part of the ongoing change story of the United States. While population growth has more direct impacts on the land, there is little doubt that racial, ethnic, and cultural changes within the population also are important, particularly to the future of Wilderness. Research has clearly shown that people of different cultural backgrounds view the natural environment and public lands differently (see Chapter 7). In 1900, 87.9 percent of the U.S. population was White, mostly non-Hispanic White. Blacks (mostly non-Hispanic) made up 11.6 percent of the population. The remaining 0.5 percent of the population was mostly either American Indian or Asian-Pacific Islander. By 1950, Whites composed almost 89.5 percent of the population and Blacks 10 percent. Very few among the population then were of other races or ethnicity. By 1980, however, as a result of major changes in the immigration laws, this racial mix had begun to change. The proportion of Whites had fallen to 83.1 percent, Blacks had risen to 11.7 percent, and others composed the remaining 5.1 percent. In 1990 a much smaller 75.6 percent of the population was non-Hispanic White, while the remaining 24.4 percent was of other races or ethnicity, including 9 percent who were Hispanic. By 2000, non-Hispanic Whites were just 69.1 percent, a dramatically smaller proportion than in the 1960s when the Wilderness Act was passed. Hispanics comprised 12.5 percent of the U.S. population in 2000, slightly exceeding for the first time in this country's history the percentage of the population who were Blacks. Asians were 3.6 percent and American Indians were just 0.9 percent in 2000. Recent [August 2004] population estimates from the 2000 Census showed the proportion of Hispanics in the United States continued to grow to 14.1 percent, with Whites dipping slightly to 67.3 percent (Cordell, Bergstrom, Betz & Green, 2004).

As population and cultural backgrounds have changed, other changes as well have been evident. Economic growth is one of them. Growth in economic activity as it creates demand for raw materials, land, and other resources has led to greater pressures on public and private rural land and is driving urban expansion. The lower 48 states include a total of over 1.9 billion acres of land and water (USDA Natural Resources Conservation Service, 2004). The majority of this area (74% or 1.4 billion acres) is nonfederal and rural. Between 1982 and 2002, an estimated 34.5 million acres of nonfederal rural lands were developed, a rate of more than 1.7 million acres per year nationally. Between 1997 and 2002, in just five years, the estimated annual rate of development of nonfederal rural land was almost 2 million acres. While the area of nonfederal rural land has been shrinking, the urban land base has been growing. Growing also, and massively so, are the numbers of people who live and work in urban areas. Living in urban areas, many today seem to have little direct connection with or knowledge of the natural environment. This built, urban orientation likely applies as much today to government employees and politicians who make decisions affecting Wilderness as it does to the general public at large. With such rapid growth of population and the economy, new immigration, rising diversity and urbanization, one has to wonder what Wilderness means to people today, especially to those who have the most "say" or influence over its future. The champions of the 1940s, 1950s, and 1960s are no longer with us. So, it is with this concern over bringing greater clarity to the question of what the meaning and value of Wilderness is to contemporary America that we devote this book.

The overall purpose of this book, then, has been to explore what is known about values contemporary Americans hold toward the National Wilderness Preservation System. We have attempted to clarify the meaning of different types of Wilderness values and to present replicable, science-based evidence of these values. Our intended audience is everyone and anyone of any persuasion who can and will have power over the future of the U.S. National Wilderness Preservation System—including ordinary citizens. We hope this book might also be a valuable resource for teachers, students, and all other curious and inquisitive people involved in either formal or informal learning institutions and research programs. It is our view that the values American citizens broadly hold are most important in determining the future of Wilderness. It is the value-laden and diverse voices of our country's public, individually and collectively, that are featured in this book. The fundamental question motivating this book is: "To what degrees and in what ways does the National Wilderness Preservation System add value in 21st century America?" Value perspectives inventoried and discussed in this book include social, economic, ecological, and ethical ones.

Summary of Chapters

Chapters 2 and 3 describe the origins and creation of the National Wilderness Preservation System. The discussions in these chapters highlight a deep commitment that existed in the United States in the 1960s to the idea of preserving wildlands. This commitment was based on the feelings people had about wilderness as both a noble idea and as unique and special places. As discussed in Chapter 4, the multiple values of Wilderness are derived from Wilderness attributes, functions, and services. In this book, we are concerned specifically with the multiple values of statutory Wilderness, that is, federal lands designated by Congress as areas within the National Wilderness Preservation System. Various attributes of the current National Wilderness Preservation System are presented in Chapters 5 and 6.

We organized the descriptions of the multiple values of Wilderness into four major categories or perspectives—social, economic, ecologic, and ethical. These categories originate from different scientific disciplines, each of which has developed its own perspectives and approaches for examining Wilderness values. Social perspectives on Wilderness values, as developed by psychologists, sociologists, social psychologists, and anthropologists, are discussed in Chapters 7 and 8. Chapter 7 discusses two general approaches for defining and assessing the social values of Wilderness: the social construction approach and the goal-directed approach. Both approaches have a relatively holistic perspective of values, and how people form those values. In the social construction approach, shared social meanings and values for Wilderness are created through historical, cultural, and political experiences over time. For example, shared Wilderness experiences, including taking Wilderness trips or working to protect Wilderness with neighbors, may improve the ability of people in a community to better organize and cooperate as a group to address common needs and problems. In the goal-directed approach, social values are formed through benefits from Wilderness that contribute to more utilitarian goals related to individual preferences. For example, Wilderness experiences, such as a challenging and inspirational trip into a wild and pristine area, may help a person develop and achieve individual physical, mental, and spiritual goals.

The discussion in Chapter 8 provides additional insight, primarily from a sociological perspective, into the views that peripheral groups (e.g., immigrants, ethnic/racial minorities, low-income groups) have on the meanings and values of Wilderness. Some social critics of the National Wilderness Preservation System charge that Wilderness is important mainly to an elite segment of American society, primarily middle-to-upper income, educated Whites. Research results discussed in Chapter 8 support this assertion to a degree, especially with regard to on-site use of Wilderness areas. Examples of on-site use would be Wilderness camping or hiking trips. However, research results indicate that native-born Americans and immigrants appear to have very similar preferences and priorities with regard to the broader, off-site, and passive-use benefits of Wilderness, such as support of the benefits of clean air and water from Wilderness. Additionally, U.S.-born Whites and ethnic/racial minorities, females and males, and people across different income groups appear to have similar preferences and priorities with respect to the broader off-site and passive-use benefits of Wilderness.

Chapters 7 and 8 both point out that Wilderness meanings and values are influenced by the important distinction between benefits derived from on-site active-use benefits of areas (e.g., Wilderness camping and hiking trips) and off-site passive benefits (e.g., contributions of Wilderness to air and water quality). As indicated in Chapter 9, economists also recognize the importance of these different use benefits. From an economist's perspective, Wilderness contributes to both national and regional economic development. The willingness-to-pay or net economic benefits for both on-site and passive uses as summarized in Chapter 9 indicate contribution to national economic development. National economic development is concerned with economic efficiency and the overall policy question of, "Which use or management of Wilderness will generate the highest net benefits to the nation as a whole?" Regional economic development is concerned with the distribution of economic benefits across communities and addresses the overall policy question of, "What are the effects on local and regional economies of the use and management of Wilderness?" These regional effects, measured in terms of community-wide income, population, and employment levels, are discussed in Chapter 10.

As indicated previously, measures of net economic value or willingness-to-pay, as reported in Chapter 9, are broadly divided into benefits from on-site recreation visits and the more passive-use benefits contributing broadly to quality of life. Based on published literature, average individual consumer surplus or willingness-to-pay for visiting a Wilderness area for recreation (i.e., on-site benefits) was estimated at about $20 for a single-day visit and about $68 for a visit lasting several days. For passive use, average annual consumer surplus or willingness-to-pay per household was estimated at about $67. Aggregation of these three values over appropriate numbers of visitors and population resulted in an estimated annual net economic value for the National Wilderness Preservation System of approximately $4 billion, or about $40 per acre per year.

As discussed in Chapter 10, research has shown that the presence of land in a county protected as part of the National Wilderness Preservation System positively contributes to the county's economy through recreation-and-tourism–related expenditures by Wilderness visitors. Research to date suggests that total numbers of nonlocal visitors to Wilderness areas across different regions of the country are not sufficient by themselves to sustain a significant local recreation and tourism industry. Local community citizens sometimes worry that "locking up" public land as Wilderness will negatively impact economic growth. However, research reviewed in Chapter 10 suggests that Wilderness does not, in aggregate, negatively affect employment trends in either the eastern or western United States. Moreover, evidence indicates that natural amenities, including designated Wilderness areas, attract new residents to rural areas who place a high priority on environmental quality, scenic beauty, and nearby recreational opportunities. Local communities can then benefit from increased business and jobs that tend to follow the new residents into these natural, amenity-rich rural areas.

The social and economic benefits of direct, on-site use of Wilderness, discussed in Chapters 7, 8, 9 and 10, including recreational, therapeutic and spiritual uses, are apparently substantial at all levels, including individual, small group, and selected community scales. However, because total numbers of Wilderness users are few, the total social and economic benefits of on-site use across the United States are small in comparison to the off-site and passive use benefits of Wilderness which spread across the population. Because of this difference in magnitude, debates in the future over Wilderness preservation are likely to focus more on broad, off-site environmental and passive-use benefits, such as provision of clean air and water, biodiversity, and continued existence of plants and animals. Continued provision of these broad off-site environmental and passive-use benefits depends on healthy ecosystems.

The degree to which designated lands under the National Wilderness Preservation System represent healthy ecosystems and high ecological value is discussed in Chapter 11. In that chapter, the ecological value of Wilderness is defined as the capacity of Wilderness to support endemic life. In general, research shows a positive relationship between the naturalness of land, eco-logical health and natural life-support capacity. Thus, as naturalness of the land increases, so should its ecological health and value. In Chapter 11, four surro-gate measures of naturalness, including fragmentation, natural land cover, distance from roads, and ecosystem representation were used to assess the naturalness of designated Wilderness compared to other lands. The results of this assessment indicate designated Wilderness is less fragmented, has greater natural cover, and has greater proportions that are remote from roads as compared to lands outside of designated Wilderness. By protecting different broad-scale ecosystem types from coastal wetlands to alpine tundra, designated Wilderness is also an important contributor to the regional, national, and global stocks or pools of natural biodiversity.

An overall conclusion of Chapter 11 is that designated Wilderness areas preserve naturalness and wildness, thus they better support healthy ecosystems and the living and nonliving elements of these ecosystems relative to other lands. Chapters 7, 8, 9, and 10 provide social and economic perspectives pri-marily on what philosophers term the instrumental value of plants, animals, and nonliving physical attributes of designated lands under the National Wil-derness Preservation System described in Chapters 5 and 6. As indicated by the philosophical discussion of wilderness values in Chapter 12, instrumental value (generally across all wildlands) refers broadly to its value as an input into or instrument of human preferences. For example, the instrumental value of Wilderness includes its value as a setting for enjoying recreational experi-ences and improving human physical, mental, and spiritual health.

The philosophical discussion in Chapter 12 also indicates that wilderness may have intrinsic value. Intrinsic wilderness value is defined as the value of its existence even in the absence of people and their on-site and off-site passive uses. The viewpoint that wilderness has value beyond instrumental ones can come from diverse personal beliefs and values including one's environmental ethics and religious beliefs. The topic of intrinsic value, however, takes discus-sion of the multiple values of Wilderness to the edge and beyond what can be defined from a human-centered perspective. Ultimately, recognition of the pure intrinsic value of Wilderness means taking a "step or leap of faith" over that edge to accept that there are values beyond what humans want or need. This includes recognition of the inherent rights of Wilderness lands to their own con-tinued natural existence. In a book aimed at providing practical information, it is important to note that recognition, appreciation, and protection of both the instrumental and intrinsic values of Wilderness, and all that is found there, are not mutually exclusive policy goals and management perspectives.

Data and Research Gaps

Throughout the course of this book, we have presented what is known about the multiple values of Wilderness using the perspectives from four different fields of science—social, economic, ecologic, and philosophic. The goal was to contribute this basic knowledge of Wilderness values to forums for social choice and natural resources policy. The question remains, "What more do we need to know about these values?" The values framework and philosophical chapters (Chapters 4 and 12) provide a foundation for organizing and better understanding what has been written thus far about Wilderness values. They provide an important basis for exploring the other chapters of the book. However, what we don't know about Wilderness values will most likely be affected by the advances in factual information emanating from ecological sciences and how this information about the benefits, products, or results of Wilderness affect and inform individual and collective social values, and ultimately social choice.

The ecological values chapter (Chapter 11) provides the beginning of a foundation for assessing biophysical and ecological differences between lands inside and outside of the National Wilderness Preservation System. The chapter presents us with a few initial objective measures that allow for systematic and scientifically informed comparisons—both statistically and intertemporally. There is little doubt that much more ecological research is needed to understand and quantify the differences between ecosystems in Wilderness and the various levels of managed ecosystems outside Wilderness. Moreover, it will be essential for science to continue to inform us about the ecological consequences associated with the loss of "naturalness" from conversion of lands from unmanaged to managed uses. Maintaining ecosystems or parts thereof through Wilderness designation will afford us the living laboratories that provide society with objective measures by which to gauge the fruits as well as consequences of our increased attempts to manage nature. The idea of Wilderness as an ecological preserve serves as a hedge against unknown risks associated with ecological transformation induced by human activities. However, as with all hedges, their value is dynamic and emanates from our ability and willingness to forego one stream of benefits and their inherent risks for another.

The social science brought to bear in Chapters 7 through 10 provides us with frameworks, methods, and results by which an informed public and their elected representatives can assess the tradeoffs to current and future generations associated with Wilderness policy and management. For example, framing and evaluating information about the benefits and costs of Wilderness (including things many would consider outside the purview of conventional economics) helps to determine how much Wilderness is the "right" amount at a given point in time. Dollar values accorded to on-site recreation and off-site passive benefits from Wilderness, as reported in Chapter 9, are a crude estimated snapshot in time. Moreover, they are unlikely to accurately reflect all of the economic values of ecological services from Wilderness discussed in Chapter 11. The answers to relative scarcity questions will depend heavily on technological change and the ability of substitutes to compensate for services—environmentally and personally—that Wilderness provides. Scientists will need not only to provide decisionmakers with information to help determine the "right amount" of Wilderness but also, as these lands are not homogeneous, the "right compo-sition." Indeed the economic benefits of Wilderness "services" are but one side of the equation. Information about the opportunity costs of keeping land in the Wilderness system must also be considered. For example, some lands may add more Wilderness benefits than others; however, various economic and social opportunity costs may dictate the political or bureaucratic selection of lands for designation that are less desirable strictly from the Wilderness benefits or values side.

Demands and preferences by society are likely to change over time as competing uses for land and relative scarcity of resources change. Addition-ally, as Chapter 8 points out, society is changing and with it, so too is the mix of preferences and ultimately benefits the American public ascribes to Wilder-ness. For now, the growing minority (heading someday to become the majority) and immigrant populations in the United States indicate less desire to visit Wilderness to experience the type of on-site recreational and spiritual benefits discussed in Chapters 7, 8, and 9. However, it appears that this population segment's preferences for the off-site environmental services and benefits of Wilderness, such as provision of clean air and water, are similar to the rest of the U.S. population. This convergence of preferences may signal that the dom-inant source of support for Wilderness in the future across the U.S. population will be off-site rather than on-site benefits and beneficiaries Wilderness. Yet, a related and somewhat sobering piece of information comes from a recent public opinion survey, which serves as a source for much of the social analysis reported in this book. Currently, less than half of the U.S. adult public (48%) is currently aware that the National Wilderness Preservation System formally exists (Cordell, Tarrant & Green, 2003). And it is likely that even fewer are aware of the history, physical aspects, and multiple values of Wilderness dis-cussed in this book. Considering that more than half of the public is unaware of the National Wilderness Preservation System, much less the benefits, values, and opportunity costs thereof, a greater controversy could come as more people become aware of the system.

Ultimately, Wilderness is a social and political construct. As such, the survival of Wilderness will continue to be determined in social and political arenas, fed by information from the biological, physical, and social sciences, and from other less formal sources. Designation of federal land as Wilderness, although not guaranteed permanency, locks in the defining criteria with a level of certainty unsurpassed by private and most forms of government land ownership. However, as a recent article in the *New York Times* indicates, loss of designation is possible if the opposing values are sufficiently convincing to sway Congress (Barringer, 2005). In a recent case, pressure from interests concerned with historical area tourism on Cumberland Island National Seashore precipitated a contest between the National Historic Preservation Act and the Wilderness Act. Local tourism interests and their elected government representatives tended in this case to favor a different balance between historical preservation and Wilderness protection on the island. The result was a loss of designation for a part of the island. Hence, to the extent that the social, economic, ecological, and ethical values of Wilderness and competing land uses drive the political process and bureaucratic decisions, the allocation and distribution of Wilderness will depend on, or at least be heavily influenced by, information feeding this process, including knowledge and appreciation of the multiple values of Wilderness.

Closing Thoughts

Throughout human history and the existence of any and all living and nonliving beings, those closest to or most intertwined with a place, idea, or issue have had the greatest influence on that place, idea, or issue. However, creation of the National Wilderness Preservation System, and indeed of our entire system of public lands, has been somehow different. In creating these systems, the greatest force or influence seemed to have been a broad collective concern. Certainly the concerns of Aldo Leopold, John Muir, Arthur Carhart, Howard Zahniser, Bob Marshall, and other champions of Wilderness in earlier decades were not primarily local. Their concerns were national and they had to do with the welfare of both the land and the people. Their concerns had to do with future generations as well as with current generations.

Wilderness within the federal land system is a national entity. It is of national interest. It is owned by all citizens of the United States. Local interests without doubt are a part of that citizenry, or public, but only one part. Generally, the public can be viewed as three categories of interest—local interests of the people who live nearby, special interests (e.g., commercial, tourism, grazing, environmental, others who may or may not live nearby) and general population-wide interests (i.e., all citizenry). Every Wilderness Bill that has added new areas or expanded existing areas has had some level of local or special-interest provision. Typically these are not the main driving interests represented in the language of Wilderness Bills or in the original Wilderness Act. The primary interest has been protecting the naturalness of the land for the broader good of all—present and future.

This book represents for the most part society-wide interests in Wilderness. The values described through the lenses of the various disciplines in Chapters 7 through 12 address citizenry values in the broadest sense. Local and special interests in public lands and Wilderness are usually well-represented at the "table" when the status and use of such lands are under consideration. Usually not at the table are the collective concerns and values of the Nation's general public. This is not said out of any disrespect for local and special land interests. All of us in one way or another have our own personal local and special interests in public lands. But in all things balance is needed. We feel that by presenting what research we could find about the public values of Wilderness, we have moved one step further toward providing the decisionmakers at whatever "table" there may be, an avenue to achieve balance in hearing all the voices of interest—narrow to broad. As summarized here, the chapters of this book indicate there is a very broad array of benefits that the public gains from Wilderness. Among these benefits, some are valued more so than others. Perhaps our summaries of Wilderness values research from different disciplinary perspectives will serve to inform those charged with making decisions about those aspects and benefits of Wilderness that the general citizenry finds most alluring. As social and political pendulums swing, it will be important to keep this information fresh and visible. We or others will need to update our understanding and assessments of the multiple values of Wilderness based on new research that will surely be forthcoming in the future.

Literature Cited

Barringer, F. (2005). *Georgia islanders take lead in feud over land use.* Retrieved April 1, 2005, from http://www.nathpo.org/News/Sacred_Sites/News_Sacred_Sites104.htm

Carstensen, V.R. (1962). *The public lands: Studies in the history of the public domain.* Madison, WI: University of Wisconsin Press.

Cordell, H.K., Bergstrom, J.C., Betz, C.J., and Green, G.T. (2004). *Trends in United States' population, demographics, urban development and recreation.* Unpublished manuscript. Athens, GA: USDA Forest Service, Recreation, Wilderness, Urban Forest & Demographic Trend Research.

Cordell, H.K., Tarrant, M.A., and Green, G.T. (2003). Is the public viewpoint of wilderness shifting? *International Journal of Wilderness, 9*(2), 27–32.

U.S. Census Bureau. (2004). *U.S. interim projections by age, sex, race, and Hispanic origin.* Retrieved November 3, 2004, from http://www.census.gov/ipc/www/usinterimproj/

USDA Natural Resources Conservation Service. (2004). *National Resources Inventory 2002: Land use report.* Retrieved November 4, 2004, from http://www.nrcs.usda.gov/technical/land/nri02/nri02lu.html

Appendix
Maps

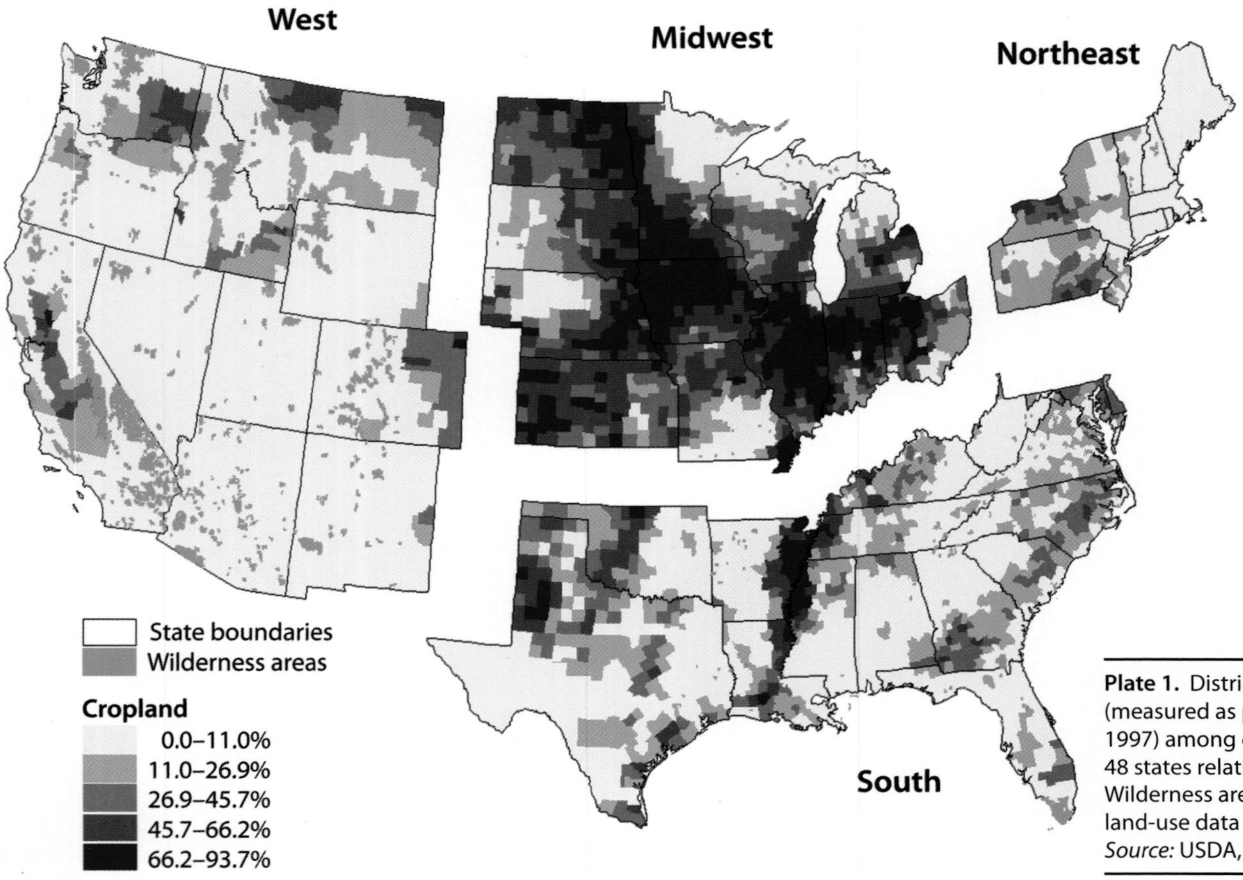

Plate 1. Distribution of cropland (measured as percent of total land area in 1997) among counties of the contiguous 48 states relative to the locations of Wilderness areas, 2004. (Comparable land-use data do not exist for Alaska) *Source:* USDA, 2001

Plate 1

Northeast

Midwest

West

South

State boundaries
Wilderness areas

Cropland
0.0–11.0%
11.0–26.9%
26.9–45.7%
45.7–66.2%
66.2–93.7%

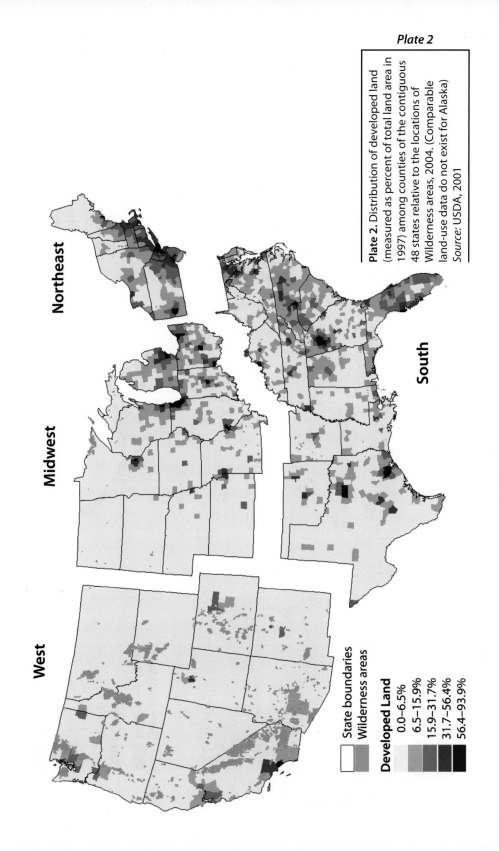

Plate 2

Plate 2. Distribution of developed land (measured as percent of total land area in 1997) among counties of the contiguous 48 states relative to the locations of Wilderness areas, 2004. (Comparable land-use data do not exist for Alaska) *Source:* USDA, 2001

Northeast

Midwest

West

South

State boundaries

Wilderness areas

Developed Land

0.0–6.5%

6.5–15.9%

15.9–31.7%

31.7–56.4%

56.4–93.9%

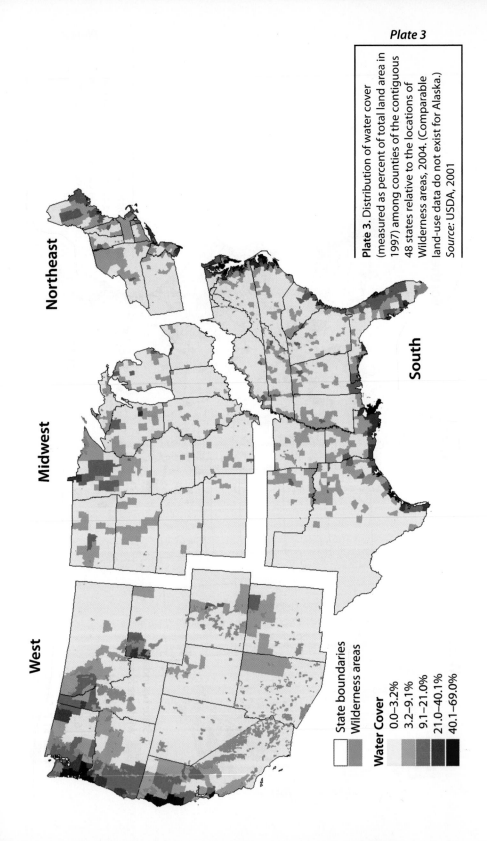

Northeast

Midwest

West

South

Plate 3

Plate 3. Distribution of water cover (measured as percent of total land area in 1997) among counties of the contiguous 48 states relative to the locations of Wilderness areas, 2004. (Comparable land-use data do not exist for Alaska.)
Source: USDA, 2001

State boundaries
Wilderness areas

Water Cover
0.0–3.2%
3.2–9.1%
9.1–21.0%
21.0–40.1%
40.1–69.0%

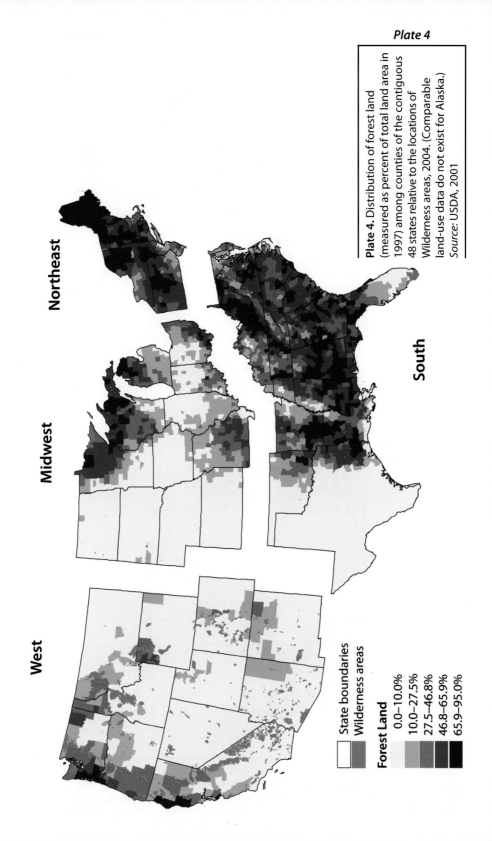

Plate 4

Plate 4. Distribution of forest land (measured as percent of total land area in 1997) among counties of the contiguous 48 states relative to the locations of Wilderness areas, 2004. (Comparable land-use data do not exist for Alaska.) *Source:* USDA, 2001

Northeast

Midwest

West

South

State boundaries

Wilderness areas

Forest Land

0.0–10.0%

10.0–27.5%

27.5–46.8%

46.8–65.9%

65.9–95.0%

Plate 5

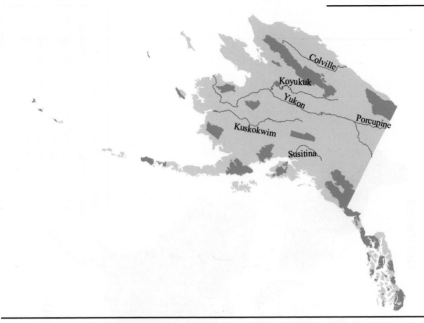

Plate 5. Location of Wilderness areas relative to major rivers in Alaska (Comparable road data not available for Alaska). *Sources:* States and rivers shape files from ESRI, 1999; Wilderness areas from Wilderness Institute, 2003

Plate 6

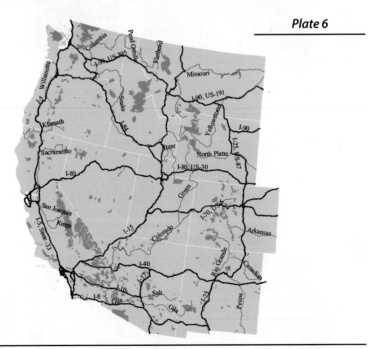

Plate 6. Location of Wilderness areas relative to major roads and rivers in the West Census Region (not including Alaska). *Sources:* States and rivers shape files from ESRI, 1999; Interstate data from USGS, 1999; Wilderness areas from Wilderness Institute, 2003

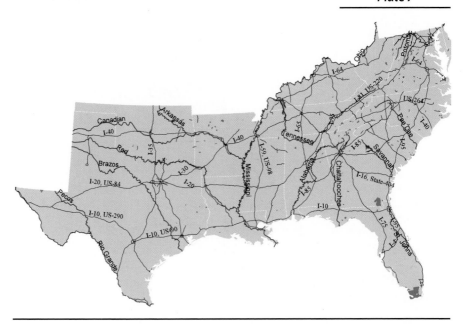

Plate 7

Plate 7. Location of Wilderness areas relative to major roads and rivers in the South Census Region. *Sources:* States and rivers shape files from ESRI, 1999; Interstate data from USGS, 1999; Wilderness areas from Wilderness Institute, 2003

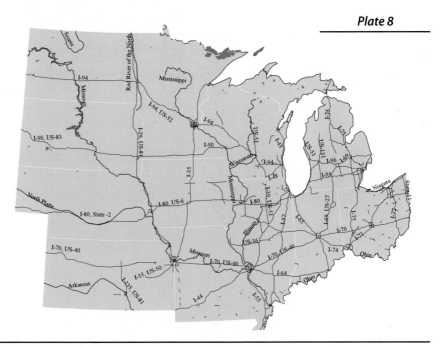

Plate 8

Plate 8. Location of Wilderness areas relative to major roads and rivers in Midwest Census Region. *Sources:* States and rivers shape files from ESRI, 1999; Interstate data from USGS, 1999; Wilderness areas from Wilderness Institute, 2003

Plate 9

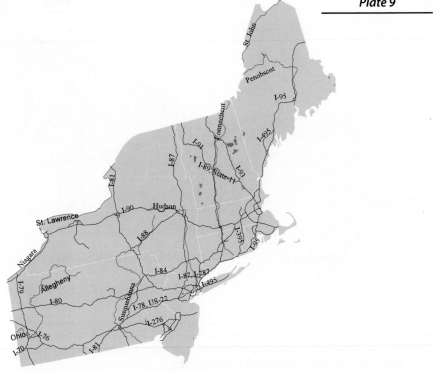

Plate 9. Location of Wilderness areas relative to major roads and rivers in Northeast Census Region. *Sources:* States and rivers shape files from ESRI, 1999; Interstate data from USGS, 1999; Wilderness areas from Wilderness Institute, 2003

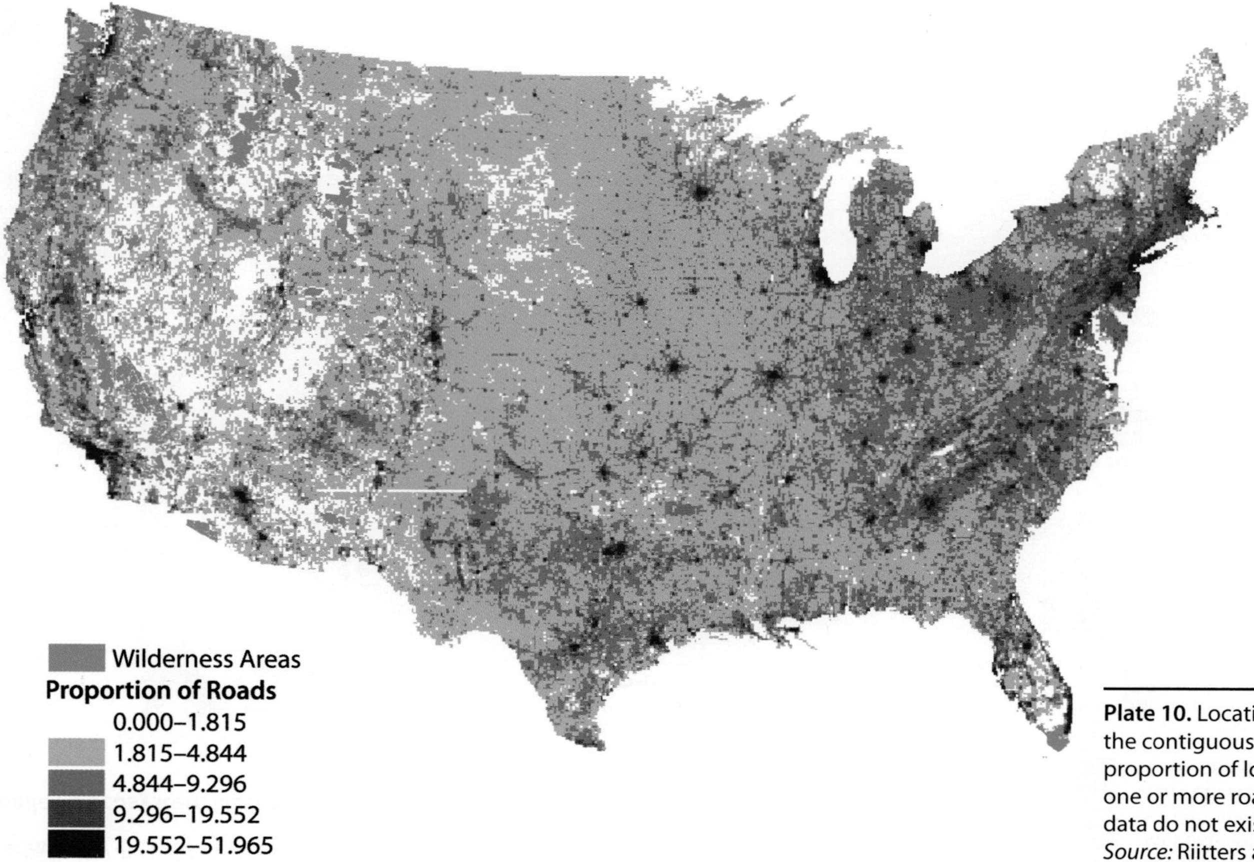

Plate 10

Plate 10. Location of Wilderness areas in the contiguous 48 states relative to the proportion of local land area containing one or more roads (Comparable roads data do not exist for Alaska).
Source: Riitters and Wickham, 2003

Wilderness Areas
Proportion of Roads
0.000–1.815
1.815–4.844
4.844–9.296
9.296–19.552
19.552–51.965

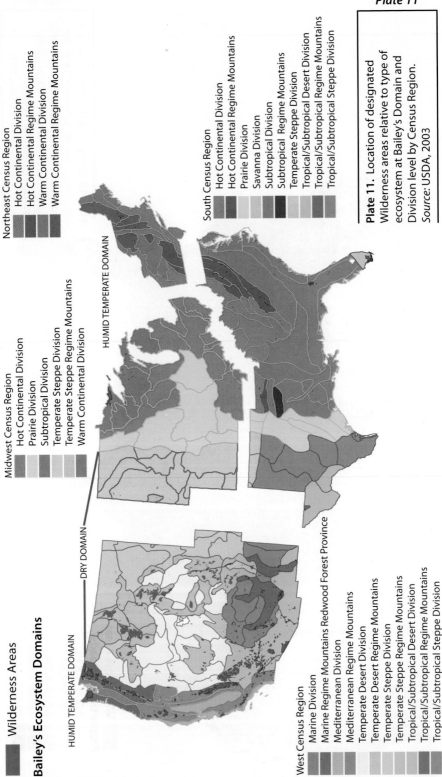

Plate 11

Wilderness Areas

Bailey's Ecosystem Domains

HUMID TEMPERATE DOMAIN

DRY DOMAIN

HUMID TEMPERATE DOMAIN

Northeast Census Region
Hot Continental Division
Hot Continental Regime Mountains
Warm Continental Division
Warm Continental Regime Mountains

Midwest Census Region
Hot Continental Division
Prairie Division
Subtropical Division
Temperate Steppe Division
Temperate Steppe Regime Mountains
Warm Continental Division

South Census Region
Hot Continental Division
Hot Continental Regime Mountains
Prairie Division
Savanna Division
Subtropical Division
Subtropical Regime Mountains
Temperate Steppe Division
Tropical/Subtropical Desert Division
Tropical/Subtropical Regime Mountains
Tropical/Subtropical Steppe Division

West Census Region
Marine Division
Marine Regime Mountains Redwood Forest Province
Mediterranean Division
Mediterranean Regime Mountains
Temperate Desert Division
Temperate Desert Regime Mountains
Temperate Steppe Division
Temperate Steppe Regime Mountains
Tropical/Subtropical Desert Division
Tropical/Subtropical Regime Mountains
Tropical/Subtropical Steppe Division

Plate 11. Location of designated Wilderness areas relative to type of ecosystem at Bailey's Domain and Division level by Census Region. *Source:* USDA, 2003

Plate 12

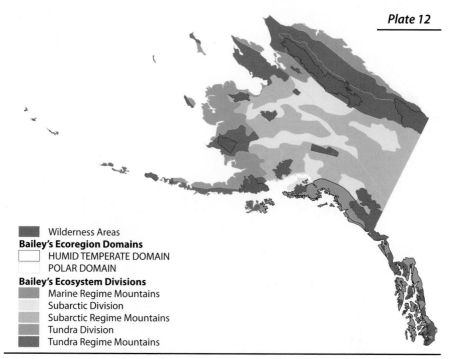

Wilderness Areas
Bailey's Ecoregion Domains
  HUMID TEMPERATE DOMAIN
  POLAR DOMAIN
Bailey's Ecosystem Divisions
  Marine Regime Mountains
  Subarctic Division
  Subarctic Regime Mountains
  Tundra Division
  Tundra Regime Mountains

Plate 12. Wilderness areas in Alaska in Relation to Bailey's Ecoregions at Domain and Division levels. *Source:* USDA, 2003

Plate 13

Plate 13.
Relative wildness of the lower 48 states.

Wildness Score

6

30

Plate 14

Wilderness areas

30   Wildness Score   6

Plate 14. Wildness in the eastern United States

Plate 15

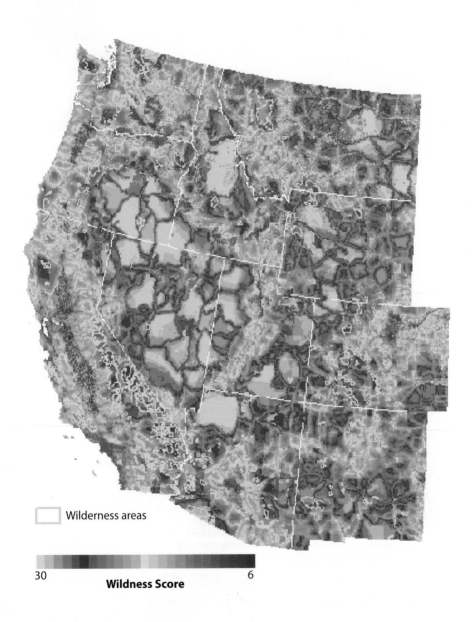

Wilderness areas

30   6
Wildness Score

Plate 15. Wildness in the western United States

Plate 16

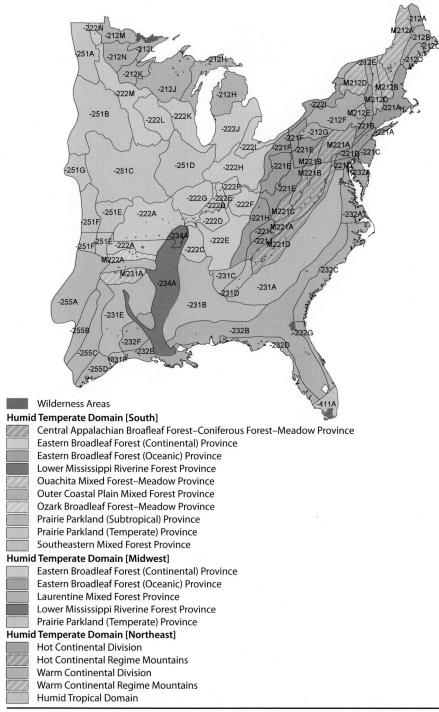

Wilderness Areas

Humid Temperate Domain [South]
Central Appalachian Broafleaf Forest–Coniferous Forest–Meadow Province
Eastern Broadleaf Forest (Continental) Province
Eastern Broadleaf Forest (Oceanic) Province
Lower Mississippi Riverine Forest Province
Ouachita Mixed Forest–Meadow Province
Outer Coastal Plain Mixed Forest Province
Ozark Broadleaf Forest–Meadow Province
Prairie Parkland (Subtropical) Province
Prairie Parkland (Temperate) Province
Southeastern Mixed Forest Province

Humid Temperate Domain [Midwest]
Eastern Broadleaf Forest (Continental) Province
Eastern Broadleaf Forest (Oceanic) Province
Laurentine Mixed Forest Province
Lower Mississippi Riverine Forest Province
Prairie Parkland (Temperate) Province

Humid Temperate Domain [Northeast]
Hot Continental Division
Hot Continental Regime Mountains
Warm Continental Division
Warm Continental Regime Mountains
Humid Tropical Domain

Plate 16. Bailey's ecosystem types and locatons of Wilderness areas at province level for Humid Temperate Region in the eastern United States. *Source:* http://www.fs.fed.us/colorimagemap/ecoregion1_provinces.html

Plate 17

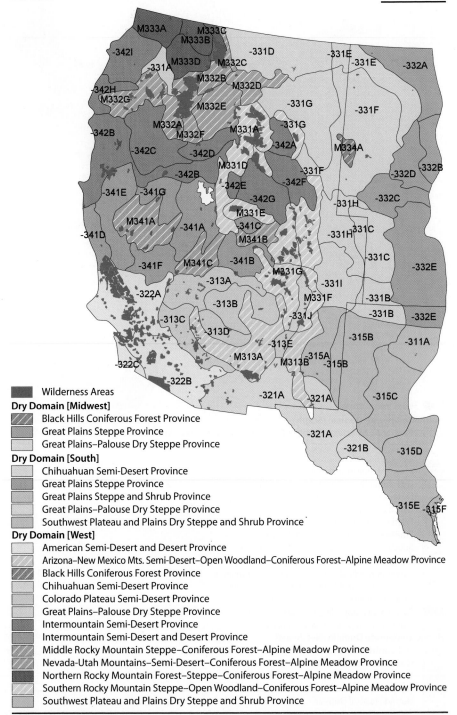

Plate 17. Bailey's ecosystem types and location of Wilderness areas at province level for the Dry Domain of the United States. *Source:* http://www.fs.fed.us/colorimagemap/ecoreg1_provinces.html

Plate 18

-242A

M242A

M242B

M261A M242C

M261G

M261D

M261B
M261C M261E
-263A M261F

-261A

-262A

M262A

M262B

-261B

■ Wilderness Areas

Humid Temperate Domain [West]

California Coastal Chapparral Forest and Shrub Province
California Coastal Range Open Woodland–Shrub–Coniferous Forest–Meadow Province
California Coastal Steppe, Mixed Forest, and Redwood Forest
California Dry Steppe Province
Cascade Mixed Forest–Coniferous Forest–Alpine Meadow Province
Pacific Lowland Mixed Forest Province
Sierran Steppe–Mixed Forest–Coniferous Forest–Alpine Meadow Province

Plate 18. Bailey's ecosystem types and location of Wilderness areas at province level for the Humid Temperate Domain of the western United States. *Source:* http://www.fs.fed.us/colorimagemap/ecoreg1_provinces.html

Plate 19

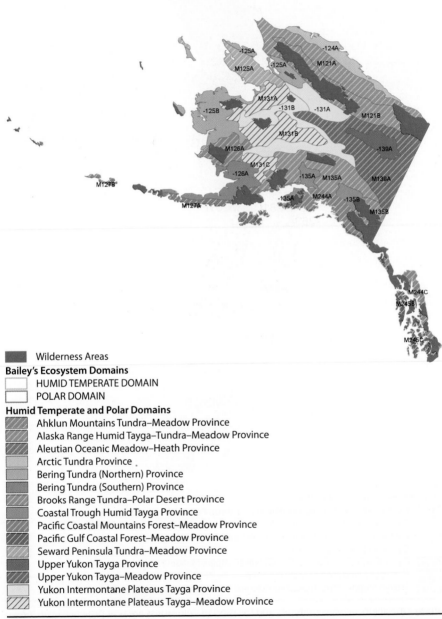

Wilderness Areas

Bailey's Ecosystem Domains
☐ HUMID TEMPERATE DOMAIN
☐ POLAR DOMAIN

Humid Temperate and Polar Domains
Ahklun Mountains Tundra–Meadow Province
Alaska Range Humid Tayga–Tundra–Meadow Province
Aleutian Oceanic Meadow–Heath Province
Arctic Tundra Province
Bering Tundra (Northern) Province
Bering Tundra (Southern) Province
Brooks Range Tundra–Polar Desert Province
Coastal Trough Humid Tayga Province
Pacific Coastal Mountains Forest–Meadow Province
Pacific Gulf Coastal Forest–Meadow Province
Seward Peninsula Tundra–Meadow Province
Upper Yukon Tayga Province
Upper Yukon Tayga–Meadow Province
Yukon Intermontane Plateaus Tayga Province
Yukon Intermontane Plateaus Tayga–Meadow Province

Plate 19. Bailey's ecosystem types and location of Wilderness areas at province level for Alaska. *Source:* http://www.fs.fed.us/colorimagemap/ecoreg1_provinces.html

Literature Cited

Environmental Systems Research Institute, Inc. [ESRI]. (1999). ArcView GIS (Version 3.2) [Computer software]. Redlands, CA: ESRI.

Riitters, K.H, and Wickham, J.D. (2003). How far to the nearest road? *Frontiers in Ecology and the Environment, 1*(3), 125–129.

U.S. Department of Agriculture, Forest Service, Inventory and Monitoring Institute. (2003). Map data. Retrieved September 17, 2003, from http://www.fs.fed.us/institute/ftp/maps/na_regns.shp.zip

U.S. Department of Agriculture, Natural Resources Conservation Service. (2001). *1997 national resources inventory* (rev. December 2000) [CD-ROM, Version 1]. Washington, DC: Author.

U.S. Geological Survey. (1999). Major roads of the United States. In U.S. Department of Interior, *National atlas of the United States*. Retrieved on September 17, 2003, from http://nationalatlas.gov/roadsm.html

Wilderness Institute. (2003). *Wilderness Information Network, National Wilderness Preservation System database*. Retrieved on September 19, 2003, from http://www.wilderness.net

http://www.fs.fed.us/colorimagemap/ecoregion1_provinces.html

Other Books by Venture Publishing, Inc.

The Game Finder—A Leader's Guide to Great Activities
by Annette C. Moore

Getting People Involved in Life and Activities: Effective Motivating Techniques
by Jeanne Adams

Glossary of Recreation Therapy and Occupational Therapy
by David R. Austin

Great Special Events and Activities
by Annie Morton, Angie Prosser, and Sue Spangler

Group Games & Activity Leadership
by Kenneth J. Bulik

Growing With Care: Using Greenery, Gardens, and Nature With Aging and Special Populations
by Betsy Kreidler

Hands On! Children's Activities for Fairs, Festivals, and Special Events
by Karen L. Ramey

In Search of the Starfish: Creating a Caring Environment
by Mary Hart, Karen Primm, and Kathy Cranisky

Inclusion: Including People With Disabilities in Parks and Recreation Opportunities
by Lynn Anderson and Carla Brown Kress

Inclusive Leisure Services: Responding to the Rights of People with Disabilities, Second Edition
by John Dattilo

Innovations: A Recreation Therapy Approach to Restorative Programs
by Dawn R. De Vries and Julie M. Lake

Internships in Recreation and Leisure Services: A Practical Guide for Students, Third Edition
by Edward E. Seagle, Jr. and Ralph W. Smith

Interpretation of Cultural and Natural Resources, Second Edition
by Douglas M. Knudson, Ted T. Cable, and Larry Beck

Intervention Activities for At-Risk Youth
by Norma J. Stumbo

Introduction to Outdoor Recreation: Providing and Managing Resource Based Opportunities
by Roger L. Moore and B.L. Driver

Introduction to Recreation and Leisure Services, Eighth Edition
by Karla A. Henderson, M. Deborah Bialeschki, John L. Hemingway, Jan S. Hodges, Beth D. Kivel, and H. Douglas Sessoms

Introduction to Therapeutic Recreation: U.S. and Canadian Perspectives
by Kenneth Mobily and Lisa Ostiguy

Introduction to Writing Goals and Objectives: A Manual for Recreation Therapy Students and Entry-Level Professionals
by Suzanne Melcher

Leadership and Administration of Outdoor Pursuits, Second Edition
by Phyllis Ford and James Blanchard

Leadership in Leisure Services: Making a Difference, Second Edition
by Debra J. Jordan

Leisure and Leisure Services in the 21st Century
by Geoffrey Godbey

The Leisure Diagnostic Battery: Users Manual and Sample Forms
by Peter A. Witt and Gary Ellis

Leisure Education I: A Manual of Activities and Resources, Second Edition
by Norma J. Stumbo

Leisure Education II: More Activities and Resources, Second Edition
by Norma J. Stumbo

Leisure Education III: More Goal-Oriented Activities
by Norma J. Stumbo

Leisure Education IV: Activities for Individuals with Substance Addictions
by Norma J. Stumbo

Leisure Education Program Planning: A Systematic Approach, Second Edition
by John Dattilo

Leisure Education Specific Programs
by John Dattilo

Leisure in Your Life: An Exploration, Sixth Edition
by Geoffrey Godbey

Leisure Services in Canada: An Introduction, Second Edition
by Mark S. Searle and Russell E. Brayley

Leisure Studies: Prospects for the Twenty-First Century
edited by Edgar L. Jackson and Thomas L. Burton

The Lifestory Re-Play Circle: A Manual of Activities and Techniques
by Rosilyn Wilder

The Melody Lingers On: A Complete Music Activities Program for Older Adults
by Bill Messenger

Models of Change in Municipal Parks and Recreation: A Book of Innovative Case Studies
edited by Mark E. Havitz

More Than a Game: A New Focus on Senior Activity Services
by Brenda Corbett

Nature and the Human Spirit: Toward an Expanded Land Management Ethic
edited by B. L. Driver, Daniel Dustin, Tony Baltic, Gary Elsner, and George Peterson

The Organizational Basis of Leisure Participation: A Motivational Exploration
by Robert A. Stebbins

Outdoor Recreation for 21st Century America
by H. Ken Cordell

Outdoor Recreation Management: Theory and Application, Third Edition
by Alan Jubenville and Ben Twight

Planning Parks for People, Second Edition
by John Hultsman, Richard L. Cottrell, and Wendy Z. Hultsman

The Process of Recreation Programming Theory and Technique, Third Edition
by Patricia Farrell and Herberta M. Lundegren

Programming for Parks, Recreation, and Leisure Services: A Servant Leadership Approach, Second Edition
by Debra J. Jordan, Donald G. DeGraaf, and Kathy H. DeGraaf

Protocols for Recreation Therapy Programs
edited by Jill Kelland, along with the Recreation Therapy Staff at Alberta Hospital Edmonton

Quality Management: Applications for Therapeutic Recreation
edited by Bob Riley

A Recovery Workbook: The Road Back from Substance Abuse
by April K. Neal and Michael J. Taleff

Recreation and Leisure: Issues in an Era of Change, Third Edition
edited by Thomas Goodale and Peter A. Witt

Recreation Economic Decisions: Comparing Benefits and Costs, Second Edition
by John B. Loomis and Richard G. Walsh

Recreation for Older Adults: Individual and Group Activities
by Judith A. Elliott and Jerold E. Elliott

Recreation Programming and Activities for Older Adults
by Jerold E. Elliott and Judith A. Sorg-Elliott

Reference Manual for Writing Rehabilitation Therapy Treatment Plans
by Penny Hogberg and Mary Johnson

Research in Therapeutic Recreation: Concepts and Methods
edited by Marjorie J. Malkin and Christine Z. Howe

Simple Expressions: Creative and Therapeutic Arts for the Elderly in Long-Term Care Facilities
by Vicki Parsons

A Social History of Leisure Since 1600
by Gary Cross

A Social Psychology of Leisure
by Roger C. Mannell and Douglas A. Kleiber

Special Events and Festivals: How to Organize, Plan, and Implement
by Angie Prosser and Ashli Rutledge

Steps to Successful Programming: A Student Handbook to Accompany Programming for Parks, Recreation, and Leisure Services
by Donald G. DeGraaf, Debra J. Jordan, and Kathy H. DeGraaf

Stretch Your Mind and Body: Tai Chi as an Adaptive Activity
by Duane A. Crider and William R. Klinger

Therapeutic Activity Intervention with the Elderly: Foundations and Practices
by Barbara A. Hawkins, Marti E. May, and Nancy Brattain Rogers

Therapeutic Recreation and the Nature of Disabilities
by Kenneth E. Mobily and Richard D. MacNeil

Therapeutic Recreation: Cases and Exercises, Second Edition
by Barbara C. Wilhite and M. Jean Keller

Therapeutic Recreation in Health Promotion and Rehabilitation
by John Shank and Catherine Coyle

Therapeutic Recreation in the Nursing Home
by Linda Buettner and Shelley L. Martin

Therapeutic Recreation Programming: Theory and Practice
by Charles Sylvester, Judith E. Voelkl, and Gary D. Ellis

Therapeutic Recreation Protocol for Treatment of Substance Addictions
by Rozanne W. Faulkner

The Therapeutic Recreation Stress Management Primer
by Cynthia Mascott

The Therapeutic Value of Creative Writing
by Paul M. Spicer

Tourism and Society: A Guide to Problems and Issues
by Robert W. Wyllie

Traditions: Improving Quality of Life in Caregiving
by Janelle Sellick

 Venture Publishing, Inc.
1999 Cato Avenue
State College, PA 16801
Phone: 814-234-4561
Fax: 814-234-1651